Machiavelli Then and Now

Machiavelli's ideas are as important in our time as in his own. His insights and prescriptions help us make sense of today's political upheavals and natural calamities, and reduce them to a working order. The essays in this volume explore Machiavelli's central concerns: statecraft and order, liberty and citizenship, diplomacy and leadership, modes of strategization, the quest for empire—all set against the basic contention between autarchy, oligarchy, and democracy. They also address the ethical and behaviourial factors behind political practice, such as force, suasion, ambition, corruption, and vigilance in public discourse. Several essays consider the role of language, text, and the imagination in Machiavelli. Two pieces bring the Machiavellian discourse closer to our own times, in relation to Gandhi, Gramsci, and Althusser.

Sukanta Chaudhuri is Emeritus Professor of English, Jadavpur University.
Prasanta Chakravarty teaches English at the University of Delhi.

Machiavelli Then and Now

History, Politics, Literature

Edited by
Sukanta Chaudhuri
Prasanta Chakravarty

CAMBRIDGE
UNIVERSITY PRESS

University Printing House, Cambridge CB2 8BS, United Kingdom

One Liberty Plaza, 20th Floor, New York, NY 10006, USA

477 Williamstown Road, Port Melbourne, vic 3207, Australia

314 to 321, 3rd Floor, Plot No.3, Splendor Forum, Jasola District Centre, New Delhi 110025, India

103 Penang Road, #05–06/07, Visioncrest Commercial, Singapore 238467

Cambridge University Press is part of the University of Cambridge.

It furthers the University's mission by disseminating knowledge in the pursuit of education, learning and research at the highest international levels of excellence.

www.cambridge.org
Information on this title: www.cambridge.org/9781316516720

© Cambridge University Press 2022

This publication is in copyright. Subject to statutory exception and to the provisions of relevant collective licensing agreements, no reproduction of any part may take place without the written permission of Cambridge University Press.

First published 2022

Printed in India by Thomson Press India Ltd.

A catalogue record for this publication is available from the British Library

ISBN 978-1-316-51672-0 Hardback

Cambridge University Press has no responsibility for the persistence or accuracy of URLs for external or third-party internet websites referred to in this publication, and does not guarantee that any content on such websites is, or will remain, accurate or appropriate.

*To the memory of Swapan Chakravorty,
scholar and humanist*

Contents

Preface		ix
Abbreviations and Editions Used		xi
1.	Introduction—*Prasanta Chakravarty*	1

Power, Citizenship, Strategies

2.	Machiavelli on Relationships: Knowledge of the Occasion—*Thomas Berns*	21
3.	The Anatomy of an Error: Machiavelli's Supposed Commitment to a 'Citizen' Militia—*Paul A. Rahe*	31
4.	Machiavelli and Tyranny—*Doyeeta Majumder*	54
5.	Machiavelli's Turn to Xenophon—*Christopher Nadon and Christopher Lynch*	73
6.	Machiavelli and the Solitary Discipline of Hunting—*Prasanta Chakravarty*	96
7.	'To Give Reputation to One': Machiavelli the Populist and Other Variations on *Il Principe*, Chapter 9—*Guido Cappelli*	121

History

8.	Riscontro: Machiavelli's Art of History—*Francesco Marchesi*	145
9.	'Letters as Oracles': Machiavelli's Foresight in His Letters—*Marcello Simonetta*	162
10.	Machiavelli's Lucretia and the Origins of the Roman Republic: Rape, Gender, and Founding Violence—*Yves Winter*	174

Words and Dispositions

11.	Thinking with Animals: Machiavelli's *L'asino* and the Metamorphoses of Power—*Supriya Chaudhuri*	193
12.	Machiavellian Rhetoric Revisited—*Victoria Kahn*	219
13.	Machiavelli Reading—*Swapan Chakravorty*	235
14.	A Language for Politics and a Language of Politics: Words as a Tool of Understanding and of Action in Machiavelli —*Jean-Louis Fournel*	262

Afterlife

15.	Machiavelli and Gandhi—*Sukanta Chaudhuri*	281
16.	*The Prince* between Gramsci and Althusser—*Vittorio Morfino*	296

The Contributors	316
Index	321

Preface

Sometime in 2016, the idea of a seminar on Niccolò Machiavelli, at once contextualizing his writings and studying their impact on our own times, took root in Prasanta Chakravarty's mind. It was a diffident intuition. Was the thought historically too adventurous? Was it tenable to universalize Machiavelli and read him from an Indian location after so many centuries? On what grounds could one advance such a politically charged proposal to a literature department? His nebulous thoughts began to take shape when Christel Devadawson, then Head of the Department of English, University of Delhi, said she would back the idea. By the latter half of 2017, Prasanta was mailing a host of Machiavelli scholars across the world, asking whether they would be willing to travel to New Delhi in October 2018 for a conference on Machiavelli and his ideas. The Department could offer hospitality and three days of strenuous jousting with the man. A number of scholars immediately agreed. Those who could not, offered enormous support and goodwill. Thus, in the autumn of 2018, the Department came to host a conference entitled 'Machiavelli in His Time, and Ours'. Most of the chapters in this book originated in that conference. The rest are by scholars who could not make it there but have been an integral part of the larger collective. Our thanks to all these distinguished contributors.

Rajeev Bhargava and Sukanta Chaudhuri were involved from the start as advisers to the project. Professor Bhargava has continued his exchanges with Prasanta on the political and philosophical ramifications of classical and Early Modern thought in our times. Sukanta Chaudhuri's association culminated in his co-editorship of this volume.

Sincere thanks are due to Rimli Bhattacharya, Rahul Govind, and Madhvi Zutshi, who participated untiringly, over a year and more, in academic and logistical planning of the conference. It would have been impossible to conceive the seminar and the book without their grace and guidance. Tanya Roy, Department of Germanic and Romance Studies, University of Delhi, and her co-participants brought the comic power of *Mandragola* to life before the conference audience by their spirited play-reading.

The Ambasciata d'Italia, Nuova Delhi, generously supported the conference. Our gratitude to them.

Finally, we thank Qudsiya Ahmed, Anwesha Rana, Aniruddha De, and Purvi Gadia of the Cambridge University Press, New Delhi.

August 2021

Sukanta Chaudhuri
Prasanta Chakravarty

Abbreviations and Editions Used

Abbreviations

Disc. Niccolò Machiavelli, *Discorsi sopra la prima Deca di Tito Livio* (*Discourses on the First Ten Books of Titus Livius*)
Pr. Niccolò Machiavelli, *Il Principe* (*The Prince*)

Editions Used

Contributors were left free to cite editions and translations of their choice for all works by Machiavelli and other authors, or to make their own translations. All sources are documented in the endnotes.

1

Introduction

Prasanta Chakravarty

Niccolo Machiavelli is an idea, an enduring *author-function*. In no other time is this idea more relevant than in ours. But in order to reassess this function, we have to place Machiavelli in his historical context. We are forever perplexed by the twin threads of profound admiration and lasting unease in the reception of his methods and writings. Was Machiavelli the first detached empiricist in matters political and artistic? Or did he simply refine and reinvent certain genres of expression, including modern forms of treatises and letters? Was he a punctilious realist, a neutral strategist—no more, no less? Or is it his patriotism that actually shines forth as he repeatedly emphasizes solidarity, cohesion, and order in public discourse? Was not Machiavelli also the forerunner of the argumentative modern citizen who cries out against slavery and political bondage to the will and dominion of rulers, however benign?[1] Or should we refrain from taking his radical solutions at face value and instead view his texts and tales as satirical and cautionary? What about the moral force of Machiavelli's pronouncements? Or is he one of the originary voices to have helped usher in the modern ideal of value-neutrality? Are his methods of amalgamating the past with the contemporary so unique that they come across as visionary and fantastical?

The idea of Machiavelli forces us to wrestle with difficult issues of moral strength, magnanimity, suasion, vigour, vitality, public spirit, civic sense, dedication, glory, expansion, and the *patria*. At the same time, he is also profoundly and uniquely identified with a certain solitude and detachment, even as he grapples at close quarters with the most pressing diplomatic and political questions of his time. But most of all, it is evident that he places a powerful wager on *verità effettuale*,[2] truth tested by success and experience (though Antonio Gramsci had stated long ago that the effectual reality is never static, but an outcome of relations of force that alter the meaning of a project,[3] and John McCormick calls such a truth 'elusive'[4]). As Isaiah Berlin puts it, for Machiavelli effectiveness and order must always precede *ozio*, quietism, and indolence.[5] This book will give us an opportunity to take a fresh look into Machiavelli's engagement with issues of statecraft and order, liberty and citizenship, modes of strategization, lessons of diplomacy and leadership, the classical heritage, the quest for empire, ethics and normativity, and modes of history writing, as well as questions regarding force, suasion, ambition, corruption, subversion, and vigilance in public discourse.

One of the most powerful and popular early vernacular translators of Machiavelli was the Frenchman Jacques Gohory. His sixteenth-century translation of the *Discourses on Livy* has been specially lauded by generations of readers. Gohory describes Machiavelli metaphorically as the Florentine merchant, a sincere man with good wares to offer each and every one. He further emphasizes that Machiavelli only sells in gross (that is, comprehensively— no retail business here), and his merchandise is neither painted nor decked out: with a word, he reveals things in clear daylight to whoever wishes to see. That is quite a felicitous description of how we have conceived this book: to delve into his 'neither painted nor decked out' merchandise.[6] The merchandise is both subtle and brutal, imbued with a strange and singular kind of inverse sentimentalism that numerous commentators have noted over the centuries. There is indeed a quest for wisdom, but only by trying to match, perhaps often unsuccessfully, antiquity and universal ideas with contingent moments. The pursuit drifts into the uncharted, so as to mark all the stumbling human transactions of this world.

In this context, one recalls Fyodor Dostoevsky's 'underground man'. Dostoevsky savagely parodies the idea of self-knowledge through a method of consistent negation. But simultaneously, he gives us the vision of the forms where creatures face the sting of the gods. While speaking of Dostoevsky, we should explicitly cite Raskolnikov's article 'On Crime', wherein he praises the introducer of 'new modes and orders'—the legislator or the lawgiver. The new authority, the founder, will and must advocate new laws and contravene the old in order to become master of the future. The new laws are the creation of the exceptional man, like Napoleon or Moses.[7] But the exceptional always has to be tested under conditions of ground reality and the constant threat of no-rule or anarchy. How can one conceive of any lasting order if the world is in flux and torment? Conversely put, how can the freedom of beginning something new also prove to be foundational, stable, and tangible in actual terms? Can we be truly free yet simultaneously accept a stable normative order? This singular conundrum is unequivocally repeated through Machiavelli's works.

Form, Event, Initiative

In fact, Machiavelli plays out the scope of the paradox to the hilt. On the one hand, the new man is a modern romantic equivalent of the subject inspired by the divine from within, such as we see in Plato's *Phaedrus*. On the other hand, his innovation, insofar as he helps the new world to institute itself, can only happen on contingent and practical grounds, since human agency is severely buffeted by some larger, lurking force that besets us all the time. This is something akin to the vision of forms that Socrates describes in the ascent of the soul to the hyperouranian realm. One is entitled to bring it back to the world and quell resistance, even kill and destroy if need be, in order to promote order by disseminating a certain vision of codification and organization. Machiavelli activates this traffic between heaven, earth, and the netherworld—most obviously in *Belfagor*—but often metaphorically and mythically, seeking truth in forms, and then working out a relationship between form and event in his major treatises. This allows him to define and demarcate a unique idea of freedom in the political, historical, and literary domains.

In this book, the chapter by Christopher Nadon and Christopher Lynch reconsiders this question of order deriving from Machiavelli's interest in Xenophon and his teachings, as a classical prototype of the way he himself thinks about determinism, discipline, and initiative in public life. In another chapter, Prasanta Chakravarty, extending this very theme taken from Xenophon, considers the vocation of hunting and maps the triangulation of solitude, preparation, and action in Machiavelli.

On the other hand, the idea of well-ordered government is also about protecting and upholding another kind of rule of law: law that yet is not, and perhaps never will be, naturalized as the modern mind would like to believe but that will operate at the cusp of custom, divinity, and *fortuna*, leading to some form of communitarian and public deliberation. One way (though not the only one) to read the neo-Roman idea of freedom is to bring legality and decision-making in tandem with *discordia concors*, marking a mode of civil association that enables citizens to become free. If we accept this reading of Machiavelli, the notion of the people and the popular will—that is, the sum of the wills of each individual citizen—in this communitarian and republican sense is redefined in a version of liberty that challenges slavery, protects manumission from the promulgations and dicta of rulers, affirms the importance of representation in running an ordered society, emphasizes a mixed constitution, and upholds the setting up and continuation of the institution of tribunes.

Such a notion of the people may stop just short of the formation of a citizen militia, which would take us in a more populist direction. Among others, this republican Machiavelli inspired John Milton, who in *The Tenure of Kings and Magistrates* (1649) declared that no one 'can be so stupid to deny that all men naturally were born free, being the image and resemblance of God himself'.[8] To Milton the relentless patriot, this would mean celebrating a life of freedom, being part of a social body that is politically alive in deliberative associations of free people.

The question of liberty can be further radicalized, set against both the Straussian and the Cambridge School readings. In various avatars of this third reading, it is suggested that Machiavelli should be read as a contentious populist or plebiscitarian, standing against the oligarchy. Still others have seen Machiavelli as a forerunner of the revolutionary tradition. These scholars particularly emphasize Machiavelli's acute and positive understanding of the role of violence, conflicts, and tumults in public life.[9]

Although ideas travel transhistorically, and we try to grapple with the powerful afterlife of Machiavelli in this book, it would be a presentist error to see sharp divergences among the three Machiavellis: one beholden to the ruthless principles of founding and maintaining the state; another who celebrates the free association of civic principles; and yet a third who is the harbinger of dissent and subversion in civic life, and therefore a prophet of political innovation and change. There are multiple and heterogeneous thoughts and imaginings in Machiavelli's writings: all the elements do not and need not cohere. This is because Machiavelli is not an abstract thinker or an ideologue in the modern sense of the term. The two functions that he performed in his political life—as part of the administration of the republic and as a diplomat across the Alps—made him aware of the rapid changes in the European political scene, hence the necessity of building a strong and formidable Florence, based on the laws and principles of the times. He steadfastly keeps away from abstract speculation and divine revelation. Corrado Vivanti has rightly said that 'the sole principle governing his judgment, which combined his experience as Florentine secretary with his later thoughts in *The Prince* and the *Discourses*, was the necessity to adapt to his times, according to the needs and the diverse behaviors of people'.[10]

One way to read the question of order and freedom in the Machiavellian scheme of things is to conceive the problem in terms of an *encounter* (*riscontro*) between political form and historical event. In recent times, this thesis has been most forcefully put by Miguel Vatter, who argues that neither natural inevitability nor relativization of form, but historical freedom or change, is what runs across Machiavelli's conception of the political.[11] Political freedom can convert not only the contingent into the necessary but also the fixed and seemingly permanent into the contingent and even the subversive. Freedom emerges from the clash among human action, natural forces, and historical twists and turns. The essence of historical becoming lies in the collision or encounter between human action and circumstances (*virtù* and *fortuna*) such that, in these fateful meetings, time itself undergoes a transformation. Necessity or order, and contingency or spontaneity, cannot be easily detached from or opposed to each other. The dimensions of the event or encounter determine its form, and vice versa.

In this book, Thomas Berns has extended this theme by considering the notion of opportunity (*occasione*) in Machiavelli. Berns thinks that the idea of opportunity works between *virtù* or decision-making on one side and *fortuna* on the other. Knowledge in Machiavelli is purely contingent and experiential, so that it is forever deferred; yet in actuality, various encounters take place that lead to relationships, tensions, and some form of order. 'Opportunity' is therefore the name of a space which Althusser has called 'conjecture'. In another chapter, Francesco Marchesi, after enquiring into the multiple meanings of the *riscontro*, suggests that the hypothesis does not end with the dichotomy between determinism and prudence, fortune and *adaequatio*, but includes a third option, that of forcing (*sforzare*) the historical conjuncture, which is not just a variation of the possibility of adaptation. The forcing of time happens by a combination of impetuosity and prudence. Hence, Marchesi finds such encounters to be acts of *poiesis* and not the simple outcomes of action. Such a concept of the encounter seems almost to adumbrate a Hegelian schema whereby history becomes autonomous. Naturally, it denies the ancient solution of a return to beginnings or historical repetition as a means of ensuring order and governance. But it also keeps clear of the opposite position, whereby Machiavelli would be seen as promoting nihilism and a politics of delegitimacy by stressing no-rule and contingent expediency.

That is one reason why Machiavelli laid so much stress on time and occasion for taking the right decision. In war and politics, what worried him was the 'folly of procrastination, the danger of appearing irresolute'.[12] But the endeavour to capture the occasion does not mean taking recourse to a romantic idea of political decisionism, as formulated by the theorists of sovereignty and *auctoritas*, from Francisco Suárez through Hans Kelsen to Carl Schmitt. In fact, the role of the non-rational forces in human and political lives is central whenever Machiavelli assesses the role of action and human initiative in matters political. The forces of *fortuna* are placed against all metaphysical solutions.

Man's addressing of such forces is, rather, an empirical issue. This approach in Machiavelli is what Louis Althusser, like all those treating of form and spontaneity, has called the *materialism of encounter or conjunction*.[13] It is important to address this aspect of Machiavelli's thought in order to understand how a powerful realist, advancing the tenets of early modernity in a protoscientific way, tries at the same time to grapple with the forces of the non-rational and the cosmic by bringing them within the ambit of the social and the political.

This is not to evade the question of historicity but to place conjectures about human and historical forces within a cosmic frame. It is evident, for instance, that Machiavelli's God is a providential force, a master deity, a God who loves the fatherland, rule of law, and freedom for the citizen. Religion, for Machiavelli, as Maurizio Viroli has explained, is at one level an *instrumentum regni*, the medium through which an intelligent legislator can work extraordinary achievements.[14] At a second level, religion is a constructive moral force, outside of mere utility. Hence Machiavelli is neither an atheist nor a straightforward pagan.

Another productive approach would be to place the Machiavellian cosmos against the backdrop of the astrological debate and Early Modern naturalism. What do 'celestial signs', for instance, mean in matters political? What role does *fortuna* play in the political destinies of countries? How are the metaphors of the body and the humours deployed in evolving an organically integrated cosmos? How do natural motions affect the fate of whole principalities? A third coordinate in matters non-rational is to take stock of Machiavelli's pronouncements on *eros* and affect, especially since he is also the formulator of the art of war. Whether it is better to be loved or feared is a constant theme in his writings; his poetry and epistles consistently address the question of love and affection, friendship and desire.[15] How does he place his idea of love vis-à-vis the prevailing Ovidian and Neoplatonic forms? Was he himself a youthful archer, or did he consider love as Cupid's punishment, a powerful but ultimately random force? What is the nature of masculine friendship in his scheme of things? Undoubtedly, there is an implicit critique of Christian love in his writings.

Machiavelli's concentrated, constructive approach to life and politics is thus paradoxically marked by a conjectural description of all the Italian principalities and republics. The very nature of the flux that besets Machiavelli's world seems at once heightened, fictive yet all too real. He moves towards political practice by emphasizing the particular characteristic of each political conjecture. Yet his world is shot through and through with imagination and innovation, expressing the subversive and the irreverent: a trait that befits only a dogged sentimentalist.

Reception and Transmigration

The discourse on rights in Europe, beginning in the seventeenth century, and subsequent legacies of the eighteenth-century Enlightenment have fallen severely short of explaining the human, social, and natural phenomena in large parts of the world in our own times. Consequently, that space has been taken over by irrational, populist, sentimentalist, and uncritical claimants. In fact, in some instances, the votaries of rights discourse and legal positivism have begun to fraternize with identity politics and fideism as rightful options to challenge the excesses of fascism and moderate mainstream liberalism. Consequently, there has been a sharp attack on the enterprise of thinking itself from both sides of the political spectrum. It is almost impossible to consider the prospect of 'thinking without a banister' at this time; such is the power of the rhetorical and the perceptual in our times and their disjuncture from genuine action.[16] All judgement has turned contingent and reactionary. As I have tried to argue, this dissociation of sensibility between thought and imagination, feeling and objectivity, is simply non-existent in Machiavelli. He can hold on to the tense balance between the two, because of his singularly dispassionate mind that simultaneously distrusts abstraction. It is for this reason that he focuses deeply and analytically on human vices and follies, pleasures and ambition alike. It would be sweeping and precipitate to call this approach the result and effect of instrumental reason, as David Wootton has recently hinted.[17] The capacity to be analytical, the power of fantasy, and the perception of the scourge of *fortuna* simply cannot be separated in Machiavelli.

There is something far more complex, elusive, and therefore profitable in Machiavelli than what radical democratic moralists like Wootton would like us to believe. One approach would be to assess the reception history of his works. The tension begins right from the Renaissance reading of rhetoric and suasion, which was genuinely historicist, acutely aware of the changing and differing circumstances of the speaker (or writer) and audience (or reader). At the same time, the humanist ethical ideal, whereby writers and performers calibrate their art in order to prompt goodness and help inculcate dialogic values in the audience, puts a constraint on such skeptical historicism that could lead us to value neutrality and relativism. Machiavelli's famed 'ambidexterity' about human values, about the rules of the game so to say, sharpened this contradiction to its limits. Victoria Kahn has directed us elsewhere to the preface to the 1532 Giunta edition of *The Prince*, where four fundamental elements of the later reception of the treatise are already present:

> (1) the view of Machiavelli as a teacher of tyrants; (2) the view of Machiavelli as a secret critic of tyranny; (3) the view that Machiavelli was merely describing the world of politics, not recommending a particular course of behaviour; or (4) that he was peddling a particular art or skill, a technique of political power, that could be used well or badly.[18]

In his chapter for this book, Swapan Chakravorty, on the other hand, has tried to capture the very idea of a dialogic humanist reception through 'metatextual signposts that look forward and backward'. The reading and reception of Machiavelli is, for Chakravorty, symptomatic of an ongoing process.[19] As he says,

> Reading directed toward action, performative reading, dialogue with the dead, polemical engagement with anterior texts, metatextual signposting, anachronous reading—all such elements contribute to our understanding of Machiavelli's practice as reader and commentator. At the same time, an eclectic mix of these strategies might increase the perplexities of present-day readers of Machiavelli instead of dispelling them.

Indeed, the reception and 'transmigration' of Machiavelli (Marlowe: 'Albeit the world thinke *Machevill* is dead,/Yet was his soule but flowne beyond the *Alpes*'[20]) have often been highly polarized. Wootton is following a line of thought initiated by the sixteenth-century Huguenot jurisconsult Innocent Gentillet in *Contre-Machivel* and carried forward by the likes of Louis Leroy. There were others, of course, who came to value the finer points of Machiavelli's life and writings. In France, some of them, like Gohory, appreciated the world set up in the *Discourses* and hailed Machiavelli as the least Machiavellian of men. Others like Claude de Seyssel analysed the institution of monarchy in practical and realistic terms. Yet others tried to stem the charge of irreligion against Machiavelli. Jean Bodin, who gradually distanced himself from Machiavelli, largely shared and extended the latter's emphasis on realism, order, and disciplinary action. In England, occasional praise for Machiavelli's sharp realism was more often punctured by the notion of the dreaded unethical and insidious figure.

We have already mentioned neo-Roman republican ideals in Machiavelli scholarship. After the Restoration, it is with James Harrington, Algernon Sidney, and Henry Neville that the republican strains in the writings begin to receive more traction. The view of Machiavelli as a classic republican is frequently found in the humanist and rational tradition inaugurated by Hans Baron and taken forward by the Skinner–Pocock–Pettit line of twentieth-century Anglo-American thought.[21] Focusing on Machiavelli's republicanism has some merits. It shows the emergence of a new political language in Europe. But to introduce modern liberal communitarian thinking into republicanism may be an unwarranted conflation. At other times, such an approach not only keeps the writer of *The Prince* at a distance from the concerns of *realpolitik* but also maintains silence on (*a*) the more democratic and radical possibilities of his political claims; (*b*) the inverse romanticism and Rousseau-like tendencies; and (*c*) much of his imaginative and literary forays, except when reading those as buttressing republican thought in general. As hinted earlier, both the autarchic and the republican traditions of reception have recently been taken in conflict-filled and democratic directions by more contentious and populist readings of Machiavelli by scholars like John McCormick, Miguel Vatter, Yves Winter, and Anthony Brunello. This turn towards assessing Machiavelli as a radical democrat and people's creature is put to test in Marcello Simonetta's chapter in this book. The one-sided paternalistic assessment of Machiavelli by the Cambridge School notwithstanding, Simonetta feels it is uncritical to valorize and idealize the tribunes and the people. Such evaluations of Machiavelli wrongly tip the scales in the other direction. Machiavelli is not uncritical of people's fickleness.

The present century places us in a more challenging situation. How can one be respectful of the historical and critical tools provided to us by five centuries of Machiavellian scholarship and at the same time reconsider the man and his thoughts vis-à-vis the specific and contingent issues and problems of our own time? Perhaps a singular need of the organically thinking person today is to explore the causes of populist overtures and retributive tendencies in public life. Does Machiavelli provide us with some idea of how to conceive of institutions and order in public life, statecraft, and human relationships?

To begin with, he seems to provide us with a wonderful opportunity to engage with the issue of popular will and eruption of irrationality in the *socius*. With Savanorola's rise and eventual fall, we realize the possibilities and limits of the politics of demagoguery. But the obverse of such fanatical fervour can also allow a successful channelling of people's power, whereby the irrational yet ingrained groundswell of opinion is given a certain order and shape. As someone keenly aware of the power of the rhetorical as against absolute communicative dialogue, Machiavelli tried to work out the implications of freedom and order between these two opposites. The power of populism and scandalmongering is a constant factor that cannot be wished away.

Irrational and aggressive forces might perhaps be given a direction by imagining politics in a wholly new way. This is the question that scholars like John McCormick and Miguel Vatter raise in their works. In this book, Paul A. Rahe, examining the question of citizen militia in Machiavelli, advances a thesis sometimes hinted at but seldom spelt out so clearly, that the disruptive and militant populism latent in Machiavelli's prescriptions also suggests he was a 'precocious Bonapartist'. Jacobinism and Bonapartism are two sides of the same coin. This question has been raised from the opposite direction in Vittorio Morfino's chapter. Taking a cue from Antonio Gramsci, Morfino suggests that in *The Prince*, Jacobinism and Bolshevism come together in a single myth to construct the foundations of a national state, even though this is never openly expressed. This is the 'double perspective of political and state action'. Thereafter, he considers Althusser's suggestion that Machiavelli is trying to fill up a political void by radically reorganizing an imaginary theoretical space where new laws emerge out of solitude. This is a far-reaching extension of the Gramscian wager. Such an emerging space is the new prince's tryst with historical conjecture. In this manner, Morfino tries to bring together the aleatory and historicist forms of materialism. These issues resonate with the strategies often adopted by the 'new demagogues' and 'democratic dictators' of our times from radical rightist and populist countermeasures and the demands of identity politics.

Why Now?

In fact, several issues of our times seem far more resonant when read in a Machiavellian light—not least matters of populism and order, belief and detachment, language and performance. This does not mean that the lessons of an ancient wisdom have been exhausted and have nothing to offer when reading Machiavelli in our time. In fact, questions of classical political philosophy—the pursuit of truth and lucidity, imperial impulses, the factor of necessity in decision-making—have been constant themes besetting human beings after Machiavelli. This is a curious phenomenon that we are witnessing across the globe today: the leaders of people are using rhetoric and demaguery to rule and extend their power, yet modernity, with all its scaffoldings, has not been exhausted. It is a historical cusp.

Of course, market forces and the post-Westphalian state create a very different milieu from the city-states of ancient times that interest Machiavelli.

Colonialism and its aftermath have also complicated the very European set-up within which Machiavelli was operating. Modern forms of nationalism are also considerably different from the love for and dedication to the *patria* in ancient and Early Modern times. But there is surely a mock re-feudalization of our surroundings in a new and tangible manner. Hence, the central questions raised by Leo Strauss and others with reference to the Machiavellian scheme of things—pursuit of glory, excellence in human endeavour, inculcation of *virtù* and freedom of will, the role of charity and gratitude, fidelity, the relationship between arms and the law, the role of unforeseen accidents (contra chance) and their control, justified terror and cruelty, and proud patriotism—are all relevant today, to the extent that those heroic notions have been cheapened and made marketable by the demagogues and democratic populists of our times. In the context of political absolutism, Doyeeta Majumder has argued persuasively in this book about the ingenious way in which Machiavelli turns the classical definition of tyranny inside out: by overlooking the new prince's lack of titular legitimacy, rationalizing his tyrannical acts, and simultaneously disparaging the inviolate title of the hereditary prince and identifying the latter's sovereignty with tyranny. Indeed, assessing the classical evaluation of Machiavelli in the light of fresh scholarly interventions always helps us to maintain a healthy scepticism towards humanist orthodoxies—not least because such exercises might also help us to distinguish the political and cultural motivations of the demi-elites from the more exclusive elites at any given point in time by considering what constitutes 'new' in the absolutist vocabulary.[22]

That Machiavelli helps to inculcate prudence in the art of statecraft is an equally ancient universalism. That the foundations of power and able governance are key issues in understanding Machiavelli is a view that goes directly against the Cambridge School of republican thought, as well as the democratic and socialist readings of more recent vintage. But the strong association of successful governance with Machiavelli's thought comes back to us as the world evolves and we begin to grapple with domination and power in new ways. Those who try to relate order and prudence believe directly in the discursive scope of his works, especially *The Prince*, which demonstrates to emerging princes and leaders the relationship between rules and actual cases, between thought and action. Machiavelli's works have actual and practical utility. All prudential action takes place in the space between providence and the human practice of rule, through interruptions and reordering. There is no escaping the cycles of tumult and reorganization in our political existence.

This very question of prudence is ingeniously treated in Guido Cappelli's chapter in this book. Cappelli delves into a Machiavellian system of governance that produces at once subjects and citizens, so that often there is no sharp distinction between a monarchy and a republic. Instead, the idea of the civic itself gets expanded. In this form of 'fortunate astuteness', Cappelli finds a prudent admixture of consent and suasion, so that during certain populist moments of governance, the sovereignty might be willingly given to an exceptional individual by the citizens themselves.[23] In another chapter, Sukanta Chaudhuri has tackled the issue of expediency by ingeniously bringing together the Gandhian *satyagrahi* and the Machiavellian man of *virtù* as moral entities. What unites the two, according to Chaudhuri, is their intense engagement with *realpolitik*, their refusal to take recourse to any transcendent, extrapolitical, or absolute source of authority in dealing with the practical issues of politics. Owing to the peculiar revolutionary force of the moral, it is impossible to demarcate the intellectual from the ethical power of *satyagraha* and *virtù* in the two thinkers.

The imperial and aggrandizing tendencies in Machiavelli in particular, and among proponents of the republican tradition in general, have often been acknowledged. In this book, Yves Winter points out, bearing the gender factor in mind, how Machiavelli assigns incoherent and contradictory value to political violence in his scheme of things.[24] The idea of destruction, stability, and the growth of Florentine power is directly proportional to the imperial acts that Florence undertakes, along with securing its internal stability and freedom. Mikael Hörnqvist has shown how Machiavelli repeatedly draws on Livy and Quintilian in order to highlight the benefits of successful Roman imperialism:

> On the one hand it involved a policy of destruction that included the razing of cities, mass executions, and the deportation of people; and on the other hand, it included a policy of benefits, such as the granting of citizenship, spectacular displays of mercy, and the resettlement of the vanquished in Rome.[25]

Such carrot-and-stick policies find uncanny resonance in the strategies employed by modern-day dictators and demagogues to aggrandize and consolidate their regimes.

Machiavelli, the Man of Letters

But there is another reason, perhaps even more pressing, that makes us address Machiavelli's contribution to human thought and action. Machiavelli is often thought and taught in literary circles and departments, especially in the Indian subcontinent, as merely providing certain items of civil and political context for the study of literature. He is placed alongside other books written for the education or orientation of courtiers—notably, Baldassare Castiglione's *The Book of the Courtier* and Erasmus's *The Education of a Christian Prince*—so that (to invoke Norbert Elias) we may understand the machinations of court society. He is hardly ever placed by the liberal arts establishment vis-à-vis Guicciardini or Alamanno Rinuccini: that would immediately have politicized and contextualized *The Prince* in a different manner. Instead, the reigning approach makes the cited writers and texts vaguely apolitical by placing their ideas in the civil domain, delineating mostly the model courtier and his behavioural traits, and tracing the circuits of patronage.

In fact, such a method narrows down the ambit of Machiavelli studies in particular and Early Modern discourse in general in two distinct ways. On the one hand, it eliminates all serious and systematic political engagement associated with the man and his thoughts by pushing him, most anachronistically, into the civil domain. On the other hand, it excludes almost his entire *oeuvre* on sheer generic grounds. Moreover, it deprives us of an excellent opportunity to apply the finer analytic tools relating to form in the literary sense: issues of rhetoric, textual proliferation, ideas and modes of fictionality, allegorical moves, and, most importantly, nurturing our universe in and through fantasy and imagination.

Victoria Kahn has been one of the most influential of Machiavelli scholars in persuading us to look more closely into the rhetorical strategies of his writings. In her contribution to this book, Kahn argues against Ernst Cassirer's reading of Machiavelli as a scientific thinker. Instead, she impels us to read Machiavelli as an astute political rhetor who could argue both sides of a question. He could therefore simultaneously stress human passion (for instance, fear as opposed to love) in order to affirm a politics of the status quo, of security and order, yet also advance a kind of dialectical rhetoric that could undermine humanism and the role of the prince. In fact, Machiavelli shows how deliberative rhetoric can be a potent weapon for mounting a political critique.

Jean-Louis Fournel, on the other hand, argues for a philology and rhetoric that affirms the autonomy of political language. We must be attuned to the intrinsic functions of Machiavelli's utterances rather than to their effect on the audience. Fournel excavates a remarkable history of the effective language of politics in Machiavelli, which in turn becomes *effectual truth*: such a language encounters historical rearrangement, and its semantic valance begins to alter and transform itself. It is through this constant process of semantic alteration that Machiavelli is able to bring together *res* and *verba*, substance and rhetoric, history and text, in his works.

The question of allegory, symbolism, and bestiality in Machiavelli is treated expansively by Supriya Chaudhuri as she focuses on the travails of the ass-human in *L'asino*. Chaudhuri's chapter asks the crucial question that complicates the very idea of humanism: Do animals in Machiavelli (lion, fox, and ass, for instance) serve more as symbols whose natures must be 'used' by the prince as they suit his needs? Or do they suggest a more performative repertory of means or styles? What exactly do we gain or lose if we extend the scope of the human beyond the Neoplatonic model? If we switch states from the human to the animal, does the knowledge gained thereby become more instrumental than mystical?

These various Machiavellis often remain hidden from us. Once alerted to such nuances, we come to form a very different idea about the fiendish arch-realist Machiavel. A central aim of this book is to expand the notion of the literary in the spectrum of cultural discourse available to Machiavelli and to locate his singular ways of approaching literature within the disciplinary shifts and evolving modes of writing in Early Modern Europe. Who or what was Machiavelli *the man of letters*? As we have just noted, the ahistorical man of letters is a mirage in Machiavelli; yet he is deeply attached to the world of art and literature. In fact, he felt affronted on finding that Ariosto had left him out of the latter's list of Tuscan poets.[26] This question becomes pressing when we see that Machiavelli embraces the literary techniques of humanist rhetoric, yet at the same time disparages and distances himself from the purely theoretical and abstract in humanist rhetoric, as being ineffective and airy. Were literature and art idle pastimes for him, merely a way to engage with the Orti Oricellari circle of republicans? Or did he take various literary tools like myth, figure, and narrative strategies seriously and use them to good effect in formulating his political treatises, reflections, letters, and poetry? How far does his particular fusion of the Tuscan vernacular with Roman traditions reorient the prevailing tendencies of Florentine literary humanism?

Over the last few centuries, we have seen a magnificent attempt at giving shape to human destiny by using natural law to resolve our conflicts and improve our understanding of human relationships. But we have not thereby been able to systematize and rationalize history, politics, and cultural production. Rumblings of an ancient disquiet can again be heard all around us, rising to a deafening cacophony that tries to defy Enlightenment values *tout court*. Machiavelli offers the possibility of engaging with our own times as well as understanding his by amplifying and diversifying the very ideas of the political and the literary. How do ideas of liberalism, socialism, and modern nationalism fare vis-à-vis Machiavellian principles in addressing the issues that beset us? Can the fundamental questions of human ambition, belief, the ravages of *fortuna*, rules of collective engagement, strategies of ordering and thriving, and, most importantly, ways to attain lasting political and natural freedom be newly framed in the light of our current tumultuous predicament, nationally and globally?

Hence, the final section of the book engages with the afterlife of Machiavelli. Along with the initial outcry and discontent with the 'murderous Machiavel' traced earlier, we notice an alteration, a repositioning. For instance, quite early on, Justus Lipsius reinstates him as a patriot and pragmatist, a label later extended by Hegel and Macaulay. For Ernst Cassirer and Eric Voegelin, he is a kind of technician who successfully applied inductive methods in political thought. Fichte and Herder thought that Machiavelli was an extraordinary mirror of his age, providing deep insights into real historical forces. Marx and Engels refer to him as one of the giants of the Enlightenment. Antonio Gramsci, Claude Lefort, and Louis Althusser have advanced and refined this view in powerful ways. Benedetto Croce has carefully considered the emancipation of politics from ethical concerns in Machiavelli, especially against the backdrop of the Christian and Aristotelian frameworks.[27] The twentieth century has seen a spate of readings: from the civic republican to the feminist, from the autobiographical to the deep empirical.

The present century seems to be truly revisiting Machiavelli in its very ethos and modes of interaction, sometimes by way of sharp contrast. But Machiavelli as *author-function* is apparent everywhere. We seem to be restoring the permanent interrogation mark that he placed in the path of posterity, the de facto recognition that equally sacred ends and entire systems of value may contradict each other without the possibility of rational arbitration. To be buffeted by these contraries is a creaturely predicament and an agonizing experience. Yet it would be foolhardy to seek any easy escape from such a predicament. The unfairness of fortune's vagaries must rather be tackled in a forthright yet strategic manner.

Notes

1. For an elaboration on this point, see Quentin Skinner, *Liberty before Liberalism* (Cambridge: Cambridge University Press, 2014).
2. *Pr.*, ch. 15.

3. See Antonio Gramsci, *Selections from the Prison Notebooks*, ed. and tr. Quentin Hoare and Geoffrey Nowell Smith (New York: International Publishers, 1971), 171–3.
4. See 'Introduction' in John P. McCormick, *Reading Machiavelli: Scandalous Books, Suspect Engagements, and Virtue of Populist Politics* (Princeton, NJ: Princeton University Press, 2018), 9–15.
5. See Isaiah Berlin, 'The Originality of Machiavelli', in *Against the Current: Essays in the History of Ideas* (Princeton, NJ: Princeton University Press, 2013), 25–79, 47.
6. See Sydney Anglo, *Machiavelli, the First Century: Studies in Enthusiasm, Hostility and Irreverence* (Oxford: Oxford University Press, 2005), 207.
7. See Fyodor Dostoevsky, *Crime and Punishment*, tr. Nicolas Pasternak Slater (Oxford: Oxford University Press, 2017), part 3 ch. 5, 219–37. For a masterly elaboration of this point about Dostoevsky, see Jeff Love, *The Black Circle: A Life of Alexandre Kojeve* (New York: Columbia University Press, 2018). On the question of sovereign exception, see Giorgio Agamben, *Homo Sacer: Sovereign Power and Bare Life*, tr. D. Heller-Roazen (Stanford, CA: Stanford University Press, 1998), and Jacques Derrida, 'Force of Law: The Mystical Foundations of Authority', tr. Mary Quaintance, *Cardoza Law Review* 11, no. 919 (1989–90), 920–1045.
8. John Milton, *Prose: Major Writings on Liberty, Politics, Religion and Education*, ed. David Loewenstein: *The Tenure of Kings and Magistrates* (Chichester: Wiley-Blackwell, 2013), 249.
9. For a democratic take on Machiavelli, see John P. McCormick, *Machiavellian Democracy* (Cambridge: Cambridge University Press, 2011), and McCormick, *Reading Machiavelli*. For more revolutionary evaluations, see Filippo Del Lucchese, Fabio Frosini, and Vittorio Morfino, eds., *The Radical Machiavelli: Politics, Philosophy and Language* (Leiden: Brill, 2015); Claude Lefort, *Machiavelli in the Making* (Evanston, IL: Northwestern University Press, 2012); Marie Gaille, *Machiavelli on Freedom and Political Conflict: An Historical and Medical Approach to Political Thinking* (Leiden: Brill, 2018); and Gabrielle Pedullà, *Machiavelli in Tumult: The Discourses on Livy and the Origins of Political Conflictualism* (Cambridge: Cambridge University Press, 2018). For a Spinoza-like take, see Mikko Lahtinen, *Niccolò Machiavelli and Louis Althusser's Aleatory Materialism* (Leiden: Brill, 2009).
10. Corrado Vivanti, *Niccolò Machiavelli: An Intellectual Biography* (Princeton, NJ: Princeton University Press, 2013), Preface, xi.
11. See Miguel Vatter, *Between Form and Event: Machiavelli's Theory of Political Freedom* (New York: Fordham University Press, 2014).

12. Quentin Skinner, *Machiavelli: A Very Short Introduction* (Oxford: Oxford University Press, 1981), 9.
13. See Louis Althusser, *Machiavelli and Us*, tr. Gregory Elliott, ed. Francois Matheron (London: Verso, 2011), 53–80.
14. Maurizio Viroli, *Machiavelli's God* (Princeton, NJ: Princeton University Press, 2012), 5–6. See also Anthony Parel, *The Machiavellian Cosmos* (New Haven, CT: Yale University Press, 1992); John M. Najemy, 'Papirius and the Chickens, or Machiavelli on the Necessity of Interpreting Religion', *Journal of the History of Ideas* 60, no. 4 (1999), 659–81. On the same point, see the two excellent chapters titled 'God's Friends and Machiavelli's' and 'The Heavenly Host' in Sebastian de Grazia, *Machiavelli in Hell* (New York: Vintage Books, 1992).
15. On the question of *eros* and the romantic strain in Machiavelli, see Haig Patapan, *Machiavelli in Love: The Modern Politics of Love and Fear* (Lanham, MD: Rowman and Littlefield, 2007), and Guido Ruggiero, *Machiavelli in Love: Sex, Self and Society in the Italian Renaissance* (Baltimore, MD: Johns Hopkins University Press, 2011).
16. See Hannah Arendt, *Thinking without a Bannister: Essays in Understanding, 1953–1975* (New York: Schocken Books, 2018).
17. David Wootton, *Power, Pleasure and Profit: Insatiable Appetites from Machiavelli to Madison* (Cambridge, MA: Belknap Press, 2018), 5.
18. Victoria Kahn, 'Machiavelli's Afterlife and Reputation to the Eighteenth Century', in *The Cambridge Companion to Machiavelli*, ed. John M. Najem (Cambridge: Cambridge University Press, 2010), 239–55, 241.
19. Chakravorty has used Althusser's notion of the *symptomatic* in the sense of making works and pronouncements visible, as a method of engaging with what he calls *anterior texts*.
20. Christopher Marlowe, *The Jew of Malta*, Prologue 1–2, in Christopher Marlowe, *Complete Works*, ed. Fredson Bowers (Cambridge: Cambridge University Press, 1973), 263.
21. See Donald R. Kelly, 'Murd'rous Machiavel in France: A Post-Mortem', *Political Science Quarterly* 85, no. 4 (1970), 545–59. See also Edmond M. Beame, 'The Use and Abuse of Machiavelli: The Sixteenth-Century French Adaptation', *Journal of the History of Ideas* 43, no. 1 (1982), 33–54; Gisela Bock and Quentin Skinner, *Machiavelli and Republicanism* (Cambridge: Cambridge University Press, 2011). For evaluations of the English reception of Machiavelli, see Felix Raab, *The English Face of Machiavelli* (London: Routledge and Kegal Paul, 1964); Mario Praz, *Machiavelli and the Elizabethans* (London: Oxford University Press, 1928). For a literary take on republicanism, see David Norbrook, *Writing*

the English Republic: Poetry, Rhetoric and Politics, 1627–1660 (Cambridge: Cambridge University Press, 2004).

22. See Friedrich Meinecke, *Machiavellism: The Doctrine of Raison d'État and Its Place in Modern History*, tr. Douglas Scott (New Haven, CT: Yale University Press, 1957); Leo Strauss, *Thoughts on Machiavelli* (Glencoe, IL: The Free Press, 1958). See also Harvey C. Mansfield, *Machiavelli's Virtue* (Chicago, IL: University of Chicago Press, 1996).

23. In this context, see Eugene Garver, *Machiavelli and the History of Prudence* (Madison, WI: University of Wisconsin Press, 1987).

24. For a wider analysis by Winter of the theme of public and performative violence in politics, see Yves Winter, *Machiavelli and the Orders of Violence* (Cambridge: Cambridge University Press, 2018).

25. Mikael Hörnqvist, *Machiavelli and Empire* (Cambridge: Cambridge University Press, 2004), 227. For understanding the functions of power and political alignment in Renaissance Florence, see Humphrey Butters, *Governors and Government in Early Sixteenth Century Florence, 1502–1519* (Oxford: Clarendon Press, 1985). For a comprehensive appreciation of the principles of monarchy in Rome and its relationship to the Renaissance prince, see Peter Stacey, *Roman Monarchy and the Renaissance Prince* (Cambridge: Cambridge University Press, 2007). See also Mark Jurdjevic, *A Wretched and Great City: Promise and Failure in Machiavelli's Florentine Political Thought* (Cambridge, MA: Harvard University Press, 2014).

26. For Machiavelli's reaction against Ariosto, see J. B. Atkinson and D. Sices, eds. and tr., *Machiavelli and His Friends: Their Personal Correspondence* (DeKalb, IL: Northern Illinois University Press, 1996).

27. For a genealogy of the critical turns in Machiavelli scholarship, see Joseph V. Femia, *Machiavelli Revisited* (Cardiff: University of Wales Press, 2002).

Power, Citizenship, Strategies

2

Machiavelli on Relationships

Knowledge of the Occasion[*]

Thomas Berns

I would like to describe the way in which Machiavelli develops the idea of knowledge of the opportunity or occasion. I will try to substantiate the idea, first, by showing the shocks resulting from the clash of temporalities within it; second, by addressing two related issues, the question of 'forcing belief' and the classic argument of the new prince giving form to matter; and third, by widening my scope and making Machiavelli a philosopher of relationships.

Knowing the Occasion

In Chapter 6 of *The Prince*, Machiavelli says that founders of states or communities like Moses, Cyrus, Romulus, and Theseus received nothing from fortune except the occasion or opportunity that gave them the matter or substance to imbue with a form.[1] Without this encounter between opportunity and *virtù*, the first would have been in vain and the second would have languished. This means that the fortune of a founder and the opportunities that he encounters essentially consist of disorder and hardship that are, however, suitable for putting into order: as I will point out later, this is particularly clear in the *Discourses on Livy* (Book 1, Chapter 2). Occasion, fortune, and *virtù* draw their respective meanings solely from their relations with each other: none of them can have substantive value without the other two. This tense relationship between occasion, fortune, and *virtù* rules out both historical determinism and determinism of will, or even a harmonization of the two through the idea of a constant willingness or acceptance of what happens, or of a simple versatility as defended by Pontano in his *De prudentia* (1496).

As Machiavelli points out in the same chapter of *The Prince*, this encounter of fortune and *virtù* produces nothing less than a specific kind of knowledge. The excellent *virtù* of these founders makes it possible for the opportunity to be met or, more literally, to be known.[2] I propose to strictly respect the terms of this remark: identifying an opportunity in this way constitutes a genuine act of knowledge, understood as an experience that affords a representation of reality. Such knowledge has the nature of an encounter, just as we can claim we have 'known' a hardship or 'known' a woman or a man through sexual intercourse. It would be an interesting exercise to give such experience a more general validity by endowing it with cognitive consistency.

We can consider other instances of such appeal to the register of knowledge, deriving from a specific encounter or experience rather than from a general exercise of reason. In *The Art of War*, Book 7, Machiavelli proposes a few 'general rules' for the practice of war, specifying that in war, we must have the skill or ability ('sapere') to know ('conoscere') the opportunity and to seize it.[3] The distinction between *sapere* and *conoscere*, and the fact that the latter is not equivalent to seizing ('pigliare') the opportunity, clearly testifies that we are dealing with a cognitive experience.

We may interpret in the same way a passage in the *Capitolo dell'Occasione* where, following an epigram by Ausonius, opportunity is said to be 'known by few' ('a pochi nota'): she turns, runs, slinks away, so that 'one does not '[re]cognize' ("conosca") me when I pass by'.[4] Given man's incapacity to know or to recognize her, opportunity is apprehended only in a context of regret, from the repentance ('penitenzia') of those who have let her pass them by: for he who lets the occasion pass by is, above all, the very one who doubts or questions it and, 'occupied by many futile thoughts'[5] (that is to say, wasting time in weighing the opportunity), ends up by letting it flee. In short, we let the opportunity slip away just when we might hope to master it through our knowledge, to plan or determine the terms of the encounter. Encounters with opportunity necessarily depend on a different kind of knowledge: opportunity is truly apprehended only after it has been seized.

The Clash of Temporalities

In Machiavelli's work, especially *The Prince*, knowledge of the occasion is always expressed as a bringing together of multiple temporalities, with the resultant shock or impact. Needless to say, seizing the opportunity calls for speed, excess, audacity, and cruelty: that is why, in *The Prince*, ch. 25, Machiavelli says that Fortune loves young people, who are more fierce and audacious in commanding her. Here, Machiavelli departs radically from the Aristotelian vocabulary of the right measure, the middle way, lukewarmness, balance, and prudence. Even his praise of youth is opposed to the Aristotelian vocabulary of middle age.

The seized occasion is revealed as entirely necessary in terms of the resulting history and the new order generated thereby—for it would surely be wrong to consider knowledge of the opportunity as temporally limited to the moment of its seizure, however essential the latter might be. In Chapter 6 of *The Prince*, this seizing of opportunity is expressed exclusively in the past tense: it *was* necessary, it *was* required, it *was* fitting ('era necessario', 'bisognava', 'conveniva'). Machiavelli uses such words to describe each encounter of a founding figure with a specific reality—a reality that is not obviously favourable but rather full of hardship and obstacles, yet apt for ordering. The essential conditions for seizing an opportunity cannot be expressed in the present tense, as a general rule. They can only be expressed by the effects which appear to be inherent to the concerned encounter or relationship.

If opportunity presents itself as slinking by, resisting a certain type of rational mastery, if regret is a constitutive albeit negative concomitant of its being, and if the truth of the encounter can only be expressed in the past tense after its outcome is determined, it is because that determinate necessity only comes into operation later. Opportunity is only *known* when order, as form entering into matter at the moment of their encounter, is prolonged and confirmed: only then does it appear to be an effective order, towards which that encounter and all results thereof were necessarily striving, and only then does an apparently adverse situation reveal itself as a fit convergence of circumstances, providing an opportunity for the *virtù* of the founder to find expression.

The clash of temporalities is particularly visible in the early chapters of the *Discourses* in the context of Roman history. Machiavelli truly confronts the originary moment of Roman history in *Discourses* 1:9, plainly legitimizing[6] the fratricidal violence of the founder of Rome. Earlier, in *Discourses* 1:2, he had evoked this origin in a negative way, as incomplete and not perfect. On the contrary, the origin of the fortunate city of Sparta is entirely defined by the *logos* of its good legislator (the *logos* of Lycurgus, as Polybius puts it), leading on to a political history that can only be understood as the preservation of this *logos*, the conservation of a perfect and rational rule. By contrast, the violent and imperfect origin of the Roman *civitas* means that its outcome is always 'deferred', and that at two levels. It is deferred in respect of the structure of Machiavelli's discourse: he starts by outlining the intrinsically indeterminate institutions of Rome, born of its conflict-torn history, and only then reverts to what had started this history, an act of violence. He thereby sees that act as underlying the changes or differences marking the history of the institutions, deferring the effect of the originary violence. But the impact of that initial act is also deferred in its content. Properly speaking, the originating violence described in *Discourses* 1:9, providing an apparent rationale for the leap from

Machiavelli to Machiavellism, does not *determine* anything, nor is it endowed with any content; what determines Roman institutions are the later political conflicts that have impelled the history of the state. The origin remains absolutely undetermined: it only opens the way to an ever-deferred history. As in Derrida, the initiating premise is a difference whose meaning is deferred.

Knowing an opportunity thus implies knowledge of an encounter made valid and consistent by reaching a point where it comes to express a necessity. We could say that a function of Machiavelli's thought is to manifest this necessity by unravelling the relations that constitute it, thus revealing the opportunity presented by the encounter. Chapter 6 of *The Prince* analyses this process, which alone testifies that the opportunity has been encountered and that matter has thereby taken form—the form of an enduring order which, in turn, allows knowledge of the occasion that brought it into being.

Forms of Matter

Let me now turn to this process whereby opportunity is encountered and the matter of history acquires form. Putting it this way implies a materialistic conception of the relation between form and matter. Here, Machiavelli evokes the notion of force. As we will see, the issue of force confronts us with a difficulty: intuitively, from a perspective we might call 'instrumentalist', we conceive of force as separating form from matter, because force is mobilized towards and justified by an order that is already given. Machiavelli's text actively resists such an interpretation. It suggests there was no such preexstant order—that is to say, an instrumentalist reading cannot validate the idea of knowledge of the opportunity.

Let us examine, then, how Machiavelli inscribes an enduring order, not underpinned by preexstant necessities, into what I have already presented as the encounter between *virtù* and fortune. The problem with *nuovi ordini*, says Machiavelli, is not only that they hurt those who were profiting from the earlier dispensation and are therefore 'enemies' of the new, but even more (and it is not trivial that Machiavelli emphasizes this aspect) that they are supported only in a mild or lukewarm way by those they are meant to benefit. This is due to the incredulity of the latter group: people do not believe in new things ('non credano in verità le cose nuove') until they acquire firm experience ('una ferma esperienza') of them.[7] This factor of novelty should be borne in mind, while admitting that such firm experience is by definition deferred, so that acceptance is indeed reduced to a question of 'belief'.

Forcing Belief

Here again, Machiavelli premises not a cognitive register based on firm experience but a belief that must be forced. The latter part of Chapter 6 consists entirely of driving home, repeatedly and insistently, the precariousness of a new order and the need to force belief in it. New princes cannot merely play the prophet, or pray ('preghino', which can be interpreted as repeating or reiterating the article of belief): they must enforce belief through force. Machiavelli uses the verb *forzare* twice without an object or complement. Force is not external to what it acts upon. It does not force something else but sites its operation within itself: it does not force an order upon matter from outside. In contrast to Savonarola, an effective prophet must therefore be armed to sustain a belief that would otherwise crumble. It is necessary to 'force belief' ('fare … credere per forza')[8] to establish a new order. Machiavelli repeats the idea several times, always combining the registers of belief and force.

What is this force that is so essential to construct and sustain belief? By linking force with belief in this way, Machiavelli implicitly dismisses two alternative possibilities, one dispensing with force and the other with belief.

The first possibility, which he explicitly raises and dismisses, is that prayer or prophecy might be enough in itself to induce belief in a new order—in other words, merely repeating the prophecy would suffice. We know that Savonarola, in his *Trattato sul governo di Firenze*, and particularly in the opening lines of the third part, utterly excludes the possibility of establishing a political regime by the force of arms. He justifies this stand by arguing that force has no common ground with reason, as the latter is unable to resist force.[9] He affirms in the clearest way, mainly in his *Sermons* but also in his texts about prophecy (the *Compiendio di rivelazioni* and the *Dialogus de veritate prophetica*), that the divine will acts directly upon his prophetic speech, making it an instrument for guiding the Christian community without need for mediation. Machiavelli responds radically to this unmediated power of prophecy by insisting upon the insufficiency of prophecy by itself to found a new order. To understand his position, we need revisit his premise of the lukewarm engagement of the political majority to the new order. Already in his letter to Ricciardo Becchi (9 March 1498), Machiavelli recounts that Savonarola's mistake lies in the fact that he considers, beyond the 'bad' that opposed him and the 'good' that supported him, a third type of person, neither good nor bad, unable to tell good from evil but, in a direct conflict between the good and the bad, would side with the good.[10] In Chapter 6 of *The Prince*, Machiavelli again rejects the notion that this third type of person will spontaneously join the 'good' in the event of a serious conflict with the 'bad'. The incredulity of the majority cannot be tackled through the prophetic message alone. It requires the addition of force to prophecy, 'fare ... credere per forza'.[11]

Yet Machiavelli is equally, if only implicitly, opposed to the idea that force by itself can ensure obedience to a new order—as if this order was not at all a matter of belief, as if it was founded independently of what it involves, as if it was already fully established and grounded in firm experience. Such a scenario might be credited to cities such as Sparta, which had, since its origin, enjoyed a perfect constitution that needed only to be preserved. In the *Discourses*, Machiavelli consistently dismisses such an ordered and well-defined scenario with respect to Rome. In the absence of a firm proven order, the lack of belief of the lukewarm majority can only be tackled in terms of belief, even if the belief has to be forced: it cannot simply rely on the founded and rational character of the intended reform.

These two rival possibilities are what Machiavelli avoids by binding belief to force: in other words, adopting Savonarola's perspective to a certain point but finally diverging on the question of arms. Both these viewpoints being eschewed, it is evident that the use of the classic antithesis of form versus matter cannot, in Machiavelli, be understood as if the latter entity is passive. In fact, the two viewpoints are rejected precisely because they assume the unilateral imposition of an autonomous form upon passive matter. Instead, form and matter are placed in an interactive relationship: order, resulting from form infused in matter, is not the actualization of a potential enshrined in prayer or obedience but the expression of a state of power that is perpetually being enacted, a belief that is constantly being forced. 'Forcing belief' in Machiavelli's sense thus allows us to dispense with both religious and juridical assumptions in and for themselves.

To sum up my argument so far: for opportunity to be *known*, it is necessary to *force belief* in a new order, rather than relying on prophetic speech as sufficient to establish the belief, so that thereafter one need only ensure its formal legitimacy. This way of thinking about the relation between order and matter does not assume the exteriority and autonomy of the former. Another, even broader way of saying this is to consider the specificity of political knowledge in Machiavelli to be entirely shaped by a series of 'pure' or 'raw' relations: not so much links between cause and effect, or means and ends, as associations that Machiavelli endows with necessity. The concomitant of this raw materiality of relations is, of course, that their meaning or purport is always postponed, deferred. I will now demonstrate this from some famous passages in the early chapters of the *Discourses*.

Thinking Relations

In *Discourses* 1:2, Machiavelli presents various possible scenarios for a mixed constitution. First, he describes the constitutions of cities such as Sparta, which had the good fortune to have, since their founding, a perfect constitution which they needed only to preserve. Such a scenario relies on the exceptional virtue and rationality of one good founding legislator, which in turn depends on fortune (both of which factors can be considered totally extrinsic): in a larger sense, these cities are condemned to conserve themselves. In such a situation, Machiavelli contrasts the history of Rome, which had not benefited from the same initial good fortune. On the contrary, Rome worked out its own fortune through a series of hardships and upsets. The fact that Rome did not have a prudent legislator like Lycurgus at the outset, but an inconclusive origin followed by persistent internal dissensions, was the driving force behind its own kind of order, an order immanent in the disorder that produced and forced it.

The difference between these two possible scenarios, one inscribed at the time of origin and the other always deferred, produces a basic and lasting distinction in the history of political thought: between a city or state whose form and fortune have been determined at its foundation, and one whose form and fortune evolve through its history. The former is necessarily limited from the demographic and institutional point of view: it might certainly be peaceful but can only maintain and preserve its own original form. The latter is plural and populous, open as regards its institutions, and imbued by conflict; it can change and expand.[12]

The distinction is essentially qualitative: it defines two possible designs, two ways of thinking about civic order. Machiavelli is drawn to the 'Roman' design, with the series of relations that constitute it, as providing a singular model even though, he acknowledges, it appears contrary to the true *vivere politico*.[13] He thereby elevates a non-model to the rank of a model. Both models seem legitimate; which one we choose depends on whether we wish to consider a republic that would set up an empire or a republic that seeks only to maintain itself in its current state.[14] Both models are constituted, equally and exclusively, by a set of relations: as determined by origin (closed, aristocratic, peaceful, limited, and conservative) or as determined by subsequent history (open, popular, tumultuous, and expansive). Here, then, are two magisterial equations enshrined in two opposed models of a republic.

At the start of *Discourses* 1:4, Machiavelli deconstructs the traditional reading of Roman history, which, by conceiving of the Roman disorder as a mere lack or absence of order, has to seek an external force to explain its greatness, either divine providence or military virtue:

> [T]he opinion of many that Rome, having been a tumultuous republic and full of much confusion, would have remained inferior to all other republics if good fortune and military virtue had not had compensated for these flaws.[15]

Machiavelli's reading does not deny the disorder but finds a strength in it, linking it to Roman liberty and expansionism. Again, there is no passive element in the equation.

We can go further and consider that Machiavelli's choice of Rome as the subject of his study, against the traditional idea of a model as stable and balanced, makes it apparent that we are contemplating a series of pure relations. What counts here is that this series of relations is impermeable, hermetically exclusive of other possible relations. There can be no middle path between the two models, such as would result from an Aristotelian approach; no possible balance between them, taking into consideration the apparent advantages of each, peace in the aristocratic model and power in the Roman model. Even worse, says Machiavelli in *Discourses* 1:6, given the fact that history is a perennial movement, and that 'necessity pushes you to many things that reason does not',[16] Rome represents *in fine* the most interesting grounds for refuting the claims of reason. The last word is thereby given precisely by the impossibility of conceiving of a form external to the matter of history: that is to say, the last word is deferred, and so is the sense of opportunity.

In *The Prince* as well as the *Discourses*, force or conflict is the expression of a collective experiment of belief in something that, being new or being linked to the unstable 'course of events' ('occorrenzia degli accidenti'),[17] resists the classic cognitive experience and must therefore be viewed as deferred. Because it is difficult to believe in such new things, force must be invoked to make it possible. To put it positively, this means that we are led by force to believe in new things, the experience of which is by definition difficult, unavailable, deferred, reliant on the course of events. And this idea can only be expressed through these suites of 'pure' or 'raw' relations proposed by Machiavelli, whose meaning is always postponed or deferred.[18]

Knowing opportunity, forcing belief, thinking politics on the basis of these sets of pure relations—all these are expressions of a certain kind of knowledge: a knowledge that does not support any previous certainty about the adequacy of the order created by form instilled in matter. At the same time, such knowledge is oriented to that order: it is an acknowledgement that a belief has been forced—that is to say, an event has occurred, behind which lies a series of relations and tensions (constitutive elements of what Althusser calls a 'conjuncture'[19]) confirmed by a collective process. These elements are never referred to an external, anterior order that could dissolve those relations or bypass the tensions that inhabit them. Machiavellian thought is fully oriented towards this kind of knowledge.

Notes

* In this chapter, I recapitulate and develop arguments already presented in Thomas Berns, 'Prophetic Efficacy: The Relationship between Force and Belief', in *The Radical Machiavelli: Politics, Philosophy and Language*, ed. Filippo del Lucchese, Fabio Frosini, and Vittorio Morfino (Leiden: Brill, 2015), 230–45.
1. '[L]a occasione[,] la quale dette loro materia a potere introdurvi dentro quella forma': *Pr.*, ch. 6; Machiavelli, *Tutte le opere*, ed. Mario Martelli (Florence: Sansoni, 1971), 264. All Machiavelli's Italian texts are cited from this edition (henceforth *Opere*). The translations are my own.
2. '[L]a eccellente virtù loro fece quella occasione essere *conosciuta*' (emphasis added): *Pr.*, ch. 6, *Opere* 265.
3. 'Sapere nella guerra conoscere l'occasione e pigliarla': Machiavelli, *Dell'arte della guerra*, lib. 7, *Opere* 385.
4. '[N]on mi conosca quando io vengo': Machiavellli, 'Dell'Occasione', *Opere* 987.
5. '[O]ccupato da molti pensier vani': ibid.
6. For the first time in the historiography of Rome: see Thomas Berns, *Violence de la loi à la Renaissance: L'originaire du politique chez Machiavel et Montaigne* (Paris: Kimé, 2000), 43–70.
7. *Pr.*, ch. 6, *Opere* 265.
8. Ibid.
9. See Girolamo Savonarola, *Treatise on the Rule and Government of the City of Florence*, 3:1, in *Selected Writings of Girolamo Savonarola: Religion and Politics, 1490–1498*, ed. and tr. Anne Borelli et al. (New Haven, CT: Yale University Press, 2006), 197–8.
10. Letter to Ricciardo Becchi, 9 March 1498: *Opere* 1011.
11. *Pr.*, ch. 6, *Opere* 265.
12. *Disc.* 1:2–6.
13. *Disc.* 1:6.
14. *Disc.* 1:5.
15. '[L]a opinione di molti che dicono, Roma essere stata una republica tumultuaria, e piena di tanta confusione che, se la buona fortuna e la virtù

militare non avesse sopperito a' loro difetti, sarebbe stata inferiore a ogni altra republica': *Disc.* 1:4, *Opere* 82. This interpretation, which we find, for example, in St. Augustine and which Machiavelli here reverses, is based on the same equation linking an originating act of violence (Romulus killing his brother, opening the doors of Rome to the brigands, the rape of the Sabine women, and so on) to the internal conflicts of the city and to external wars: see Thomas Berns, 'Penser le politique depuis le caractère expansif de la liberté', *Historia philosophica* 11 (2013), 35–45.
16. '[A] molte cose che la ragione non t'induce, t'induce la necessità': *Disc.* 1:6, *Opere* 86.
17. *Disc.* 1:2, *Opere* 79.
18. In *Disc.* 1:5–6, the conquests undertaken by Rome are seen as the deferred expression of the same phenomenon: they are not the achievements of a *virtù* independent of disorder or external to it but the deferred order of the disorder itself, an expression of the order inherent in the conflicts. The conquests are a sign of the expansive character of freedom, which means freedom of the largest number; hence, internal conflict can produce order. On this subject, see Thomas Berns, *La guerre des philosophes* (Paris: Presses Universitaires de France, 2019).
19. More precisely, this immanent necessity is what Althusser called 'penser *sous* la catégorie de conjoncture' (emphasis added), thinking *under* (not *about* or *sur*) the category of conjuncture: Louis Althusser, *Machiavel et nous* (Paris: Tallandier, 2009), 55. This is also what Deleuze, situating himself in the tradition of Spinoza, Nietzsche, and Foucault, called thinking of the 'content of possibilities' of a situation, the potential inherent in it (which does not contradict the 'liberty or creativity' of a *dispositif* or a mode of existence), in order to express the possibility of weighing it 'without any appeal to transcendental values': Gilles Deleuze, 'What Is a *Dispositif?*' in *Michel Foucault Philosopher*, tr. Timothy J. Armstrong (New York: Routledge, 1992), 159–66, 163.

3

The Anatomy of an Error
Machiavelli's Supposed Commitment to a 'Citizen' Militia

Paul A. Rahe

If there is one thing that in our time everyone knows concerning Niccolò Machiavelli, it is that he favoured the establishment of a citizen militia. Aristotle had made the case for a citizen army in his *Politics*.[1] In his *De militia*, Leonardo Bruni had advocated the establishment of an order of civic knights composed of the leading citizens of Florence (although not, as some suppose, a civic militia, including a large body of infantry, of the sort that had existed in the thirteenth century).[2] Machiavelli followed these predecessors. So at least we are told by luminaries such as Hans Baron, Cecil H. Clough, J. G. A. Pocock—who made 'arms-bearing citizenship' the mainstay of his argument concerning the so-called civic humanist tradition—and Quentin Skinner in *The Foundations of Modern Political Thought*;[3] and on their authority, this claim has been bandied about ever since.[4]

However, as I have noted in passing more than once,[5] the claim does not survive close scrutiny. Machiavelli agreed with Aristotle and Bruni that mercenary soldiers are unreliable. He firmly favoured reliance on 'populations armed' ('populationi armate'),[6] but nowhere in any of his correspondence or works did he ever insist that those armed be drawn from the citizenry or that they be made citizens.

In Florence, when he was secretary of the Second Chancery, Machiavelli championed the institution of a popular militia, as is well known. He proposed and succeeded in securing the passage of what came to be known as the *ordinanza*. He personally oversaw the militia's establishment. He hired a mercenary captain to see to its training, he selected the officers, he managed this little conscript army throughout its existence, and he was justly proud when his *ordinanza* secured the surrender of Pisa and brought that city back into the Florentine territorial state.[7]

Moreover, nine years after the Medici had been restored to power and his militia been partially disbanded, reconfigured, and reconstituted by the city's new masters, Machiavelli published his dialogue *The Art of War*, where he had his chief interlocutor, a distinguished mercenary captain named Fabrizio Colonna, defend the *ordinanza* and lay out his understanding of the manner in which a popular militia along such lines should be organized, trained, and deployed in battle.[8] It would be fair to say that arming the population was for Machiavelli a persistent or even a central concern. Where there are 'good arms' ('buone arme'), he intimates in *The Prince*, there will be 'good laws' ('buone legge').[9]

The Florentine Militia

The Florentine population that Machiavelli armed was not limited to the citizen body. In fact, there were next to no citizens in Machiavelli's militia. Those who were recruited and who served were Florence's subjects, not her citizens. They were *contadini*, not *cittadini*.

Initially, to be sure, early in the fall of 1506, when Machiavelli first formally proposed organizing a popular militia for the defence of Florence and that city's territorial state, he wished to start with the *contadini*, but then in time add to them a force of *cittadini*, and ultimately join with them a similar force drawn from the *distretto*—that is to say, the once-independent and sometimes rebellious communities that had been incorporated within Florence's dominion. Later, however, on 6 December, when the *ordinanza* was passed, no mention was made of either of the latter two categories.[10]

There was a logic to their omission. Pisa was in revolt; the rest of the *distretto* was restive; and thanks to their experience in the late fourteenth century with the Ciompi, the Florentines accorded full citizen rights were wary of arming the lower orders within the *città*. Moreover, there was ample precedent for the recruitment of *contadini*. In the past, in times of military exigency, this had been done with some frequency.[11] Moreover, upon reflection, it must have seemed a dictate of prudence to Machiavelli's political masters that they play down and obscure the radical, transformative character of their institution of a sizable permanent military establishment along the lines specified in the *ordinanza*.[12] Piero Soderini, the first and only Gonfaloniere to be elected in Florence for life, and his politically ambitious, tough-minded younger brother Francesco Soderini, bishop and cardinal of Volterra, were not fools.[13]

In his original proposal, Machiavelli mentioned the *cittadini* only once, almost as an afterthought, and he never spoke or wrote about their subsequent exclusion from his militia as a defect. Indeed, he may, from the outset, have thought the opposite. Certainly, by the time he penned

The Art of War—though he was prepared to draw on the *città* for cavalry and no doubt also for smiths, carpenters, ferriers, stonecutters, and the like—he had come to prefer as infantrymen the residents of Florence's *contado*. He may have been alert, as the ancient Greeks were,[14] to the fact that the rural population of a territory has a greater stake in victory than do its city-dwellers—that the property of farmers is not sheltered by the town's walls; that they possess farms which may be looted, ravaged, or even confiscated should a war be lost; and that those who cannot take their skills and money elsewhere should the community be conquered make better soldiers than do merchants, bankers, artisans, and skilled craftsmen. This, however, it would have been impolitic to stress in a book written in Tuscan and addressed, at least in the first instance, to the merchants, bankers, artisans, and skilled craftsmen of his native Florence. So the grounds that Machiavelli made Fabrizio Colonna stress in his dialogue are those mentioned by Vegetius, the Roman writer on whom, in this work, Machiavelli most frequently drew: that the *contadini*, being peasants, are toughened up by hard labour in the sun.[15]

My main point, however, is simply this: that to all appearances, Machiavelli was indifferent to the question of citizenship. All that seems to have mattered was that the soldiers be stakeholders, apt to lose something of vital importance to them should a war be lost. Only then would they be willing to risk their lives to defend the territory of the pertinent principality or republic, and only then would their arms be the arms of the prince or of the republic.

One's Own Arms

This is what Machiavelli emphasizes in the books he penned. In the twelfth and thirteenth chapters of *The Prince*, for example, he takes up the question of 'offence' and 'defence' (*le offese e difese*).[16] It is in this context that he emphasizes the importance of good laws and good arms. It is in these chapters that he observes, 'And because it is not possible for there to be good laws where there are not good arms and where there are good arms there must be good laws, I shall leave out the reasoning concerning laws and speak of arms.'[17]

Machiavelli's theme is that 'mercenary and auxiliary arms are useless and dangerous': that mercenaries are 'disunited, ambitious, bereft of discipline, unfaithful, gallant among friends, among enemies cowardly' and that they exhibit 'no fear of God' and 'no faith with men'. Ruin, he says, 'is delayed only so long as attack is delayed; and in peace you are by them despoiled, in war by the enemy'.[18] These mercenaries are useless because, although they will take their pay, they will not risk their lives. They are dangerous because they are sometimes in a position to seize the city that hired them, and auxiliary arms—those supplied by a foreign prince or city – are, for the same reason, if anything more dangerous still.

In this connection, Machiavelli engages in a heartfelt diatribe against the practices adopted by the Italian cities after the Guelfs in the towns, with the help of the Church, overcame the militia deployed by the Ghibelline nobles based in the countryside and subjected the *contado* to the *città*.[19] In his view, these practices—above all, the reliance on mercenaries—left Italy vulnerable to the invasion that Charles VIII of France staged in 1494 and to subsequent interventions by his successor Louis XII and the formidable husband of Isabella of Castile, Ferdinand of Aragon.

When Machiavelli offers examples of cities that managed 'offence' and 'defence' properly, he mentions the Romans, the Spartans, and the Swiss before any other communities. This might be taken as evidence that he was a champion of 'arms-bearing citizenship'. But in the thirteenth chapter of his treatise, when he makes positive recommendations, he harps on a simple theme: that a prince must have his own arms. 'Without possessing its own arms,' he concludes, 'no principality is secure; indeed it is entirely obliged to fortune since it cannot rely on virtue for its defense in adversity.' He adds an explanation that 'one's own arms are those which are made up of either your subjects, or citizens, or your creatures'.[20] When he returns to this theme in the twentieth chapter of *The Prince*, while discussing whether fortresses are a help or a hindrance, he observes with some exaggeration:

> It has never happened, then, that a new prince has disarmed his subjects; on the contrary, whenever he has found them unarmed, he has always armed them. For when you arm them, those arms become yours; those suspected by you become faithful, and those who were faithful remain so; and from subjects they are made into your partisans.[21]

At least in *The Prince*, when Machiavelli argues that one needs to arm the population, he does not give preference to citizens over subjects, and the fact that he mentions the prince's 'creatures' suggests that he would be perfectly happy to see a new prince set his 'creatures' over the citizens and subjects to be found in a particular community, as the mercenary captain Francesco Sforza had done when he seized control in Milan.[22] We should not underestimate the ruthlessness of the man whose example was thought by some to have occasioned the devil's coming to be called 'Old Nick'.[23]

One could, of course, argue that in his *Discourses on Livy* Machiavelli adopts a different stance, and there, where he rarely discusses 'new princes' as such,[24] he does drop all mention of such a prince's 'creatures'. But when he turns to 'defence and offence' in Book 1, Chapter 21, of that supposedly republican work, his theme, as the chapter title indicates, is that princes and republics alike must have 'their own arms' ('armi proprie'), and the exemplars to whom he points are monarchs, not republican magistrates: Tullus Hostilius of Rome and Henry VIII of England.[25] Moreover, when he returns to this subject in Book 1, Chapter 43, he insists that republics and kingdoms alike must arm their 'subjects' ('sudditi').[26]

He repeats these points in Book 2, Chapter 10, where he denies that 'money is the sinews of war' ('I danari non sono il nervo della guerra'), arguing that a prince will fool himself if he measures his forces

> by money, or by the site, or by the benevolence of men, while lacking his own arms. For the things just mentioned increase your forces well, but do not give them to you well, and by themselves are nothing and do not help in any way in the absence of faithful arms. For without these, ample money does not suffice, nor does the strength of the country come to your aid; the faith and benevolence of men do not last, for they cannot be faithful to you if you are unable to defend them. Every mountain, every lake, every inaccessible place becomes a plain in the absence of strong defenders. Money also—not only does it not defend you, it makes you into prey the sooner.[27]

It is, as he pointedly puts it soon thereafter, the countryside or *paese* that must be armed, not the citizens as such. In this particular, he can praise the Romans and the Swiss while criticizing the Carthaginians, the Italians of his own day, and tellingly, in the same discussion, the current king of France.[28]

There are other chapters in the second book of the *Discourses*[29] in which Machiavelli returns to the military matters first explored in *The Prince*, such as mercenaries, auxiliaries, and fortresses; and in these chapters he frequently refers to *The Prince* and restates the themes that he developed in that work. What is striking about these chapters is that Machiavelli persistently discusses principalities and republics as if, in this important regard, there is no difference between them. By this expedient, Machiavelli deliberately and ostentatiously distances his critique of the Italian communes' dependence on mercenaries and auxiliary troops from that advanced by the 'civic humanists'.

Ordinanza

But, one might ask, what about *The Art of War*? Does Machiavelli not repeatedly refer there to the need for a 'citizen militia'? This is certainly what one would suppose if one were to rely on Allan H. Gilbert's translation of Machiavelli's works, as Pocock and Skinner did; and I suspect this is the proximate origin of the error they propagated. Had they attended closely to the original, they might well have stopped short of making the claims they advanced.

If one examines the Italian text, one discovers that every time that Gilbert's Machiavelli uses the phrase 'citizen militia', 'citizen army', 'citizen force', 'citizen armies', or 'citizen forces', the real Machiavelli used the term *ordinanza*.[30] Put simply, Gilbert's translation is not a translation; it is a paraphrase—at times, an exceedingly inaccurate paraphrase. Or, rather, it is an interpretation—a demonstrably false interpretation given that the Florentine military, to which the term *ordinanza* in this context refers, was almost entirely made up of *contadini*, who were in no way citizens.

The word *ordinanza* deserves more attention than it has received, for it has a history. It goes back to Charles VII of France, who managed to recover his kingdom from Henry VI of England, son of Henry V and Catherine of France—in part, of course, because of the popular uprising inspired by Joan of Arc, but also because this Charles had the good sense to issue an *ordonnance* providing for the organization of what were called the *compagnies d'ordonnance*: that is to say, he made provision for arming and training the French peasantry so that as infantrymen they could defend themselves, the land they farmed, and their king against the depredations of the English and their French adherents.[31]

As the choice of name suggests, Machiavelli's *ordinanza* was a Florentine imitation of the French *ordonnance* designed to enable Florence to withstand Louis XII of France and Ferdinand of Aragon. Machiavelli's popular army was an imitation of the popular army raised by Charles VII and abandoned by his successors. If this claim seems far-fetched, one need only consult—preferably in the original—the thirteenth chapter of *The Prince*, where Machiavelli singles out Charles VII for praise, noting that he 'recognized this necessity of arming oneself with one's own arms, and laid down within his kingdom an *ordinanza* for men-at-arms and infantry'.[32]

There is something else that needs mention. In Machiavelli's lifetime, Europe was undergoing a military revolution.[33] The successes of Charles VII's *compagnies d'ordonnance* foreshadowed what was to come, but they were not the most indicative and startling events. These would be the repeated, dramatic defeats and ultimate death that the lowly pikemen of Switzerland inflicted in 1476 and 1477, when Machiavelli was a boy, on Charles the Bold of Burgundy, who was leading the greatest armies of mounted knights ever assembled.

It was this shocking series of events that brought home to the monarchs of Europe the need for disciplined infantry, and it was this that inspired Machiavelli's critique of the mounted mercenaries of his native Italy and of cavalry more generally. It was his conviction that in the future the infantry would command the battlefield, as it had in antiquity in Greece and in the Mediterranean more generally; and, if one naturally looked to the landed aristocracy for cavalry, it was to the ordinary peasants who tilled the soil that one looked for infantry,[34] as the ancient Greeks and Romans had done. It is no accident that in the *Discourses*, when he insists that money is not the sinews of war, Machiavelli alludes to the Swiss defeat of Charles the Bold. Their achievements and example loomed large in his thinking.[35] Nor is it fortuitous that towards the end of that book, he addresses a prince, saying, 'The military cannot be good unless it is put through its paces; and it cannot be put through its paces unless it is made up of your subjects.'[36]

All of this suggests that it makes no sense to think of Machiavelli as a 'civic humanist' or 'classical republican'. He is, in fact, sui generis. He departs, as he himself claims, 'from the orders of others' ('dagli ordini degli altri'),[37] and he does so in nearly every regard.

Political and Military Populism

One question remains. Was there a larger political programme lurking behind Machiavelli's preference for arming the population? According to Francesco Guicciardini, there were prominent men at Florence who opposed Machiavelli's *ordinanza* because they suspected as much. They wondered whether the intentions of the secretary of the Second Chancery and of the Soderini brothers were not revolutionary.

Prior to 1494, the Florentines had frequently hired a mercenary cavalry force but kept it at arm's length lest it seize the city. At least in the fourteenth century, as William Caferro has recently shown, this practice, supplemented by the hiring of infantrymen and infantry captains from within the Florentine territorial state and also from without, had served the military interests of the commune rather well.[38] It was one thing to do this. It was another to arm on a considerable scale and train as a permanent force a segment of the city's rural population—a body of men who belonged to Florence but who were not among its citizens. The fact that Piero Soderini had been elected *Gonfaloniere di Justizia* for life made Florence's *primi cittadini* nervous, and, of course, it inspired envy and resentment. It was unprecedented for the Standard-bearer of Justice to serve for more than a few months, and Soderini's election for life had the appearance of being the first step in a process that would transform the republic into a principality. Should this Soderini find himself in political trouble, they asked, would he not make use of what looked like a praetorian guard to install himself as tyrant? So, at least, we are told.[39]

The notables who, for the most part, ran Florence even under the post-1494 *governo popolare* were, by and large, well-educated. Many of them were steeped in ancient history and in the Greek and Roman classics; even those—and they were numerous—who had no desire to reconstruct Florence on the ancient Roman model tended to be civic humanists of a sort, inclined to quote Latin tags and classical examples and to think in classical terms.[40] They had read Plato, Aristotle, Cicero, Sallust, and Livy; they knew the work of Leonardo Bruni. They did not have to be told that there is nearly always a symbiotic connection between the political regime governing a community and the army that defends it, and that trouble is apt to result where the two are not carefully coordinated. Political scientists know this even today, as Stephen Peter Rosen's 1996 book *Societies and Military Power: India and Its Armies* testifies.[41]

Even if the opposition to the *ordinanza* reported by Guicciardini was a figment of the man's imagination, as one distinguished scholar has recently argued,[42] or if its opponents were unduly suspicious, the legal safeguards were more than sufficient to prevent abuse. Machiavelli and the Soderini were not up to anything untoward in Florence, as many other scholars believe. But it remains a question whether, in advocating arming the population everywhere, the author of *The Prince*, the *Discourses on Livy*, and *The Art of War* did not have a radical agenda in mind. Machiavelli was, after all, a populist. He strongly advised princes to favour the *popolo* in preference to the *grandi*, and he gave the same advice to those wanting to found or rejuvenate republics.

This posture, in fact, set him radically at odds with Plato, Aristotle, Cicero, Sallust, Livy, and the civic humanists and classical republicans of his own time. His stance was closely linked with the critique of morality that he articulated in chapters fifteen to eighteen of *The Prince*. It was his view that moral superiority is a delusion and that the ideal of the gentleman peddled in the *Nicomachean Ethics*, *De officiis*, and elsewhere is fraudulent. He therefore argued a position that no classical republican had ever argued or ever would argue: that anyone who contemplates founding a republic must suppose every man a rogue. This debunking of morality, and of the claim that some men are morally superior to others, is the ground of his commitment to equality. One must assume, he said, that everyone is wicked.[43]

In promoting the infantry and calling for the populace to be armed, was Machiavelli not preparing the ground for a populist politics? The fact that from a military perspective, he was right about the central importance of the infantry, and the need to use the population residing in the rural regions of a polity's territory to defend it, does not rule out the possibility that he had another ulterior motive for pushing such a programme. This, according to Guicciardini, was what worried those in Florence who opposed Machiavelli's *ordinanza*, and they had a point. The establishment of a highly disciplined army of *contadini* on so great a scale ought to have made every last *cittadino* nervous, especially since the condottiere hired to train the troops was the Spaniard Don Miguel de Corella (known in Italy as Don Michele or Don Michelotto). Don Miguel had earned notoriety as a henchman of Cesare Borgia. As ambassadorial colleagues, Francesco Soderini and Machiavelli had witnessed this man's efforts to form and train a militia in the Romagna on behalf of his employer,[44] and the latter had been present when, at his master's behest, Don Miguel had employed this militia to commit a host of crimes, among them a massacre of Borgia's allies and likely future enemies at Senigaglia.[45]

The *primi cittadini* of Florence may well have had another reason for concern. As William Connell has explained to me, Machiavelli's *ordinanza* encroached in the *contado* on the rural patronage networks run by many of the city's patricians. With the support of their clients, these prominent families—above all, the Medici—had hitherto been able to field private armies and, in times of crisis, to turn their palaces within the *città* into fortresses guarded by armed retainers who camped out in their courtyards.[46] In effect, the scheme proposed by Machiavelli and the Soderini, and implemented in December 1506 by the Florentine state, threatened to transform the clients of these great families into retainers of the *governo popolare* that had made Piero Soderini *Gonfaloniere di Justizia a vita* and, as such, the permanent presiding officer of its *Signoria*, the governing body at Florence authorized to initiate legislation and pass ordinances.

I will not discuss here the accuracy of Guicciardini's report regarding the concerns of those who opposed the *ordinanza*, except to note that in late October 1504, Cardinal Soderini wrote a letter to Machiavelli intimating that there was already opposition to the plan on the very grounds mentioned by Guicciardini; and that much later, in *The Art of War*, Machiavelli had Cosimo Rucellai confirm the nervousness on this score and articulate the grounds for its presence.[47] Nor will I deal with the question of the immediate intentions of Machiavelli and the Soderini, except to make two points: that Cardinal Soderini, the more ruthless and audacious of the two siblings, appears to have supposed that the militia would be a support for his brother's rule[48] and that Machiavelli was later highly critical of Piero Soderini's failure to use force in 1512 to liquidate those among the *grandi* of Florence who were attempting to overturn the republic and restore the Medici.[49]

There is a substantial literature on the two questions in dispute,[50] and I am inclined both to credit Guicciardini and to suppose that, if Machiavelli's advice had been taken or Francesco Soderini had occupied the office held by his elder brother, there might well have been genuine grounds for the fears that Guicciardini reported. But for my purpose, the debates concerning the fears of Florence's *primi cittadini* and the calculations of Francesco and Piero Soderini do not matter.

A Precocious Jacobin?

The question that I want to explore instead is that of Machiavelli's long-term intentions. Was he, as Antonio Gramsci once suggested, 'a precocious Jacobin'? In addressing this matter, Gramsci voiced his suspicion that 'Machiavelli's goal was to create links between the city and the country and to broaden the role of the urban classes—to the point of asking them to divest themselves of certain feudal-corporative privileges with respect to the countryside, in order to incorporate the rural classes into the State.' It was Gramsci's conviction that 'no formation of national popular will is possible unless the masses of peasant farmers enter *simultaneously* into political life'. He was aware that this was what 'the Jacobins achieved in the French revolution', and inclined to think that 'this was what Machiavelli wanted to happen through the reform of the militia'.[51]

Gramsci's suggestion is attractive for two reasons. To begin with, it reminds us of certain facts that Marxist and Marxisant scholars in our day sometimes forget. First, while the *governo popolare* between 1494 and 1512 was quite democratic by the standards of the time, it was in fact a closed oligarchy in which no more than 13,000 of the 55,000 residents of the *città* were accorded citizenship. Of these, 3,000–3,500 were authorized to attend and vote at the meetings of the Grand Council, and not many more than 1,000 from this select group ordinarily showed up. Second, those elected to positions of leadership—to high office, the Council of Eighty, and the *Signoria*—were almost without exception selected from among the city's *primi cittadini*. Third, the sharp juridical distinction drawn between the *contadini* and the *cittadini* was no less apt, and perhaps even more so, to give rise to political conflict than the socio-economic distinctions between the Florentine *grandi* and the *popolo*. And fourth, one of the principal tasks assigned to Machiavelli's *ordinanza* was policing the *contado* and suppressing resistance to the dictates of the Florentine government.[52] Gramsci's suggestion also raises the question whether a man of Machiavelli's acumen could have failed to consider the probable long-term consequences of permanently arming the *contado*. The logic of Machiavelli's populism and the likely long-term result of arming the population fit all too neatly together.[53]

I have not found evidence proving beyond a doubt that Machiavelli linked the two. The one serious attempt to make the case, following Gramsci's suggestion, seems to me to be based on special pleading throughout. I have in mind Jérémie Barthas's recent book *L'Argent n'est pas le nerf de la guerre*, and the articles in English derived from it.[54]

Barthas's argument is ingenious. His focus is the fiscal-military state, which emerged in northern Italy—that is to say, in Venice and Florence—centuries before it appeared in Holland and England. Barthas bases his argument on the fine work on the Florentine fisc and the Florentine communal debt, the so-called Monte, carried out by Louis Marks and Anthony Molho, who demonstrate that there was a recurring fiscal crisis at Florence, that it was occasioned by frequent military emergencies, and that the city's wealthy merchants and bankers profited from the circumstances by making short-term loans to the commune at ridiculously high rates of interest. That this species of corruption was a serious problem in Florence is clear.[55] That it was a regime question, setting the *grandi* of Florence (as opposed to a handful of the wealthier families) resolutely against the city's *popolo* and the *contadini* in the territorial state, is another matter. The same can be said even more emphatically of Barthas's contention that the class struggle to which the communal debt and the fiscal-military state supposedly gave rise was the central problem facing the polities of Early Modern Europe. Wherever it existed, the system of public debt was at times an irritant (as it still is): of that there can be no doubt. At Florence, as Barthas points out, it caused Guicciardini to exclaim more than once in exasperation that the city must destroy the Monte or the Monte would destroy the city. But it was not the paramount issue. The great struggles at Florence turned on questions other than the public debt. Barthas takes a small piece in the puzzle that was Florence and treats it as the whole.

Even more to the point, however, at least for our present purposes, Barthas fails to show that the question of public debt plays any role at all in Machiavelli's thinking. The author of *The Prince*, the *Discourses on Livy*, *The Art of War*, and the *Florentine Histories* was, of course, aware that some of the *grandi* were engaged in milking the commune in this way.

As Barthas notes, he was present at the debates; in his capacity as a civil servant, he even took official notes at some of the *pratiche e consulte* held early in his time as secretary of the Second Chancery to discuss proposals to alleviate the problem. But if he really cared about this matter and thought it of central importance, he never reveals it. In his letters and books, he does not say a word about the problem as being serious.

Moreover, although in his reports on the affairs of France and the Holy Roman Empire,[56] the secretary of the Second Chancery displays an awareness that it was cheaper to train and, in a crisis, deploy a militia than to hire mercenaries, and although in the course of budgeting for such a militia in Florence, he must have become aware of the fiscal advantages, he never mentions those advantages while arguing in favour of such a militia in preference to mercenaries. All that can be said is that in *The Art of War* he has Fabrizio Colonna allude in passing to the high cost of maintaining a standing army.[57] In fact, not one of the passages from Machiavelli that Barthas cites in support of his case actually supports it. Even when Machiavelli argues that 'money is not the sinews of war',[58] alluding to an ancient dictum sometimes deployed in Florence by advocates of mercenary armies, his focus, as we have seen, is solely on military effectiveness. In that passage, which is central to Barthas's argument, Machiavelli says not one word about public debt. In any case, finance was not Machiavelli's long suit, as he readily admitted. He writes to a friend,

> If I were able to speak to you, I would be unable to refrain from filling your head with castles in the air [*castelluci*] because Fortune has brought it about that, since I do not know how to reason about either the silk or the wool trade, either gains or losses, it is necessary that I reason concerning matters of state [*stato*].[59]

Although he was born in a commune of tradesmen and bankers, Machiavelli devoted his attention primarily to ancient polities governed by warriors and farmers. However, he was by no means an economic ignoramus. He was sensitive to the fact that his beloved Romans had financed their wars by enslaving the conquered and confiscating their land. He regretted that changes in the *ius gentium* ruled out such a policy in Christian Europe and opined that in this particular, the *ius gentium* needed reform.[60] Nowhere else does he address the question of how one should pay for modern wars. Repeatedly, however, he denies that money is 'the sinews of war', and he means what he says in quoting a statement attributed by Lucian to Solon that war is made with steel, not gold, and that the one with more steel could easily seize the gold. Gold of itself, he adds, does not suffice for finding good soldiers, but 'good soldiers suffice for finding gold'.[61]

Of course, Barthas's inability to uphold his case does not of itself mean Gramsci was wrong. The fact remains that Machiavelli's military populism dovetails exceedingly well with his political populism. There is one other circumstance pertinent to our interpretive puzzle.

It would not have been counterproductive for Machiavelli to stress the financial advantages of relying on a militia. It would, in fact, have greatly enhanced the attractiveness of the idea both in Florence and abroad. For this reason, we can judge Machiavelli's silence as indicating a decided lack of interest on his part. By the same token, it would have been counterproductive, and quite possibly fatal to his cause, to stress the revolutionary political implications inherent in arming the countryside. That would have brought home to the *grandi*, who managed Europe's governments and commanded its armies, and who were apt to be attracted by the military and fiscal advantages attendant on such a reform, of the grave political dangers of its implementation.

As was politic, instead of broadcasting a radical political purpose, Machiavelli did the precise opposite. In *The Art of War*, the only work of political prose he ushered into print in his lifetime, he has Fabrizio Colonna respond to Cosimo Rucellai's worries in this regard by firmly denying that arming 'one's own citizens or subjects' ('suoi cittadini o sudditi'), when done in accordance with law, ever does any real damage. Rucellai alludes to the role played by the army in destroying Roman liberty and cites the precautions taken by the Venetians and the current king of France against a comparable political upheaval: for this reason, he tells us, they keep their citizens and subjects disarmed, relying instead on 'the arms of others' ('le armi d'altri'). Colonna responds by pointing to the longevity of the Roman and Spartan republics. The community, he asserts, 'that employs its very own arms fears nothing—apart from its own citizen'.[62]

Yet Colonna is tellingly silent in this passage about the perils of such a community arming its subject population. He has nothing to say about the Social War and the extension of Roman citizenship rights that was required to quell it; he is equally silent about the threat posed to the Lacedaemonian regime by the helots and *perioikoi*. Moreover, he makes no mention of the consequences, fatal to Roman liberty, of the decision made in the late republic to arm the unpropertied *capite censi* and *proletarii*, so that they could serve in place of the reluctant, property-holding 'settled men' (*adsidui*) who had hitherto made up Rome's legions.[63] It would be an understatement to argue that this aspect of Colonna's response to Rucellai was disingenuous: Machiavelli, who was thoroughly familiar with the history of ancient Sparta and Rome, was surely aware of the dodge.[64]

Elsewhere, in an under-appreciated passage of his *Discourses on Livy*, Machiavelli tacitly concedes that Cosimo Rucellai's argument has considerable force by noting in passing the advantage that a new prince, intent on fomenting a revolution within a republic and defending it, can gain from rallying the unenfranchized countryside, as Nabis had done at Sparta when he armed 'the *contado* to perform the office that the [urban] plebs ought to have performed'. In the same passage, Machiavelli asserts that the Roman republic was invulnerable in the face of such a manoeuvre since, as he puts it, 'at Rome the *contado* was the *città*'.[65] Given his deep admiration for Rome, it is easy to imagine Machiavelli thinking that all would be well if the *contado* were once again the *città*, and if the Florentines were to incorporate the *distretto* within their civic community by gradually extending citizenship to its residents. There is no question that he thought it necessary to arm the countryside; and abolishing the distinction between the country folk and their compatriots in the *città* was, as he was well aware, the only way that, in the long run, this could safely be done.[66]

I would only qualify Gramsci's suggestion in one particular: if one is to view the Florentine as 'a precocious Jacobin', one must also see him as a precocious Bonapartist. John Pocock once suggested to me that Napoleon was the first genuinely Machiavellian prince; and as I have elsewhere argued, he was surely right.[67] It is also good to ruminate on the fact that, as Standard-bearer of Justice for life from 1502, Piero Soderini qualified, from Machiavelli's perspective, as a 'new prince', albeit one lacking the *virtù* required in 1512 to turn an emergency into an *occasione*.[68]

The attempts to depict Machiavelli as a civic humanist or classical republican, as a liberal democrat, or even as a radical democrat in the Jacobin mode, reflect a tendency that I believe scholars should eschew. I have in mind the propensity to moralize the Florentine and to turn the man who rejected not just moralism but morality itself into an idealist, an enthusiast for stances that the scholars in question themselves find attractive.

Machiavelli's thinking is, I believe, far more radical and disturbing than this. If he is a forerunner of anyone, it is Friedrich Nietzsche. Both figures cherish and embrace spiritedness for its own sake; and, if the former sees Christianity as a source of human weakness and displays contempt for it,[69] it is for reasons akin to those that induced Nietzsche to find Christianity, liberal democracy, and socialism loathsome.[70] Moreover, just as both thinkers blur or even deny the bifurcation between good and evil, so the earlier ostentatiously refrains from drawing a moral distinction between republics and principalities. If Machiavelli prefers one form of government or the other, generally or in particular circumstances, it is always with an eye to the projection of power.[71] His populism is not rooted in a genuine sympathy for the *popolo*. It derives, instead, from his preference that, as in ancient Rome, there be an 'infinite' succession of 'virtuous princes'[72] and 'a people numerous and armed'[73] dedicated to the imperial expansion that, in his opinion, constitutes the common good.[74] It is a grave error to suppose that the man said to have supplied Satan with his nickname 'Old Nick' can be tamed.

Notes

1. Aristotle, *Politics* 1297b:1–17; see also Aristotle, *Nicomachean Ethics* 1116b.
2. Compare Charles Calvert Bayley, *War and Society in Renaissance Florence: The* De Militia *of Leonardo Bruni* (Toronto: University of Toronto Press, 1961), with James Hankins, 'Civic Knighthood in the Early Renaissance: Leonardo Bruni's *De militia* (ca. 1420)', *Noctua: International Online Journal of the History of Philosophy* 1, no. 2 (2014), 260–82. A lengthier version of Hankins's essay is to be found in James Hankins, *Virtue Politics: Political Thought in Renaissance Italy between Petrarch and Machiavelli* (Cambridge, MA: Harvard University Press, 2019).
3. See Hans Baron, *The Crisis of the Early Italian Renaissance: Civic Humanism and Republican Liberty in an Age of Classicism and Tyranny* (Princeton, NJ: Princeton University Press, 1966 [1955]), 430–9; Cecil H. Clough, 'Niccolò Machiavelli's Political Assumptions and Objectives', *Bulletin of the John Rylands Library* 53, no. 1 (1970), 30–74 (esp. 71–3); J. G. A. Pocock, *The Machiavellian Moment: Florentine Political Thought and the Atlantic Republican Tradition* (Princeton, NJ: Princeton University Press, 1975), 194–218 (esp. 199–203, 208–14), 384–6; Quentin Skinner, *The Foundations of Modern Political Thought* I: *The Renaissance* (Cambridge: Cambridge University Press, 1978), 173–5. See also J. G. A. Pocock, 'Historical Introduction', in *The Political Works of James Harrington*, ed. J. G. A. Pocock (Cambridge: Cambridge University Press, 1977), 18–19, 43–4.
4. A full list of examples would be immense. Recent publications include Erica Benner, *Machiavelli's Ethics* (Princeton, NJ: Princeton University Press, 2009), 441; Erica Benner, *Machiavelli's Prince: A New Reading* (Oxford: Oxford University Press, 2013), 155; Erica Benner, *Be Like the Fox: Machiavelli in His World* (New York: W. W. Norton, 2017), 179, 257–8, 298–9; John P. McCormick, *Machiavellian Democracy* (New York: Cambridge University Press, 2011), 58, 93, 102–3; John P. McCormick,

Reading Machiavelli: Scandalous Books, Suspect Engagements, and the Virtue of Populist Politics (Princeton, NJ: Princeton University Press, 2018), 11, 102–3; Alissa M. Ardito, *Machiavelli and the Modern State: The Prince, the Discourses on Livy, and the Extended Territorial State* (New York: Cambridge University Press, 2015), 23, 77, 90, 180–2, 275, 277–81, 291; Alexander Lee, *Machiavelli: His Life and Times* (London: Picador, 2020), 256–8, 389, 452, 707n75. For notable exceptions to this propensity, see Niccolò Capponi, *An Unlikely Prince: The Life and Times of Machiavelli* (Cambridge, MA: Da Capo Press, 2010), 150–3, 219–28; Catherine H. Zuckert, *Machiavelli's Politics* (Chicago, IL: University of Chicago Press, 2017); and Gabriele Pedullà, *Machiavelli in Tumult: The Discourses on Livy and the Origins of Political Conflictualism*, tr. Patricia Gaborik and Richard Nybakken, rev. edn (Cambridge: Cambridge University Press, 2018).

5. See Paul A. Rahe, *Republics Ancient and Modern* II: *New Modes and Orders in Early Modern Political Thought* (Chapel Hill, NC: University of North Carolina Press, 1994), 324; Paul A. Rahe, *Against Throne and Altar: Machiavelli and Political Theory under the English Republic* (Cambridge: Cambridge University Press, 2008), 239–40.

6. Letter to Francesco Vettori, 26 August 1513: Niccolò Machiavelli, *Tutte le opere*, ed. Mario Martelli (Florence: Sansoni, 1971), 1156. All Machiavelli's works except *L'Arte della guerra* are cited from this edition (henceforth *Opere*). All translations are my own unless otherwise stated.

7. For recent discussions of the evidence, see Mikael Hörnqvist, '*Perché non si usa allegar i Romani*: Machiavelli and the Florentine Militia of 1506', *Renaissance Quarterly* 55, no. 1 (2002), 148–91, and Andrea Guidi, *Un Segretario militante: Politica, diplomazia e armi nel Cancelliere Machiavelli* (Bologna: Società Editrice Il Mulino, 2009), 159–386 (esp. 196–386), which is admirably attentive to Florentine conditions and institutions and to the outlook of Machiavelli's compatriots.

8. Niccolò Machiavelli, *L'Arte della guerra; Scritti politici minori*, ed. Jean-Jacques Marchand, Denis Fachard, and Giorgio Masi (Rome: Salerno, 2001), 27–311. All later references to *L'Arte della guerra* are to this edition by book and sentence number.

9. *Pr.*, ch. 12, *Opere* 275. See Nathan Tarcov, 'Arms and Politics in Machiavelli's *Prince*', in *Entre Kant et Kosovo: Études offertes à Pierre Hassner*, ed. Anne-Marie Le Gloannec and Aleksander Smolar (Paris: Presses de Sciences Po, 2003), 109–21.

10. Cf. Machiavelli's 'La cagione dell'ordinanza, dove la si truovi, e quel che bisogni fare' with his 'Provisione della ordinanza' in *L'Arte della guerra*, 470–92.

11. See Philip J. Jones, 'The Machiavellian Militia: Innovation or Renovation', in *La Toscane et les toscans autour de la Renaissance: Cadres de vie, société, croyances* (Aix-en-Provence: Université de Provence, 1999), 11–52; Guidi, *Un Segretario militante*, 196–210.
12. See Jean-Jacques Marchand, *Niccolò Machiavelli: I primi scritti politici (1499–1512): Nascita di un pensiero e di uno stile* (Padua: Antenore, 1975), 133–41; Hörnqvist, '*Perché non si usa allegar i Romani*', 148–91.
13. See K. J. P. Lowe, *Church and Politics in Renaissance Italy: The Life and Career of Cardinal Francesco Soderini, 1453–1524* (Cambridge: Cambridge University Press, 1993); Roslyn Pesman Cooper, *Pier Soderini and the Ruling Class in Renaissance Florence* (Goldbach: Keip Verlag, 2002). For a narrative of the period in which these two men were dominant, see Humphrey C. Butters, *Governors and Government in Early Sixteenth Century Florence, 1502–1519* (Oxford: Clarendon Press, 1985), 1–165. Regarding their family background, see Paula C. Clarke, *The Soderini and the Medici: Power and Patronage in Fifteenth Century Florence* (Oxford: Clarendon Press, 1991).
14. See Paul A. Rahe, *Republics Ancient and Modern: Classical Republicanism and the American Revolution* (Chapel Hill, NC: University of North Carolina Press, 1992), 1:3:1.
15. See *L'Arte della guerra*, 1:129–42, 193–7. See also Clough, 'Niccolò Machiavelli's Political Assumptions and Objectives', 71–3. It is telling that in and after November 1510, when Machiavelli received permission to recruit a unit of cavalry, the recruiting took place in the *contado* and not in the *città*: Guidi, *Un Segretario militante*, 254–59.
16. *Pr.*, ch. 12, *Opere* 275.
17. '[E] perché non può essere buone legge dove non sono buone arme, e dove sono buone arme conviene sieno buone legge, io lascerò indrieto el ragionare delle legge e parlerò delle arme': ibid.
18. 'Le mercenarie e ausiliarie sono inutile e periculose: … disunite, ambiziose, sanza disciplina, infedele; gagliarde far gli amici; fra e' nimici, vile; … e tanto si differisce la ruina quanto si differisce lo assalto; e nella pace se' spogliato da loro, nella guerra da' nimici': ibid.
19. For the twelfth and thirteenth centuries, see Daniel Waley, 'The Army of Florence from the Twelfth to the Fourteenth Century', in *Florentine Studies: Politics and Society in Renaissance Florence*, ed. Nicolai Rubinstein (Evanston, IL: Northwestern University Press, 1968), 70–108; Daniel Waley, 'Condotta and Condottieri in the Thirteenth Century', *Proceedings of the British Academy* 61 (1975), 337–71. For the fourteenth century, see note 37.

20. 'Concludo, adunque, che, sanza avere arme proprie, nessuno principato è securo; anzi è tutto obligato alla fortuna, non avendo virtù che nella avversità con fede lo difenda. ... E l'armi proprie son quelle che sono composte o di sudditi o di cittadini o di creati tuoi: ...': *Opere* 278. Machiavelli was already pressing this argument, in precisely the same terms, before the authorities of Florence in November 1502: see Niccolò Machiavelli, *Legazioni, Commissarie, Scritti di governo*, vol. 2, ed. Denis Fachard and Emanuele Cutinelli-Rèndina (Rome: Salerno Editrice, 2002–11), 465–6.

21. 'Non fu mai, adunque, che uno principe nuovo disarmassi e' sua sudditi; anzi, quando gli ha trovati disarmati, sempre gli ha armati; perché, armandosi, quelle arme diventano tua; diventano fedeli quelli che ti sono sospetti; e quelli che erano fedeli si mantengono e di sudditi si fanno tuoi partigiani': *Opere* 289.

22. See *Pr.*, chs 1, 7, 12, 14, 20, *Disc.* 2:24, and *L'Arte della guerra* 1:56–62, 96–102, 174–5, in the light of the *Istorie fiorentine* 6:13, 17–27. See also Séan Erwin, 'A War of One's Own: Mercenaries and the Theme of *Arma Aliena* in Machiavelli's *Il Principe*', *British Journal for the History of Philosophy* 18, no. 4 (2010), 541–74.

23. See, for example, Samuel Butler, *Hudibras*, ed. John Wilders (Oxford: Clarendon Press, 1967), 3:1:1313–16. Whether the devil's moniker is so derived is a matter of controversy; see Ernst Leisi, 'On the Trail of Old Nick', in *The History and the Dialects of English: Festchrift for Eduard Kolb*, ed. Andreas Fischer (Heidelberg: Carl Winter, 1989), 53–7.

24. Note, however, *Disc.* 1:25–7.

25. Ibid., 1:21.

26. *Opere* 126.

27. '[O]gni volta s'ingannerà, quando le misuri o dai danari, o dal sito, o dalla benivolenza degli uomini, mancando, dall'altra parte, d'armi proprie. Perché le cose predette ti accrescono bene le forze, ma ben non te le danno; e per se medesime sono nulla; e non giovono alcuna cosa sanza l'armi fedeli. Perché i danari assai non ti bastano sanza quelle; non ti giova la fortezza del paese; e la fede e benivolenza degli uomini non dura, perché questi non ti possono essere fedeli, non gli potendo difendere. Ogni monte, ogni lago, ogni luogo inaccessibile diventa piano, dove i forti difensori mancano. I danari ancora, non solo non ti difendono, ma ti fanno predare più presto': *Opere* 159.

28. *Disc.* 2:12. Machiavelli makes the same point about political communities and their *paesi* in *L'Arte della guerra* 1:123.

29. *Disc.* 2:20, 24, 30.

30. Compare *The Art of War* in Machiavelli, *The Chief Works and Others*, tr. Allan H. Gilbert (Durham, NC: Duke University Press, 1965), 2:580, 583, 585,

587–8, 590–92, 594, 611, 725, with *L'Arte della guerra* 1:104, 148, 151, 154, 170, 189, 201, 220, 222, 227, 234, 238, 240, 260, 263; 2:171; 7:241. For a far more reliable English translation, see Niccolò Machiavelli, *Art of War*, ed. and tr. Christopher Lynch (Chicago, IL: University of Chicago Press, 2003).
31. See Clifford J. Rogers, 'The Military Revolutions of the Hundred Years' War', *Journal of Military History* 57, no. 2 (1993), 241–78.
32. '[C]onobbe questa necessità di armarsi di arme proprie, e ordinò nel suo regno l'ordinanza delle gente d'arme e delle fanterie': *Opere* 278. Note also *Disc.* 2:30.
33. For an overview, see Geoffrey Parker, *The Military Revolution: Military Innovation and the Rise of the West, 1500–1800* (Cambridge: Cambridge University Press, 1988). For a recent study focused on Machiavelli's contribution, see Andrea Guidi, *Books, People, and Military Thought: Machiavelli's Art of War and the Fortune of the Militia in Sixteenth-Century Florence and Europe* (Leiden: Brill, 2020).
34. See *L'Arte della guerra* 1:196.
35. Consider *Disc.* 2:10, 3:10 in the light of Machiavelli's letters to Francesco Vettori on 10 and 26 August 1513 and 10 December 1514: *Opere* 1147–50 (esp. 1149–50), 1154–7, 1180–5 (esp. 1183–4); also *Pr.*, chs 12–13; *Disc.* 2:4, 12, 16–19, 30; *L'Arte della guerra* 1:208; 2:18, 29, 50–2, 56–8, 144; 3:27–30, 33, 36, 134, 140–6, 165; 6:120; 7:226–8, in the light of Bernard Wicht, *L'Idée de milice et le modèle suisse dans la pensée de Machiavel* (Lausanne: L'Age d'Homme, 1995).
36. '[L]a milizia non puote essere buona, se la non è esercitata; e ... la non si può esercitare, se la non è composta di tuoi sudditi': *Disc.* 3:31, *Opere* 239.
37. *Pr.*, ch. 15, *Opere* 280.
38. See William P. Caferro, 'Continuity, Long-Term Service, and Permanent Forces: A Reassessment of the Florentine Army in the Fourteenth Century', *Journal of Modern History* 80, no. 2 (2008), 219–51. Note also William P. Caferro, *Petrarch's War: Florence and the Black Death in Context* (Cambridge: Cambridge University Press, 2018), 49–146 (esp. 49–83).
39. See Francesco Guicciardini, *Storie fiorentine*, ed. Alessandro Montevecchi (Milan: Rizzoli, 1998), 423.
40. See Felix Gilbert, 'Florentine Political Assumptions in the Period of Savonarola and Soderini', *Journal of the Warburg and Courtauld Institutes* 20 (1957), 187–214. Also note Hörnqvist, '*Perché non si usa allegar i Romani*', 148–91; Guidi, *Un Segretario militante*, 159–96.
41. Stephen Peter Rosen, *Societies and Military Power: India and Its Armies* (Ithaca, NY: Cornell University Press, 1996).

42. See John M. Najemy, '"*Occupare la tirannide*": Machiavelli, the Militia, and Guicciardini's Accusation of Tyranny', in *Della tirannia: Machiavelli con Bartolo*, ed. Jérémie Barthas (Florence: Leo S. Olschki Editore, 2007), 75–108.
43. On Machiavelli's populism and its foundations, see Paul A. Rahe, 'Situating Machiavelli', in *Renaissance Civic Humanism: Reappraisals and Reflections*, ed. James Hankins (Cambridge: Cambridge University Press, 2000), 270–308; Rahe, *Against Throne and Altar*, 22–55. On the stance taken by the Renaissance humanists more generally, see Hankins, *Virtue Politics*, passim.
44. For our purposes here, it does not matter that this militia turned out to be more a matter of aspiration than achievement: see John Larner, 'Cesare Borgia, Machiavelli, and the Romagnol Militia', *Studi romagnoli* 17 (1966), 253–68; John M. Najemy, 'Machiavelli and Cesare Borgia: A Reconsideration of Chapter 7 of *The Prince*', *Review of Politics* 75, no. 4 (2013), 539–56.
45. For a list of Don Miguel's crimes, see Hörnqvist, '*Perché non si usa allegar i Romani*', 177–8. With regard to the man, his employment by Cesare Borgia, and his subsequent employment by Florence, see also Guidi, *Un Segretario militante*, 210–13, 259–61, 277–320, 348–53.
46. See F. W. Kent, 'Politics and Society in Fifteenth-Century Florence', *I Tatti Studies* 2, no. 1 (1987), 41–70; William J. Connell, '"*I Fautori delle parti*": Citizen Interest and the Treatment of a Subject Town, *ca.* 1500', in *Istituzioni e società in Toscana in età moderna: Atti delle giornate di studio dedicate à Giuseppe Pansini*, ed. Claudio Lamioni (Rome: Pubblicazioni degli Archivi di Stato, 1994), 1:118–47; and then William J. Connell, *La Città dei crucci: Fazioni e clientele in uno stato repubblicano del '400* (Florence: Nuova Toscana Editrice, 2000).
47. See Letter from Francesco Soderini, 26 October 1504 (*Opere* 1066); *L'Arte della guerra* 1:151–61.
48. See Robert Black, 'Machiavelli and the Militia: New Thoughts', *Italian Studies* 69, no. 1 (2014), 41–50.
49. See *Disc.* 3:3, 30; note also *Disc.*, 3:9.
50. Compare, for example, Carlo Dionisotti, 'Machiavelli, Cesare Borgia, e don Michelotto', *Rivista storica italiana* 79 (1967), 960–75, rpt. in Carlo Dionisotti, *Machiavellerie* (Turin: Einaudi, 1980), 3–59, with Gennaro Sasso, 'Ancora su Machiavelli e Cesare Borgia', *La Cultura* 7, no. 1 (1969), 1–36, rev. as 'Machiavelli, Cesare Borgia, Don Micheletto e la questione della milizia' in Gennaro Sasso, *Machiavelli e gli antichi e altri saggi* (Milan: Riccardo Ricciardi, 1987–97), 2:57–117, and with Roslyn Pesman Cooper, 'Pier Soderini: Aspiring Prince or Civic Leader?', *Studies in Medieval and*

Renaissance History n.s. 1 (1978), 69–126, and Roslyn Pesman Cooper, 'Machiavelli, Francesco Soderini and Don Michelotto', *Nuova rivista storica* 66 (1982), 342–57, both reprinted in Cooper, *Pier Soderini*, 43–114. For additional bibliography, see Pedullà, *Machiavelli in Tumult*, 111–12n78–9.

51. Antonio Gramsci, *Prison Notebooks*, ed. and trans. Joseph Buttigieg (New York: Columbia University Press, 2007), 3:248, 327 (notebook 8 §§21, 162).
52. On the last point, note *L'Arte della guerra* 1:241–9, and see Mikael Hörnqvist, 'Machiavelli's Military Project and the *Art of War*', in *The Cambridge Companion to Machiavelli*, ed. John Najemy (Cambridge: Cambridge University Press, 2010), 112–27; Guidi, *Un Segretario militante*, 159–72, 320–25. On Florence's leadership cadre, see Roslyn Pesman Cooper, 'The Florentine Ruling Group under the *Governo Popolare*, 1494–1512', *Studies in Medieval and Renaissance History* n.s. 7 (1985), 69–181, rpt. in Cooper, *Pier Soderini*, 141–251.
53. See Timothy J. Lukes, 'Martialing Machiavelli: Reassessing the Military Reflections', *Journal of Politics* 66, no. 4 (2004), 1099–102. One should not be put off by Lukes's propensity to sneer at scholars of genuine erudition. There is value in the pages he devotes to the makeup of Machiavelli's militia. In this connection, note also Guidi, *Un Segretario militante*, 159–80, 325–37.
54. See Jérémie Barthas, *L'Argent n'est pas le nerf de la guerre: Essai sur une prétendue erreur de Machiavel* (Rome: École française de Rome, 2011), alongside Jérémie Barthas, 'Machiavelli, Public Debt, and the Origins of Political Economy: An Introduction', in *The Radical Machiavelli: Politics, Philosophy and Language*, ed. Filippo del Lucchese, Fabio Frosini, and Vittorio Morfino (Brill: Leiden, 2015), 273–305, and Jérémie Barthas, 'Machiavelli, the Republic, and the Financial Crisis', in *Machiavelli on Liberty and Conflict*, ed. David Johnston, Nadia Urbinati, and Camila Vergara (Chicago, IL: University of Chicago Press, 2017), 257–79. Note also Jérémie Barthas, '"Altra volta ne ragionai a lungo": A Reinterpretation of Niccolò Machiavelli's Cryptic Clause in *The Prince*', in *The Art and Language of Power in Renaissance Florence: Essays for Alison Brown*, ed. Amy R. Bloch, Carolyn James, and Camilla Russell (Toronto: Centre for Reformation and Renaissance Studies, 2019), 155–86 (esp. 172–9), where special pleading concerning the reference intended at the opening of *Pr.*, ch. 2 is no less in evidence.
55. See Louis Marks, 'La Crisi finanziaria a Firenze dal 1494 al 1502', *Archivio storico italiano* 112, no. 1 (1954), 40–72; Anthony Molho, *Florentine Public Finances in the Early Renaissance (1400–1433)* (Cambridge, MA: Harvard University Press, 1971); Anthony Mohlo, 'L'Amministrazione del debito

pubblico a Firenze nel quindesimo secolo', in *I Ceti dirigenti nella Toscana del Quattrocento*, ed. Riccardo Fubini (Pisa: Papafava, 1987), 191–207; Anthony Mohlo, *Firenze nel Quattrocento*, 1: *Politica e fiscalità* (Rome: Collezione di Storia e Letteratura, 2006).

56. See Machiavelli's 'Ritratto di cose di Francia' and 'Ritratto delle cose della Magna', in *L'Arte della guerra*, 546–66, 570–8.
57. See *L'Arte della guerra* 1:82–4.
58. 'I dinari non sono il nervo della guerra': *Disc.* 2:10, title, *Opere* 159.
59. 'Pure, se io vi potessi parlare, non potre' fare che io non vi empiessi il capo di castellucci, perché la Fortuna ha fatto che, non sapendo ragionare né dell'arte della seta et dell'arte della lana, né de' guadagni né delle perdite, e' mi conviene ragionare dello stato': Letter to Francesco Vettori, 9 April 1513: *Opere* 1131.
60. See *L'Arte della guerra* 2:305–9.
61. '[I] buoni soldati sono bene sufficienti a trovare l'oro': *Disc.* 2:10, *Opere* 159–60. See also *L'Arte della guerra*, 7:178.
62. 'Quella che usa l'arme proprie, non teme se non il suo cittadino': see ibid., 1:151–88.
63. See Claude Nicolet, *The World of the Citizen in Republican Rome*, tr. P. S. Falla (Berkeley, CA: University of California Press, 1980); Paul A. Rahe, *The Spartan Regime: Its Character, Origins, and Grand Strategy* (New Haven, CT: Yale University Press, 2016).
64. See *L'Arte della guerra* 1:63–76, where Fabrizio indicates his awareness of what had happened to Rome's armies in the late republic, but eschews close analysis.
65. '[I]l contado, che faccia quello ufficio che arebbe a fare la plebe; … una medesimo cosa il contado e Roma': *Disc.* 1:40, *Opere* 125.
66. See *Disc.* 2:23; also *Disc.* 2:3.
67. See Paul A. Rahe, 'Machiavelli and the Modern Tyrant', in *Machiavelli on Liberty and Conflict*, 207–31.
68. See Roslyn Pesman Cooper, 'Machiavelli, Pier Soderni, and *Il Principe*', in *Altro Polo: A Volume of Italian Renaissance Studies*, ed. Conal Condren and Roslyn Pesman Cooper (Sydney: Frederick May Foundation, 1982), 119–44, rpt. in Cooper, *Pier Soderini*, 115–40.
69. Cf. Machiavelli, *Disc.* 1: Praefatio with *Disc.* 2:2, 3:1.
70. For an argument tending in this direction, see J. Patrick Coby, 'Machiavelli's Philanthropy', *History of Political Thought* 20, no. 4 (1999), 605–26; J. Patrick Coby, *Machiavelli's Romans: Liberty and Greatness in the Discourses on Livy* (Lanham, MD: Lexington Books, 1999).

71. See William J. Connell, 'Machiavelli on Growth as an End', in *Historians and Ideologues: Essays in Honor of Donald R. Kelley*, ed. Anthony T. Grafton and J. H. M. Salmon (Rochester, NY: University of Rochester Press, 2001), 259–77; Mikael Hörnqvist, *Machiavelli and Empire* (Cambridge: Cambridge University Press, 2004); Pedullà, *Machiavelli in Tumult*, 10–180 (esp. 170–80).
72. '[I]nfiniti principi virtuosssimi che sono l'uno dell'altro successori': *Disc.* 1:20, *Opere* 105.
73. '[G]ran numero di uomini, e bene armati': *Disc.* 1:6, *Opere* 86.
74. Consider *Disc.* 2:1–4 in the light of *Disc.* 1:5–6, 1:20.

4

Machiavelli and Tyranny

Doyeeta Majumder

Lamenting the failure of modern political scientists in grasping the real meaning of tyranny, Leo Strauss asserts, 'One cannot overcome this limitation without reflecting on the basis, or the origin, of present-day political science. Present-day political science often traces its origin to Machiavelli.'[1] A decade later, he adds, '[C]ontemporary tyranny has its roots in Machiavelli's thought, in the Machiavellian principle that the good end justifies every means… In the *Discourses* Machiavelli sometimes acts explicitly as an adviser of tyrants; in *The Prince* he acts in this capacity only silently.'[2] Strauss traces the horror of the Third Reich back to the writings of a sixteenth-century Florentine bureaucrat. In this he is not alone amongst twentieth-century theorists. Ernst Cassirer, for instance, locates in Machiavelli's writings the instrument that severed the connections between the state and the 'organic whole of human existence', which in turn precipitated the crises of twentieth-century Europe.[3] Strauss goes beyond the measured critique of Cassirer and calls Machiavelli 'a teacher of evil', adding that modern scholars choose to ignore this evil 'because they are the heirs of the Machiavellian tradition; because they, or the forgotten teachers of their teachers, have been corrupted by Machiavelli'.[4]

Strauss's account, if a little too melodramatic in tone, is however representative of a five-century-long tradition of reading and making meaning of Machiavelli's writings, particularly prevalent in English and French traditions of political thought. In fact, Strauss's words, laden with satanic implications, are an uncanny echo of the first known English critique of Machiavellian thought, formulated by Reginald Pole in *Apologia ad Carolum Quintum* (1539). There Henry VIII, Pole's erstwhile patron and mentor, is denounced not only as a tyrant but as the Antichrist,[5] who derives his tyranny from Machiavelli's occult teachings, which Pole goes on to describe as the writings of the 'enemy of mankind, giving all the advice of the enemy'.[6] As soon as Pole chanced upon the book, he knew it was written by the finger of Satan ('Satanae digito scriptum'[7]). The most famous denunciation of Machiavelli as the tutor of tyrants comes later in the sixteenth century, in the *Discours contre Machiavel* (1576) of the Huguenot writer Innocent Gentillet. Countering those readers of Machiavelli who attributed to him the invention of a science of politics, Gentillet accuses Machiavelli of having created

> not a political, but a tyrannical science … as all they who read my writings, shall give their judgment, and acknowledge that Machiavelli was altogether ignorant in that [political] science, and that his scope and intent in his writings is nothing else but to frame a very true and perfect tyranny.[8]

Like the twentieth-century political theorists cited previously, Gentillet tries to attribute a brutal political genocide, the massacre of Huguenots on St Bartholomew's Day, to the teachings of Machiavelli and to convince his readers that Machiavelli's 'only purpose was to instruct a prince to be a true tyrant and to teach him the art of tyranny'.[9]

Curiously, as Sydney Anglo observes, while Gentillet's invective associates Machiavelli with a specific form of Catholic tyranny manifesting itself in the oppression of Protestants, Pole's critique is an invective against the persecution of Catholics at the hands of the newly minted apostate, Henry VIII. Anglo writes:

> [E]ach polemicist believed that, in Machiavelli's writings, he had discovered the theoretical enunciation of the principles upon which a specific tyranny had been built. Both authors attacked the theory and its practice; and both have been remembered more for Machiavelli's sake than for the tyrants they opposed. Yet in both cases the tyrants were the real objects of disgust. Their use, real or imaginary, of Machiavelli was simply the stick with which it seemed appropriate to beat them.[10]

This chapter will try to investigate why Machiavelli lends himself to this kind of appropriation, why he casts his shadow across the spectrum of tyranny: modern, Early Modern, Catholic, Protestant, Fascist, Aryan supremacist. The focus of my discussion will be the way in which his writings challenge conventional Early Modern formulations of tyranny, with special attention to England and France, but hopefully also gesturing beyond England in order to make sense of the enduring historical association between tyranny and Machiavellian thought.

Contre Leo Strauss, I argue that neither does Machiavelli collapse the distinction between the good king and the bad tyrant nor does he set out to be a declared advisor to tyrants. Nevertheless, Machiavelli's configuration of tyranny marks a momentous rupture in the medieval and Early Modern European discourses on tyranny and monarchy, as he consciously moves away from received definitions of tyranny and deliberately upsets age-old structures. The elusive term *tirannia*, which is entirely absent from *The Prince*, and only very cautiously used in the *Discourses*, becomes an inverted reflection of the Machiavellian *virtù*—which is stretched to its semantic limits through excessive use.

Etymologically, 'tyrant' is derived from the Greek *turannos*, a morally neutral word meaning a ruler whose power is singular and uncircumscribed. However, by the sixteenth century, the word had acquired a host of negative connotations. The two most common usages denoted, respectively, a bad king and an illegitimate king. Broadly speaking, both meanings could be plotted along the axis of illegality or unlawfulness. The monarch who acquired his power through illegitimate means transgressed the law, even if his manner of ruling was entirely just and fair. Conversely, the monarch who ascended the throne lawfully but contravened the juridical norm of the country at will was rendered illegitimate by his abuse of power. The word 'tyrant' in the Early Modern period became imbued with these two overlapping notions of legitimacy and the absence thereof.

The earliest theoretical exposition of this dual meaning of 'tyrant', as a usurper or a tyrant *ex defectu tituli* and/or an unjust ruler with criminal tendencies or a tyrant *ex parte exercitii*, is found in Bartolus of Sassoferrato, the trecento jurist whose work acquired unprecedented celebrity in medieval and Early Modern jurisprudence. One of the principal aims of his *De tyrannia* is to 'inquire how many kinds of tyrants there may be in a commonwealth'. Bartolus explains:

> [A] tyrant is one who rules not according to law (*non jure*), and since there are various ways of ruling contrary to law there are various types of tyrants ... One may be openly a tyrant by reason of his conduct, another by defect of title.[11]

Ephraim Emerton reminds us that Bartolus was a jurist steeped in the 'old Roman imperial tradition', for whom 'Italian sovereignties were dependent on an imperial overlordship'.[12] Thus, for Bartolus, the tyrant's lack of title bears the very specific connotation of not having imperial sanction. But through subsequent centuries and rapidly changing politico-historical circumstances, the rhetorical shape of Bartolus's conflation of usurpation and tyranny resurfaces in the works of later writers with altered political connotations. Half a century after Bartolus, Coluccio Salutati, the famous humanist and chancellor of the republic of Florence, builds his definition of tyranny on the precepts of Pope Gregory, and following the contours of Bartolus's argument thence, he concludes that 'a tyrant is either one who usurps government, having no legal title for his rule, or one who governs *superbe* or rules unjustly or does not observe law or equity'.[13]

For Salutati, the context of imperial overlordship is not really an obstacle in the path of legitimacy. Standing at the brink of Medicean dynastic rule, the connotations of tyranny and usurpation have begun to change for Salutati. Nearly a century and a half later, at the other end of Europe, Thomas Smith rehearses the formal division between two kinds of tyranny in *De republica anglorum*:

> So as one may be a tyrant by the entrie and getting of the rule and a king in the administration thereof. As a man may thinke of *Octavius* and peradventure of *Sylla*. For they both comming by tyranny and violence to the rule did seeme to travaile verie much for the better ordering of the common wealth, although each after a diverse maner. An other may be a king by the entrie, and a tyrant by the administration, as *Nero*, *Domitian*, and *Commodus*: for the empire came to them by succession, their administration was utterly tyrannicall.[14]

Smith was a mid-Tudor jurist, whose political milieu had endowed the institution of hereditary monarchy with a sacrosanct inviolability that would have been entirely alien to Bartolus or Salutati. But this conflation of misgovernment with the lack of legitimate title persists in the work of continental political thinkers, even as the meaning of what constitutes titular legitimacy keeps changing.

The first difficulty with Machiavelli's formulation of tyranny arises from the fact that the double meaning the word 'tyrant' had acquired by the sixteenth century is unacknowledged by Machiavelli, who mostly bypasses the question of titular legitimacy altogether. Machiavelli removed the contingent question of legitimacy from his discussions of sovereignty and tyranny, thus rendering unstable the more or less accepted understanding of what constitutes misgovernment. He offers no consistent theoretical distinction between the tyrant and the good prince; instead, he unmoors both ideas from the bedrock of timeless and universal precepts of good and bad governance, making them, for the most part, dependent on historical circumstances.

In *The Prince* he effects a radical revision of the question of legitimacy by recasting the oft-reviled figure of the usurper–tyrant as the *principe nuove*, the new prince, who becomes the protagonist and addressee of this rather unusual *speculum principis*. At the outset, Machiavelli makes a distinction between hereditary principalities and new ones; 'new' is also used as a euphemistic reference to usurped kingdoms. The crucial point of difference for him is that hereditary sovereignty does not allow much scope for developing or displaying political virtuosity; hence, the study of such principalities did not interest him. It is the new prince who emerges as the poster child of Machiavellian *virtù*. Machiavelli freely admits that the hereditary prince has less cause to offend.[15] A hereditary prince of average capability can rule without trouble, but he is not a man of *virtù* and holds no fascination for Machiavelli. Neither is Machiavelli concerned with the figure of the tyrant per se. His focus is entirely on the prince, who, as Dollimore puts it, is 'no longer the agent of God', whose 'identity is dictated by the necessities of political intervention', and who might be forced to commit tyrannous acts due to the 'pressures of the contingent historical moment'.[16]

The basic premise of the work is that not all monarchies or *principati* are hereditary; or even if they are, they cannot remain that way till the end of time: an enterprising outsider may come and assume power. That is a political and historical fact that Machiavelli accepts without attempting to criticize or rationalize it.[17] That a private individual may rise through the ranks and acquire sovereign power through his personal capability or his good fortune does not seem reprehensible to the Florentine because 'it is perfectly natural and ordinary that men should want to acquire things'.[18] Machiavelli's work foregrounds the usurper without insinuating oppressive rule. At the same time, it offers an entirely logical explanation as to why the usurper must commit certain outrageously cruel and tyrannical acts in order to maintain his authority. 'A new prince, above all others, cannot possibly avoid a name for cruelty',[19] because new political orders are tenuous and under constant threat. It is important to note that the words *tiranno* or *tirannia* do not occur in the text of *Il Principe*, but the acts attributed by Machiavelli to exemplary new princes such as Cesare Borgia would have been instantly identified by contemporary readers as acts traditionally associated with tyranny in the sense of inhumane and oppressive rule. Without ever explicitly referring to either form of tyranny, or using words corresponding to 'usurper' or 'tyrant', Machiavelli shows us how this lawmaking violence, which the usurper must perforce commit, could potentially effect his transformation into the other kind of tyrant: a transformation from *ex defectu tituli* to *ex parte exercitii*, as, one could argue, happens with Agathocles.

Chapter 26 of the first book of the *Discourses* reinforces this with the example of Philip of Macedon:

> Whoever becomes prince of a city or state, especially if the foundation of his power is feeble, and does not wish to establish there either a monarchy or a republic, will find the best means for holding that principality to organize the government entirely anew (he being himself a new prince there) ... He should take Philip of Macedon, father of Alexander, for his model, who by proceeding in that manner became, from a petty king, master of all Greece ... [H]e transferred the inhabitants from one province to another, as shepherds move their flocks from place to place. Doubtless these means are cruel and destructive of all civilized life ... Nevertheless, whoever is unwilling to adopt the first and humane course must, if he wishes to maintain his power, follow the latter evil course.[20]

The processes by which a new prince may become a tyrant are drawn out more explicitly and held up for scrutiny here. It is almost as if the author himself wants to comprehend the rationale for the centuries-long association between usurpation and tyranny to tease out the various possible theories. But Machiavelli is still loth to admit that the monarch's lack of titular legitimacy in itself, by default, constitutes tyranny. The stereotype of Machiavelli as an advocate of tyranny can then be seen as stemming not so much from the fact that he collapses the traditional binary between the good king and the bad tyrant, as from his firm refusal to recognize one of the two faces of the Janus-like figure of the Early Modern tyrant.

For Machiavelli, writing in the first decades of the sixteenth century, the legitimizing authority of the imperial overlords that had driven Bartolus's understanding of tyranny has ceased to be a consideration for the Florentine political thinker. In fact, in *The Prince*, his fantasy of a pan-Italian nation state led by a new prince, preferably Florentine, emphatically rejects the idea of looking towards any higher legitimating authority. This is pushed further in the *Discourses*, where the dynastic legitimacy of the hereditary model is seen as an unacceptable abomination and, paradoxically enough, as the source of all tyranny in the sense of misrule. The question of 'sovereign right' as a given is dismissed peremptorily in the dedicatory epistle addressed to Cosimo Rucellai, in which Machiavelli says he has chosen to dedicate the sum of his political knowledge not to a prince but to an acute reader because men ought to esteem 'those who would know how to govern states, rather than those who have the right to govern, but lack the knowledge'.[21]

The second chapter of Book 1 of the *Discourses* takes this argument further. Machiavelli begins by invoking the Aristotelian theory of six types of government and links them together in a Polybian sequence of historical succession, arguing that tyranny stems directly and indisputably from hereditary sovereignty:

> But when they began to make sovereignty hereditary and non-elective, the children quickly degenerated from their fathers; and, so far from trying to equal their virtues, they considered that a prince had nothing else to do than to excel all the rest in luxury, indulgence, and every other variety of pleasure. The prince consequently soon drew upon himself the general hatred. An object of hatred, he naturally felt fear; fear in turn dictated to him precautions and wrongs, and thus tyranny quickly developed itself.[22]

This is a direct paraphrase of Polybius, who writes in Book 6 of his *Histories*:

> But when their royal power became hereditary in their family, and they found every necessity for security ready to their hands, as well as more than was necessary for their personal support, then they gave the rein to their appetites; imagined that rulers must needs wear different clothes from those of subjects; have different and elaborate luxuries of the table; and must even seek sensual indulgence, however unlawful the source, without fear of denial. These things having given rise in the one case to jealousy and offence, in the other to outburst of hatred and passionate resentment, the kingship became a tyranny.[23]

Machiavelli was not unique, but definitely unusual, in his adherence to Polybius. The lowest common denominator which tied nearly all humanist political taxonomies together was the Aristotelian model of six kinds of government, one-third of which are examples of the good-king–bad-tyrant binary. Aristotle, however, is equivocal about hereditary monarchies and even believes them to be desirable under some circumstances:

> How about the family of the king? Are his children to succeed him? If they are no better than anybody else, that will be mischievous. But, says the lover of royalty, the king, though he might, will not hand on his power to his children. That, however, is hardly to be expected, and is too much to ask of human nature … But when a whole family … happens to be so pre-eminent in virtue as to surpass all others, then it is just that they should be the royal family and supreme over all.[24]

At any rate, there is no explicit link binding tyranny to the corruption of hereditary sovereignty in Aristotle's understanding. Instead, in Aristotle's version of the sequence of governments, tyranny follows oligarchy:

> The first governments were kingships, probably for this reason, because of old, when cities were small, men of eminent virtue were few ... But when many persons equal in merit arose, no longer enduring the pre-eminence of one, they desired to have a commonwealth, and set up a constitution. The ruling class soon deteriorated and enriched themselves out of the public treasury; riches became the path to honour, and so oligarchies naturally grew up. These passed into tyrannies and tyrannies into democracies.[25]

For later humanist writers, the link between kingship and tyranny was often more direct. For instance, Salutati writes that the word 'tyrant' came from *tyros*, meaning brave, as in the earliest Greek polities these leaders were brave kings who protected communities; but 'as evil increased and kings began to rule oppressively [*superbe*] the name "tyrant" was confined to those who abused their power "tyrannically"'.[26] The idea grew pervasive that the origins of tyranny lie in a general atmosphere of corruption and degeneration that has plagued the history of human civilization. For instance, two centuries later, the Scottish writer George Buchanan's *De iure regni apud scotos* also begins with the kings-versus-tyrants gambit and, in trying to historicize kingship and tyranny, invokes the inevitability of human corruption. In an echo of Salutati, Buchanan writes:

> It is credible that the first magistrates to be so called were good men, if only from the fact that the name was at one time held in such honour that it was even applied to the gods. It was their successors who made it so shameful by their crimes that everyone shunned it as if it were contagious and pestilential, deeming it a milder insult to be called a hangman than a tyrant.[27]

In the entire history of European political thought, there is no writer who displays the kind of deep, unshakably pessimistic faith in the infinite corruptibility of human beings that Machiavelli does. Yet in describing the inception of tyranny, he deliberately eschews the premise of generalized and universal corruption, focusing instead on the specific context of hereditary sovereignty, as derived from Polybius. This is because, for Machiavelli, hereditary monarchy presents the *only* non-contingent, non-negotiable basis of tyranny. Every other aspect of tyrannical behaviour can be construed as contingent. Acts traditionally associated with tyranny could potentially, under certain circumstances, lead to effective governance, in which case Machiavelli would not call such acts tyrannous. Illegitimate seizing of power is not tyranny by default, as that too may result in the establishment of a stable, orderly state. Cruelty, when administered judiciously in dire circumstances, could be effective and therefore non-tyrannous. For Machiavelli, the only inevitable circumstance of tyranny, then, is the context of hereditary kingship.

The abhorrence he feels for a model of monarchy that was fast becoming normative in sixteenth-century Europe, coupled with his equanimity towards the figure who posed the greatest threat to this dynastic model of monarchy, namely the new prince and his acts of lawmaking violence, makes Machiavelli's definition of tyranny a misfit in its historical milieu and therefore especially vulnerable to misreadings and misappropriations. This deliberately controversial reading of tyranny is etched out in sharp relief in *Discourses* 1:9 and 1:10 by juxtaposing the figures of Romulus and Julius Caesar. In particular, I would like to examine the curious positioning of Julius Caesar in the Machiavellian universe as the Petri dish in which Machiavelli's slippery notions of tyranny can be glimpsed in a consolidated manner: Caesar, who is the new prince par excellence, who fulfils almost every criterion of political greatness outlined by Machiavelli in *The Prince*, is barely mentioned in that text but becomes the prototype of the tyrant in the *Discourses*.

Julius Caesar was one of the most polarizing historical figures for Early Modern historians and political theorists. On the one hand, the greatest narrative poem of trecento Italy placed Caesar's assassins in the lowest circle of hell, along with Judas, the prototype of treachery for believing Christians.[28] On the other hand, as Hans Baron shows, whether or not Caesar qualified as a tyrant was hotly debated by luminaries such as Salutati, Bruni, Poggio, and Guarino, and Caesar's reputation had to withstand the vicissitudes of an intensifying resurgence of republican ideology in Early Modern Europe. Once again, a useful counterpoint to Machiavelli is Coluccio Salutati, whose treatise on tyranny follows the traditional characterization of the usurper as the tyrant *ex defectu tituli* but who chooses to exonerate Caesar from the charges of tyranny, arguing that his actions as a ruler more than made up for the less-than-ideal way in which he came by his power. Writing at a time when the Florentine republic was reeling under the threat of destruction, Salutati, himself one of the greatest defenders of republican values, sees Caesar not as the nemesis of the Roman republic but as a just ruler who did not deserve the appellation of tyrant, 'seeing as he held his principate in a commonwealth, lawfully and not by abuse of law'.[29]

Though Salutati's historical position mirrors Machiavelli's, the latter's views on tyranny and Caesar form Salutati's chiastic obverse. For Machiavelli, neither the ambitious title of Dictator nor the exercise of extra-juridical powers is *ipso facto* tyrannical. In fact, he writes:

> And therefore all republics should have some institution similar to the dictatorship. The republic of Venice, which is pre-eminent amongst modern ones, had reserved to a small number of citizens the power of deciding all urgent matters without referring their decisions to a larger council. And when a republic lacks some such system, a strict observance of the established laws will expose her to ruin; or, to save her from such danger, the laws will have to be disregarded.[30]

Machiavelli asserts that at times, abrogating the rule of law is entirely necessary for the survival of a republic.

Additionally, Plutarch's biography of Caesar shows him as the textbook example of the Machiavellian new prince. Plutarch's account tells us that Caesar kept striving for higher ambitions and greater glories, just as Machiavelli advises the new prince. He knew how to use cruelty well and when to be clement. For instance, he did not stop with the defeat of Pompey but went to Spain to exterminate the latter's progeny. But once his dictatorial powers were consolidated,

> he pardoned many of those who had fought against him, and to some he even gave honours and offices besides, as to Brutus and Cassius, both of whom were now praetors. The statues of Pompey, which had been thrown down, he would not suffer to remain so, but set them up again, at which Cicero said that in setting up Pompey's statues Caesar firmly fixed his own. When his friends thought it best that he should have a bodyguard, and many of them volunteered for this service, he would not consent, saying that it was better to die once for all than to be always expecting death. And in the effort to surround himself with men's good will as the fairest and at the same time the securest protection, he again courted the people with banquets and distributions of grain, and his soldiers with newly planted colonies.[31]

In *The Art of War*, Machiavelli himself acknowledges Caesar's military valour, while also withholding from him the distinction of being a 'good man'.[32] In *Discourses* 3:6 he highlights Caesar's popularity, calling him 'beloved by the people';[33] yet in a most un-Machiavellian way, he remains unwavering in his denunciation of Caesar's tyranny:

> Nor let any one be deceived by the glory of that Cæsar who has been so much celebrated by writers; for those who praised him were corrupted by his fortune, and frightened by the long duration of the empire that was maintained under his name, and which did not permit writers to speak of him with freedom. And if any one wishes to know what would have been said of him if writers had been free to speak their minds, let them read what Catiline said of him. Cæsar is as much more to be condemned, as he who commits an evil deed is more guilty than he who merely has the evil intention.[34]

Of course, pro-republican humanist writers often reviled Caesar as the person who ended the glorious days of the Roman republic. Normally dictators, even in the Roman republic, were wholly subject to the Senate and other bodies. Their extraordinary powers lasted only as long as extraordinary circumstances did, but with Caesar there was a breakdown in the constitutional machinery. Therefore, one obvious way to read Machiavelli's indictment of Caesar is by invoking a slightly reductive version of the Cambridge School's view of Machiavelli as the uncompromising upholder of republican values, who bows to Medicean authority owing to the exigencies of history; but when released from those pressures, his preference for republican forms of governance shines forth. His exaltation, in other texts and contexts, of authoritarian new princes resembling Caesar can be shown, then, to be a dissembling act. The threat of oversimplification which often underlies such readings has been pointed out by historians like John McCormick who have also seriously questioned Machiavelli's commitment to republican government or at least to what Quentin Skinner understands by Machiavelli's republicanism.[35]

But even if we accept Machiavelli's republicanism unsceptically and unreservedly, Machiavelli himself acknowledges that even before Caesar assumed power, the Roman republic was 'already corrupt' ('venuta alla corruzione').[36] This explicit admission, when read in conjunction with his praise of constitutional dictatorships in dire circumstances, would seem to exonerate Caesar. In fact, while talking about the foundation of new political orders, he states clearly that at the point of inception, extra-juridical rule by one person is preferable to the rule of many:

> But we must assume, as a general rule, that it never or rarely happens that a republic or monarchy is well constituted, or its old institutions entirely reformed, unless it is done by only one individual ... The above views might be corroborated by any number of examples, such as those of Moses, Lycurgus, Solon, and other founders of monarchies and republics, who were enabled to establish laws suitable for the general good only by keeping for themselves an exclusive authority.[37]

What damns Caesar in Machiavelli's eyes is not his disruption of republican government, nor his usurpation of exclusive authority, nor the acts of cruelty committed in the process. As Plutarch writes, Caesar is deemed a tyrant because 'the monarchy, besides the element of irresponsibility, now took on that of permanence'.[38] He was responsible for the inception of a dynastic monarchical form of government, as after his assassination, the Julio-Claudian dynasty became the arbiters of the fate of Rome, which spiralled downward into an abyss of corruption and tyranny.

Through the contrasting examples of Romulus and Caesar, Machiavelli drives home the crucial difference between the new prince who commits an act of lawmaking violence in order to craft a new political order and the conqueror who initiates a hereditary model of sovereignty. Through this contrast between the two, Machiavelli redraws the Early Modern parameters of tyranny altogether. Romulus, the founder of Rome and the man who killed his own brother to consolidate the stability of the state, is a man of *virtù* precisely because he is a 'sagacious legislator of a republic' ('una prudente ordinatore d'una republica'). Such a ruler, who, like Romulus, seeks to

> promote the public good, and not his private interests, and who prefers his country to his own successors, should concentrate all authority in himself; and a wise mind will never censure any one for having employed any extraordinary means for the purpose of establishing a kingdom or constituting a republic ... The lawgiver should, however, be sufficiently wise and virtuous not to leave this authority which he has assumed either to his heirs or to any one else; for mankind, being more prone to evil than to good, his successor might employ for evil purposes the power which he had used only for good ends.[39]

Having founded the new political order, Romulus does call the Senate but still retains his exclusive prerogative, particularly his control over the army. What he does not do is leave the state to his biological heirs: this marks the crucial difference between him and Caesar. In the next chapter of the *Discourses*, Machiavelli expands upon this idea by dividing the entire history of imperial Rome into two sections: the regimes of emperors who obtained the throne through inheritance and those who came to power by dint of their own *virtù*:

> For of the twenty-six Emperors that reigned from the time of Cæsar to that of Maximinius, sixteen were assassinated, and only ten died a natural death ... [A]ll the Emperors that succeeded to the throne by inheritance, except Titus, were bad, and those who became Emperors by adoption were all good, such as the five from Nerva to Marcus Aurelius; and when the Empire became hereditary, it came to ruin.[40]

At this point, Machiavelli displays no nostalgic hankering for the republic that had fallen into decay and paved the way for the Empire. His hatred of dynastic inheritance, however, remains unaltered. The Emperors from Nerva to Marcus Aurelius were not tyrants, because unlike the Julio-Claudian line, the rulers of the Nerva–Antonine line adopted the most prominent man of the Empire as their heir. This practice stopped with Commodus, the biological son of Marcus Aurelius who became emperor after his father and immediately revealed himself to be a cruel and rapacious tyrant.

Machiavelli's initial apathy towards hereditary princes in *The Prince* develops into an almost pathological hatred of the institution of hereditary monarchy in the *Discourses*. And in Machiavelli's analysis, the blame rests with Julius Caesar: he is not a tyrant in the sense of an ungodly, oppressive monarch; he is a tyrant because his reign marks the transformation of the sovereignty of Rome into heritable authority.

As more and more Western European kingdoms moved towards a model of centralized hereditary monarchy in the Early Modern period, the anxieties surrounding usurpation became increasingly acute. Machiavelli's association of tyranny with hereditary kingship rather than usurped power could, then, be seen as the relic of an older political milieu which was becoming increasingly outdated. Two centuries prior to this, it was acceptable for Marsiglio of Padua to hint in his *Defensor pacis* that hereditary kings often govern to ensure their own benefit and the succession of their progeny, which makes this kind of regime akin to tyranny.[41] But in the sixteenth century, particularly in kingdoms like France and England, hereditary monarchy had come to be championed as the bulwark against the tyranny of the upstart new prince.

As J. H. Burns argues in his brilliant study of Western European absolutism, what set Early Modern theories of monarchical absolutism apart from the medieval tradition was that Early Modern thinkers conflated 'the "divinity" or sacred character of kingship' with 'hereditary succession'. Whereas medieval European polities often followed more elective forms of kingship, by the fifteenth century it was more or less accepted, at least in theory, that 'hereditary monarchy was the superior and in some sense the more "natural" form'.[42] In England, for instance, the idea of 'indefeasible hereditary right', or succession by primogeniture, was a relatively recent development, first appearing as late as the mid-fifteenth century;[43] however, once it made an appearance, it quickly became the ideological norm and began to be seen as an eternal and immutable principle of sovereignty to which most political writers at least paid lip service. The more the hereditary prince was upheld as God's deputy, the blacker appeared the sins of the tyrant *ex defectu tituli*. Discerning a pattern in late Elizabethan drama where the usurper is identified as a tyrant and routinely punished, W. A. Armstrong can thus posit that the Elizabethan tyrant is conceived in a milieu of 'dynastic nationalism': that is why the drama of this period is much more concerned with the 'civic disasters wrought by unlawful kings' than with the tyrant's 'wilful passion and a patent contempt for God's commandments'.[44]

At a time when even the erstwhile Italian republics were devolving into principalities, to say nothing of the apotheosis of the dynastic prince in kingdoms such as England, Machiavelli's redefining of tyranny runs counter to every single existing convention. He extols the new prince, overlooks his lack of titular legitimacy, and rationalizes his tyrannical acts, while simultaneously vilifying the sacrosanct title of the hereditary prince, automatically identifying hereditary sovereignty with tyranny. He not only upsets the extant discourse on tyranny but also turns the customary definitions of tyranny inside out. It might be possible to argue that because Machiavelli describes tyranny by totally inverting the terms of engagement with it, he has been seen as an advocate of what classical and medieval political thought traditionally categorized as tyranny, particularly in the contemporary English and French traditions of political writing, which could only view his deliberately contrarian views in incredulous horror with occasional lapses into a satanic vocabulary. As traditional Christian notions of titular legitimacy and non-contingent ideas of virtuous governance persist unhindered through subsequent centuries, so does Machiavelli's reputation as the founder of the science of tyranny. With the gradual devaluation of hereditary sovereignty, Machiavelli's abiding discomfort with the institution ceased to be a disruptive issue.

The politico-theological crises that ripped Europe apart in the first half of the twentieth century compelled a number of theorists from either side of the political divide to look back to Early Modern writers, particularly Machiavelli, to make sense of their own chaotic milieu. The four-hundred-year-old association between Machiavelli and tyranny left a lasting impact on this discourse. His rejection of hereditary sovereignty was normalized by that time. Instead, his intensely pragmatic but morally neutral rationalization of the new prince's acts of lawmaking violence became a crucial point of theorization. But that is material for a wholly different paper.

Notes

1. Leo Strauss, *On Tyranny*, ed. Victor Gourevitch and Michael S. Roth (Chicago, IL: University of Chicago Press, 2000), 23–4.
2. Leo Strauss, *Thoughts on Machiavelli* (Chicago, IL: University of Chicago Press, 1958), 13, 26.
3. Cassirer says: 'The political world has lost its connexion not only with religion or metaphysics but also with all the other forms of man's ethical and cultural life. It stands alone—in an empty space.' Ernst Cassirer, *The Myth of the State* (New Haven, CT: Yale University Press, 1946), 140.
4. Strauss, *Thoughts on Machiavelli*, 12.
5. Pole writes that Henry VIII 'so embodies the form of the reign of Antichrist that it had never been seen, these many centuries, in such open form in any other king or tyrant, Christian or infidel' ('formam imperii Antichristi sic expressit (ut in nullo unquam Rege vel tyranno, nec fideli, nec infideli, multis saeculis tam aperte cognosci possit)'): Reginald Pole, *Apologia Reginaldi Poli ad Carolum V. Caesarem*, in *Epistolarum Reginaldi Poli Collectio* (Brescia: Rizzardi, 1744), 167–8; tr. Peter S. Donaldson, *Machiavelli and the Mystery of the State* (Cambridge: Cambridge University Press, 1988), 14.
6. '[H]oste humani generis, in quo omnia hostis consilia explicantur': Pole, *Apologia*, 136; tr. Alessandra Petrina, 'Machiavelli's *Principe* and Its Early Appearance in the British Isles', in *Machiavellian Encounters in Tudor and Stuart England*, ed. Alessandro Arienzo and Alessandra Petrina (Farnham: Ashgate, 2013), 15.
7. Pole, *Apologia*, 137.
8. '[N]on une science politique mais tyrannique … que tous ceux qui liront mes escrits, en feront bon iugement, et conoistront que Machiauel a esté du tout ignorant en ceste science [politique], et que son but n'a tendu et ne tend par ses escrits qu'à former une vraye tyrannie': Innocent Gentillet, *Discours, sur les moyens de bien govverner … contre Nicolas Machiauel Florentin* (1576), Book 1, Preface, 3; tr. Simon Patericke, *A Discourse upon the Meanes of Well Governing* (London: Adam Islip, 1608), Preface, sig.A2r.
9. '[S]on but à esté d'instruire le Prince à estre vn vray Tyran, et à luy enseigner l'art de Tyrannie …': Gentillet, *Discours*, Book 3, Preface, 251; tr. Patericke, 142.
10. Sydney Anglo, *Machiavelli: The First Century* (Oxford: Oxford University Press, 2005), 289.
11. '[T]yrannus ciuitatis est qui in ciuitate non iure principatur, sicut autem non iure principatus multis modis contingit: ita multae sunt tyrannorum species … Item esse quem tyrannum manifeste contingit, quandoque ex parte exercitus, quandoque ex defectu tituli': Bartolus Saxoferratus,

Consilia Bartoli Saxoferratei (Lyons: Jacques and Jean Senneton, 1546), fol.115r; tr. Ephraim Emerton in *Humanism and Tyranny: Studies in the Italian Trecento* (Cambridge, MA: Harvard University Press, 1925), 132.
12. Emerton, *Humanism and Tyranny*, 64.
13. 'Tyrannus autem, licet omnibus opponatur, quia tamen eius proprium est pessundare leges, superbe se gerere, suisque non subditorum utilitatibus providere': Coluccio Salutati, *De Tyranno*, ch. 1: *Il Trattato 'De Tyranno' e lettere scelte*, ed. Francesco Ercole (Bologna: Zanichelli, 1942), 9; tr. Emerton, *Humanism and Tyranny*, 78.
14. Thomas Smith, *De Republica Anglorum*, facsimile of the 1583 edition (New York: Da Capo Press, 1970), sig.B3v.
15. 'Dico, adunque, che negli stati ereditarii e assuefatti al sangue del loro principe sono assai minori difficultà a mantenerli che ne' nuovi; ... in modo che, se tale principe è di ordinaria industria, sempre si manterrà nel suo stato, se non è una estraordinaria ed eccessiva forza che ne lo privi ...' (*Pr.*, ch. 2): Niccolò Machiavelli, *Tutte le opere*, ed. Mario Martelli (Florence: Sansoni, 1971), 258. All citations of Machiavelli's Italian texts are from this edition (henceforth *Opere*) ('Let me say, then, that hereditary states which have grown used to the family of their ruler are much less trouble to keep in hand than new ones are ... Hence, if a prince is just ordinarily industrious, he can always keep his position, unless some unusual or excessive act of force deprives him of it': Niccolò Machiavelli, *The Prince*, tr. and ed. Robert M. Adams, 2nd edn [London: W. W. Norton, 1992]. 4. All translations of *Il Principe* are from this version).
16. Jonathan Dollimore, *Radical Tragedy: Religion, Ideology and Power in the Drama of Shakespeare and His Contemporaries*, 2nd edn (London: Harvester Wheatsheaf, 1989), 179.
17. It is of course important to remember that the political organization of Italy was vastly different from that of England or even Western Europe. Quattrocento Italy witnessed the birth and rise of properly republican states, while in England, a semi-feudal polity was in force. So to imagine a political community devoid of a hereditary monarch in Florence was a very different matter from doing so in England in the sixteenth century. On the rather short-lived republican states of quattrocento Italy, see Quentin Skinner, *Foundations of Modern Political Thought* (Cambridge: Cambridge University Press, 1978), vol. 1, esp. 1–22.
18. 'È cosa veramente molto naturale e ordinaria desiderare di acquistare': *Pr.*, ch. 3, *Opere* 261; tr. Adams, 10.
19. 'E intra tutti e' principi, al principe nuovo è impossibile fuggire el nome del crudele': *Pr.*, ch. 17, *Opere* 282; tr. Adams, 45.

20. 'Qualunque diventa principe o d'una città o d'uno stato, e tanto più quando i fondamenti suoi fussono deboli, e non si volga o per via di regno o di republica alla vita civile; il megliore rimedio che egli abbia, a tenere quel principato, è, sendo egli nuovo principe, fare ogni cosa, in quello stato, di nuovo: ... e pigliae per sua mira Filippo di Macedonia, padre di Alessandro, il quale, con questi modi, di piccol re, diventò principe di Grecia. E ... tramutava gli uomini di provincia in provincia, come e' mandriani tramutano le mandrie loro ... [N]ondimeno, colui che non vuole pigliare quella prima via del bene, quando si voglia mantenere conviene che entri in questo male': *Opere* 109; tr. Christian Detmold in *Historical, Political, and Diplomatic Writings of Machiavelli*, 4 vols. (Boston, MA: James R. Osgood, 1882), 2:155–6. All translations of *Discorsi* are from this version.
21. '[Q]uelli che sanno, non quelli che, sanza sapere, possono governare uno regno': *Opere* 75; tr. Detmold, 2:92.
22. 'Ma come dipoi si cominciò a fare il principe per successione, e non per elezione, subito cominciarono li eredi a degenerare dai loro antichi; e, lasciando l'opere virtuose, pensavano che i principi non avessero a fare altro che superare gli altri di sontuosità e di lascivia e d'ogni altra qualità di licenza: in modo che, cominciando il principe a essere odiato, e per tale odio a temere, e passando tosto dal timore all'offese, ne nasceva presto una tirannide': *Opere* 80; tr. Detmold, 2:100.
23. Polybius, *The Histories*, tr. Evelyn S. Shuckburgh (London: Macmillan, 1889), 1:464.
24. *Politics*, 3:15; tr. from *The Politics of Aristotle*, tr. Benjamin Jowett (Oxford: Clarendon Press, 1885).
25. Ibid.
26. 'Crescente vero malitia, cum superbe regnare reges incepissent, nomen tyranni restrictum est ad illos, qui per insolentiam imperii viribus abutuntur': Salutati, *De tyranno*, 7; tr. Emerton, *Humanism and Tyranny*, 74–5.
27. 'Primos enim magistratus, qui ita appellabantur, viros bonos fuisse credibile est, vel hinc, quod nomen id aliquando tam fuerit honorificum, ut ad deos etiam transferretur. Posteri suis sceleribus ita reddiderunt infame, ut omnes tanquam contagiosum et pestilens id fugerent: leuiusque putarent conuicium, carnificem quam tyrannum appellari': George Buchanan, *De iure regni apud Scotos* (Edinburgh: John Ross, 1579), 51; tr. from Buchanan, *A Dialogue on the Law of Kingship among Scots*, tr. and ed. Roger Mason and Martin Smith (Farnham: Ashgate, 2004), 83.
28. See Dante, *Inferno*, Canto 34:61–9.
29. '[U]t statum illum rei publice qui resedit in Cesare non ad tyrannidem, sed ad rem publicam pertinere vir libertatis avidissimus iudicavit': Salutati, *De tyranno*, 23; tr. Emerton, *Humanism and Tyranny*, 100.

Machiavelli and Tyranny

30. 'E però le republiche debbano intra loro ordini avere uno simile modo: e la Republica viniziana, la quale intra le moderne republiche è eccellente, ha riservato autorità a pochi cittadini, che ne' bisogni urgenti, sanza maggiore consulta, tutti d'accordo possino deliberare. Perché, quando in una republica manca uno simile modo, è necessario, o, servando gli ordini, rovinare, o, per non ruinare, rompergli': *Disc.* 1:34, *Opere* 117; tr. Detmold, 2:170.
31. Plutarch, Life of Caesar: *Lives*, tr. Bernadotte Perrin, Loeb Classical Library (Cambridge, MA: Harvard University Press, 1919), 7:577.
32. Like Pompey and other Roman generals, he acquired fame 'come valenti uomini, non come buoni': *L'Arte della guerra*, Book 1, *Opere* 306; tr. from Machiavelli, *The Art of War*, ed. and tr. Christopher Lynch (Chicago, IL: University of Chicago Press, 2003), 15.
33. 'Cesare, il quale, per avere il popolo di Roma amico …': *Opere* 209; tr. Detmold, 2:345.
34. 'Né sia alcuno che s'inganni, per la gloria di Cesare, sentendolo, massime, celebrare dagli scrittori: perché quegli che lo laudano, sono corrotti dalla fortuna sua, e spauriti dalla lunghezza dello imperio, il quale, reggendosi sotto quel nome, non permetteva che gli scrittori parlassono liberamente di lui. Ma chi vuole conoscere quello che gli scrittori liberi ne direbbono, vegga quello che dicono di Catilina. E tanto è più biasimevole Cesare, quanto più è da biasimare quello che ha fatto, che quello che ha voluto fare un male': *Disc.* 1:10, *Opere* 92; tr. Detmold, 2:123.
35. See John P. McCormick, 'Machiavelli against Republicanism: On the Cambridge School's "Guicciardinian Moments"', *Political Theory* 31, no. 5 (2003), 615–43. For a persuasive account of Machiavelli's republicanism, see Gisela Bock, Quentin Skinner, and Maurizio Viroli, eds., *Machiavelli and Republicanism* (Cambridge: Cambridge University Press, 1993).
36. *Disc.* 1:29, *Opere* 111; tr. Detmold, 2:160.
37. 'E debbesi pigliare questo per una regola generale: che mai o rado occorre che alcuna republica o regno sia, da principio, ordinato bene, o al tutto di nuovo, fuora degli ordini vecchi, riformato, se non è ordinato da uno; … Potrebbesi dare in sostentamento delle cose soprascritte infiniti esempli; come Moises, Licurgo, Solone, ed altri fondatori di regni e di republiche, e' quali poterono, per aversi attribuito un'autorità, formare leggi a proposito del bene comune': *Disc.* 1:9, *Opere* 90–1; tr. Detmold, 2:120–1.
38. Plutarch, Life of Caesar: *Lives*, 7:575.
39. '[V]olere giovare non a sé ma al bene comune, non alla sua propria successione ma alla comune patria, debbe ingegnarsi di avere l'autorità, solo; né mai uno ingegno savio riprenderà alcuno di alcuna azione straordinaria, che, per ordinare un regno o constituire una republica, usasse

... Debbi bene in tanto essere prudente e virtuoso, che quella autorità che si ha presa non la lasci ereditaria a un altro: perché, sendo gli uomini più proni al male che al bene, potrebbe il suo successore usare ambiziosamente quello che virtuosamente da lui fusse stato usato': *Disc.* 1:9, *Opere* 90; tr. Detmold, 2:120–1.

40. 'Perché, di ventisei imperadori che furono da Cesare a Massimino, sedici ne furono ammazzati, dieci morirono ordinariamente; ... [T]utti gl'imperadori che succederono all'imperio per eredità, eccetto Tito, furono cattivi; quelli che per adozione, furono tutti buoni, come furono quei cinque da Nerva a Marco: e come l'imperio cadde negli eredi, e' ritornò nella sua rovina': *Disc.* 1:10, *Opere* 92; tr. Detmold, 2:124. By 'cinque da Nerva a Marco', Machiavelli obviously means the five emperors who followed Nerva, down to Marcus Aurelius. Detmold's translation wrongly reads 'Nero' for 'Nerva' at this point, though 'Nerva' correctly in the next sentence.
41. In this connexion, see *Disc.* 1:9, 1:16.
42. J. H. Burns, 'The Idea of Absolutism', in *Absolutism in Seventeenth-Century Europe*, ed. John Miller (London: Macmillan, 1990), 21–42, 31.
43. John Neville Figgis, *The Divine Right of Kings* (Cambridge: Cambridge University Press, 1914), 82.
44. W. A. Armstrong, 'The Elizabethan Conception of the Tyrant', *Review of English Studies* 22, no. 87 (1946), 161–81 (esp. 180).

5

Machiavelli's Turn to Xenophon

Christopher Nadon and Christopher Lynch

Machiavelli's treatment of Cyrus, king and founder of the Persian Empire, followed in the tradition of scholars who later came to be known as the Italian Renaissance humanists, who had laboured from the beginning of the fifteenth century to restore the direct knowledge of classical antiquity. In doing so, they made Xenophon part of the common intellectual heritage of sixteenth-century Italians. Machiavelli enrolled in this movement when he listed Cyrus among the chief examples of those who became princes by their own virtue and not by fortune, when he compared him to no less a figure than Moses, and when he exhorted his readers to consult Xenophon's account of Cyrus's life, the only book so honoured in *The Prince*. Machiavelli was unable, however, simply to follow in the path of others. A sign of the difference between them is that whereas the humanists also took great interest in Plato and Aristotle, Machiavelli harboured doubts, much as Hobbes would later,[1] as to the wisdom of reinstating these figures as intellectual authorities. Indeed, for Machiavelli, Xenophon's particular understanding of politics and philosophy and his manner of writing on these subjects are important elements of the remedy or antidote to the ills he thought produced, in part, by other philosophers from the classical tradition.

The Rediscovery of Xenophon

The rediscovery of Xenophon in Italy began when Coluccio Salutati, Chancellor of the Florentine Republic, persuaded the Byzantine scholar Manuel Chrysoloras to come to Florence to lecture and teach Greek from 1397 to 1400. Chrysoloras seems to have used Xenophon as a basic text for teaching the language. The Greek texts of all Xenophon's works were available in Italy well before the fall of Constantinople in 1453, and Chrysoloras's students were interested enough in their substance to begin translating them into Latin.[2] The first to do so was Leonardo Bruni (1370–1444) in 1403, perhaps guided in his choice of Xenophon's *Hiero* by his mentor Salutati's earlier treatise, *De tyranno*. He followed this in 1407 with a translation of *The Apology of Socrates*.[3] In 1432, Franceso Filelfo (1398–1481) translated both the *Constitution of the Lacedaemonians* and the *Agesilaus* while residing as a scholar in Florence. The choice of these particular works, denouncing tyranny and largely focusing on Sparta, probably testifies to the republican politics of the translators, for at this time Sparta was considered the classic model of a republican regime and Xenophon was well known and even esteemed for his philo-laconism.

However, the political flexibility of Xenophon's writings allowed the similarly flexible Filelfo, who had meanwhile moved to Milan under the patronage of Duke Filippo Maria Visconti and remained there under Duke Francesco Sforza, to translate and present the *Cyropaedia* in 1467 as a full endorsement of one-man rule. In the dedication to Pope Paul II, Filelfo claims that Xenophon's Cyrus is a 'most wise, most just king' ('sapientissimo iustissimoque principe') whom he places, as will Machiavelli in *The Prince*, in the company of Moses.[4] The favourable reception of the translation was no doubt gratifying to Filelfo, as it superseded the loose and often inaccurate paraphrase produced in 1446 by his bitter rival Poggio Bracciolini (1380–1459), itself an improvement on the brief translation by Lorenzo Valla (1407–57) of the first four chapters of the *Cyropaedia* in 1438.[5] Yet it was Poggio's Latin version that formed the basis for the first and only Italian translation of Xenophon to be published in Machiavelli's lifetime. The rendering was by Poggio's son Jacopo.[6]

Xenophon's *Oeconomius* is known to have been translated in classical times by Cicero. The first Early Modern rendering, by Giovanni Aurispa (1376–1459), is also lost. The first extant translation from the fifteenth century is by Lampugnino Birago (1390–1472). It was dedicated to Pope Nicholas V and probably completed before 1453. Birago also translated the *Anabasis*, but only his preface, dated 1452, remains. The *Memorabilia*, given that name by Johannes Levvenklaius in his 1572 edition of Xenophon's complete works, was first translated in its entirety by Cardinal Basilios Bessarion (1403–72) as *De dictis et factis Socratis*. The last Socratic work to be translated into Latin was Xenophon's *Symposium* by Janus Cornarius, published at Frankfurt but not until 1546. Its rather blunt presentation of Greek sexual mores, and lack of any mystical or sublime rhetoric no doubt combine to explain its absence from the Italian humanist canon.[7] All the remaining minor works—including the *Athenian Constitution* and the *Letters*, now considered by many to be spurious—were available in Latin by 1561.

If we go by the number of editions published, Xenophon's *Hiero* seems to have been his most popular work in the fifteenth century. Yet the *Cyropaedia* was often considered his masterpiece, and references and citations to it far outnumber those to any other of his works. Moreover, the *Cyropaedia* allows us to gauge the impact of Xenophon on Renaissance thinkers, since prior to its recovery, its title character, Cyrus the Great, seems to have been known primarily from the account in Herodotus's *Histories*, where he is outwitted and slain by the Massagette Queen Tomyris: she has his severed head plunged in a bucket of blood so that he might finally have his fill of gore.[8] Despite a more favourable presentation in the Old Testament (Ezra 1–6, Isaiah 44–5), Cyrus figures in pre-Renaissance literature as a rapacious and violent king.[9] His fortune changes dramatically when Italians begin to take their bearings by Xenophon's account.

In his *De principe* (1470), Bartolomeo Sacchi di Platina claims that 'the Socratic philosopher' Xenophon shows that the good ruler differs in no way from the good parent in preferring the public advantage to his own private good. He illustrates this by citing the example of Cyrus, who also serves as a model of piety and benevolence.[10] Around the same time, in a work also bearing the title *De principe* (1468), Giovanni Pontano elaborates on Virgil's exhortation, 'learn justice and despise not the gods'.[11]

> For all bear with a calm mind the rule of him in whom there is justice and even subject themselves willingly to his governance; which we read about that Cyrus, who was believed to be not only the model of justice but of all the other kingly virtues.[12]

Pontano's Cyrus, 'whom I very much wish you to imitate',[13] also took care to make himself loved by practising a *humanitas* manifested in sharing in his subjects' toils, practising liberality by not appropriating their goods and wealth, and devoting himself to making all the citizenry happy.

The praise or blame of Cyrus seems not to have been closely connected to the question with which Francesco Patrizi opens his *De institutione reipublicae* (c. 1470): whether it is better to have a republic or a principality. In this work, Patrizi comes down on the side of republics. Yet he, much like Machiavelli later, also wrote a companion work, *De regno et regis institutione* (c. 1480), in which he seems to take the opposite view. He was alive to the apparent contradiction between the two stands and sought to dismiss it on the rather specious grounds that men are free to praise and disprase whomever they wish.[14] Yet the two works are not so much at odds as their titles might lead one to believe.

This can be seen in the philosophically unified treatment he accords Cyrus in both. Even in his republican work, Patrizi admits that Cyrus 'ruled happily all his life with the great support of the people, just like the Stoic Marcus Aurelius, whose innocence and holiness made him pre-eminent among all the Roman emperors'. He can do this because he prefaces this praise with 'if we wish to believe what Xenophon says of Cyrus'.[15] But for Patrizi, Xenophon's Cyrus is not a historical figure but a model of imagined perfection, just as the city in Plato's *Republic* is an imagined city. According to Patrizi, no actual man is perfect, and a regime that presupposes the existence of perfect virtue in its ruler will quickly degenerate. Thus, a regime 'mixed of all classes of men' ('ex omni genere hominum commixta'[16]) and ruled by law is preferable in practice, even though itself by no means perfect. Needless to say, these arguments apply to his portrait of the ideal prince in *De regno*, though Patrizi stresses, even in this monarchic book, that such a figure 'may never have existed' and is as imaginary as Plato's 'perfect city ... which never was nor will be'.[17]

There is a deeper issue at stake behind the debate over the real or imagined character of Xenophon's prince and the interest and praise the humanists lavish on him—indeed, on ancient political thought altogether. This is the issue of the conflict or harmony between the pagan or classical understanding of goodness and the understanding of goodness based on biblical faith. If the classical conception of the good man or ruler is essentially the same as the biblical—if, as Filelfo claims, Cyrus can properly be ranked with Moses— there is no essential conflict between the classical position and the Christian faith, even if God's grace may be required to make the imagined perfection actual. Drawing on a passage from Xenophon's *Education of Cyrus*, Patrizi asserts the theoretical self-sufficiency of classical political thought.

> The laws of the Persians, as Xenophon writes, commanded one to be just as one's first duty; and thus from early childhood the citizens were taught to desire nothing dishonest or foul. According to me, this is the best course of all. And inasmuch as it were possible to have everyone instructed in this doctrine, it appears to me that it would be superfluous to lay down precepts of good living, because all the citizens of the republic would be just. *And all other precepts, that have to do with human society, would be superfluous.* When everyone does what is required, they will be altogether honest and without any lascivious desire or perturbation. Nor would anyone, having been conquered at the beginning, depart from *true reason* out of ambition, avarice, hate, or envy. Nor would anyone wish to follow private interest or crazed desires rather than the common good and *true reason*. But men being imperfect, and having only the simulacra of virtue, the laws require being asserted by force. (Emphasis added)[18]

Classical thought can safely be revived because it teaches the rational basis of the good political community. It must therefore conform to the genuine requirements of the political dimension of scriptural faith and could perhaps even help to resolve the doctrinal and political schisms afflicting the Church in the fifteenth century.

Whether the humanists' revival of classical thought was intended as a support and aid to faith, or whether they wished to reverse this relation and use the test of reason to 'purify' or possibly moderate religious doctrine is hard to tell; no doubt the position varied from author to author. In Patrizi's case, the mere fact that he was Bishop of Gaeta in no way decides the issue. Consider also Leonardo Bruni, the first translator of Xenophon into Latin. As should be stressed with almost all the humanists, Bruni's interest in Xenophon paled before his interest in Plato and Socrates. Of the *Gorgias*, Bruni claimed in a letter to Pope Eugene IV that

> in this book Socrates teaches that if someone does us an injury, we should not seek vengeance. What kind of teachings, by God, are these? Are they not divine, are they not very similar to Christian perfection?[19]

The historian James Hankins argues: 'Bruni's translations of Socratica, with their accompanying prefaces and arguments, were designed to show that [contemporary concerns about Socrates's heretical character] were untrue, and that in fact Socrates had been practically a Christian before Christ.'[20] But while Bruni draws on Plato's *Apology* to portray Socrates as a martyr who believes in an afterlife, on the *Crito* for his meek submission to the laws, on the *Phaedo* for his teaching about the immortality of the soul, and on the *Symposium* for a metaphysics of love that leads upward to the divine, he is quite selective as to which passages from these works make it into his Latin translations. For example, he removes all mentions of pederasty from the *Symposium* and also drops the discussion of true and false rhetoric from the *Phaedrus*.[21] Again, is Bruni, as a good Christian, simply suppressing those elements of Plato that he thought non-essential yet potential stumbling blocks for his Christian audience? Or has he been schooled by those parts of *Phaedrus* that he suppresses and is himself engaged in a kind of medicinal rhetoric to make it easier for his readers to swallow principles that will eventually transform their religious beliefs into something politically more salutary?

Hankins considers Bruni to be most concerned with reviving republican politics and therefore thinks 'his real affinity is with the Socrates of Xenophon: with Socrates the moral teacher and ideal citizen of Athens'.

Hankins is therefore surprised that 'there is (as yet) no evidence that Bruni ever studied Xenophon's *Memorabilia* or *Symposium*'.[22] But if certain Christian doctrines are what stand in the way of sound politics, perhaps Bruni thought it better to focus on Plato precisely because the greater overlap between Platonism and Christian doctrine would allow for a greater degree of influence or refraction. Such a strategy is not without its risks, since assimilation can work both ways. No sooner might Plato be recovered as an alternative to Christian thought and politics than he could perhaps be re-Christianized, as happened earlier under the early Church Fathers. Marsilio Ficino, a humanist with relatively little interest in Xenophon, none whatsoever in the *Cyropaedia*, but a great deal in Plato, seems to have set himself this task:

> With just a few changes, [Augustine] maintained, the Platonists would be Christians. Relying on Augustine's authority, and moved by an immense love of humanity, I long ago decided that I would try to paint a portrait of Plato as close as possible to the Christian truth.[23]

He succeeded so well that in Machiavelli's view, Ficino and his followers proved unable to resist the political machinations of an ambitious priest like Savonarola, who, adopting Augustine's motto from Isaiah as his own, again used philosophy against itself to subordinate it to faith: 'Unless you believe, you will not understand.'[24] And while it is true that Ficino ultimately broke with and repudiated Savonarola, he did so on grounds friendly to the Friar's position of the supremacy of faith over reason:

> God has arisen and dispersed His enemies in Anti-Christ, all who hate God have fled before his face ... He, the All-Powerful, Who certainly resists the proud, but gives his grace to the humble has shown strength with His arm [in delivering the Florentines from Savonarola and his followers].[25]

Platonism and Aristotelianism Rejected

When Machiavelli made his only published mentions of Ficino and his disciple Pico della Mirandola, he was clearly concerned with the relative status of faith and reason in his time and place. Ficino and Pico were Plato's greatest disciples in Machiavelli's age, arguably in the entire Italian Renaissance and perhaps even in the Renaissance *tout court*, and Pico must be considered a disciple of both Plato and Aristotle, since he was also a great synthesizer of disparate approaches to truth. In his *Florentine Histories*, Machiavelli implies that the close relationship between these two men of letters and their great Medici patrons ultimately reflects the confused or improperly ordered relationships between faith and reason, religion and philosophy, within Ficino's and Pico's thoughts and writings.

Machiavelli is unusual among contemporary thinkers in making little mention of Plato and Aristotle. His near silence constitutes his basic judgement and perhaps his most telling treatment, evoking as it does the latter-day Noah imagined by Machiavelli in the *Discourses on Livy*, 2:5. Machiavelli's Noah figure seeks to order the future in his own mode by suppressing and perverting his knowledge of past writings. And just as he names Plato and Aristotle only once each in his greatest work, the *Discourses*, so too does he name Ficino and Pico just once each in his longest work, the *Florentine Histories*.[26] Ficino and Pico are mentioned at the peak of the culminating chapters on the putative heroes of this otherwise bleak history: Cosimo and Lorenzo de' Medici, the rulers of Florence during the roughly six decades of relative peace, prosperity, and power for the city. Only Cosimo and Lorenzo seem to have succeeded in dispersing the political darkness that pervaded Florentine and Italian politics, by ameliorating the party strife that is the explicit theme of the *Florentine Histories* as a whole. The Medici's patronage of these men of letters is presented as the crowning achievement or best use of their well-known liberality. As Cosimo was the patron of Ficino from the 1460s, so was Lorenzo of Pico from the 1480s. Machiavelli's eulogy of Cosimo attains its peak by listing the men of letters he brought to Florence, most prominently Ficino. Although he loved and exalted many literary men, Ficino 'he loved extremely', 'took him into his home', and 'gave him a property near his own'.[27] Pico is similarly featured among the most impressive aspects of Lorenzo's awe-inspiring life. Of the five 'marvels' mentioned in connection with Lorenzo, the first is his marvellous love for men who excelled in any art, but especially in letters. Among the men of letters, he especially loved Pico.[28] Yet a careful look at the contexts of Machiavelli's glowing presentation of the Medici patronage of Ficino and Pico darkens the picture: it reveals his fuller judgement on the shaky foundations and ultimately disastrous effects of Medici rule over Florence.

Machiavelli's mention of Ficino calls to mind the abject condition of Cosimo at the time of his death and Ficino's famous role as Cosimo's consoler. Immediately before he speaks of Ficino, Machiavelli notes only one other man of letters, the Greek Argyropoulos whose Aristotelian works, along with Ficino's translations of Plato, were, by Ficino's own account, Cosimo's chief consolations.

Ficino reports that Cosimo 'discussed many things concerning the contempt of this life, since he already aspired to that supernal beatitude'.[29] When Ficino told him that a student of Plato had written on such matters, Cosimo asked him to translate the work into Latin. And not long after, according to Ficino's account, Cosimo read

> the book of Plato on the origin of all things [the *Parmenides*] and that one on the highest good [the *Philebus*]—twelve days thereafter, as if about to return to enjoy that 'origin' and that 'highest good', he was recalled from this shadow of life and drew near the supernal light.[30]

When Machiavelli recounts these same events in the *Florentine Histories*, he casts Cosimo's end in an altogether different and less heavenly light, reflecting the weakness of Medici rule owing to Cosimo's lack of his own arms and his consequent abject dependence on the arms of the treacherous Francesco Sforza. In what might seem the most inappropriate of places—namely the eulogy of the greatest Medici in a book dedicated to a Medici pope—Machiavelli recounts in detail how deeply 'it distressed the greatness of his [Cosimo's] spirit [*animo*] that he ... had not increased the Florentine empire' because 'he had been deceived by Francesco Sforza'. This 'caused him very great annoyance' and contributed to his 'passing the last years of his life in disquiet'.[31] While Ficino portrays a dying Cosimo, who contemns the things of this world in Platonic anticipation of other-worldly beatitude, Machiavelli portrays a spirit vexed unto death by his failure to secure arms of his own. Indeed, this chapter is the culmination of the *Florentine Histories* as a whole, whose purpose is to detail and diagnose the ills that attend the reliance on mercenary captains such as Francesco Sforza and, more particularly, the unarmed condition of Florence.[32]

Machiavelli's treatment of Pico similarly places him at the summit of Lorenzo's patronage but notes how this is ineffectual in overcoming the latter's continued dependence on the House of Sforza. The final chapter of the *Florentine Histories* opens with a hopeful reflection on Lorenzo's great potential. Especially promising is the cardinalate of his son Giovanni, who would later ascend to the papacy. Yet by the end of the chapter, Machiavelli offers, as proof of Lorenzo's magnificence, what is in fact the most compelling indication that his legacy will be a poor one: for Machiavelli wryly asserts that the measure of Lorenzo's greatness was how everything came to total ruin shortly after his death. The chapter and book conclude: 'As soon as Lorenzo was dead, those bad seeds began to grow which, not long after, since the one who knew how to eliminate them was not alive, ruined and are still ruining Italy.'[33] The same metaphor for the ruination of Italy is used towards the beginning of the work to explain the origins of the Guelf and Ghibelline factions, which are said to be the seeds of the ruin of all Italy.[34] Nothing has fundamentally changed. Ludovico Sforza, the son of the Sforza who more than tarnished Cosimo's life, does the same for Lorenzo.

The gist of Machiavelli's sole discussions of Ficino and Pico is that even the most worldly of rulers will find themselves vulnerable if they surround themselves with philosophers or intellectuals who would revive Plato and Aristotle, teach contempt for worldly things, and value supernal beatitude. Indeed, especially in light of Ficino's well-known Christianized commentaries on Plato, it is difficult to distinguish Machiavelli's veiled criticism of Ficino and Pico from his all but open criticism of Christianity in the *Discourses*. There Machiavelli says,

> the ancient religion did not beatify men if they were not full of worldly glory, as were captains of armies and princes of republics. Our religion has glorified humble and contemplative more than active men. It has then placed the highest good in humility, abjectness, and contempt of things human … and if our religion asks that you have strength in yourself, it wishes you to be capable more of suffering than of doing something strong.[35]

If Christianity has glorified contemplative men over active men, so too has the reigning philosophy of Machiavelli's day. The opening lines of Ficino's commentary on Plato's *Republic* read:

> As the eye surpasses the hand, the head the feet, reason the senses, the soul the body, the end all that is directed towards the end, stillness movement, and eternity time, so the contemplative life is seen to surpass the active life. For contemplation is the beginning and end of action … Thus, from the very contemplation of God all the movements and actions of the heavens and of nature are guided as if from their inception to their end.[36]

To be sure, Ficino is elsewhere careful to qualify this sweeping exaltation of contemplative over-active men.[37] But the essence of the assertion is not retracted. Although prioritizing contemplation over action is important, for Ficino it is perhaps even more important to situate that priority within a providential cosmic context. The entry to Ficino's commentary on Plato's most fundamental book on politics is guarded by the contemplated God himself as the beginning and the end of all action.

Ficino leaves no doubt that he places 'our Plato' among the founders of states, surpassing all other founders because of the priority of contemplation over action:

> It is for this reason that our Plato surpasses all other founders of states and lawgivers in this respect at least, that while all the others, as human beings, have organized the states mainly for action, Plato, as if divine, guides the entire activity ... of the state mainly towards contemplation and establishes his state as the mistress of the world, not that it may be feared by many but rather that it may be reverenced by all peoples as the heavenly Jerusalem fully manifest on earth.[38]

Machiavelli mentions neither Plato nor Aristotle when he famously warns against taking one's bearings by 'imagined republics and principalities that have never been seen or known to exist in truth'.[39] This omission is perhaps because he had seen how 'the effectual truth of the thing' ('verità effettuale della cosa')[40] begun by those philosophers lived and breathed in Machiavelli's own time in the career of Marsilio Ficino and his sometime master, Savonarola.

The only time Machiavelli comments on Plato and Aristotle together appears designed to counter Ficino's understanding and admiration of them and to diminish the influence that arose out of reverence for their writings. Towards the end of a proposal for political reforms of Florence written at the request of the Medici Pope, Machiavelli asserts that 'the greatest good one can do is to one's fatherland'—hastening to add, for the Pope's benefit, that this is also most pleasing to God.[41] He goes on to proclaim that none are more exalted than those who have reformed republics and kingdoms with laws and institutions. Indeed, they are the first to be praised among all men ('after', that is, 'those who have been gods'[42]). He continues:

> This glory has been so much esteemed by men who never long for anything other than glory, that those who have not been able to make a republic in deed have done it in writing, like Aristotle, Plato, and many others. They have wanted to show to the world that if they have not, like Solon and Lycurgus, been able to found a civil way of life, this omission was not from ignorance but from lack of power to do it in deed.[43]

Machiavelli risibly presents the two philosophers as frustrated local reformers who would have devoted themselves entirely to public life if they had only had the opportunity. For want of that, they were forced to settle for becoming two of the most influential authors in the Western world. If the actual effect of their works was perhaps not what they had intended, Machiavelli's own activity as a writer, oppressed as he was by 'the malignity of fortune', shows that he thought it could be done better and perhaps without giving rise to the ills that attend 'imagined republics and principalities'. His predecessor, and in some sense his model, was Xenophon.

The Reign of Machiavelli's Cyrus

In *The Prince*, Machiavelli follows the Renaissance humanist tradition that enlists Cyrus the Great in the ranks of the 'most excellent' princes of the past, including no less a figure than Moses. Like his humanist predecessors, Machiavelli attributes the success of these men not to good fortune but to their *virtù*. Unlike the humanists, however, Machiavelli lays stress on their also having had their own arms. Arms, indeed, he regards as decisive:

> Moses, Cyrus, Theseus, and Romulus would not have been able to make their peoples observe their constitutions for long if they had been unarmed, as happened in our times to Brother Girolamo Savonarola.[44]

As for the quality or character of these constitutions, Machiavelli seems to consider the kind of discussion or enquiry conducted by the Athenian stranger in Plato's *Laws*, Socrates in the *Republic*, or Aristotle in the *Politics* to be altogether unnecessary. Reasoning about good arms could even take the place of reasoning about good laws, since 'there cannot be good laws where there are not good arms, and where there are good arms there must be good laws'.[45] Xenophon, who presents himself as both a student of Socrates and a successful general, is recommended in a passage that stresses the necessity of military virtue. His *Life of Cyrus* is singled out by name and even suggested as a source for future reading—the only book, apart from Machiavelli's own, to be so honoured in *The Prince*.[46]

The context of Machiavelli's turn to the *Education of Cyrus* is the need for a prince to 'have no other object, nor any other thought, nor to take anything else as his art but the art of war and its orders and discipline; for that is the only art which is of concern to one who commands'.[47] Other Renaissance authors praise Xenophon's account of the Persians' devotion to hunting and Cyrus's lifelong practice of this sport as apt to develop and maintain the physical demands of warfare. Machiavelli, too, praises hunting but does so in his own name without recourse to authority: 'And as to deeds, besides keeping his armies well ordered and exercised, he [the prince] should always be out hunting, and through this accustom the body to hardships.'[48] In *The Prince*, Machiavelli reserves the example of Xenophon's Cyrus for the exercise of the prince's mind. It falls into the category of 'histories [recounting] the actions of excellent men, ... how they conducted themselves in wars, ... the causes of their victories and losses, so as to be able to avoid the latter and imitate the former'.[49] Of course, not all the subjects of these histories were themselves great readers. As the creations of those who wrote books, Achilles and Cyrus did not need books in the usual sense, for they could develop the requisite knowledge of the art of war through the unmediated and continuous observation and study of 'the nature of sites' ('la natura de' siti').[50] But the invention and circulation of books, the influence of authors as authorities, have changed the world even on the battlefield, and the prince must change with it.[51] In reading those histories, the prince is to

> do as some excellent man has done in the past who found someone to imitate who had been praised and glorified before him, whose exploits and actions he always kept beside himself, as they say Alexander the Great imitated Achilles; Caesar, Alexander; Scipio, Cyrus. And whoever reads the life of Cyrus written by Xenophon will then recognize in the life of Scipio how much glory that imitation brought him, how much [*quanto*] in chastity, affability, humanity, and liberality Scipio conformed to what had been written of Cyrus by Xenophon.[52]

Strictly speaking, the prince should imitate an imitator.[53] He should be like Caesar, not Aristotle's student Alexander, nor Scipio, the hero of the Italian humanists. Machiavelli explains this preference for Caesar over Scipio in *The Prince*, Chapter 16, devoted to liberality.

In Machiavelli's analysis, bounty on a large scale makes a prince 'held to be liberal' ('tenuto liberale'), something which in itself should admittedly be good. But the lavish displays this requires consume his substance, compel him to raise taxes, and result in his becoming 'hated by his subjects'. Liberality requires harming many, while rewarding but a few. The end result is damage to the prince himself. It would therefore seem much better to practice parsimony, which allows the prince to 'use liberality with all those from whom he does not take, who are infinite, and meanness with all those to whom he does not give, who are few'; and prudence counsels 'not [to] care about a name for meanness'. Yet this economic and fiscally sensible path fails to moderate or satisfy a certain 'someone' ('alcuno') who objects that 'Caesar attained empire with liberality' and that 'many others, because they have been and have been held to be liberal, have attained very great rank'. Machiavelli admits that for a prince with an army, 'which feeds on booty, pillage, and ransom', liberality is necessary to make the soldiers follow him. Moreover, one can be a bigger giver 'of what is not yours or your subjects', as were Cyrus, Caesar, and Alexander, because 'spending what is someone else's does not take reputation from you but adds it to you; only spending your own is what harms you'.[54] Absent from this list is Scipio, about whom we can now read the remark quoted earlier in a new light, indicating how *little* [*quanto*] he 'conformed to what had been written of Cyrus by Xenophon', at least as regards liberality.[55] Yet the 'agreeable nature' ('natura facile') that Scipio cultivated out of a mistaken understanding of Xenophon's Cyrus would also have proved his ruin had he not had the good fortune of being under the control of the Roman Senate, which enabled him to hide this 'damaging quality' ('qualità dannosa').[56]

Machiavelli's understanding of the virtues follows from his wish 'to go directly to the effectual truth of the thing [rather] than to the imagination of it',[57] much as Xenophon's Cyrus understood the traditional Persian virtues: not in terms of their effect on the Persians' souls or goodness, but in the light of the tangible things they produced either for themselves or their community.[58] It then follows that a prince must 'learn to be able not to be good, and to use this [ability] and not use it, according to necessity'[59]—a conclusion drawn and explicitly stated in the *Cyropaedia* in a passage that seems to have provided the model for Machiavelli's formulation. On the eve of Cyrus's departure to help his Median uncle, Cyaxares, fight an invading Assyrian army, his father instructs him that to take advantage of the enemy he must be 'a plotter, a dissembler, wily, a cheat, a thief, and rapacious'. Moreover, such a man is 'both most just and most lawful'. Of course, by 'most lawful' Cambyses does not mean someone who adheres to the letter of the law or precedent, for Cyrus must also himself become 'a poet of stratagems against the enemy, just as musicians not only play the tunes they learn but also try to compose other new ones'. And if the stress on effectual truth grants equal if not greater power to a reputation for virtue than its reality, it allows deception to become the key to mastery, which in turn encourages independence and innovation. 'For in music, fresh tunes are extremely well regarded; but in military affairs, new stratagems win still higher regard by far, for they are even more able to deceive opponents.'[60]

Thus, Xenophon's Cyrus can become for Machiavelli in the *Discourses* the exemplar of the maxim: 'That one comes from base to great fortune more through fraud than through force.'[61]

> Xenophon in his life of Cyrus shows this necessity to deceive, considering that the first expedition he has Cyrus make against the king of Armenia is full of fraud, and that he makes him seize his kingdom through deception and not

through force. And he does not conclude otherwise from this action than that it is necessary for a prince who wishes to do great things to learn to deceive. Besides this, he makes him deceive Cyaxares, king of the Medes, his maternal uncle, in several modes; without which fraud he shows that Cyrus could not have attained that greatness to which he came.[62]

Xenophon, like Machiavelli, takes his bearings in politics from the effectual truth of political virtue. More important, his analysis of political life builds from the ground up and remains firmly attached to the ground. He introduces no doctrines, either conceptual or metaphysical, that could stifle political life or philosophic thought by becoming authoritative. Machiavelli prefers Xenophon to the other classical philosophers because there is no such thing as Xenophonism. If his Persians and his Socrates cannot help but say something about the higher powers, they profess but might not altogether believe that the gods help those who help themselves: a teaching, like Machiavelli's own invocations of Fortuna, that encourages human enterprise, independence, and striving.[63] Were Machiavelli to level any criticism at all against Xenophon, it might only be that he took too much trouble—whether out of delicacy, bashfulness, or perhaps an unwillingness to brave a reputation for 'Manlian'[64] or Machiavellian harshness—to attribute to Cyrus the princely qualities of affability, humanity, and mercy in a way that could mislead a poor reader like the republican general Scipio, to say nothing of the sophisticated philologists of his own or any other age, by obscuring the true causes of Cyrus's success.[65]

One can see Machiavelli's influence on his contemporaries' understanding of Xenophon and his Cyrus in the Italian translations of Xenophon that were made after the publication of the *Discourses* and *The Prince* in 1531 and 1532, respectively. In 1547, Lodovico Domenichi published a collection, *Le opere morali di Senofonte*, including a translation of the *Hiero* that rendered its traditional subtitle, *De tyranno*, simply as *Il Principe*. A year later, Domenichi dedicated his *Della vita di Ciro re de' Persi* to Lucantonio Cuppano, at the time a colonel under the Duke of Florence, in which he identified Xenophon not as a Socratic but as an Athenian military man whose works were of great utility to other 'captains'. Similarly, Antonio Gandini entitled his 1588 four-volume translation of Xenophon's complete works *Le opere de Senofonte molto utile a capitani di guerra, et al viver morale, et civile*. As for Xenophon's Cyrus, one now finds him cited, not simply as a most just and virtuous ruler but as an important exemplar of the need for deception in politics, by the writers on *ragione di stato* who elaborated and popularized Machiavelli.[66] Scipione Ammirato follows Machiavelli precisely, stressing the unusually large scope granted by Xenophon to his Cyrus when he has him deceive not only his formal enemies but also his maternal uncle Cyaxares.[67] In a world deprived of providence, deception becomes the key to political mastery.

By showing some of his contemporaries that at least one classical political philosopher was concerned not with giving a systematic defence or grounding of traditional morality but rather with bringing out the problems and tensions that beset it, Machiavelli achieved some small measure of success in his philosophic effort to liberate men's minds and to initiate a 'golden age when each can hold and defend the opinion he wishes',[68] where it would be possible to argue 'without any respect' ('sanza alcuno respetto')[69]—that is, without any recourse or regard for authority. Yet the political project that accompanied this effort, whether to unify Italy or simply establish a republic in Florence that would be independent of foreign powers, was not so fortunate. Unification had to wait until the nineteenth century. The Republic of Florence that he sought to arm did manage to re-establish itself in 1527, not long before his death. But by 1530, Florence had fallen to Charles V acting in concert with the Medici Pope Clement VII, its military weakness exacerbated by the kind of spiritual or intellectual dependence Machiavelli had wished to overcome. Benedetto Varchi, poet and eyewitness to the Siege of Florence, described the mentality of a people who had expelled the Medici princes while yet remaining under the influence of another:

> Because of the words and sermons of Fra Girolomo, which they called prophecies, the more their enemies pressed Florence, the more greatly they rejoiced, holding firmly to the belief that when the city had been reduced to such a point that she had no remedy left and could not be defended by human power in any way, then, at last, and not before then, angels would be sent from heaven to the walls of the city to liberate her with their swords. Not only common and uneducated men believed this, but also noble and learned ones.[70]

Although Machiavelli himself gave rise to what we may call a school of thought or of political action, *ragione di stato* or Machiavellianism, it was a school with few if any hard and fast rules, perhaps the only one being a rule against such rules. And if, like Xenophon, he omitted to present his own thinking in a systematic or doctrinaire form so as to avoid becoming himself an intellectual authority threatening to suffocate free thought, this may have come at the expense of a certain direct influence on political life. His practical aim, to establish a kind of secular politics that submits religion to political necessities, was better accomplished by thinkers such as Hobbes and Locke, who took Machiavelli's insights and formulated them in terms of the state of nature, natural rights, and the social contract—theories that transformed the world, partly owing to their systematic and doctrinaire character. Yet when these theories themselves quickly—and inevitably—became a new kind of orthodoxy,[71] it is remarkable to find one of their most thoughtful critics, Lord Shaftesbury, turning again to reinvigorate his mind in the writings left behind by Xenophon.[72]

Notes

1. 'And when the same error is confirmed by the authority of men in reputation for their writings on this subject, it is no wonder if it produce sedition and change of government. In these western parts of the world we are made to receive our opinions concerning the institution and rights of Commonwealths from Aristotle, Cicero, and other men, Greeks and Romans ... And by reading of these Greek and Latin authors, men from their childhood have gotten a habit, under a false show of liberty, of favouring tumults, and of licentious controlling the actions of their sovereigns; and again of controlling those controllers; with the effusion of so much blood, as I think I may truly say there was never anything so dearly bought as these western parts have bought the learning of the Greek and Latin tongues': Thomas Hobbes, *Leviathan*, ed. Richard Tuck (Cambridge: Cambridge University Press, 1991), 150; see also 254.
2. 'In 1427 Aurispa brought all of Xenophon's works, "omnia quicquid scripsit", back with him from Byzantium': Hans Baron, *In Search of Florentine Humanism* (Princeton, NJ: Princeton University Press, 1988), 237.
3. For bibliographical information on Latin translations of Xenophon, we have relied for the most part on David Marsh, 'Xenophon', in *Catalogus translationum et commentariorum: Mediaeval and Renaissance Latin Translations and Commentaries: Annotated Lists and Guides*, ed. Paul Kristeller, vol. 1 (Washington, DC: Catholic University Press, 1960), which also contains excerpts from some of the translators' prefaces. This work has recently been supplemented by a number of outstanding critical editions by Jeroen De Keyser of fifteenth-century Latin translations of Xenophon.
4. Francesco Filelfo, *Traduzioni da Senofonte e Plutarco*, ed. Jeroen De Keyser (Alessandria: Edizione dell'Orso, 2012), 102, 104–5; English translation by the present authors.
5. For the superiority of Filelfo's translation over Poggio's, see the judgement of Jakob Spiegel (Lo Spiegellio) cited by Michelangelo Grisolia in his annotated Italian translation of Pontano's *De principe* (Naples: M. Morelli, 1784), 87n4.

6. *Vita di Ciro dal greco messa in latino dal vecchio Poggio, indi tradotta in italiano da Jacopo suo figliuolo*. The first edition, published from Florence, has no date. The second edition, 'tradotto in lingua Toscana', is dated 1521. For early translations of Xenophon into Italian, see Filippo Argelati, *Biblioteca degli volgarizzatori, o sia notizia dall'opere d'autore che scrissero in lingue morte prima del secolo XV*, vol. 3 (Milan: Federico Agnelli, 1767), 372–82.
7. For example, Xenophon's Socrates explains his marriage to Xanthippe on the less than elevated grounds that if he could endure her, he would have no trouble getting along with the rest of mankind (Xenophon, *Symposium*, 2:10).
8. Herodotus, *Histories*, tr. David Grene (Chicago, IL: University of Chicago Press, 1988), 92–4.
9. For instance, Dante, *Purgatorio*, 12:55–7; Dante, *De monarchia*, 2:8; Boccaccio, *Ameto: comedia delle ninphe fiorentine*, 3; Petrarch, 'Trionfi della Pudicizia', 104–5; and Petrarch, 'Trionfi della Fama', 2:94.
10. See Bartolomeo Sacchi di Platina, *De principe*, ed. G. Ferrau (Palermo: Il Vespro, 1979), 55, 57, 72, 172.
11. '[D]iscite iustitiam moniti et non temnere divos': *Aeneid* 6:620: *Virgil*, ed. and tr. H. R. Fairclough, rev. edn (Cambridge, MA: Loeb Classical Library, 1978).
12. 'Justitia enim in quo fuerit, ejus imperium aequo omnes animo patiuntur, illiusque moderationi se se etiam sponte subiiciunt; quod de Cyro illo legimus, quem non justitiae solum, sed omnium etiam regiarum virtutum exemplum fuisse creditum est': Giovanni Pontano, *De principe*, with Italian tr. by Michelangiolo Grisolia (Naples: Morelli, 1784), 86–8; translation by the present authors.
13. '[Q]uem imitari te maxime cupio': ibid., 138.
14. '[L]ibera hominum esse iudicia, et posse quempiam alterum laudare sine alterius vituperatione, vel vtrunque etiam si placuerit probare': Francesco Patrizi, *De regno et regis insitutione libri ix* (Paris: Galiot a Prato, 1531), 7.
15. 'Principes etiam legimus secundo populi rumore omni vita imperasse, et Cyrum in primis Persarum Regem, si vera sint quae de eo a Xenophonte scribuntur, et Antoninum, Stoicum Philosophum, quem propter vitae innocentiam ac sanctitatem omnibus Romanis Principibus praetulerunt': Francesco Patrizi, *De institutione reipublicae libri ix* (Strassburg: Zetzner, 1608), 13; translation by the present authors.
16. Ibid., 24.
17. '[Q]ualis fortasse nemo unquam fuit … quae civitas nunquam fuit, et nunquam futura est': Patrizi, *De regno*, 61; translation by the present authors.

18. 'Persarum leges, ut Xenophon scribit, in primis ad justiciae cultum instituunt, et ita ab ipsa pueritia cives erudiunt, ut nihil in honestum, nihil turpe aut injustum appetant: quae quidem persuasio omnium optima mihi esse videtur. Et si quo pacto fieri posset, ut omnes hac doctrina instituantur, magna parte laboris nostri liberati essemus. Nam si cives optime animati, aequi bonique studio adducta ad Rempublicam accederent, supervacua praecepta essent, quibus humana societas instituitur. Unusquisque enim sibi praescriberet quid facto opus esset, et simul cunjuncti, nulla cupiditate, aut alia omni perturbatione affecti, optime de rebus consulerent; nec alium ambitio, alium auaritia, alium simultas, alium invidia, adeo aversum raperet, ut a veri ratione distraheretur, et privatam utilitatem, aut insanam voluntarem potius quam commodum publicum aut veram rationem sequeretur. Sed quoniam non cum perfectis hominibus vivitur, sed cum his, quos et laudamus et admiramur, si simulacrum alique virtutis prae se ferunt, adhibenda sunt praecepta...': Patrizi, *De institutione reipublicae*, 19–20; translation by the present authors.

19. 'In eodem libro Socrates docet: Si iniuriam quis nobis fecerit, non esse vindictam a nobis faciendam. Haec per deum qualia sunt? An non divina, an non Christianae perfectionis simillima?' Bruni, *Humanistisch-philosophische Schriften: Mit Einer Chronologie Seiner Werke und Briefe*, ed. Hans Baron (Leipzig: Tübner, 1928), 71; tr. Gordon Griffiths, from Bruni, *The Humanism of Leonardo Bruni: Selected Texts*, ed. and tr. Gordon Griffiths, James Hankins, and David Thompson (New York: Renaissance Society of America, 1987), 158.

20. James Hankins, 'Socrates in the Italian Renaissance', in *Socrates, from Antiquity to the Enlightenment*, ed. Michael Trapp (London: Routledge, 2007), 186.

21. Ibid., 187.

22. 'Xenophon's picture of Socrates as a great moral teacher of youth and an active participant in the life of his city would certainly have appealed to Bruni; he would have heard with relief Xenophon's declarations that Socrates never engaged in homosexual practices; and he would have agreed enthusiastically with the Xenophontean Socrates's advice to master language and the art of speaking': ibid., 188.

23. 'Aurelius Augustinus ... asserueritque Platonicos, mutatis paucis, christianos fore. Ego vero cum iampridem Aureliana auctoritate fretus summaque in genus humanum caritate adductus, Platonis ipsius simulacrum quoddam christianae veritati simillimum expremirere statuissem': Marsilio Ficino, *Théologie Platonicienne*, Book 1, 'Prohenium': ed. Raymond Marcel, 3 vols. (Paris: Société d'Édition 'Les Belles Lettres', 1964), 1:36; tr. from

Ficino, *Platonic Theology*, tr. Michael J. B. Allen, ed. James Hankins, I Tatti Renaissance Library (Cambridge, MA: Harvard University Press, 2001), 1:11.

24. 'Nisi credideritis, non intelligetis': Girolamo Savonarola, 'Open Letter to a Friend', in *Selected Writings of Girolamo Savonarola: Religion and Politics, 1490–1498*, ed. Anne Borelli, Maria Pastore Passaro, and Donald P. R. Beebe (New Haven, CT: Yale University Press, 2006), 280–9, 285.

25. 'Exsurrexit Deus et dissipavit inimicos in Antichristos suos, fugerunt a facie Dei omnes qui oderunt Deum ... Quoniam omnipotens ille, qui superbis quidem resistit, humilibus autem dat gratiam, fecit potentiam in brachio suo, dispersit cum Lucifero superbos mente cordis sui': Marsilio Ficino, *Apologia contra Savonarolam*, in *Supplementum Ficinianum: Marsilii Ficini Florentini philosophi Platonici opuscula inedita et dispersa* (Florence: Olschki, 1937), 78–9; tr. Borelli, *Selected Writings of Girolamo Savonarola*, 358.

26. Plato and Aristotle are mentioned respectively in *Disc.* 3:6 and *Disc.* 3:26, Ficino and Pico in *Florentine Histories* 7:6 and 8:36 respectively.

27. '[N]utrì nelle sue case Marsilio Ficino, ... il quale sommamente amò; e ... una possessione propinqua alla sua di Careggi gli donò': *Florentine Histories* 7:6: Machiavelli, *Tutte le opere*, ed. Mario Martelli (Florence: Sansoni, 1971), 797. All Machiavelli's Italian texts from this volume (henceforth *Opere*) unless otherwise stated. Translation from *Florentine Histories*, tr. L. Banfield and H. Mansfield (Princeton, NJ: Princeton University Press, 1988). All translations of *Florentine Histories* are from this version.

28. *Florentine Histories* 8:36, *Opere* 843.

29. '[C]opiose de huius uitae contemptu disseruit, utpote qui iam ad supernam beatitudinem adspiraret': Ficino, Preface to the Latin translation of Xenocrates's *De morte*: Ficino, *Opera omnia* (Basel: Henricus Petrus, 1576), 1965; tr. from George W. McClure, *Sorrow and Consolation in Italian Humanism* (Princeton, NJ: Princeton University Press, 2014), 140.

30. 'Platonis librum de uno rerum omnium principio, et de summo boni iam peregisset, duodecima deinde die, quasi ad id principium bonumque fruendum rediturus, ex hac vitae umbra, ad supernam lucem revocatus accessit': Ficino, *Opera omnia*, 1965; tr. McClure, 140.

31. 'Angustiava ancora la grandezza dello animo suo non gli parere di avere accresciuto lo imperio fiorentino ... [G]li pareva essere stato da Francesco Sforza ingannato; ... Il che fu di noia grandissima a Cosimo cagione ... Tutte queste cose gli feciono passare gli ultimi tempi della sua vita inquieti': *Florentine Histories* 7:6, *Opere* 797.

32. Christopher Lynch, 'War and Foreign Affairs in Machiavelli's *Florentine Histories*', *Review of Politics* 74, no. 1 (2012), 1–26.

33. '[S]ubito morto Lorenzo cominciorono a nascere quegli cattivi semi i quali, non dopo molto tempo, non sendo vivo chi gli sapesse spegnere, rovinorono, e ancora rovinano, la Italia': *Florentine Histories* 8:36, *Opere* 844.
34. *Florentine Histories* 1:21, *Opere* 647–8.
35. 'La religione antica ... non beatificava se non uomini pieni di mondana gloria; come erano capitani di eserciti e principi di republiche. La nostra religione ha glorificato più gli uomini umili e contemplativi, che gli attivi. Ha dipoi posto il sommo bene nella umiltà, abiezione, e nel dispregio delle cose umane: ... E se la religione nostra richiede che tu abbi in te fortezza, vuole che tu sia atto a patire più che a fare una cosa forte': *Disc.* 2:2, *Opere* 149; tr. as in Machiavelli, *Discourses on Livy*, tr. Harvey C. Mansfield and Nathan Tarcov (Chicago, IL: University of Chicago Press, 1995), 131.
36. 'Quanto oculus praestat manibus, caput pedibus, ratio sensibus, anima corpori, finis omnibus quae diriguntur ad finem, status motui, aeternitas tempori, tanto contemplativa vita activae praestare videtur. Contemplatio enim actionis et principium est et finis ... Sic utique ab ipsa contemplatione Dei coelestes naturalesque motus, et actiones omnes tanquam a principio ducuntur, et reducuntur, veluti ad finem': Ficino, *Divini Platonis opera omnia Marsilio Ficino interprete* (Leiden: Antonius Vincentius, 1557), 360; tr. Arthur Farndell, *When Philosophers Rule: Ficino on Plato's Republic, Laws, and Epinomis* (London: Shepheard-Walwyn, 2009), 3.
37. See, for example, the opening of Ficino's Commentary on Plato's *Laws* (Farndell, *When Philosophers Rule*, 73). For the complementarity of contemplation and action as argued by some of Ficino's fellow humanists, consider Erica Benner, *Machiavelli's Ethics* (Princeton, NJ: Princeton University Press, 2009), 41–3.
38. 'Quamobrem Plato noster eo saltem caeteris civitatum legumque conditoribus est excellentior, quo caeteri quidem velut humani ad actionem magis civitatem instituerunt, ipse vero quasi divinus actionem civitatis omnem tam publicam quam privatam potissimum perducit ad contemplandum, civitatemque constituit suijpsius antequam orbis dominam, neque tam multis timendam, quam cunctis gentibus venerandam, coelestem quasi Hierusalem pro viribus in terris expressam ...': Plato, *Opera*, 360; tr. Farndell, *When Philosophers Rule*, 3.
39. '[I]maginati republiche e principati che non si sono mai visti né conosciuti essere in vero': *Pr.*, ch. 15, *Opere* 280; tr. Harvey C. Mansfield, Machiavelli, *The Prince*, 2nd edn (Chicago, IL: University of Chicago Press, 1998), 61. All translations from *Il Principe* are from this version.
40. Ibid.

41. '[I]l maggiore onore che possono avere gli uomini ... è loro dato dalla loro patria': *Discursus florentinarum rerum post mortem iunioris Laurentii Medices*: *Opere* 30. All translations from this work by the present authors.
42. '[Q]uesti sono, dopo quegli che sono stati Iddii, i primi laudati': ibid.
43. '[È] stata stimata tanto questa gloria dagli uomini che non hanno mai atteso ad altro che a gloria, che non avendo possuto fare una repubblica in atto, l'hanno fatta in iscritto; come Aristotile, Platone e molti altri: e' quali hanno voluto mostrare al mondo, che se, come Solone e Licurgo, non hanno potuto fondare un vivere civile, non è mancato dalla ignoranza loro, ma dalla impotenza di metterlo in atto': ibid., 30–1.
44. 'Moisè, Ciro, Teseo e Romulo non arebbono possuto fare osservare loro lungamente le loro constituzioni, se fussino stati disarmati: come ne' nostri tempi intervenne a fra' Girolamo Savonerola': *Pr.*, ch. 6, *Opere* 265; tr. Mansfield, 24.
45. '[N]on può essere buone legge dove non sono buone arme, e dove sono buone arme conviene sieno buone legge': *Pr.*, ch. 12, *Opere* 275; tr. Mansfield, 48.
46. *Pr.*, ch. 14.
47. 'Debbe, adunque, uno principe non avere altro obietto né altro pensiero, né prendere cosa alcuna per sua arte, fuora della guerra e ordini e disciplina di essa; perché quella è sola arte che si espetta a chi comanda': *Pr.*, ch. 14, *Opere* 278; tr. Mansfield, 58.
48. 'E, quanto alle opere, oltre al tenere bene ordinati ed esercitati li suoi, debbe stare sempre in sulle cacce, e mediante quelle assuefare el corpo a' disagi': *Pr.*, ch. 14, *Opere* 279; tr. Mansfield, 59.
49. '[L]e istorie, e in quelle considerare le azioni degli uomini eccellenti; vedere come si sono governati nelle guerre; esaminare le cagioni delle vittorie e perdite loro, per potere queste fuggire, e quelle imitare': *Pr.*, ch. 14, *Opere* 279; tr. Mansfield, 60.
50. *Pr.*, ch. 14, *Opere* 279; tr. Mansfield, 59.
51. '[N]on ho trovato, intra la mia suppellettile, cosa quale io abbi più cara o tanto esìstimi quanto la cognizione delle azioni delli uomini grandi, imparata da me con una lunga esperienzia delle cose moderne e una continua lezione delle antique' ('I have found nothing in my belongings that I care so much for and esteem so greatly as the knowledge of the actions of great men, learned by me from long experience with modern things and a continuous reading of ancient ones'): *Pr.*, ch. 14, 'Dedica', *Opere* 257; tr. Mansfield, 3. Direct experience itself is no longer sufficient.
52. '[F]are come ha fatto per lo adrieto qualche uomo eccellente, che ha preso ad imitare se alcuno innanzi a lui è stato laudato e gloriato, e di quello ha tenuto sempre e' gesti ed azioni appresso di sé: come si dice che Alessandro

Magno imitava Achille; Cesare, Alessandro; Scipione, Ciro. E qualunque legge la vita di Ciro scritta da Senofonte, riconosce di poi nella vita di Scipione quanto quella imitazione li fu di gloria, e quanto, nella castità, affabilità, umanità, liberalità Scipione si conformassi con quelle cose che di Ciro da Senofonte sono sute scritte': *Pr.*, ch. 14, *Opere* 279; tr. Mansfield 60.

53. Christopher Nadon, *Xenophon's Prince* (Berkeley, CA: University of California Press, 2001), 15.
54. '[U]sare liberalità a tutti quelli a chi non toglie, che sono infiniti, e miseria a tutti coloro a chi non dà, che sono pochi'; 'non si curare del nome del misero'; 'Cesare con la liberalità pervenne allo imperio, e molti altri, per essere stati ed essere tenuti liberali, sono venuti a gradi grandissimi'; 'che si pasce di prede, di sacchi e di taglie'; 'di quello che non è tuo, o de' sudditi tuoi'; '[L]o spendere quello d'altri non ti toglie reputazione, ma te ne aggiugne: solamente lo spendere el tuo è quello che ti nuoce': *Pr.*, ch. 16, *Opere* 281; tr. Mansfield 62–4.
55. '[Q]uanto, nella castità, affabilità, umanità, liberalità Scipione si conformassi con quelle cose che di Ciro da Senofonte sono sute scritte': *Pr.*, ch. 14, *Opere* 279; tr. Mansfield 60. For *quanto* meaning 'how little', see the first sentence of *Pr.*, ch. 18; also *Disc.* 2:17, 1:55, 3:23. See Nathan Tarcov, 'Quentin Skinner's Method and Machiavelli's *Prince*', *Ethics* 92, no. 4 (1982), 692–709, 707.
56. *Pr.*, ch. 17, *Opere* 283; tr. Mansfield, 68.
57. '[A]ndare drieto alla verità effettuale della cosa, che alla imaginazione di essa': *Pr.*, ch. 15, *Opere* 280.
58. See Xenophon, *Cyropaedia*, 1:5:7–12; 1:2:3, 15.
59. 'Onde è necessario a uno principe, volendosi mantenere, imparare a potere essere non buono, e usarlo e non l'usare secondo la necessità': *Pr.*, ch. 15, *Opere* 280; tr. Mansfield, 61.
60. Xenophon, *Cyropaedia*, 1:6:27, 38.
61. 'Che si viene di bassa a gran fortuna più con la fraude che con la forza': *Disc.* 2:13, title, *Opere* 163.
62. 'Mostra Senofonte, nella sua vita di Ciro, questa necessità dello ingannare; considerato che la prima ispedizione che fe' fare a Ciro contro al re di Armenia è piena di fraude, e come con inganno, e non con forza, gli fe' occupare il suo regno; e non conchiude altro, per tale azione, se non che a un principe che voglia fare gran cose, è necessario imparare a ingannare. Fegli ingannare, oltra di questo. Ciassare, re de' Medii, suo zio materno, in più modi; sanza la quale fraude mostra che Ciro non poteva pervenire a quella grandezza che venne': ibid.
63. *Pr.*, ch. 25, *Disc.* 2:30; cf. Xenophon, *Cyropaedia*, 1:6:5–6, 46; *Oeconomicus*, 5:12.

64. As characterizing Manlius Torquatus: see *Disc.* 3:22.
65. *Disc.* 3:20; see also *Disc.* 3:23.
66. See Girolamo Frachetta, *Il Prencipe* (Venice: Ciotti, 1599), 255, 325, 328.
67. Scipione Ammirato, *Discorsi sopra Cornelio Tacito* (Brescia: Compania Bresciana, 1599), Discorso VI, 108–9.
68. '[I] tempi aurei, dove ciascuno può tenere e difendere quella opinione che vuole': *Disc.* 1:10, *Opere* 93.
69. *Disc.* 1, Preface, *Opere* 76.
70. '[D]alle parole mossi delle prediche di fra Girolamo, le quali chiamavano profezie, quanto più i nimici stringevano Firenze, tanto si rallegravano essi maggiormente, avendo per fermo, che quando la città fosse in termine ridotta ch' ella più rimedio nessuno non avesse nè forza umana potesse in verun modo difenderla, allora finalmente, e non prima, dovessero essere mandati dal cielo in sulle mura gli angioli a liberarla miracolosamente colle spade: nè erano questi che ciò credevano uomini di volgo solamente e idioti, ma eziandio nobilissimi ... e letterati ...': Benedetto Varchi, *Storia fiorentina*, ed. Gaetano Milanesi, 3 vols. (Florence: Felice Le Monnier, 1858), 2:320; tr. Donald Weinstein, *Savonarola and Florence: Prophecy and Patriotism in the Renaissance* (Princeton, NJ: Princeton University Press, 1970), 372*n*170.
71. 'At all times there will be men destined to be subjugated by the opinions of their century, their country, their society. A man who plays the free thinker and philosopher today would, for the same reason, have been only a fanatic at the time of the Holy League': Rousseau, *First Discourse*, tr. Roger Masters (New York: St. Martin's Press, 1969), 33.
72. See, for instance, Benjamin Rand, ed., *The Life, Unpublished Letters, and Philosophical Regimen of Antony, Earl of Shaftesbury* (London: Swan Sonnenschein, 1900), 29, 94, 98–9, 226; Lord Shaftesbury, *Characteristics of Men, Manners, Opinions, Times*, ed. Lawrence Klein (Cambridge: Cambridge University Press, 1999), xxii, 101, 261, 443.

6

Machiavelli and the Solitary Discipline of Hunting

Prasanta Chakravarty

From his well-known letter of 10 December 1513, written to Francesco Vettori, we have come to know about Machiavelli's snaring of thrushes with his own hands: rising well before dawn, he would prepare his snares and go off with a pile of cages on his back, looking like 'Geta returning from the port with Amphityron's books'.[1] We also know from the same source that once the migration of the thrushes came to an end by early December, Machiavelli, after talking to the woodcutters on his daily rounds, would often leave the woods to visit a stream and proceed thence to some bird traps. On such trips, he would take a book with him—Ovid, Tibullus, Dante, or Petrarch. Reading about their amorous passions and recalling his own, he would dwell pleasurably on those thoughts for a while.

As Italy marked the 500th anniversary of *The Prince*, there came to light a previously unknown poem, signed with the initials N. M.: an epigram in memory of the banker Lorenzo Strozzi's beloved dog, where the poet extols the virtues of hunting dogs. It is probably a commissioned work. The poem, just four lines long, extols the speed and strength of the dog, 'born in Etruria' and called Furia or Fury, suggesting it may have been a mastiff or hound. The verses describe how it could 'beat the hare at running and the deer at jumping'.[2] There are also the three 'prison sonnets' addressed to Giuliano de' Medici. In one of those, Machiavelli encounters the creaturely world in much more trying circumstances: 'These walls exude lice,/ sick with the heaves no less, that [are as big as] butterflies,/ nor was there ever such a stench in [the massacre of] Roncesvalles.'[3]

Such biographical details depict Machiavelli's occasional encounters with the zoological world. However, he also highlights certain eternal confrontations that are, at the same time, ways of maintaining an order of life, involving a different kind of creaturely encounter. Such encounters pertain to questions of leadership and order by means of inculcating *virtù*. But the process of acquiring *virtù* is perhaps the most difficult topic to pinpoint in his oeuvre. One way of doing so might be to study the underlying motif of hunting in some of his works and parts of his own life. Such an enquiry might also open up a space where we would see how Machiavelli makes a subtle claim for theory and practice, contemplation and action, fiction and *Realpolitik*, to combine in a kind of cyclical relay race.

Leisure as Dedication

Machiavelli's use of his leisure time interests us. How does he convert such apparently fallow and lean periods into productive time? Machiavelli does not view leisure negatively, merely as the obverse of war or negotiation. Even as viewed positively, it is not a vacant time of diversion either. I will argue that the standard Renaissance distinction between action and contemplation, *negotium* and *otium* does not work for a certain category of thinkers. Machiavelli is one such, for whom life is an eternal vigil. Leisure, therefore, instead of being fallow, is a time for consolidation.

Leisure can be minimally defined as what a man does when he is free to do what he pleases. The Neolithic being, says José Ortega y Gasset,[4] has an advantage over the Palaeolithic in that the former is no more a mere hunter-gatherer seeking subsistence. Hunting is now a sport—an act of using time in a considered manner. It is no longer simply an obligation or compulsion.

If leisure is not an obligation, it constitutes a different use of time for the free man: dedication. Dedication is the prerogative and affliction of our species. Dedication in the aristocrat, a person liberated from compulsion, is a use of time that addresses not his *métier*—combat, burdens of the government, care of his own wealth and property—but a thoughtful and controlled use of the fortunate moments of contemplation. The pursuits of such felicitous moments of consolidation in the free man are, according to Ortega, hunting, dancing, racing, and conversing. Hunting marks an archetypal pursuit of consolidation and dedication, a privilege granted to such a person, satisfying a permanent yearning of the human condition. With hunting, it is as if we have 'poked a trigeminal nerve'.[5]

Chapter 14 of *The Prince* evaluates the ruler's relationship with military matters. In such matters, a wise prince 'diligently makes capital on which he can draw in periods of distress',[6] and a prince ought not to concern himself with anything beyond them or superfluous to them. The art of war must be honed with a certain leisurely yet vigilant dedication. How are military matters conducted during peacetime? We are told that there are two ways of doing this: one is by going on exercise, the other is by study—'the first with his actions; the second with his mind'.[7] The rest of the chapter illustrates how these two methods are curiously intertwined.

With regard to exercise, besides keeping his troops well disciplined and trained, the free man should frequently engage in hunting. This second form of exercise, Machiavelli says, does two things: it hardens his body and also makes him familiar with the terrain—how the mountains rise, how valleys open and plains spread out, as well as the characteristics of rivers and swamps. Though these seem like practical concerns for the prince—knowing the natural defences of one's country and exploring new terrains in order to have a total sense of one's domain—such drills help later in achieving other objectives of war: it enables one to track down the enemy, camp the army properly, lead it towards the enemy, and prepare for battle.

The idea of dedication in peacetime means paying heed to an ontological condition. Dedication is an ever-vigilant inner comportment, a journey of continual contemplation of action. Hunting, therefore, is first and foremost *a condition of alertness*, complete with chase and falconry, and alertness ever comes from a certain discipline, which might arise equally out of monastic rule or military order. To begin with, however, it harbours a potential, an opportunity to show daring, endurance, and dexterity. At the heart of Chapter 14 is the realization that hunting as an exercise of the aristocratic spirit is a hard, constant task. At the everyday level, it helps to keep one fit, face extreme fatigue, and accept danger. Inwardly, it requires a complete code of ethics that the hunter secretly treasures within him. He nurtures his edicts and imperatives in the greatest solitude, with no witness or audience.

I will return to the theme of solitude, and a rhetoric entwined in simultaneous hope and despair. Meanwhile, it is fascinating to witness a kind of sublunary imagination in many of Machiavelli's writings. With the hunter, we are literally and metaphorically at the bottom tier of the harmonious and ordered cosmos, a zone of imperfection and fluidity—the terrestrial *stato mortale*, which must be assailed. Success often depends on our interpreting the cycles of sublunar existence without necessarily understanding their origin or purpose. The hunter strategizes in and for this sublunar existence. Fortune is indeed the arbiter of half our actions; the other half is realized by the potential hunter in the aristocrat.

Mikael Hörnqvist offers a major insight into this concept: why does the wise man, in spite of his wisdom and caution, fail while facing fortune's ravages?[8] Nature inclines us to certain moods. There is a time to act impetuously; but instead of discussing impetuosity, Machiavelli lets a sublunar mood, a certain flux, spread across many of his writings. It may be because in such cases, when it is a fit time to act impetuously, his agency is not in accord with fortune. We need caution and impetuosity in equal measure, as we do circumspection and violence, patience and action, injunctions to be humane and cruel. There are always two kinds of time that beset the aristocrat: a time of deep solitude, when he prepares for action, and the here and now, when he must take decisive, impetuous action.

In Machiavelli's *Life of Castruccio Castracani*, we notice the rewards of such prior dedication to the mode of the hunter:

> But Castruccio, having in the night without uproar taken Serravalle, about midnight left Montecarlo and in silence arrived with his soldiers in the morning at the foot of the hill. Thus at the same time the Florentine army and he, each from his own direction, began to climb the slope … [The Florentines] were not expecting to find Castruccio on the hill, because they did not know that he had mastered the town. Hence the Florentine cavalry, having climbed the slope, unexpectedly beheld Castruccio's infantry; the cavalry were so near as scarcely to have time to lace their helmets. Since, therefore, *the unprepared were attacked by the prepared and the well ordered*, with great spirit Castruccio's soldiers pressed upon the Florentines. (emphasis added)[9]

Here is the hunter on the prowl, fulfilling his potential that must have been prepared and enacted many times in conception and in actual reconnoitres. Precision and single-mindedness are his markers.

Power is always territorial. What is space has to be converted into territory. The founder of a city must therefore have a *cynegetic sensibility*. He hunts in order to construct and expand his territory. Hunting is a way of gathering whatever is scattered and unaccumulated. The hunter finds his prey unprepared. Castruccio has first mastered the topography of the hill, then of the town, and uses each against the other. There lies his victory, in a thought that was *acted out*. What is most instructive in this passage is that the abstract dedication is finally given shape in the here and now: hopelessness and caution are turned on their heads by Castruccio's capacity for impetuous decision-making. When the abstract and metaphorical entities that determine our lives—God, fortune, war, hatred, a river in flood, and so on—turn into the reality of action and material entities, the hunter is aroused: he breaks out of his solitude—*but in solitude, too, he was ever vigilant*.

This sense of concentrated discipline is a key element in Machiavelli's conceptual framework. This subtle exactitude is derived from ancient wisdom. Machiavelli has to say this in Book 2 of *The Art of War*, on 'the wisdom of the ancient training':

> In the estimation of the ancients nothing was more valuable to a republic than to contain many men trained in arms, because not the splendor of gems and gold makes enemies submit to you, but only the fear of arms ... They [the ancients] taught them also to shoot with the bow and with the sling. They had teachers in charge of all these matters. Thus when citizens were chosen to go to war, they *already had the disposition and courage of soldiers*. (emphasis added)[10]

Indeed, the fear of arms is an essential motivation in making others submit to you. It makes the enemy respect your power. Fear works in two directions: others fear your (the hunter's) arms, while the hunter loses all fear since he inwardly comprehends the rationale of using arms. Besides, mistakes made in war cannot be corrected, since the penalty comes at once. There is no second chance. The prey will be swift in retaliation. Knowing how to fight makes men bolder, because nobody fears to do what he believes he knows how to do. This is not only an investment in practical epistemology but also a confidence booster at the psychological level. Furthermore, hands-on practice in the use of arms, even in peacetime, makes an army suppler and stronger. Under such a regimen, when citizens are chosen to go to war, they already have the disposition and courage of soldiers. There is something pre-emptive in igniting what is already latent in oneself. The decision to fight is a dispositional struggle that comes from within.

Of course, hunting in itself cannot bring about fundamental progress, nor is it a reasoned pursuit. It reveals a potential that has to be converted into action.

Energetic Effort

In other words, *a certain fusion of leisure and action* characterizes the hunter. The hunter seeks a particular kind of happiness. That happiness is not pleasure, since there are lots of trials and inconveniences in this vocation. It is an energetic striving, whereby leisure is converted into a more focused state of being. It is a calling, not just a sport.

What is the inherent goal of the act of hunting? The first significant aspect of hunting is that it is not simply about killing but equally about *retrieving the beast alive and owning it*. It is hardly about eliminating the foe or moving it out of sight. Its goal is the final act whereby, in retrieving the beast, the process of hunting is completed and the hunting expedition is successful. The hunter takes possession of the prey, dead or alive. You cannot foreswear your prey and proceed to other dealings. Before you can do so, you must reclaim your prey.

So, with Ortega y Gasset, we can now define hunting in precise terms: 'hunting is what an animal does to take possession, dead or alive, of some other being that belongs to a species basically inferior to its own.'[11] We might link this to a particular tendency in Machiavelli—his ways and methods of linking imperial greatness with republican liberty. There is a distinctive if implicit message that 'a ruler who understands how to honour and to draw benefit from his valorous subjects is destined for imperial greatness'.[12]

The idea of the *imperium* is directly related to the classical triumph. The triumph is not only a sacramental right but also a celebration of justice, virtue, fame, and glory, culminating in a tribute to the ancestral gods. After having brought a campaign or expedition to a victorious end, the prince 'returned to the same site, to the same temple and appeared before the same gods with the gifts and trophies he had promised them in his vow'.[13]

The triumph re-establishes the boundary between war and peace, the military and the civil realms. The ceremonial commemoration of the victory reaffirms the right to possess and acts as an *imprimatur* of the sovereign. The triumph, therefore, is a process by which one redeems and recuperates a space by celebrating the appropriation of the vanquished and his territory within one's own. It is a sacramental act to mark the real accruing of fresh territories. The prince shapes the material of his rule into the form that seems best to him. The triumphant hunter is a great innovator, who understands that accrual of the prey to his possession is the key to augmenting his stature.

Xenophon's *On Hunting*

Hunting is education for warfare, nurtured and performed under the sign of Artemis. But more than that, it is 'a sure route to excellence in thought, speech and action'.[14] In Chapters 12 and 13 of Xenophon's *On Hunting*, the author reflects on hunting after eleven chapters of detailed and practical insights into its actual practice and vocation. More than hunting itself, he highlights *the strong desire to hunt*, which is an existential disposition, the cultivation of a distinctive manner of living. Besides, hunting fosters physical fitness, improves sight and hearing, slows down the process of ageing, and, above all, is good training for warfare. Building up stamina is the key to hunting, which is always a silent act.

Xenophon makes several key points about this particular disposition. To begin with, the hunter converts potential into action by his habit of carrying weapons when hunting. There is also a practical and laborious side to the vocation. The hunter has to sleep rough and guard the spot that he is assigned.

He must maintain that position in the face of danger and not break ranks. Fitness and courage are key elements of the pursuit and hence cultivated by trained hunters. The man who would rule must be trained to resist hunger and thirst, to forestall sleep, to put off sex, and to endure heat and cold. These are essential qualities in order to undertake the great toil that the vocation demands.

Xenophon suggests that the primitive skill of hunting has always been part of the free man's curriculum. Hunters can freely follow game through fields bearing any kind of crop: 'It brings them [young people] up surrounded by reality, and so gives them self-restraint and honesty.'[15] Such men are of outstanding worth, for they will not let anyone escape after wronging their city or harming their land. Inculcating *virtù* is a matter of hard work, which hunting instils early on.

It is instructive to note that Xenophon takes up hunting as a subject in order to critique the sophists trenchantly. Sophists, he feels, are concerned with trivialities, not life. They represent academics, not action, and indulge in vain enjoyment, not virtue. Moreover, they are not practical but marked by a smugness of style rather than genuine substance.

Hunters, on the other end, are plain and straightforward people. Their vocation inculcates alertness and poise, which sophists lack altogether. To argue endlessly is not genuine wisdom. Further, sophists seek out wealthy young men as targets. True philosophers are thoughtful, active, agile in everyone's cause. Hunters often present themselves and their property for the common good of their fellow citizens in the spirit of true generosity. They go after wild animals while others go after their friends (an amazing metaphor for both socializing and lynching). In hunting, the agonistic impulse that drives elite competition and weakens elite solidarity is deflected from rivalry with other aristocrats and directed towards the animals that are the object of the hunt. Finally, the hunter identifies and acts against the common enemy of the community, unlike a lynch mob, which acts divisively and in bad faith. I will have more to say on this aspect soon.

The object of the hunter's expedition is never to satisfy his own greed or harm another man. His very engagement in hunting makes him a superior being, for the reason that he will never capture his prey without an extraordinary amount of effort and a great deal of thought and study. Unlike politicians, hunters train themselves to defeat public enemies.

However, Xenophon adds one caveat: hunters ought not to be impetuous. They must eschew all sordid greed and moral corruption. Above all, they are elegant beings, masterly in their pursuit. Gods find great pleasure in hunting, whether doing it or watching it. Hunters are thus the favourites of the gods: there is a pietistic relationship between the two. All devotees of hunting, men and women, will come to be imbued with genuine virtue.

Such a virtue is marked by intensive toil. Toil is an enhanced version of labour that engages the virtuous and the practical-minded. At the heart of the reformed aristocratic spirit is an amalgam of suffering and valorized effort. Such a combination can lead to self-control through continual training. Xenophon's manual is a work of far-ranging exhortation and advice, including a prescription of 'what activities to pursue, what to avoid, what company to keep, how to live'.[16] This is, in fact, an ideological apologia, directing the aristocrat to practice the mode of life appropriate to him. So also must the whole ceremony of the hunt be imbued with exquisite and overwhelming beauty: 'So charming is the spectacle that if anyone saw a hare tracked, found, chased, and caught, he would forget whatever else he loved.'[17]

Clemency as Valour

But there is a subtler point here: *your relation with the animal or prey cannot be too unequal*, as Ortega rightly observes. Weapons and advances in technology—marks of rational superiority—are a hindrance in this respect. The animal must be free to practice its wily defences, since hunting is not pure killing or destroying at all.

In order to appreciate this singular aspect of hunting, one must revisit the Roman notion of the *princeps*. How does the *res publica* delineate the relationship between the notional qualities of *gloria*, *honour*, and *fama*, and the scope of their proper exercise?

Peter Stacey has provided us with a useful entry point into the metaphysical sources of the idea of the *princeps*. It lies in the Stoic doctrine of divine providence—something that J. G. A. Pocock does not at all mention in the early chapters of his *The Machiavellian Moment*,[18] when he deals with the subject of providence and fortune. The universe the Stoics held was organized and animated purposefully and benevolently by an immanent force which they identified as the *logos* or *ratio*. The *logos* is personified in various ways: sometimes as fate or providence and at other times as nature, the gods, or even Zeus himself. The dicta of nature are common to both divine and human beings; this shared ability to reason enables both god and men to participate in the divine scheme of happenings. Being universal and divine, the *civitas* belongs to both man and God. Those who follow this line of thinking follow natural law, the dictum of the *vir sapiens*. And *fortuna* is related and derived from whatever is natural. The Roman *civitas* could be therefore the same as the cosmic city. Seneca, for instance, exults to 'measure the bounds of our citizenship by the path of the sun'.[19] Stoic reason is a cornerstone of Roman imperial ideology. The prince is bound by this higher and universal law and not by local argumentative tradition. The earthly *civitas* is an analogue of the universal cosmic *civitas*. The *princeps* can be equated with the heroic figure of the Stoic *vir sapiens*.

It is in this context that Seneca proposes *clementia*—mercy or clemency— to be exercised by the *vir sapiens*. Clemency is the greatest of virtues. The emperor is the embodiment of *sapientia* (sagacity) because he works in conformity with universal *ius* (right) and *lex* (law). He is the epitome of *iustitia*, the virtue of justice. Seneca insists that his prince be *mitis* (mild), because there is always the need to cultivate the virtues of *moderatio* (moderation), *temperantia* (temperance), *mansuetudo* (gentleness), *lenitas* (leniency), *humanitas* (kindness), and *patientia* (patience). These are psychological qualities necessary for the successful performance of acts of clemency and magnanimity, as distinct from and indeed the obverse of pity. The prince holds up a mirror. In fact, he shows forth his own image and splits it in order to cultivate clemency and thereby take on his adversaries. Pity implies weakness of vision, while the *vir sapiens*, above all else, is clear-sighted. Conversely, pity looks at the world as contingent and irrational and succumbs to it. Instead of surrendering to circumstance by feeling pity, the hunter-prince takes precisely the opposite stand: he reads the course of *fortuna*, waits patiently, hones his skills, and acts when the time comes. Clemency is the willed gift of the ruler: he first withholds and then bestows it. He has to assert and parry, much like a successful orator. Before interacting with his interlocutors, the prince or *imperator* holds forth to himself. This is because he is held to act in place of the gods, as their vice-regent on the temporal realm. The *imperator* grants occasional clemency to his subjects since he is a trustee of the divine.

Hunting, therefore, is never akin to killing: rather, it is its obverse—*to be able to offer clemency after possessing the prey*. The hunter, the supreme Stoic, improves his state constantly by restructuring the practices of his life. True mercy means exercising supreme power with the truest *temperantia* (self-control), an embracing love for the human race as though it is deployed for oneself. Stacey tells us that the aim of the Senecan Stoic is to make us good archers: 'The archer ought not to hit the mark only sometimes; he ought to miss it only sometimes. That which takes effect by chance is not an art. Now wisdom is an art; it should have a definite aim, choosing only those who will make progress.'[20] The ability to grant clemency on the right occasion is akin to this skill in archery.

Indeed, mercy is crucial for the *imperium* to function. The merciful ruler acts with felicity. Hunting is the private and innermost practice of such felicity in peacetime that will yield results at a time of true crisis. It ensures that the faculties of the *imperator* never rust. All acts of *virtù* must be tested in order to flourish; *virtù* shrivels without an adversary, a prey. Hunting affords scope for such trial. Much more than physical fortitude, it is moral strength and magnanimity that the hunter must practice in his art. The wise hunter makes himself *invictus*, morally invincible. The battle with his prey is an externalized projection of his internal struggle for self-conquest.

Seigniorial ideology shows exactly these ethical qualities. In this context, one can refer to Mark Jurdjevic's discussion of the term *generosità* in Machiavelli's *Florentine Histories*.[21] Machiavelli uses the word in its martial connotation of boldness, as opposed to liberality, which he regards as a weak ideology. Those who are engaged in the defence of the city must be generous of spirit: they will not attack the enemy unexpectedly. Generosity is the obverse of abjectness. It is sometimes related to ambition and entitlement; but above all else, it is a condition of *givingness*. It makes the *imperator* forge an undying bond even with his adversaries by the exercise and exchange of boldness and martial capacity on both sides. If one is stripped of arms and generosity, it is cause for lament not only for the decline of the warrior class but also for the loss of a martial culture that inspires the warrior-hunter to undertake bold actions. One cannot buy security: one has to confront the prey that is one's existential other. Liberalism, by contrast, is a term reserved by Machiavelli for scorn and sarcasm. We may recall the scathing attack on pragmatic liberals in Chapter 16 of *The Prince*.

These are delicate acts that Machiavelli speaks of. To inculcate subtlety and discreetness in every gesture and shun shrillness is therefore crucial for the hunting *vir sapiens*. The hunter must not be zealous; he must restrain oneself, limiting his intervention. Predation is above all a mystical agitation. In fact, conflict is not the key principle or activity in most of Machiavelli's texts. That is an epiphenomenon. Mutual aggression does not interest him. There is always some kind of inequality between the hunter and the hunted: indeed, the hunter owes his existence to the hunted. But although hunting involves taking possession of a lesser being, the latter, whether dead or alive, cannot be too lowly. The supremacy of the hunter over the hunted is not infinite: there are limits in actuality. It is not that the opponent is not robust and spirited: the tracked animal may sometimes be nimbler or cannier than the hunter. Yet in the general balance of gifts and faculties, the hunter will always be a notch higher than the hunted.

Sometimes, the hunter returns empty-handed. Hunting is the confrontation of two systems of instinct or intuition: the prey must be allowed to function freely with its own defensive instincts. That makes its capture difficult: the confrontation becomes primal and ontological. In the intuitive depths of its nature, the prey has already felt the hunter. Its entire life is an incessant wait for the latter's aggression and for finding ways to evade him or, if possible, strike back. The hunter, likewise, keeps honing his defensive and evasive qualities in analogy with the strategy of the prince. Such is the nature of the game; hence, hunting is also a game. Like all games, its course is regulated by the combatants.

A Magical Symphony

Hunting is an elaborate exercise in a preternatural and extramundane venture. The very beating out of the prey is a collective indulgence in magic. The desired animal is neither abundant nor everlasting but rare and extraordinary; hence, the first operation is to procure its existence. To this end, a series of operations have to be enacted. Success is demanding, almost improbable; to ensure it, the hunter-prince must exert himself in innovation.

Mandragola is such an exercise in direct, elaborate ritualizing of the hunter's activity. It is a comedy that works simultaneously in realistic and ironic registers. Its characters show a somewhat variant approach to that of the prince and therefore the notions of power and preyness take on a more contentious dimension at times. It is all the more notable that Machiavelli employs the trope of hunting in a manner consistent with his other treatments. He begins with a typology of the prey, offering a stark choice between French and Italian women. The speculation about the superiority of either nation leads to a fresh one, about the possibility of a certain tendency in womankind, exemplified here through a comment about Lucrezia: 'She's very chaste and a complete stranger to love dealings.'[22] These provide the platform for the hunting expedition to begin. Rituals of pursuit take strange and unexpected routes.

The Canzone after the first act makes it clear that love is put to test in a ritual combat. The battle must be joined:

> He who makes no test, Oh Love, of your great power, must hope in vain ever to have true faith in Heaven's highest worth. He does not know how at the same

time one can live and die, how one can search for ill and run away from good, how one can love oneself less than some other, how often the heart is frozen and melted by fear and hope; he does not know how men and gods in equal measure dread the weapons with which you're armed.[23]

Contrary sentiments merge in the game of love. Danger and evil come to pass in this game, but one cannot therefore run away from the good that love instils. In the familiar Petrarchan trope, the heart is at once frozen and melted, with simultaneous fear and hope. The hunter must take the plunge: he has nothing to fear, as he is armed with weapons dreaded by both men and gods. His prize—a nocturnal being, naïve and worried—eludes him. But the prey, too, plays the game in its own way: it hides, but it does not run away or disappear. The game is on.

Hence, in hunting, the initial labour of detecting the prey is more important than killing it. The game is basically about making the prey expose itself. Then the fateful moment arrives. The prey appears at a suitable range but may disappear in a burst. Yet to have come into the presence of the prey is a triumph in itself, because it has been achieved by a certain technique adopted by the hunter and his retinue: he takes the prey by the forelock, so to speak. It would not have appeared there on its own. The right initiative on the hunter's part is crucial.

The animal will now play a game of hide and seek. The greatest challenge to the hunter is the beast's bouts of absence. At such points, the hunter relies on the detective instincts of other beings. Man therefore hunts with an animal—the hound: he places the dog between the power of human reason and the wiles of the prey. The collaboration makes use of the dog's instinct for hunting. Xenophon lays great importance on the use of dogs in hunting. In fact, hunting—or cynegetics, in Xenophon's more formal term—is an elaborate ritual practice with dogs, beaters, and shooters. Ortega calls it a majestic symphony in progress. Dogs and falcons form a warm relationship with man, and so man hunts together with such beings. The falcons are stern and menacing; the dogs are focused and dedicated.

Such dogs and beaters are assembled in many ways in Machiavelli's comedies and allegories. Love is a great hunt, as it were. As many commentators have observed, Ligurio in *Mandragola* is a true hunter. He is divided within himself but takes the external pursuit of hunting seriously, though not the prize. The very strategizing, bringing the game into its full formal blossoming, makes him act in a calm and concerted manner. Callimaco, again, is a kind of beater, rounding up his own wife and leading her gradually towards the hunting machine.

Callimaco, Ligurio, and Messer Nicia, with the 'medicine made with mandrake' ('pozione fatta di mandragola'), plot collectively to acquire the prey. The three of them are busy in the preparatory phase of the hunting game: among other things, they try to conjure up a stratagem whereby Callimaco and Ligurio will arrange for another fantastic and fictive character to sleep with Lucrezia. Callimaco directly uses the hunting metaphor:

> Then we'll disguise ourselves, you, Ligurio, Siro, and myself, and we'll go hunting in the New Market, the Old Market, all through such places. And as soon as we find an idle young fellow, we'll pull a sack over his head, and to the music of blows, we'll take him into your house and into your bedroom in the dark.[24]

We also have the other hounds, Sostrata and Frate Timoteo. Both are actively involved right from the early stages of beating out the prey. Timoteo believes that women are the most 'liberal givers',[25] yet, at the same time, the most vexing. If men deal with women, they are likely to encounter reward and vexation together. But one must still indulge in the act of hunting, since 'it's a fact that there's no honey without flies'.[26] Sostrata helps Lucrezia acquiesce in the plan through assiduous cajoling and threats. In other words, Sostrata, along with Lucrezia's mother, are the ones who help the prey reveal herself. The beaters, the hound, and the falcon take on the shape and contours of the arrow, as it were. The arrow flies towards the prey, which now hides and now reveals itself before fleeing again. When the arrow finally strikes the prey, the collective weight of many days and hours of planning and meditation comes to bear on that compressed moment.

Mandragola is thus an extension of a certain kind of training, and its practical implementation in conquering and consolidating one's prize, which we have already encountered conceptually in *The Prince*. The canzone after the third act brings out this aspect: 'O Love, with your great power, by making others blessed, you make them rich; you conquer, with your sacred counsels alone, rocks, enchantments, and poisons.'[27] The hunter's investment in the erotic game is sacred and primal, fostered with utmost care and acumen, so much so that all rocks and hurdles, every form of enchantment and the bane that may be churned out of it, can be duly exorcized.

Lynching: A Control Scenario

At this point, we must highlight an essential element in Machiavelli's position: that the existential obverse of hunting is never the liberal democratic order,

Machiavelli and the Solitary Discipline of Hunting 109

which he views with disdain. Rather, the obverse is the act of lynching and its underlying psychology.

Lynching is the opposite of hunting: it is another kind of atavistic resurgence of primitive forces. The lynch mentality is a hidden condition of civilization. Machiavelli had seen, very closely, variations on the theme of people tearing down churches and grand buildings in the name of justice, flogging, mutilating, and maiming. He had himself suffered physically and mentally—strung up, imprisoned, and ostracized once the Gonfalonier-for-life Piero Soderini was removed from power in 1512.

Lynching is a collective act where no single person can or will take responsibility. Grégoire Chamayou calls such a formation a *pack*:

> A pack is a collective being that draws its strength from numbers. Once caught, the prey will succumb to a multitude of blows or bites: all the pack's members will have killed the prey, but none of them will be the killer. The pack deindividualizes its members. Its unity is merely temporary, however. Once the hunt is over, it disperses.[28]

In the act of lynching, a penalty is demanded by public opinion. Annihilation is a summary act. But there is a more important, though secondary, function to the act of lynching: it is a device to intimidate a group, not just the transgressor. Free born men are cautioned by sects and populist groups in the name of their brand of moral justice: the violence has a 'demonstration effect' on the rest of the population. It feels that the so-called elite have been taken to task. Hence, the actual guilt of the suspect is of no real consequence to the lynch mob: their essential objectives are intimidation and acquiescence, to establish an order sanctioned by the mob. The implicit moral strictures of the state or the community can sometimes play a prominent manipulative role in the process.

There is an endemic everyday dimension to crucifixion, for instance. We know that not just Jesus of Nazareth but thousands of Judeans were executed routinely on crosses:

> They were stripped, in order to be deprived of dignity, then paraded, mocked and whipped, pierced, derided and spat upon, and tortured for hours in the presence of jeering crowds for popular entertainment ... [T]he purpose was to strike terror in the subject community. It was to let people know that the same thing would happen to them if they did not stay in their place.[29]

Many of the victims were never buried but simply left on the cross as carrion for wild beasts. During the early Roman Empire, the *peregrini* (foreigners, people from abroad) and the *barbari* (nomads, bandits, or those from certain primitive cultural groups), who were not Roman subjects, were often dealt with in a similar manner. The *peregrini* were subject to *de plano* (summary) justice, including execution, at the discretion of the *legatus Augusti*, the provincial governor. Saint Paul himself, although Jewish, was a Roman citizen by birth. In CE 60 he was rescued by Roman soldiers from a Jewish mob at the temple of Jerusalem that accused him of blasphemy and was on the point of lynching him. Taken to the Roman fort, the commander of the unit ordered him to be interrogated under the lash until he confessed what he had done to upset the Jews. But when Paul declared himself a Roman citizen, the flogging was aborted and his chains removed. What is very revealing is the evident fear of the soldiers when they realized that they had roughly handled a Roman citizen and not a *peregrino*.

There is yet another side to lynching, as also to the rise of the militia in a state or community. I am trying to argue that the idea of hunting belongs to a necessary preparatory phase for the prince and is hence part of a body of advice to the prince; it is therefore important to consider the connection between hunting and the knowledge of territory. By extending the link, hunting becomes a necessary means of governing and securing the relationship between the prince and his territory. This naturally includes gaining knowledge of enemies as possible sources of threat, as well as the general management of violence within the territory. Following from this, it seems that the ability to assess threats efficiently and manage violence is what makes hunting a proper discipline, perhaps even the vehicle of an ethics of sorts for the prince. It thereby relates directly to the sovereignty of the prince and his monopoly over violence.

That being so, the obverse phenomenon of lynching may suggest a crisis of this sovereignty, a fragmentation of the monopoly over violence, since lynching is, so to speak, an outsourced exercise of violence. The shift to lynching becomes a symptom of the prince's insecurity and of confusion between subjects and enemies. The persistence of lynching, in defiance of the rule of law and a disciplinary management of violence, can perhaps be read as a state of exception extended into a rule. It happens when the *civitas* is dissolved and the latent presence of the state of nature within the polity manifests itself.

The position of the multitude or the populace is a constant concern in Machiavelli's *Discourses*. Soon after the famous formulation in *Discourses* 1:4 that it is the discord between the people and the senate that makes the republic free and powerful comes 1:8, where Machiavelli takes up the subject of scandalmongering. Here is his categorical take about slander:

> It can be learned from this passage how detestable slanders are in free cities and in every other kind of community, and how, to repress them, no plan that fits the conditions should be neglected. Nor can there be a better plan for getting rid of them than to give enough openings for bringing charges, because however much lawful charges help republics, so much do slanders hurt them ... And when a charge has been made and well investigated, slanderers should be severely punished ... And where this matter is not well arranged, there always follow great disorders, because slanders irritate but do not punish the citizens.[30]

One must remember that this is spoken in a republican spirit. The bedrock position is that slander weakens the civic community: it is a detestable form of killing that calls for no discipline or patience. Rumour-mongering is a way of lynching one's adversaries through contempt and shaming without any accountability. It becomes a free-for-all: anyone can slander anyone. Slander is a public spectacle: people are slandered in squares and arcades. It never ever has a goal; it vexes but does not openly punish the citizens. It is amorphous. It occurs most when cities are least organized to deal with them.

Machiavelli categorically states that slanderers ought not to be spared. They must be paid in their own coin. As a strategy, not only does slandering drain the city's energies but also turns futile and generates a cycle of retributive violence. Those who are slandered keep on thinking of avenging themselves: there is no way they can effectively be cowed down for ever. And after a point, they only hate and do not fear the things that are said against them.

He who reads the history of Florence will see how many slanders have always been put forth against citizens employed in key positions or otherwise given important assignments. One citizen might be charged with defalcation of public funds, another with receiving bribes or some other corrupt or improper action. Hatred seems to have sprung up on every side. Such vengeful animosity creates schisms, and schismatic politics eventually leads to ruination. But the basic problem lay elsewhere: Florence did not have any proper system for bringing charges against citizens, including charges of slander. Machiavelli concludes that had Florence had such a system, many troubles could have been averted. The falsely condemned would not have harboured grudges and harmed the city in the long run. It is very easy to slander someone rather than accuse him formally.

Social order, according to Machiavelli, is of prime importance. The multitude without a head is useless, he says in *Discourses* 1:44. In *Discourses*

1:17, he extends this malady to cover general corruption in the city. Corruption is a precondition for such anarchic trends to make a dent in the first place. 'So it can be concluded that where the matter is not corrupt, uprisings and other disturbances do no harm. Where it is corrupt, well planned laws are of no use.'[31]

A further subtle point is made in *Discourses* 1:29 that pathos and sentimentality must never prevent a citizen from objectively taking stock of a crisis. Too much love leads to wrong judgements.

> A city living in freedom has two ends: the first, to make gains; the second, to keep herself free. In both of these she probably will err through too much love … Her errors in keeping herself free are, among others, these: injury to citizens whom she should reward; fear of citizens whom she should trust.[32]

Recognition of merit and the right kinds of incentives are crucial, and fear or resentment of injury of those same persons fatal, for the good of the city.

The popularity of a good leader must not turn into populist worship. Private citizens would soon grow afraid of such an ambitious man: 'For the law of these matters is that when men try to escape fear, they make others fear, and the injury they push away from themselves they lay on others, as if it were necessary either to harm or to be harmed.'[33] Hence, a republic ought to have among its laws that the citizens are to be watched, so that they cannot, under cover of good, do evil to their exclusive gain. Good governance does not foster populist measures.

Machiavelli develops a curious estimation of the very category of the *popolo*. In the *Discourses*, he is at once hopeful of the power of the people yet consistently pessimistic about the people's inclination to harm themselves:

> The people, deceived by a false image of good, many times desire their own ruin. And if somebody in whom they have faith does not convince them that what they want is bad and explain what is good, countless dangers and losses come upon the republic. And when chance causes the people to have faith in no one, as sometimes happens, since they have been deceived in the past both by things and by men, of necessity the republic is ruined. Dante says about this, in his discussion *On Monarchy*, that the populace many times shouts: 'Long live its own death', and 'Down with its own life'.[34]

Much later, refining such thoughts, Gustav le Bon was to say that as with the fiercest religious sect, so too with the modern crowd, its commonly held convictions 'assume the characteristics of blind submission, fierce intolerance, and the need of violent propaganda'. Its leader is 'acclaimed as a veritable god', holding sway over its imagination by 'devising new formulas as devoid as possible of precise meaning', thus taking on whatever meaning the follower invents for it. At the same time, this leader destroys his rivals with claims devoid of substance: 'By dint of affirmation, repetition, and contagion', the leader affirms that his opponent is 'an arrant scoundrel, and that it is a matter of common knowledge that he has been guilty of several crimes'.[35] Le Bon concludes: 'It is, of course, useless to trouble about any semblance of proof.'[36]

It is again Seneca who draws our attention to the causes of factionalism within the late Roman republic and their outward manifestation in a protracted civil war. He is particularly acute on the vitiation of the Roman *populus*. Its descent into deeply divisive and irrational behaviour in the madness of civil war had caused it to lose coherence: it no longer knew how to live and think properly. Losing its virtue and rationality, it had turned into a multitude. This was the proper state of slavery of mind, a state that leads to the burgeoning of the slanderous lynch mob.

The lynch mob is also an extension of the pack, especially the lamenting pack—one that considers itself to be a victim of some real or imaginary injustice. A pack is a conglomerate that is yet to turn into a proper and formed crowd, a state that le Bon would call 'crowd-crystals'. The animal's exercise of power by seizing and ingesting or *in-corporating* the overpowered creature, and then expelling it as disgusting waste (is it disgusting to the animal?), becomes the critical model for the exercise of power in human life by the lynch mob. The communion between the members of a pack is a ceremony of increase. The basis of power in the pack rests on two factors: the psychology of seizing and incorporating, and the intuitive conviction that survival itself is power. Such a philosophy is the very opposite of hunting.

The Terminus of Hunting

Does the sovereign hunter have a goal? I do not wish to wade into the morass of trying to read Machiavelli ethically, which is a whole field unto itself. The goal is difficult to gauge theoretically, except by focusing on the moment of contact between the hunter and the prey. In *Meditations on Hunting*, Ortega y Gasset thinks that perhaps the prospect of a life about to be annulled surprises the hunter at the point when he lets go of the arrow. How can death be inflicted upon a slender, enchanting beast, he wonders. The hunter therefore turns restive. His relationship with the animal, instead of heightening his consciousness of his own existence (as Hegel would have us believe), makes him withdraw into his own interiority in an instinctual turn. The human becomes one with the animal at that point, even if equivocally so, since there is a constant and mysterious *communication with the animal within one's humanity*. If there is to be an ethics of the chase, it would centre on the realization that the enigma of death is multiplied by the enigma of the animal. How do we understand our assailants? Do all of us actually wander without group protection, fated to await our would-be assassins?

For the hunted, on the other hand, as Chamayou has suggested, there could be two possibilities at the time of the fateful confrontation.[37] First, he might confront the hunter creatively at that moment, even at the risk of dying. That would mean that he directly takes on the hunter even after looking down the power gradient: the animal might still use its will to protect its freedom and desire for life. The other possibility is that he might seek a certain kind of freedom in death. It can be actual death at the hands of the hunter or a potential death in hiding and biding, accepting the foregone relationship between hunter and prey. With respect to the first option, Chamayou makes a brilliant point about the aristocratic temperament:

> What is peculiar to manhunting, what constitutes its danger but also its supreme aristocratic attraction, is the constant possibility of a reversal of the relationship: the prey might become a predator, the hunted a hunter. Manhunting is characterized by this fundamental instability: when the prey, refusing to continue to be a prey and ceasing to run away, retaliates and tracks in turn, hunting becomes combat or a struggle.[38]

This reversal of the cycle of violence, where the hunter and the hunted merely change places, is perhaps the ultimate retribution brought about by cynegetic ways of living and dying.

In Machiavelli's *L'Asino*, Diana's chief nymph goes seeking her prey in the forest—along with bears, wolves, and lions that are fierce and cruel, and many other beasts of prey, and stags and badgers and boars. Her prey is human. She pronounces to the prey what is in store for him: 'You must know that in the world these animals you see were men like yourself.'[39] The prey knows and follows her, mesmerized by his destiny. But before she hunts him with slow ease, dining and drinking and going to bed with him, she says something extraordinary to her prey:

> But before these stars show themselves propitious toward you, you will have to travel to explore the world, covered with a different skin, because that

Providence which supports the human species intends you to bear this affliction for your greater good. Hence you must altogether lose your human semblance, and without it come with me to feed among the other beasts. There can be no change in this harsh star; by putting you in this place, the ill is deferred, not cancelled.[40]

We do not know how the whole narrative of this incomplete work might have turned out. What might have been in Machiavelli's mind when he thought of conceiving such an ominous netherworld? Why must the human being be truly and literally turned to a beast, covered in a different skin, in order to bear affliction? What is the greater good in taking us through the process of the hunt? The ordeal of being preyed upon cannot, in itself, alter one's harsh fate. The 'preyness' of the prey remains forever a condition of its existence. To realize this clearly, we must altogether lose our human semblance in every respect. The veneer of restoration and reparation of a lost human order must be totally relinquished; yet we must carry on with our accustomed chores.

The hunter kills, while the animal lying in front of him is degraded and soiled. He feels the deepest mystery of the intimate blood that oozes out, secretly and occultly, from the material body of the dead game, which is now a cadaver. It brings a literally 'sanguinary' clarity to the truth of power, the *imperium*. At that point, the cadaver loses its intimacy. The body turns to pure matter: no one is hidden inside it.

I have argued that hunting is the supreme exercise in developing restraint and ordered planning. But the actual moment of hunting is a blur. There is a line, beyond which it seems to us that what is purely our whim or obsession is the only possibility. We take a leap into pure action, turning irretrievably towards being the hunter. At such nodal points, Machiavelli fuses the acutest forms of fantasy with the real conditions of existence. At such junctures, the blood spilling out of the prey begins to intoxicate the hunter. He realizes that it is he who has produced this death: he has been *led into* the condition of having to kill. That is the point where the sovereign hunter begins to rehearse and anticipate his own death. There is pure delight in finally conquering the game. The hunter can now be benevolent. But he is also made supremely aware of the impenetrable destiny in and through which the hunter and the hunted are bound forever—a destiny now sealed with death. It is a moment of paroxysm. But it also brings with it the ethical realization that death is the finality of all action.

There is a kind of reckoning at the end. Ortega y Gasset writes about such a moment of anticipation and authenticity:

> There is a harsh confrontation with the animal's fierceness, the struggle with its energetic defense, the point of orgiastic intoxication aroused by the sight of blood, and even the hint of criminal suspicion that claws the hunter's conscience. Without these ingredients the spirit of the hunt disappears.[41]

The hunt is not the moment of death. It constitutes everything that the hunter did in order to achieve his prey. The elaborate process of hunting has hardly anything to do with killing. One does not hunt in order to kill; one kills in order to have hunted. Above all, in both Xenophon and Machiavelli, the aim is to avoid moral prudery. The animal can never descend to the level of man; but man can, as a conscious act of ethical humbling, eschew his superiority and be at par with the animal. In this manner, he actually levels with himself and brings himself closer to the creaturely elements lying within his own self.

Francesco de Sanctis has noted, and Louis Althusser reminds us, that Machiavelli 'takes us by surprise and leaves us pensive'.[42] Seeking to fill up the deficit of national unity in Florentine politics, he searches for a lasting form to contain such a unity and the preconditions it may impose. Whether fortune or *virtù* is the dominant force, such a wager will always imply being 'torn up by one's roots, cut off from them, irredeemable'.[43] Such is the hunter-prince's unwonted, untamed character. He can only innovate by working in solitude in order to found a state. He is seized by *virtù*, not always consciously but by an exercise of will and striving. Hunting allows such a platform for exercising *fortezza* (valour)—the very basis of heroic passion. It is the meeting ground of *fortuna* and *virtù*. As such, hunting is the original act of *urging*—steeped in ancient *Pathosformel* (formula for pathos) and determination through which the hunter reaches the unity of living.[44] The hunter must navigate waters that are yet uncharted.

Notes

1. '[P]arevo el Geta quando e' tornava dal porto con e libri d'Amphitrione': Machiavelli, *Tutte le opere*, ed. Mario Martelli (Florence: Sansoni, 1971), 1159. All Italian texts of Machiavelli's works are cited from this edition (henceforth *Opere*) unless otherwise mentioned; tr. from *The Letters of Machiavelli: A Selection*, tr. and ed. Allan Gilbert (Chicago, IL: University of Chicago Press, 1961), 139.

2. '[N]acqui ... nella bella e gloriosa Etruria ... le lepri vinsi al corso, i cervi à salti': report in *La Repubblica*, 27 February 2017, accessed on 17 March 2020 at https://firenze.repubblica.it/cronaca/2013/12/09/news/l_epigramma_di_machiavelli_dedicato_al_cane_furia-73137071/. See also Nick Squires, 'Poem Marks Machiavelli as a Pet Lover', *The Telegraph*, 10 December 2013, accessed on 5 October 2018 at https://www.telegraph.co.uk/news/worldnews/europe/italy/10509801/Poem-marks-Machiavelli-as-a-pet-lover.html.
3. 'Menon pidocchi queste parieti / bolsi spaccati che paion farfalle, / né fu mai tanto puzzo in Roncisvalle ...': text and tr. from Sebastian de Grazia, *Machiavelli in Hell* (Princeton, NJ: Princeton University Press, 1989), 34, 392.
4. See Jose Ortega y Gasset, *Meditations on Hunting* (New York: Charles Scribner's Sons, 1942, rpt. 1972), 29.
5. Ibid., 40.
6. '[C]on industria farne capitale, per potersene valere nelle avversità': *Opere* 280; tr. Allan Gilbert as in Machiavelli, *The Chief Works and Others*, 3 vols. (Durham, NC: Duke University Press, 1965), 1:57. All translations of Machiavelli's works cited from this version (henceforth *Chief Works*) unless otherwise mentioned.
7. '[L]uno con le opere, l'altro, con la mente': *Opere* 279; tr. *Chief Works* 1:55–6.
8. See Mikael Hörnqvist, *Machiavelli and Empire* (Cambridge: Cambridge University Press, 2009).
9. 'Ma Castruccio, avendo sanza tumulto preso la notte il castello [Serravalle], si partì in su la mezza notte da Montecarlo, e tacito con le sue genti arrivò la mattina a piè di Serravalle; in modo che a un tratto i Fiorentini ed esso, ciascuno dalla sua parte, incominciò a salire la costa ... I Fiorentini ... né credevano trovare Castruccio in sul colle, perché non sapevano ch'ei si fusse insignorito del castello. In modo che, insperatamente, i cavagli de' Fiorentini, salita la costa, scopersono le fanterie di Castruccio, e trovoronsi tanto propinqui a loro, che con fatica ebbono tempo ad allacciarsi le celate. Sendo pertanto gli impreparati assaltati dai preparati e ordinati, con grande animo li spinsono': *Opere* 622; tr. *Chief Works* 2:547.
10. 'Né istimavano gli antichi cosa più felice in una republica, che essere in quella assai uomini esercitati nell'armi; perché non lo splendore delle gemme e dell'oro fa che i nimici ti si sottomettono, ma solo il timore dell'armi ... Insegnavano ancora loro trarre con l'arco, con la fromba, e a tutte queste cose avevano preposti maestri, in modo che poi, quando egli erano eletti per andare alla guerra, egli erano già con l'animo e con la disposizione soldati': *Opere* 323; tr. *Chief Works* 1:602.
11. Ortega y Gasset, *Meditations on Hunting*, 49.

12. Hörnqvist, *Machiavelli and Empire*, 349.
13. Ibid., 151.
14. Xenophon, *Cynegetics*, in *Hiero the Tyrant and Other Treatises*, tr. Robin Waterfield (London: Penguin Books, 1997), 131. See also Steven Johnstone, 'Virtuous Toil, Vicious Work: Xenophon on Aristocratic Style', in *Oxford Readings in Classical Studies: Xenophon*, ed. Vivienne J. Gray (Oxford: Oxford University Press, 2010), 137–66.
15. Xenophon, *Hiero the Tyrant*, 158.
16. V. J. Gray. 'Xenophon's "Cynegeticus"', *Hermes* 113, no. 2 (1985), 156–72, 159.
17. Xenophon, *Hiero the Tyrant*, 141.
18. J. G. A. Pocock, *The Machiavellian Moment* (Princeton, NJ: Princeton University Press, 1975).
19. '[T]erminos civitatis nostrae cum sole metimur': Seneca, 'Ad Serenum: De otio', *Moral Essays*, vol. 2, tr. John W. Basore, Loeb Classical Library (Cambridge, MA: Harvard University Press, 1932), 180–1.
20. Peter Stacey, *Roman Monarchy and the Renaissance Prince* (Cambridge: Cambridge University Press, 2012), 66.
21. Mark Jurdjevic, *A Great and Wretched City: Promise and Failure in Machiavelli's Florentine Political Thought* (Cambridge, MA: Harvard University Press, 2014).
22. '[È] onestissima ed al tutto aliena dalle cose d'amore': Machiavelli, *Mandragola* 1:1, *Opere* 870; tr. *Chief Works* 2:780.
23. 'Chi non fa prova, Amore,/della tua gran possanza, indarno spera/di far mai fede vera/qual sia del cielo il più alto valore;/né sa come si vive, insieme, e muore,/come si segue il danno e 'l ben si fugge,/come s'ama se stesso/men d'altrui, come spesso/timore e speme i cori adiaccia e strugge;/né sa come ugualmente uomini e dèi/paventan l'arme di che armato sei': *Mandragola* 1:canzone, *Opere* 873; tr. *Chief Works* 2:785.
24. 'Dipoi ci travestiremo, voi, Ligurio, Siro ed io, e andrencene cercando in Mercato Nuovo, in Mercato Vecchio, per questi canti; ed el primo garzonaccio che noi troverremo scioperato, lo imbavaglierero, ed a suon di mazzate lo condurreno in casa ed in camera vostra al buio': *Mandragola* 2:6, *Opere* 876; tr. *Chief Works* 2:792.
25. 'Le più caritative persone': *Mandragola* 3:4, *Opere* 878; tr. *Chief Works* 2:796.
26. 'Ed è 'l vero che non è el mele sanza le mosche': ibid.
27. '[T]u, col tuo gran valore,/nel far beato altrui, fai ricco Amore;/tu vinci, sol co' tuoi consigli santi,/pietre, veneni e incanti': *Mandragola* 3: canzone, *Opere* 882; tr. *Chief Works* 2:801.
28. Grégoire Chamayou, *Manhunts: A Philosophical History*, tr. Steven Rendall (Princeton, NJ: Princeton University Press, 2010), 99–100.
29. James H. Cone, *The Cross and the Lynching Tree* (New York: Orbis Books, 2013), 88–9.

30. 'È da notare, per questo testo, quanto siano nelle città libere, ed in ogni altro modo di vivere, detestabili le calunnie; e come, per reprimerle, si debba non perdonare a ordine alcuno che vi faccia a proposito. Né può essere migliore ordine, a torle via, che aprire assai luoghi alle accuse; perché, quanto le accuse giovano alle republiche, tanto le calunnie nuocono: ... e fatto questo [*sc.*, l'accùsa], e bene osservato, debbe punire acremente i calunniatori: ... E dove non è bene ordinata questa parte, seguitano sempre disordini grandi: perché le calunnie irritano, e non castigano i cittadini': *Opere* 89; tr. *Chief Works* 1:216.

31. 'E si può fare questa conclusione, che, dove la materia non è corrotta, i tumulti ed altri scandoli non nuocono: dove la è corrotta, le leggi bene ordinate non giovano': *Opere* 102; tr. *Chief Works* 1:239–40.

32. '[A]vendo una città che vive libera, duoi fini, l'uno lo acquistare, l'altro il mantenersi libera; conviene che nell'una cosa e nell'altra per troppo amore erri ... Quanto agli errori per mantenersi libera, sono, intra gli altri, questi: di offendere quegli cittadini che la doverrebbe premiare; avere sospetto di quegli in cui la si doverrebbe confidare': *Opere* 111; tr. *Chief Works* 1:258–9.

33. 'E l'ordine di questi accidenti è che, mentre che gli uomini cercono di non temere, comincino a fare temere altrui; e quella ingiuria che gli scacciano da loro, la pongono sopra un altro; come se fusse necessario offendere o essere offeso': *Disc.* 1:46, *Opere* 128; tr. *Chief Works* 1:290.

34. '[I]l popolo molte volte, ingannato da una falsa immagine di bene, disidera la rovina sua; e se non gli è fatto capace, come quello sia male, e quale sia il bene, da alcuno in chi esso abbia fede, si porta in le republiche infiniti pericoli e danni. E quando la sorte fa che il popolo non abbi fede in alcuno, come qualche volta occorre, sendo stato ingannato per lo addietro o dalle cose o dagli uomini, si viene alla rovina, di necessità. E Dante dice a questo proposito, nel discorso suo che fa *De Monarchia*, che il popolo molte volte grida: Viva la sua morte! e Muoia la sua vita!': *Disc.* 1:53, *Opere* 134; tr. *Chief Works* 1:302–3.

35. Gustav Le Bon, *The Psychology of Crowds* (1895), as quoted in Robert Zaretsky, 'Donald Trump and the Myth of Mobocracy', *The Atlantic*, 27 July 2016, accessed on 5 June 2021 at https://www.theatlantic.com/international/archive/2016/07/trump-le-bon-mob/493118/. See also Elias Canetti, *Crowds and Power*, tr. Carol Stewart (New York: Farrar, Straus and Giroux, 1984).

36. Le Bon, *The Crowd*, 116. See also Jaap Van Ginneken, *Crowds, Psychology, and Politics, 1871–1899* (Cambridge: Cambridge University Press, 1992).

37. See Gregoire Chamayou, *Manhunts: A Philosophical History*, tr. Steven Rendall (Princeton, NJ: Princeton University Press, 2010), 60–4.

38. Ibid., 74.

39. '[S]appi che queste bestie che tu vedi,/uomini, come te, furon nel mondo': *L'asino* 2:128–9, *Opere* 959; tr. *Chief Works* 2:755.
40. 'Ma prima che si mostrin queste stelle/liete verso di te, gir ti conviene/ cercando il mondo sotto nuova pelle;/ché quella Provvidenza che mantiene/ l'umana spezie, vuol che tu sostenga/questo disagio per tuo maggior bene./ Di qui conviene al tutto che si spenga/in te l'umana effigie, e, senza quella,/ meco tra l'altre bestie a pascer venga./Né può mutarsi questa dura stella;/e, per averti in questo luogo messo,/si differisce il mal, non si cancella': *L'asino* cap.3:115–24, *Opere* 962; tr. *Chief Works* 2:758.
41. Ortega y Gasset, *Meditations on Hunting*, 109.
42. Louis Althusser, *Machiavelli and Us* (London: Verso, 2011), 117.
43. Ibid., 118.
44. For a discussion on the relationship between will, heroic passion, *fortezza* and *Pathosformel*, see Ernst Cassirer, *The Individual and Cosmos in Renaissance Philosophy*, tr. Mario Domandi (Philadelphia, PA: University of Pennsylvania Press, 1972 [1963]), 75. Ernst Gombrich describes *Pathosformel* as 'the primeval reaction of man to the universal hardships of his existence that underlies all his attempts at mental orientation' in his *Aby Warburg: An Intellectual Biography* (London: Warburg Institute, 1970), 223.

7

'To Give Reputation to One'

Machiavelli the Populist and Other Variations on Il Principe, *Chapter 9*

Guido Cappelli

One of the main problems of modern Machiavelli criticism is what might be summarized in the polarity 'philosopher *versus* politician'—that is, the distinction between a 'theorizing' Machiavelli, political scientist and political philosopher, and a 'practical' Machiavelli, little interested in doctrine, attached only to the events of his time—moreover, a Florentine Machiavelli, addressing a span of concerns from the municipal to the national. The opposition widens when interwoven with discrepant assessments of Machiavelli's culture and of the reading that feeds his knowledge. For some, that knowledge is largely second-hand and 'municipal' in character, while for others it is comparable to that of a true humanist scholar.[1]

I think it is possible to obviate this debate.[2] The opposed factors are both legitimate, and complementary. It is no doubt necessary to recover practical intentions and immediate contexts; but this can also shed light on wider issues, such as—to anticipate the critical point I will address in this chapter—the Medicean (or Soderinian) interpretation of the civil principality ('principato civile'),[3] in relation to the theoretical need for autonomy, security, and 'statehood' characterizing Machiavelli's entire treatise.[4]

To succumb entirely to the imperatives of the contingent can result in a reductionism that leaves unexplained the ideal and doctrinal influence that Machiavelli has exercised for five centuries. It restricts the range of Machiavelli's thought to the politics of the present, whether Machiavelli's present or our own. The inadequacy of this view mirrors that of its opposite: an aseptic theory that makes Machiavellism a universal vade mecum, extending even to its naïve but sinister use by the American neocon right.[5] The risk of such spectacular reductionism should not be underestimated.

It is true that Machiavelli's complexity cannot be altered to fit a theory, or a presumed 'coherence' to be defended at all costs. We cannot reconcile the countless, and sometimes contradictory, theoretical points of the treatise into a cohesive philosophical system, ignoring moments of genuine aporia.[6] But we cannot glibly admit such aporia, or even simple contradictions, as an excuse for our own interpretative limitations. We must first make every effort to grapple with the text and its contexts.

In short, between the high-flying theorist of 'scientific' method and the strategist of local operations, perhaps there is a space where we can place an *analyst* Machiavelli. The analyst speaks for the immediate, but in general terms. He studies behaviour, but by researching classifiable series of events and models of conduct—even if, as in this case, they are always partial and contingent—in an arduous effort to draw reliable knowledge from a changing and partly uncontrollable reality.[7]

Such a position has been well described as 'an extraordinary mixture of old and new',[8] with the stamp of 'extravagance',[9] a tendency or impulse to subvert the *idées reçues*. Its study requires an approach that plots Machiavelli's work (especially the two major ones) against its most immediate intellectual interlocutor—namely, political humanism. This is partly to allow us to frame Machiavelli's thought historically, measuring its gap with the humanist tradition. The gap is real enough to have inspired the invective opening the famous Chapter 15 of *The Prince*; yet the two discourses share languages, concepts, and ideological horizons. Humanism is reflected in the functioning of the polemical engine, taking the theoretical contribution of the latter beyond the merely contingent.

We therefore require an 'ecumenical' approach, though this is not without problems. It involves a simultaneous inquiry in three directions. The first looks back to the classical and humanistic framework of political and (increasingly) juridical doctrine but extends beyond sterile purism to embrace the revisions, misunderstandings, and *felices errores* of a creative intellectual, not simply a scholar or philologist. The second line of inquiry explores the author's present, the inescapable web of political and social circumstance from which this reflection of humanism takes its cue and draws its life. Finally and most challengingly, we must consider the future, or rather the 'future past' (to adapt Reinhart Koselleck's phrase) of an author who never ceases to question each and every epoch of history but can still interact fruitfully with the thought of later centuries. I hold the simultaneous presence of these three dimensions to be not only justified but necessary.

* * *

Chapter 9 of *The Prince* describes a theoretical situation, a 'case', where a change in the form of government occurs in a situation of socio-political tension. We need to clarify the nature of this tension and to establish precisely what form of government Machiavelli has in mind.

In this scenario, the city is corrupt. Traditional orders and institutions can no longer ensure social stability; the political balance is disturbed. There is no open civil war (a point to be kept very much in mind), but the two sides, the people and 'the great' ('grandi'), feel they cannot resist each other's incursions on their space. Hence, they set up a prince to advance their interests, even if their motives for doing so are opposite: self-protection for the people, oppression for the *grandi*, led by the alternative compulsions of necessity and ambition, respectively.[10] Yet the corruption is not total: there is no armed conflict. In the *Discourses*, Machiavelli observes that the Roman polity passed from being a kingdom to a republic precisely because the popular body was not corrupt. The casuistry of *The Prince*, Chapter 9, on the other hand, assumes *a certain* (unspecified) *degree* of corruption, with a temperate prince who can eliminate or at least reduce the inequality or disparity of power and political dominance between the ruling class and the people. All this is viewed in a context of exceptionality: the situation being described is an extreme case.[11] It is comparable to that of Rome in the first year of the Decemviri as described in the *Discourses* 1:40, where Appius Claudius, the leader of the Decemviri, projected himself in a new pro-popular image. The Decemviri in general behaved 'very civilly' ('assai civilmente'): despite having absolute authority, they sought the people's support for serious decisions, submitting all proposed laws to a popular vote, 'so that they might be amended before their final confirmation'.[12] This situation is not far removed from that fostered by the pro-people prince in Chapter 9 of *The Prince*.[13]

The example of Rome shows that though Machiavelli's primary concern may have been Florence in the fifteenth century or under Soderini, this need not prevent us from understanding the 'city' as *any* political community, a *civitas*, a laboratory for the theoretical speculation that infuses the entire first part of *The Prince*. Florence illustrates the state (already in itself 'extreme') of the new principality contemplated in *The Prince*, Chapter 9,[14] to which 'one ascends ... either with the support of the people or with the support of the great',[15] even if further analysis shows that only the first alternative has any real possibility of success.

Since people, as we know, have different temperaments,[16] attention is turned to the dawn of the conflict and the activating mechanism:

> For in every city these two diverse humors are found, which arises from this: that the people desire neither to be commanded nor oppressed by the great, and the great desire to command and oppress the people. From these two diverse appetites one of three effects occurs in cities: principality or liberty or license.[17]

The tone and approach confirm the strictly theoretical nature of the reflection. The initial dynamic of the conflict appears to be reduced to its more general essence, opening the path to a revolution of Copernican dimensions that goes beyond the organic metaphor to the physiology of the *polis*, 'from the anatomical hierarchy to the functioning of the body'.[18] 'Licenza' (licence) is not simply a degenerate form of the republican order but a totally arbitrary dispensation, an absolute lack of rules, a kind of state of nature. 'Appetiti' (desires or appetites) suggests the idea of *libido*. Not by chance does tradition associate libido with licence, linking the two in reciprocal echo as Cicero had done[19]—*libet* with *licet*, the latter word expressive of bad government and ultimately of tyranny. Tyranny, in fact, consists precisely in considering every *libido* lawful: 'quicquid libuerit licuerit', as Pontano writes.[20] It is power (*potentia*), as another theorist, Francesco Patrizi, states, that creates the harmful overlap:

> Power often drags men to license and injustice. We see that the opinion of Cicero is true, when he says that nothing is sadder than a prince who wants to do everything he can; and vice versa, those who believe that everything they can do is legitimate are totally unhappy.[21]

Here, then, emerges a new type of *princeps*, not produced by bloody conflict in his society; but he is called upon to temper and rescue that society from destructive *licenza*.[22] His will be an unusual principality. Although Machiavelli admits the possibility of a principality where the *grandi* prevail, he hypothesizes one that is openly grounded on a popular basis and anti-aristocratic in bent. *It is not a republic*, neither was the preferred structure of governance in the famous pages in *Discourses* 1:18 advocating an 'almost regal power' ('podestà quasi regia'),[23] given the 'impossibility' of maintaining a republic in a corrupt city, or recreating it once destroyed. Thus, Machiavelli arrives at the paradoxical solution of a republic (*principato civile*) founded on a quasi-monarchic model, a *stato regio* or 'royal State'.[24]

Although there is now a considerable body of scholarship arguing the opposite case, terms such as *civilis* are still often applied exclusively to republics and thence, broadly but invariably, equated with 'free', if not 'democratic'. What I characterized years ago as 'republican prejudice'[25] has been of little benefit to Machiavelli studies; fortunately, the tendency is on the verge of extinction and neutralization. It is now possible to explore other routes to a hermeneutic horizon and propose other doctrinal solutions.

To be defined precisely, the 'civil' nature of this principality must be conclusively detached from an abstract republican form. In this regard, it is useful to recover, if only by way of samples, the usual political connotations of the term *civilis*. It seems to be a conceptual threshold, which we may need to cross even when we are not treating specifically of republican issues. It is worth looking at a key text of fifteenth-century political theory, the *De obedientia* by Giovanni Pontano (composed c. 1470, printed 1490). There, already at the opening of Book 1 (fol. 6v), regarding the concept of *iustitia*, the author speaks of the duties relating to justice of the city or republic ('iustitiae civilis officia').[26] Distributive justice ('iustitia distributiva') is then proposed as an essential part of civic life ('vivere civile') and characterized in this way:

> It is proper [for the operation of justice] to take care and precaution that in appointing magistrates, conferring honours, dispensing rewards and assigning public duties, nothing is done either more or less than is seen to be equal and just.[27]

In such a state, a single ruler or monarch must be the leader and moderator of civic activity: 'unus esset aliquis aut magistratus aut rex qui ... dux et moderator esset civilium actionum'.[28]

In the chapter on obedience to the judiciary, Pontano says that the basis of civic obedience is respect for the rulers.[29] But perhaps the most significant passage concerns the leader of civic life, the *dux ... civilium actionum* mentioned previously. It amasses characteristics attributable to a civil prince in a context clearly foregrounding monarchy: the *rex* is the protector of liberty, averter and chastiser of wrongs, proponent and guardian of the law, and governor, father, and arbiter of matters both public and private.[30]

There is enough, I would say, to link—as was the norm in Machiavelli's time—the concept of the civil or civic (*civilis*) to a life regulated by institutions and norms, whether governed by magistrates or by a single head, avoiding the reductionist trap of limiting the *civilis* to 'what pertains to a republic'. Only in this way will we understand the innovative dimension of the principality envisaged by Machiavelli.[31]

The full meaning of the civil principality starts from this recognition, avoiding its exclusive identification with a republic. More broadly considered, *civilis* implies two features: power *based on a political-legal apparatus* and *emanating from an institutional structure*. A state ruled by law can exist outside the republican model, even if (as recounted in *The Prince*, Chapter 9) such an order must be precarious and transitory, since in Machiavelli's time the only stable forms of government were the republic and the principality. Hence, ultimately, it becomes imperative to 'ascend from a civil order to an absolute order'.[32]

This notion, however, only makes sense by recognizing the structural impossibility of a society with potential for only one of these orders. The new principality that draws Machiavelli's theoretical attention is the popularly oriented one, but the other is equally a possibility, where a 'civil' prince comes to power by the favour of the aristocracy. These two different moods or tendencies ('questi dua umori diversi') are to be found in every city.

Such a notion destabilizes the humanist view, which revolved around the idea of conquering the *populus* affectively ('devincire' in Renaissance Latin) rather than gaining or earning its favour ('il favore' in Machiavelli's Italian).[33] Instead, Machiavelli's perspective assumes a dialectic between opposed tendencies. It rests on a pessimistic conception of human nature, dismissing the humanistic notion of an emotional bond of love to foreground the political value of *utilitas*, as in the famous passage on being either feared or loved:

> [M]en have less hesitation to offend one who makes himself loved than one who makes himself feared; for love is held by a chain of obligation, which, because men are wicked, is broken at every opportunity for their own utility, but fear is held by a dread of punishment that never forsakes you.[34]

Consensus now ceases to mean an organic fusion with the *populus* in its entirety. Instead, it becomes the political strategy of winning the more or less fluctuating support or 'favour' of a section—here specifically the popular section, the most numerous and the most exempt from ambition. A populist horizon opens up before us as never before. The consensus of love would have been stable and organic; the consensus of favour is necessarily precarious, temporary, changeable, given the structural conflict (even if healthy within certain limits) in a society that has eschewed a model based on universal harmony, where an integral cohesion is assumed to be impossible.

The logical consequence at the level of concrete action, as embodied in the conduct of the *princeps*, marks another reversal of the humanist notion.

If the latter internalized *virtù* as the motive force and guarantee of mutual *amor* between the ruler and the ruled, for Machiavelli *virtù* assumes a very different guise. It expresses itself in the capacity to change, in an unprecedented dialectic between *being* and *appearing* swayed by contingent need. As elaborated in Chapter 15, 'human conditions' ('condizioni umane')[35] do not permit a civil prince to display all possible virtues but to practice prudence ('essere … prudente') instead. He can change sides from the nobles to the people, just as he must simulate a virtue if the situation requires it, on the principle that one can be good and not good as political opportunity demands, know how to do wrong, and use that knowledge according to necessity.[36]

Obtaining a principality in these conditions requires a mixture of *virtù* and fortune: the situation is not fully controllable, as it resists a 'rational interpretation of events'.[37] This 'fortunate astuteness'[38] is a form of *prudentia*—capable of predicting, creating, and then seizing the opportunity. Humanist discourse (as in Pontano's *De prudentia*) would categorically exclude the term from the ambit of political *prudentia*. *Astuzia fortunata* teaches how to adapt to an 'accident outside the normal order of things' ('accidente fuori di … ordine')—the ability which, in the famous opening chapter of Book 3 of the *Discourses*, provides the antidote to the decline of the *res publica*.[39]

The logic of the discourse of *The Prince* turns on the opposition of friend and enemy, the latter more than ever identified with the upper classes threatening the power of the prince. Machiavelli uses traditional concepts to outline, albeit in a 'literary' way using the tools of rhetoric, a technique for recognizing dissent, if only to prevent it: the great

> must be considered in two modes chiefly. Either they … are obligated in everything to your fortune, or not. Those who are obligated, and are not rapacious, must be honored and loved; those who are not obligated have to be examined in two modes. Either they do this out of pusillanimity and a natural defect of spirit; then you must make use especially of those who are of good counsel … [B]ut, when by art and for an ambitious cause, they are not obligated … the prince must be on guard against them, and fear them as if they were open enemies.[40]

At first glance, the vocabulary still seems to belong to the classical and humanistic tradition, with its emphasis on love and, above all, the classification of potential political opponents culminating in outright rebels, 'scoperti inimici'. But on closer look, Machiavelli is seen to be sensibly affected by the juridical–political theorization of various types of rebellion, originally conceived by the imperial jurists and applied in particular, in the fourteenth century, by Bartolo di Sassoferrato to the aristocratic-feudal *rebellio* of the 'great men' (*grandi*), who constitute 'the enemy' for Machiavelli as well. These were the subject of the humanistic formulation of Pontano's *De obedientia*, which echoes Bartolo's glossa on the *Corpus iuris civilis*:

> Since every precept partly commands and partly forbids and prevents, the former aspect requires action, while the other instructs one to take care and hold together. Some err in the first respect, by not doing what is ordered of them, and others by going against the command. The first type of offence is not always caused by deliberate will, but negligence or sloth. In the latter, however, the driving force is clearly either opposition or depravity, with an audacity that destroys the force of obedience and almost demolishes and subverts it.[41]

Between those who must be 'loved and honoured' and the 'open enemies', Machiavelli indicates the space for repressive action by the civil prince. Political humanism had joined the divide by the bond of *amor*. Machiavelli, on the contrary, seeks a legal prescription for social dissolution and institutional collapse, strips and reduces it to a pure balance of power, and thence broaches a principle of sovereignty. He also admits the possibility that, with the support of the people, the prince can 'make and unmake them [the nobles] every day, and take away and give them reputation at his convenience'.[42]

If the problem is with the *grandi*—that is, the aristocrats who unduly condition political management to the point of endangering the *civitas*—it is useless, even harmful, to seek an organic bond with them, since structurally, by nature, the *potentiores* (the *too* powerful whose *raison d'être* is dominion) are committed to oppressing the weaker sections of society. That is what opposes them to the *popolo*. Machiavelli brings into play the logic of a tactical, obligatory consensus in place of an organic bond: a consensus ultimately enforced by the pure compulsion of survival on the part of the common people. Once the idea of a genuine accord between the governor and the governed is dismissed, the only alternative is that the former should 'protect' or 'defend' the latter, in an atmosphere of suspicion and uncertainty:

> Therefore, one who becomes prince through the support of the people should keep them friendly to him, which should be easy for him because they ask of him only that they not be oppressed. But one who becomes prince against the people with the support of the great must before everything else seek to gain the people to himself, which should be easy for him when he takes up its protection.[43]

The humanist order of *virtutes* guaranteed the certainty of the *regula*: once that is dissolved, all political prescriptions dissolve as well. Consent is no longer obtained through certain scientific regulation: Machiavelli cannot formulate 'certain rules', and therefore the matter is 'left out' from his discussion.[44] The distance from the humanist order, which provides for a whole series of *virtutes* that involve *amor* almost in a 'scientific' way, could not be greater. Given the permanent threat inherent in political life, and the role of force in political relations, once love is excluded as the binding force of the body politic, the balance will naturally tend towards *fear*.

I have repeatedly noted the broad use of the term *civilis*, extending beyond republican contexts. Conceptually and terminologically, Machiavelli differentiates between tyranny and good governance much more than between the republic and the monarchy, since the *res publica* is not so much, or only secondarily, a specific form of government, even if according to some the only legitimate form. Basically, *res publica* is literally 'everybody's concern', the object of common good, any space in which the political and social community develops.[45] Given also the possibilities of semantic extension inherent in the term 'principality' (*principato*), it can be concluded that Machiavelli refers to a new form of government, hybrid but clear in its direction, neither republican nor monarchic but based on a new legal apparatus devised and controlled by a *princeps* strongly legitimized, at the political level, by the popular multitude.

From a historical point of view, this was reflected, of course in a rather imperfect way, not only in Medicean Florence but in other new regimes founded on more or less sovereign (rather than abstractly 'republican') civic institutions. This was a specifically Italian model of a principality. As already pointed out by the philosopher Agostino Nifo (and widely noted), such rulers include the Bentivoglios of Bologna, Pandolfo Petrucci of Siena, Simon Boccanegra of Genoa, and perhaps minor potentates of states such as Perugia[46]—not, however, the Estensi of Ferrara or the Sforzas of Milan, who were legally ducal, nor of course the Aragonesi of Naples. Perhaps it is this novel indefiniteness (rather than 'ambiguity') that explains the use of the dittology 'citizens and subjects' ('cittadini e sudditi').[47] But above all, it shows us that Machiavelli is imagining a new model of the state *because* it is not legally validated: it is new, based on ground realities.[48] Beyond the historical data, therefore, it is the theoretical design, experimenting with a new and different form of legitimacy derived from political strategy. It is born of social division and conflict, and leads to a new legality. It undermines the institutional polarity of republic *versus* monarchy, as political humanism had already discovered. The civil principality is conceivable only by emphatically attenuating this opposition, which has now been superseded by the 'actual reality'.[49] It is configured as the first proposal, concrete yet essentially conceptual, of a new political order based on the irreducibly conflict-ridden structure of society as viewed by Machiavelli.

Since the authority of the civil prince derives exclusively from political dialectics, it is almost obvious that the conflict of the classes is resolved in his rule—to the maximum possible degree, in consensus. Such a ruler progresses from a private citizen to a prince 'not through crime or other intolerable violence but with the support of his fellow citizens'.[50] Such a figure is authorized by the Aristotelian tradition: 'Sometimes one begins with persuasion and continues to govern with consent and persuasion.'[51] This ability to persuade can be considered part of the *prudentia* that, on the other hand, allows such a prince to acquire power by exploiting the historical circumstances: that is, the 'fortunate astuteness' ('astuzia fortunata') that differs from both wickedness or crime ('scelleratezza') and 'intolerable' ('intollerabile') violence[52]—an adjective that, as Larivaille noted,[53] implies the existence of another 'tolerable' form of violence needed to maintain, if not to obtain, power. That is not surprising. Machiavelli upsets many of the political categories established by tradition: his unsqueamish acceptance of tyranny, assimilated to the traits of absolute power, disoriented many of his early readers and continues to vex us.[54] The scope of classical tyranny, as codified by tradition, appears reduced and almost weakened in both *The Prince* and *The Art of War*: the term is 'formally absent',[55] but some of its traits end up being undeniably included in the new Machiavellian princehood. Machiavelli shows little belief in classical tyranny as such, and this helps to expand his reflection and liberate it from the limits of the political–legal tradition.[56]

The example of Nabis—the only *exemplum* cited in the chapter—is indicative in this sense. No humanist thinker would ever have thought of proposing Nabis as a model, but Machiavelli can easily identify the element that interests him: the ability to promote policies that bring him popular favour, disregarding the tyrannical means by which he attained and defended his power (and met his violent end). This confirms that in Chapter 9, the stress falls more on the conduct than on the origin of this type of princely rule;[57] but in my opinion, that should not lead us to confuse the civil principality with the principality *tout court*. The markedly political profile of the *princeps* of Chapter 9, much more clearly defined than the casuistry prevailing up to that point, guides all his activity and determines his spaces of action. We should not be deceived by the similarity with the general figure of the 'new prince', of which this is a subspecies.[58] As for Nabis, he appears to illustrate the specific point about maintaining popular favour: the issue is not how he gained power but his attitude towards the common people.[59] At the same time, the genesis of the prince's power has its significance, because this, much more than the concrete exercise of government, is what characterizes the 'civiltà' of the principality and ultimately distinguishes it from tyranny: with its basis in political consensus and the absence of extreme violence, the civil principality is endowed with a legitimacy of origin.[60]

As we have seen, such a principality is, in practice, tilted in favour of the people, since it is the people who guarantee solidity to the consensus and present less of a political threat, merely aspiring to the negative freedom of 'not being commanded', unlike the *grandi*, who, as a class, tend to oppression. Hence, 'the prince who rules in the people's interest' is said to be 'civil in a strong sense'.[61] Both this prince and the other pro-aristocratic one express their innate bent in this way: that is what gives each of them his *reputazione*, makes him the leader or visible head but also, in a way, a representative. However, the two cannot command the same moral justification: the aristocratic prince seeks to 'vent [the] appetite' of the *grandi* ('sfogare il loro appetito'),[62] while the popular one resists and guards against illegitimate appetites: 'The popular desire is only for tranquillity and peace… while the aristocratic will is subversive.'[63] From this point of view, the people, the only entity in the *civitas* that speaks for the collective interest or common good, legitimately constitutes itself as the true body politic, while the interests of the aristocracy are illegitimate because they are partial or sectarian. The civil prince, representing the entire people by a kind of *mise en abime*, enshrines the constituent power of a new political identity. The *populus* is constituted by the exclusion of one part; the civil prince can be the whole and the part at the same time, incorporating all factions in a 'civil' *unicum*. He resolves all dichotomies by founding a new community whose members are 'citizens and subjects' at the same time and with the same rights.

* * *

Chapter 9 of *The Prince* thus highlights an exceptional situation, a *populist moment*, holding promise of a possible political stability through the peaceful prevalence of a part of the population coinciding with the *populus* or multitude. It is not fortuitous that this formulation, which I have presented in its most stripped-down theoretical substance, is unique to Machiavelli; neither, however, is it continued or developed in the rest of his writings.[64]

All this reveals a Machiavelli who pictures an ideal state, inevitably in line with the humanist search for an organic model of the polity, perpetually valid. It is no coincidence that the populist-minded *princeps* makes himself indispensable by merging with his people, creating and embodying an ideal political totality. He will gain the prize of a virtually perpetual, valid, and effective power, 'always and in every quality of time'.[65] But this body politic is no longer the harmonious, organic totality envisaged by the humanists. Its constitution takes off with a defensive exclusion of the part of the population that is less numerous but more powerful.[66] At the same time, as we have seen, the civil prince evinces certain traits of a tyrant—not precisely the tyrant of tradition, but sometimes recalling that figure in a disturbing way.[67]

From a doctrinal and, I would say, philosophical point of view, the relationship so sketched out between the prince and the people, and *a fortiori*, the way in which his pro-people identity is formed, can plausibly be seen as relating to the populist ideological spectrum. Of course, we must take into account the obvious variants between different historical phases, and the fact (by no means unimportant) that Machiavelli seems to lack a clear sense of dialectical tension between equivalence and difference. This is what makes the formulation of 'the people' so complex in populist theory, whereas in Machiavelli the people constitute a single block, a working hypothesis.[68] But his equally crucial sense of an actual social conflict adds to our conviction that populism, as the basic attitude of politicians, can reveal certain profound mechanisms of consensus and of the relationship between the head and the body, *caput* and *corpus*, in contrast to an organicist approach, beyond what a merely republican perspective allows.[69]

As we saw at the start, Machiavelli takes off from a position of unease and tension—a series of expectations, popular issues that are not resolved; on the contrary, a rapacious and corrupt elite threatens to assume definitive control. We may read this situation through Ernesto Laclau's lenses. For Laclau as for Machiavelli, the political spectrum has become 'dichotomised', a groove been created; the 'internal antagonistic frontier separating the people from power' and 'dividing society into two camps' has been reinforced in a disturbing way.[70] A popular demand is now created and articulated in a representative who makes the will of a group (however large a group—its size, I would say, is a *conditio sine qua non*) compatible with 'the interests of the entire community'. Given that 'the construction of a "people" would be impossible without the operation of mechanisms of representation', a leader must emerge—the *princeps*—who ensures that the 'defensive' aspirations of the people are articulated and consolidated in 'a stable system of signification',[71] creating, at the end of the process, a relationship of mutual dependence between the representative and the represented. Such a leader does not necessarily have to come from the popular ranks: significantly, Machiavelli speaks of 'one of them' for the powerful and just 'one' for the popular.[72] What matters is that the leader be 'made of the same psychic substance as his followers. He is a *primus inter pares*. He epitomizes the personality of the followers and gives them an image of power.'[73] Of course, his *pares* here are not just the other nobles but all citizens. Platonically, the civil *princeps* is the soul (*anima*) of the body politic, reflecting and reflected in each and every one: in Machiavelli's words, he 'with his spirit ['lo animo'] and his orders keeps the generality [or 'the whole corpus'] of people inspired ['animato']'.[74]

All this allows us to advance a coherent explanation for the *vexata quaestio* of the dangerous progress to an *absolute* princely rule: 'These principalities customarily run into peril when they are about to ascend from a civil order to an absolute one.'[75] However, the conceptual continuity of the chapter, always focused on the civil principality, is ensured at the linguistic level by the demonstrative adjective: *these* ('questi') principalities. The transition to absolutism is essentially a question of will: first and foremost, the subversive will of the *grandi*, who 'can take away [the prince's] state with great ease either by turning against him or by not obeying him',[76] but above all the will of the citizens or the people, who support the passage to absolutism as they had supported the rise of the civil prince in the first place: the *voluntas principis* is supported and fed by the *voluntas populi*. Hence, 'absolute' here cannot mean unlimited power—despotic, diametrically opposed to the 'civil';[77] it rather indicates, in a line of ascending continuity, the internal evolution of the civil principality towards a power that discards the previous political-legal apparatus (aristocratic, oligarchic, or any other) to base itself upon the dynamic consensus of the people, thereby generating a new political order. The *magistrati*, in a clearly defined chain of command, now become the direct embodiment of the princely power built up, in its earlier 'civil' phase, through a shrewd policy of mutual dependence: 'a way by which [the prince's] citizens, always and in every quality of time, have need of the state and of himself.'[78]

In my opinion, this is what affirms and gives structure to the expression 'voltare la reputazione' (extol the reputation), as applied to the people's crying up the prince they support: without this context it is not possible to understand the experimental sense of Machiavelli's bold theoretical proposal. And this, probably, is the point where the patent agonism of Machiavelli's political discourse, the sense of conflict, is tempered and resolved into an order, an agreement, a newfound political and social organicity, at least for a moment—the populist moment.

Notes

1. I do not intend to revisit a controversy which, as will shortly be seen, I believe can be resolved. I will limit myself to noting that, among those arguing for a 'weak' Machiavelli, Mario Martelli and Francesco Bausi are the most prominent: see, for example, the latter's *Machiavelli* (Rome: Salerno, 2005), esp. 181–93, and, on *Il Principe*, 194–225. Arguments of weight for the opposite case can be found in Giorgio Inglese, 'Per una discussione sulla "cultura di Machiavelli"', *La Cultura* 25 (1987), 378–87, and his 'Introduzione' to *Per Machiavelli* (Rome: Carocci, 2006).
2. I note that in the Preface to the Spanish translation of his *Machiavelli*, tr. Marcello Alberto Barbuto (Valencia: Universitat de València, 2015), Bausi himself is much more open to a balanced resolution of the controversy.
3. *Pr.*, 9:1, as in *Il Principe*, ed. Giorgio Inglese (Turin: Einaudi, 1995); tr. from *The Prince*, tr. Harvey C. Mansfield, 2nd edn (Chicago, IL: University of Chicago Press, 1998), 38. All citations are from this text (by chapter and sentence) and translation.
4. Extending his gaze from Florence to the general nature of the principality, Gabriele Pedullà carries out this task very well in the Introduction to his commentary on *Il Principe*, Cinquecentennale edition (Rome: Donzelli, 2013), LXXXIV–LXXXIX, and notes ad loc. Mario Martelli takes a more 'Florentine' perspective in 'Machiavelli e Firenze dalla repubblica al principato', in *Niccolò Machiavelli politico storico letterato*, ed. Jean-Jacques Marchand (Rome: Salerno, 1996), 15–31.
5. See R. Dainotto, 'Machiavellism and Anti-machiavellism: Strauss and Exceptionalism', in *Machiavelli Cinquecento. Mezzo millennio del* Principe, ed. Gian Mario Anselmi, Riccardo Caporali, and Carlo Galli (Milan: Mimesis, 2013), 111–19.
6. Bausi makes this point about the *Discourses*, which reveal 'rapid tumultuous drafting' as well as various internal contradictions (*Machiavelli*, 171, 175–6), though not always as striking and irreconcilable as the author suggests.
7. Allan H. Gilbert alerts us to this aspect in *Machiavelli's Prince and Its Forerunners* (Durham, NC: Duke University Press, 1938), 235.
8. Pedullà, 'Introduzione', l.
9. On this aspect, which concerns the 'style of thought' but with subtle legal resonances, see Diego Quaglioni, *Machiavelli e la lingua della giurisprudenza* (Bologna: Il Mulino, 2011), 71–2; Romain Descendre, 'La ligne brisée ou d'une écriture "extravagante" (*Le Prince*, chap. IX)', *Bruniana and Campanelliana* 20, no. 1 (2014), 35–46.
10. Pedullà (commentary, 107–8n7) draws attention to the treatment of this process in *Disc.* 1:37, 1:46.

'To Give Reputation to One' 135

11. See Giorgio Cadoni, 'Il Principe e il popolo', *La Cultura* 23, no. 1 (1985), 180–2, on *Disc.* 1:16–17, which describes, *inter alia*, the rise of a popular prince.
12. '[P]er poterle innanzi alla confermazione loro emendare': *Disc.* 1:40: *Tutte le opere*, ed. Mario Martelli (Florence: Sansoni, 1971), 123; tr. Christian E. Detmold in Machiavelli, *The Prince and the Discourses*, intr. Max Lerner (New York: Random House, 1950), 219. I feel that Marco Geuna, in his valuable analysis of the dictatorship, may not have taken sufficient account of this beginning; hence, he uncritically condemns the Decemvirate. See his 'Extraordinary Accidents in the Life of Republics: Machiavelli and Dictatorial Authority', in *Machiavelli on Liberty and Conflict*, ed. David Johnston, Nadia Urbinati, and Camila Vergara (Chicago, IL: University of Chicago Press, 2017), 280–308, 288.
13. The parallel is noted and taken to the extreme of identifying the civil prince with the tyrant, by Giovanni G. Balestrieri, 'La posizione del capitolo IX del "Principe" nel pensiero di Machiavelli', *Teoria politica* 24, no. 3 (2008), 69–88; but see Sasso's view in note 24.
14. See Paul Larivaille, 'Il capitolo IX del Principe e la crisi del "principato civile"', in *Cultura e scrittura di Machiavelli* (Rome: Salerno, 1998), 227–8.
15. '[S]i ascende … o con il favore del populo o con quello de' grandi': *Pr.*, 9:1; tr. Mansfield, 39.
16. See also *Disc.* 1:4; Gianluca Briguglia, *Il corpo vivente dello Stato: una metafora politica* (Milan: Mondadori, 2006), 88–100; note by Pedullà, commentary, ad loc. For the underlying Aristotelian inspiration, see Arisotle, *Politics* 5, 1307a; Gilbert, *Machiavelli's Prince*, 56.
17. 'Perché in ogni città si truovono questi dua umori diversi: e nasce, da questo, che il populo desidera non essere comandato né oppresso da' grandi ed e' grandi desiderano comandare e opprimere el populo; e da questi dua appetiti diversi nasce nelle città uno de' tre effetti: o principato o libertà o licenza': *Pr.*, 9:2; tr. Mansfield, 40.
18. Briguglia, *Il Corpo vivente*, 91.
19. Cicero, *Philippic* 13:6, 14.
20. Giovanni Pontano, *De Principe*, ed. Guido M. Cappelli (Rome: Salerno, 2003), 22. For the humanistic history of this expression, see Guido Cappelli, 'La otra cara del poder. Virtud y legitimidad en el Humanismo político', in *El poder y sus límites: Figuras del tirano*, ed. Guido Cappelli and Antonio Gómez Ramos (Madrid: Dykinson, 2008), 97–121, 108, 116.
21. Francesco Patrizi, *De regno et regis institutione* (Paris: Galeotus, 1531), 2:2, 252: '[P]otentia enim saepenumero homines proclives in libidinem, iniuriamque rapit. Vera prorsus Ciceronis sententia esse cernitur, cum ait

nihil principibus infoelicius esse, quam velle agere quaecunque possunt rursusque illos miseros omnino habendos esse censet, qui omnia sibi licere existimant.' The translation is my own. The quotation from Cicero is actually an amplification of Ammianus Marcellinus, *Rerum gestarum libri*, 26:10:12: 'imperator enim promptior ad nocendum, criminantibus patens et funereas delationes adsciscens, per supplitiorum diversitates effrenatius exultavit, sententiae illius Tullianae ignarus, docentis infelices esse eos qui omnia sibi licere existimarunt' ('For the emperor, the more eager to do injury, lent his ear to accusers, listened to death-dealing denunciations, and took unbridled joy in various kinds of executions, unmindful of that saying of Cicero's which asserts that those are unlucky who think that they have power to do everything they wish'). Ammianus, *History*, ed. and tr. J. C. Rolfe, Loeb Classical Library, vol. 2 (Cambridge, MA: Harvard University Press, 1940). The 'saying of Cicero' quoted by Ammianus does not appear in that exact form in Cicero's known works but resembles a passage in *Philippic* 13.

22. Descendre, 'La ligne brisée', 37–8. Descendre points out that the rise of the civil *princeps* was the legal norm in Rome, in accord with *iussum populi*. But while this might be historically the case, in Machiavelli's theorization it seems the outcome of a situation far from normal.

23. *Disc.* 1:18, *Tutte le opere* 104; tr. Detmold, 171.

24. Bausi's commentary on the *Discorsi* (Rome: Salerno, 2001, ad loc.) is very clear about the affinity of the *principato civile* with the *stato regio*. On the various nuances of the term *civile*, consider also Cadoni's appellation, 'an unfinished form of popular principality' ('Il Principe e il popolo', 153–4, 188). On the relationship between *Disc.* 1:16–18 and *The Prince*, Chapter 9, the decadence of the republics and adoption of an already 'princely' logic, see the stimulating observations in Gennaro Sasso, 'Principato civile e tirannide', in his *Machiavelli e gli antichi e altri saggi*, vol. 2 (Milan: Ricciardi, 1988), 399, although I cannot always share Sasso's hypercritical approach.

25. See Guido M. Cappelli, 'Conceptos transversales: República y monarquía en el Humanismo político', *Res publica: Revista de filosofía política* 21 (2009), 51–69.

26. I cite the *editio princeps* of *De obedientia* (Naples: Mattia Moravo, 1490). For other occurrences of *civilis*, see 'in omni re et familiari et civili' (fol.11v); 'in civili consuetudine' (fol.64r); 'civilis libertatis' (fol.65v); 'civiles res' (fol.81v); 'civilis observantia' (fol.82v, 86v); 'civilis institutionis' (fol.82v); 'civilem societatem' (fol.83r); 'civilem decorum' (fol.83v); 'aequabilitas ... per quam civilis societas stabilis manet' (fol.94r). On the expression 'vivere civile', see Romain Descendre, 'Qu'est-ce que la "vie civile"? Machiavel et le *vivere civile*', *Transalpina* 17 (2014), 21–9. In his commentary on *The Prince*, Pedullà offers a detailed history of the syntagma in scholasticism, law, and

the classics, and links (correctly in my opinion) the 'civilization' in question with 'a particular style of princely government formally respectful of the republican traditions'. For a precedent for this view, without specific reference to the form of government, see James Hankins, 'Modern Republicanism and the History of Republics', in *Nuovi maestri, antichi testi: Umanesimo e Rinascimento alle origini del pensiero moderno*, ed. Arturo Calzona, Stefano Caroti, and Vittoria Perrone Compagni (Florence: Olschki, 2010), 109–26, 123.

27. '[P]roprium est [*scil.* iustitiae] curare et cavere ne in creandis Magistratibus, conferendis honoribus, reddendis praemiis civilibusve muneribus ... aliquid plus minusve fiat quam quod aequum iustumque videatur': *De obedientia*, Book 1, fol.25v. The translations from *De obedientia* are my own.
28. *De obedientia*, Book 4, fol.60r.
29. '[C]ivilis obedientiae fundamentum in colendis magistratibus': *De obedientia*, Book 5, fol.82r.
30. '[D]efensor libertatis, propulsator iniuriarum atque animadversor ... legum lator et custos ac public privatimque moderator, pater, rector': *De obedientia*, Book 4, fol. 63v.
31. See Bausi, *Machiavelli*, 204, and his commentary on *Disc.* 1:18: 'Civilly... in keeping with a republican state.' In more nuanced vein, Rinaldi, in his commentary on Chapter 9, speaks of 'the support given by citizens to a *prince*, that is, the social legitimacy of a principality' and 'fundamental norms ... without distinction between republican and seigniorial regimes': Machiavelli, *Il Principe*, ed. Rinaldo Rinaldi (Turin: Utet, 2006), 206. See also Descendre, 'La ligne brisée', 36–8: 'in the Roman, imperial sources, the *princeps* does not behave as an absolute ruler; he obeys the law'. On this distinction, much more significant than that between monarchy and republic, see also Descendre, 'Qu'est-ce que la "vie civile"?', 7.
32. '[S]alire da lo ordine civile allo assoluto': *Pr.*, 9:23; tr. Mansfield, 42.
33. *Pr.*, 9:1.
34. '[L]i uomini hanno meno rispetto a offendere uno che si facci amare, che uno che si facci temere: perché lo amore è tenuto da uno vinculo di obligo, il quale, per essere gl'uomini tristi, da ogni occasione di propria utilità è rotto, ma il timore è tenuto da una paura di pena che non ti abbandona mai': *Pr.*, 17:11; tr. Mansfield, 66–7.
35. *Pr.*, 15:11; tr. Mansfield, 62.
36. *Pr.*, ch. 15. On this specific point, see James Hankins, 'Machiavelli, Civic Humanism, and the Humanist Politics of Virtue', *Italian Culture* 32, no. 2 (2014), 98–100.
37. Inglese, *Per Machiavelli*, 72.

38. '[A]stuzia fortunata': *Pr.*, 9:1; tr. Mansfield, 62.
39. On *prudentia*, see also Diogo Pires Aurelio, 'Razionale e irrazionale nella politica', in *Machiavelli Cinquecento*, 142.
40. '[D]ico come e' grandi si debbono considerare i dua modi principalmente: ... che si obligano in tutto alla tua fortuna, o no. Quegli che si obligano, e non sieno rapaci, si debbono onorare e amare. Quelli che non si obligano, si hanno a esaminare in dua modi: o e' fanno questo per pusillanimità e difetto naturale d'animo,—allora tu te ne debbi servire, massime di quelli che sono di buono consiglio ... [M]a quando e' non si obligano per arte e per cagione ambiziosa, ... da quelli si debbe el principe guardare, e temergli come se fussino scoperti inimici.' *Pr.*, 9:10–13; tr. Mansfield, 40.
41. 'Cum autem praeceptum omnem partim imperet partim vetet atque deterreat atque altero opera exigatur, cavere alterum et continere iubeat in illoque peccetur imperatum quod sit minime faciendo, in hoc contra imperium nitendo, prioris vitii non semper aperta voluntas sed tum negligentia tum ignavia causa esse solet; in posteriori late regnat nunc contumacia nunc improbitas et, quae vim obedientiae labefactat ut quasi demoliatur et evertat illam, temeritas': Pontano, *De obedientia*, fol.70r. For an initial investigation into the relationship between juridical thought and humanistic reflection, drawing on the Bartolian glossa and much more, see Guido Cappelli, *Maiestas: Politica e pensiero politico nella Napoli aragonese (1443–1503)* (Rome: Carocci, 2016).
42. '[F]arne e disfarne ogni dì e tòrre e dare a sua posta reputazione loro': *Pr.*, 9:9; tr. Mansfield, 40.
43. 'Debbe pertanto uno, che diventi principe mediante el favore del populo, mantenerselo amico: il che gli fia facile, non domandando lui se non di non essere oppresso. Ma uno che, contro al populo, diventi principe con il favore de' grandi, debbe innanzi a ogni altra cosa cercare di guadagnarsi el populo: il che gli fia facile, quando pigli la protezione sua': *Pr.*, 9:14–15; tr. Mansfield, 40.
44. '[C]erta regula ... si lasceranno indreto': *Pr.*, 9:17; tr. Mansfield, 40–1.
45. On the historical roots of this confusion, see James Hankins, 'Exclusivist Republicanism and the Non-Monarchical Republic', *Political Theory* 38, no. 4 (2010), 452–82; on the conceptual implications, see Cappelli, 'Conceptos transversales'.
46. See Bausi, *Machiavelli*, 205–6.
47. *Pr.*, 9:25; tr. Mansfield, 42. See Mario Martelli, *Saggio sul Principe* (Rome: Salerno, 1999), 87.
48. Cf. a remark in this vein regarding *Disc.* 1:26 in Sasso, 'Principato civile e tirannide', 460: 'on the ruins of the old state, a new "order" has been established ... a new objective structure, dependent on the prince.'

49. According to Carl Schmitt, *Der Begriff des Politischen* (Berlin: Akademie Verlag, 2003), 'republic' is a polemical term that acquires meaning only in a competitive context, and Machiavelli, in particular, 'calls a republic all that is *not* a monarchy' (emphasis added): cited from the Spanish tr. *El concepto de lo político* (Madrid: Alianza, 1998), 60.
50. '[N]on per sceleratezza o altra intollerabile violenzia, ma con il favore delli altri sua cittadini': *Pr.*, 9:1; tr. Mansfield, 38–9.
51. Aristotle, *Politics* 5, 1304b.
52. *Pr.*, 9:1; tr. Mansfield, 38–9.
53. Sasso, 'Principato civile e tirannide', 420*n*, has already suggested that, even at the genesis of the prince's power, some form of violence, limited to containing the *grandi*, was still predictable.
54. See, in particular, *Disc.* 1:25. See also Sasso, 'Principato civile e tirannide', 446–7.
55. See Jean-Louis Fournel and Jean-Claude Zancarini, 'Tirannide', in *Enciclopedia machiavelliana*, gen. ed. Gennaro Sasso (Rome: Treccani, 2014), 612–17, 612.
56. Fournel and Zancarini ('Tirannide', 613) notes that already in the 'formal' definition of tyranny in *Disc.* 1:25, 'the rather vague reference sounds as though at a potential distance from the doxa'. Martelli makes a similar observation in his commentary (Rome: Salerno, 2006), 168, but significantly, he attributes it to specific features of the Florentine political mentality and not to general or theoretical reasons. We should also keep in mind Roberto Esposito's perceptive remarks in 'La fondazione etica della politica', in his *Ordine e conflitto* (Naples: Liguori, 1980).
57. The distinction was highlighted for the first time in Sasso, 'Principato civile e tirannide', 358–9 and n. 5.
58. For this reason, I cannot accept Descendre's argument, though brilliantly argued, that for the greater part of Chapter 9, Machiavelli does not talk about its declared subject, the civil prince ('La ligne brisée', 39–40). Pedullà makes the same point ('Introduzione', LXXXVII). The logic of the text also makes it difficult for me to imagine such contradictions and aporiae in a treatise like *The Prince*. For other observations about the coherence of the chapter, see Martelli, *Saggio sul* Principe, 86 and note.
59. See Larivaille, 'Il cap. IX del *Principe*', 232–6; however, he adheres to the idea that the second part of the treatise treats of the principality in general.
60. Precisely for this reason, personalities such as Valentino, Nabis, or Sforza cannot be counted among the civil princes proper, as Descendre rightly notes, although they might serve as analogous examples ('La ligne brisée', 341). For the opposite view, see Sasso, 'Principato civile e tirannide', 361–4.

See also Inglese, *Per Machiavelli*, 66: 'The "civil" principality is characterized by the manner in which it is acquired.'
61. Sasso, *Niccolò Machiavelli: Storia del suo pensiero politico* (Bologna: Il Mulino, 1980), 349. See also Sasso, 'Principato civile e tirannide', 359–61 and *passim*; Fabio Frosini, 'L'aporia del "principato civile"', *Filosofia politica* 19, no. 2 (2005), 199–218: 201 and *passim*.
62. *Pr.*, 9:3; tr. Mansfield, 39.
63. Sasso, 'Principato civile e tirannide', 368.
64. Cadoni ('Il Principe e il popolo', 196) shows indeed how, in a text like *Discursus florentinarum rerum*, Machiavelli seems to take the opposite path. For the same reason, while I agree with Sasso about the prevalence, for Machiavelli, of the 'popular' civil principality, I do not agree with the idea that *Il Principe* advances only 'a theory … of the civil principality' (Sasso, *Niccolò Machiavelli*, 353; see also Sasso, 'Principato civile e tirannide'). On the contrary, Machiavelli seems to draw his idea from the exceptional case as encountered in reality, uncommon and partly dependent on fortune. See also Frosini, 'L'aporia del principato civile', 201.
65. '[S]empre e in ogni qualità di tempo': *Pr.*, 9:27; tr. Mansfield, 39.
66. Laclau explains the mechanism of this transformation: 'We also know that such an abyss can only be hegemonically mediated, through a particularity which, at some point, assumes the representation of a totality which is incommensurable with it': Ernesto Laclau, *On Populist Reason*, new edn (London: Verso, 2015 [1985]), 170.
67. On this relation, see Eugenio Di Rienzo, 'Dal principato civile alla tirannide: Il "Neronis encomium" di Gerolamo Cardano', *Studi storici* 28, no. 1 (1987), 157–82.
68. On this point, see Laclau, *On Populist Reason*, 77. In any case (let it be said softly and in passing), it seems that today, the abstract division of society into only two opposing blocs, 99 per cent 'people' against 1 per cent of the privileged and powerful, has returned with greater crudeness. See, however, Frosini, 'L'aporia del principato civile', 203: 'the conjunction of the points of view of the prince and of the state takes place precisely in the people, or rather in the prince/popular relationship under the sign of freedom … The people are bearers of a universality that coincides with its irreplaceability.'
69. See James Hankins, 'Leonardo Bruni and Machiavelli on the Lessons of Florentine History', in *Le cronache vulgari in Italia*, ed. Giampaolo Francesconi and Massimo Miglio (Rome: Isime, 2017), 373–95, 383.
70. Laclau, *On Populist Reason*, 74, 77.

71. Ibid., 74.
72. See Larivaille, 'Il capitolo IX', 230.
73. José Luis Villacañas, *Populismo* (Madrid: La Huerta Grande, 2017), ch. 12.
74. '[T]enga con lo animo e ordini suoi animato l'universale': *Pr.*, 9:22; tr. Mansfield, 41. I do not think this *animo* is 'courage', as Carmine Donzelli translates it (see Pedullà, commentary; Martelli, exegesis, ad loc.). Rinaldi's phrase 'favourable disposition' (ed. *Il Principe*, commentary, ad loc.) seems to me a little too broad. But cf. the same author's 'Comunione e obbligazione. Per un profilo del consenso nel Principe', in *Machiavelli Cinquecento*, 209, where he writes of the 'mobilization of the people's friendship'. Inglese's interpretation 'to prevent the people from losing heart' appears to me to be reductive. I believe that the etymological play on *animo* and *animato* (*anima*, soul) is intentional, aimed at emphasizing the animating (*lex animata*) and life-giving function proper to the popular prince and inherent in the two terms.
75. 'Sogliono questi principati periclitare, quando sono per salire da lo ordine civile allo assoluto': *Pr.*, 9:23; tr. Mansfield, 41–2.
76. '[G]li possono tòrre con facilità grande lo stato, o con abbandonarlo o con fargli contro': *Pr.*, 9:24; tr. Mansfield, 42. The Bartolian scheme of the *duae habenae* comes into play again. It is very significant that instead of 'abbandonarlo', some manuscripts read 'non lo obedire' ('not obeying him').
77. The juridical tradition of the late Middle Ages was well aware of the limitations to a sovereign's freedom of action. The lesson would not have been lost on Machiavelli. See Diego Quaglioni, 'I limiti del "princeps legibus solutus" nel pensiero giuridico-politico della prima età moderna', in *Giustizia, potere e corpo sociale*, ed. Angela De Benedictis and Ivo Mattozzi (Bologna: Clueb, 1994), 56–71.
78. '[U]no modo per il quale e' sua cittadini, sempre e in ogni qualità di tempo, abbino bisogno dello stato e di lui': *Pr.*, 9:27; tr. Mansfield, 42. Although made from a different perspective, Pedullà's remark in his commentary (ad loc.) is significant in this context: 'For Machiavelli, the other powers are good as a direct emanation of central power or as its mask.' Cadoni ('Il Principe e il popolo', 154) draws attention to a phrase in *Pr.*, ch. 4, about the Turkish system of governance through administrators that the lord 'replaces and changes as he sees fit' ('muta e varia come pare a lui'). From our 'populist' perspective, this is possible and does not end in tyranny precisely because of the popular consensus previously obtained and subsequently maintained.

History

8

Riscontro

Machiavelli's Art of History

Francesco Marchesi

John Pocock, at the beginning of his masterpiece *The Machiavellian Moment*, claimed that

> a vital component of republican theory—and, once this had come upon the scene, if no earlier, of all political theory—consisted of ideas about time, about the occurrence of contingent events of which time was the dimension, and about the intelligibility of the sequences (it is as yet too soon to say processes) of particular happenings that made up what we should call history.[1]

An analogous caution is common among interpreters of Machiavelli's work: history, in the writings of the Florentine Secretary, is in turn an application of the knowledge of the ancients, offering a perspective on current political issues; an inventory of examples and experiences from the past;[2] and the mere practice of something analogous to chronicling.[3]

My starting point and main hypothesis is that in Machiavelli's thought, history plays a crucial role in a distinctive way. To explain in detail, history is not only a *theme*, the subject of erudite philological study with material applications, but also an *object* that needs structural analysis to define its topological role and its internal, constitutive oppositions. My hypothesis is that the keynote of Machiavelli's historical knowledge is the notion of *riscontro*, as expounded in the seminal text of the *Ghiribizzi al Soderino*, a letter of 1506 to Giovan Battista Soderini. The *riscontro*, which is elaborated for the first time in the *Ghiribizzi* and which keeps returning through the entire Machiavellian corpus, is the encounter between a form of political action, a *modo del procedere* in Machiavelli's language, and a specific historical conjuncture, the *qualità dei tempi*. This Machiavellian construct of a historical event articulates—that is to say, both separates and connects—the two factors in a diachronic sequence and allows us to identify the causes of political change.

In this chapter, I will try to substantiate my hypothesis through a philological and theoretical analysis of Machiavelli's first conceptualization of this notion, in the *Ghiribizzi al Soderino*. My analysis will be articulated in three sections, corresponding to the three figures that the structural opposition between political concepts and principles on the one hand and the events of the times on the other can assume. In the first section, I will describe the first (and apparently only) meaning of *riscontro* as a deterministic relationship governed by fortune. In the second section, I will try to illustrate a prudential form of this relationship as an *adaequatio*, establishing parity or accordance between a particular action and the general state of the times. In the third section, I will develop what Charles Singleton has called the perspective of art: that is, seeing the encounter as a *forcing* of the conjuncture by political action. In this way, I will try to demonstrate that *riscontro* is neither just a literary image nor exclusively a political concept but the chief foundation of Machiavelli's theory of history.

Political Practice, Conjuncture, Determinism

The history of the *Ghiribizzi scritti in Perugia al Soderino* has created controversies for four decades. Even if the philological debate seems to have ended, the theoretical significance of the document is still an open issue, owing to recent innovative readings.

Until 1969, the *Ghiribizzi* was interpreted as a communication to Pier Soderini, Gonfaloniere of the Florentine republic until 1512 and Machiavelli's political godfather; it was sent in 1512–13 during Soderini's Dalmatian exile. Its historical context was redefined after Jean-Jacques Marchand found the manuscript in the Vatican Library.[4] The discovery induced scholars to date it earlier, to September 1506, and to attribute the discussion of the Pope's political action to the conquest of Perugia by Pope Julius II, where Machiavelli was present as a Florentine emissary.

The *Ghiribizzi* is an answer to a letter by Giovan Battista Soderini, nephew of Piero,[5] written in a highly symbolic style. It starts by conceptualizing the problem treated in the entire text, the apparent irrelevance of the form of a political action to its outcomes:

> [S]teering along a variety of routes can bring about the same thing and that acting in different ways can bring about the same end—whatever this conviction may have lacked has been filled in by this pope's actions and their outcomes.[6]

Machiavelli expresses here for the first time[7] his feelings about the situation in Perugia, of which he had written in broad terms in a diplomatic letter to the Dieci di Balia, an extraordinary magistracy of the Florentine republic set up in 1384 to deal with foreign policy and the defence of the city.[8] Pope Julius II seized control of the city through a dangerous operation, an impetuous act carried out with the support of his Swiss guards, without a home army of his own (*armi proprie*). The success of this audacious action contrasts with the cautious approach and respect for circumstances evinced by Pier Soderini, probably the unnamed but true addressee of the letter. Yet both practices achieve good results—the former as a single event, the latter as a sustained course of political conduct: the historical experience seems incapable of suggesting which is the better form of action. Nonetheless, the author's *maraviglia* is not simple astonishment at this impasse but a kind of theoretical dissatisfaction: Machiavelli is looking for a criterion that can help to determine a general method of political, military, and diplomatic activity.

Within this framework, as commonly in Machiavelli's style of discourse, there is set an example from Roman history that allows us to better scrutinize the abstract question, in a typical dialectical relationship between 'long experience with modern things and a continuous reading of ancient ones' ('una lunga esperienzia delle cose moderne e una continua lezione delle antique').[9] The comparison between Hannibal and Scipio, starting from this text, will be one of the main Machiavellian paradigms for discussing contrasting forms of political action:

> Take Hannibal and Scipio: in addition to their military training, in which they were equally preeminent, the former kept his armies in Italy united through cruelty, treachery, and impiety and made himself admired by the populace, who, in order to follow him, rebelled against the Romans; the latter achieved the identical result among the populace in Spain with compassion, loyalty, and piety: both achieved victory upon victory.[10]

The opposed conduct of Hannibal and Scipio underlines the problem once again: in the history of ancient Rome,[11] as of modern Italy, different modes lead not to different but to similar results.

If the first theoretical strategy, the comparison between ancients and moderns, could not resolve the question, the second tries to do so through a return to strictly modern times:

> This pope, who has no scales or measuring stick in his house, obtains through chance—and disarmed—what ought to be difficult to attain even with organization and with weapons. We have seen, and continue to see, in all the examples mentioned above—and in countless other examples that could be brought in as evidence in analogous instances—that kingdoms are conquered,

or are subdued, or have fallen, as unforeseen events would have it. Sometimes the way of doing things that was praised when it led to conquest is vilified when it leads to defeat, and sometimes when defeat comes after long prosperity, people do not blame anything of their own but rather indict heaven and the will of the Fates.[12]

The key to Machiavelli's explanation is now the placing of various forms of political action ('modi di procedere') in a relational and polarized framework where the other point of reference is the quality or state of the times ('qualità dei tempi'). We see here for the first time the image of *riscontro*: the *tempi* proceed along the vertical or temporal line of history, but the forms of political action can be various, in a kind of horizontal or geographical pluralism—that is to say, during the same period of time, they can vary owing to the multiplicity of human nature. If, at a given moment, the nature of a single man or of a specific form of action agrees with the quality of the times, the result will be positive and the encounter (*riscontro*) happy ('felice'). But if their nature does not accord with the times, the *riscontro* will be unhappy. This theoretical structure explains why different types of conduct, both audacious and cautious, can obtain the same degree of success or defeat in their encounter with circumstances, rendering them either favourable or adverse. Thus, Machiavelli's main philosophical achievement in this text is to generalize the singularity of the experience by relativizing its universality.

> And, on the other hand, because times change and the pattern of events differs, one man's hopes may turn out as he prayed they would. The man who matches his way of doing things with the conditions of the times is successful; the man whose actions are at odds with the times and the pattern of events is unsuccessful. Hence, it can well be that two men can achieve the same goal by acting differently: because each one of them matches his actions to what he encounters and because there are as many patterns of events as there are regions and governments.[13]

As Machiavelli proceeds to explain, in this hidden structure of the *riscontro*, the human players appear to be static owing to their specific and localized nature, in contrast to the times that are perpetually moving. Hence, this framework is strictly deterministic: fortune alone determines whether a single man or a single form of action can or cannot agree with the historical conjuncture.

However, Machiavelli now proceeds to consider a further question: whether people can modify their natures with respect to the changing times, in order to control the course of fortune. Only by changing one's nature can one attune one's conduct to the transformations of history. Machiavelli's thought now embraces the full dimensions of the encounter between the two poles of the *riscontro* and the possibility of bridging them: on the one hand, the context of historical conjuncture and on the other, the forms of human action.

> But because times and affairs often change—both in general and in particular—and because men change neither their imaginations nor their ways of doing things accordingly, it turns out that a man has good fortune at one time and bad fortune at another. *And truly, anyone wise enough to adapt to and understand the times and the pattern of events* would always have good fortune or would always keep himself from bad fortune; and *it would come to be true that the wise man could control the stars and the Fates*. (Emphasis mine)[14]

But Machiavelli at once negates this happy possibility—that men can change their nature—by citing the irremediable shortcomings of the human state:

> But such wise men do not exist: *in the first place, men are shortsighted*; in the second place, they are unable to master their own natures; thus it follows that Fortune is fickle, controlling men and keeping them under her yoke. (Emphasis mine)[15]

Adaequatio and Prudence

Thus, the *Ghiribizzi* seems to affirm a purely deterministic view of history, guided by a theory of encounter between human action and the state of the times radically overdetermined by the caprices of fortune. However, as Eugenio Garin observes, the words 'che 'l savio comandassi alle stelle et a' fati' ('could control the stars and the Fates') can be seen as questioning this conclusion. They paraphrase a famous motto attributed to Ptolemy, 'sapiens dominabitur astris', alluding to astrological divination and prophecy.[16] This passage seems to indicate the influence on Machiavelli's thought of the widespread astrological debate of the Renaissance which questioned the immutability of both the cosmos and human action. Not only is the structural asymmetry between human action and historical change admitted but even the possibility of variations in human nature within a single conjuncture: if the wise man (*sapiens*) can respond to variations in the quality of the times by modifying his conduct accordingly, his encounter with the times can always attain to good fortune. But that is only a hypothesis in the Machiavellian discourse, immediately negated by the idea that because humans have only a limited vision, they cannot command fate. The tyranny of Fortune is reasserted: the polar opposition of the *riscontro* weighs much more heavily in favour of the times compared to the role of action. Even the hypothesis of *adaequatio* is thus denied.[17]

However, the theoretical relevance of the text does not end here. The philological debate about the *Ghiribizzi* in the Italy of the 1970s also admits a different point of view. In his letter to Machiavelli of 12 September 1506, preceding the *Ghiribizzi*, Giovan Battista Soderini talks about another letter, 'la inclusa', which some interpret to mean an actual second letter 'included' in the first[18] and perhaps written by Pier Soderini. Gennaro Sasso argues that Machiavelli's reply is certainly directed to the first, known, letter, but the context, as well as allusions in the document itself, permits us to infer a hidden communication (whether or not material to the issue) between Machiavelli and Pier Soderini.[19] Clearly, the problem is not merely philological: the final reference to Soderini's prudence, his typical mode of action, admits the hypothesis that there is scope for the exercise of human prudence, allowing the *adaequatio* of human political action or strategy with the external situation of the times.

Philology and textual interpretation prove relevant tools once again. First of all, Machiavelli writes at one point to Giovan Battista Soderini that the latter's claim that the letter is camouflaged ('in pappafico') is easily comprehended by the Secretary as implying a message from the hidden handler, Pier Soderini. But more importantly, as Ridolfi and Sasso have observed, the metaphor of navigation at the heart of the text is probably an allusion to the brilliant career of the senior Soderini, the Gonfaloniere: it cannot possibly apply to the nephew.

> I know you and the compass of your navigation; even if it could be blamed, which it cannot be, I should not, since I see what ports it has guided you to and what hopes it may foster in you. (Hence I think not according to your perspective, wherein nothing but prudence is visible, but to the perspective of the many, which must see the ends, not the means, of things.)[20]

The navigation metaphor replaces the cancelled words 'di che gradi vi habbi onorato' in the manuscript draft. Here 'gradi' (ranks, stages) is probably an image for goals as well as offices. So, while the addressee is Giovan Battista, the hidden interlocutor appears to be Piero, and the object is the prudential political action of the latter.[21]

Other parts of the text emerge as crucial from this perspective. The dichotomy between an action conducted step by step ('scaglione a scaglione'), a reference to Soderini, and another effected audaciously and instantaneously, in a burst ('lo scoppio') or a flash ('il baleno'),[22] becomes an image of the opposition between *adaequatio* and transformation, Soderini's model and Machiavelli's. Moreover, and not least, it may seem to allude to Giampaolo Baglioni, the lord of Perugia, whose cowardice could not resist the bold but inadequately armed venture of Pope Giulio II.

Other aspects of the context are also brought to light: for example, tracing the link with the astrological debates of the day, as indicated by Garin,[23] a letter to Machiavelli of 4 June 1504 from Bartolomeo Vespucci, the young Paduan cosmographer and nephew of Amerigo Vespucci. The letter is the reply to a lost missive from the Florentine Secretary:

> It is enough that your opinion proves itself most true with respect to the belief that (as you agree) was held by the ancients, *that the wise man has the power to alter the influence of the stars. In fact, such a man proceeds not with reference to the stars, since nothing mutable can intervene in what is eternal, but guided by his own wisdom, who, as he passes from one experience to another, can change and transform himself.* (Emphasis mine)[24]

If Vespucci's report is reliable, Machiavelli's position in 1504, only two years before the *Ghiribizzi*, could be summed up as follows: the wise man can move from one experience to another, changing himself in the process; his nature is not eternal like the celestial motions to which he is committed. That is to say, the uniformity of the cosmos does not extend to human nature, which can change according to the times and potentially generate a happy encounter with the historical conjuncture. Considerations negated in the immediate context of the work can thereby re-emerge to redefine a perspective of human agency, similar to that of Pico della Mirandola, even though the wise man is still completely involved in the immutability of nature and the cosmos. In this model of political action as prudence, the operative principle is not the transformation of the times but the possibility of an *adaequatio* between external and human forces.

Forcing the Times and the Art of History

This enquiry into the multiple meanings of *riscontro* does not end with the dichotomy between determinism and an autonomous human prudence, the unilateral operation of fortune and an exercise in *adaequatio*. The signification of this figure seems to include a third option, forcing (*sforzare*) of the historical conjuncture, which is more than a variation of the option of adaptation through *adaequatio*. On the contrary, forcing the times is the opposite process to adapting to the times, a contrasting investment in the historical context. It does not simply exercise either respect or audacity vis-à-vis the historical conjuncture but attempts to influence the times by political action.

The notion of forcing the times is developed by Machiavelli in a specific locus of the *Ghiribizzi*, the marginalia. As a general practice, he uses marginal glosses to note down some idea for future research. Hence, the glosses stake out a path along which Machiavelli's work can progress. These are some of the notes:

- In fine, advise no one and accept advice from no one, except for a general suggestion that each man must do what his mind prompts him to—and do it with daring.[25]
- To try Fortune, who is the friend of youth, and to change according to the times.[26]
- When Fortune slacks off it follows that a man, a family, and a city crumble. Each person's fortune is based upon his way of doing things, and each person's fortune slacks off; when it is slack, it must be regained by some other means.[27]

Gennaro Sasso notes the divergence between the logic of *adaequatio* and the image of trying your luck; but as presented by Machiavelli in the *Ghiribizzi*, trying your luck is not the same as changing according to the times. The audacious man can always try his luck; his success depends not on the audacity itself but on its conformity to the quality of the times. Changing according to the times, on the contrary, does not mean trying one's luck on one's own terms, audaciously and impetuously, but instead to alternate between prudence and impetuousity, impetuousity and prudence, as dictated by the times. These are two different formulas: the former indeed an intrinsic form of the latter but one of many such forms.[28]

Sasso illustrates the difference between the hypotheses implicit in the marginalia and in Machiavelli's position as reported in Vespucci's letter of 1504: a divergence that nonetheless manifests a common opposition to the determinism prevailing at the surface of the text. It is probably for this reason that prudent action and forcing of the times are often confused. But Sasso's description lacks theoretical accuracy: in the marginalia, audacious action is not merely an either/or selection between the prudent and the impetuous, between moderation and fury. The marginalia appears to offer a much more substantial modification of the concept of *riscontro*, because forcing is not a variant of *adaequatio*. It points to a new mode of encounter between human action and the given state of the times, based on the very fact that the two do not match. This leads to an accumulation of hypotheses and suggestions typical of a conceptual laboratory like the *Ghiribizzi*.

Obviously, the theoretical context of the *Ghiribizzi* does not permit the exclusive possibility of either *adaequatio* or forcing. But hints of these strategies return in Machiavelli's major texts, *adaequatio* in the *Discourses on Livy* and forcing of the times in the *Florentine Histories*.[29] In 1506, Machiavelli's point of view is still mainly naturalistic; hence, the spectrum of meanings of *riscontro* is limited to the deterministic tyranny of fortune. This limitation is overcome by the culturalist approach of the mature texts. The administrative experience of the Cancellario, the study of ancient modes and orders, and continuing reflection on the history of Florence all serve to reactivate the potency of both concepts, of *adaequatio* and forcing of the times. The *Ghiribizzi* thus appears as an open text that leads us beyond its own limits.

Moreover, the basic structure of the *riscontro* as a category of historical knowledge—that is, a notion of the historical event as connecting two established orders in diachronic sequence—resounds with the Machiavellian hapax of the 'art of the state' ('l'arte dello stato').[30] As Carlo Ginzburg notes, the articulation of the figures of *adaequatio* and forcing illustrates a little-known feature of the relationship between Machiavelli's thought and that of Aristotle and Aquinas.[31] Ginzburg locates this link in the prudential signification of the terms *art* and *virtue*. As Charles Singleton (cited by Ginzburg) has underlined, the philosophical meaning of art, as detailed here, allows us to separate the theoretical fields of prudence and forcing. Art, in the Aristotelian sense, implies a non-conformity between the intent of the action and its result. Hence, displacing political action from the field of prudence to that of art has a number of relevant consequences:

> Prudence and Art, then, are both concerned with practical matters and both with a good. Prudence—and, as we see, political action—with the good of the agent, first of all: *bonum operantis*; and art with the good of that which is made: *bonum operis* …
>
> [T]he perspective of art [implies] a mode of action conceived as being in the order of making because passing into external matter; and consequently viewed has having its end and its good in that external goal; a mode of action, in short, that is extra-moral, amoral, and is recognized as such in the philosophy of a medieval Christian theologian …
>
> Machiavelli [follows] the way of *making*, where *virtù* is consequently the power essentially to make, to impress a form upon matter, durably—or as durably as possible. *Virtù* is the power of the sculptor, of the forger.[32]

To impress a form upon matter is the fundamental function of art. But if we accept Singleton's reading—as also Ginzburg's, connecting this premise to the reflections in the *Ghiribizzi*—Machiavelli is displacing political action from the sphere of prudence to that of art.

What are the consequences for the theory of *riscontro* as an encounter between action, *i modi di procedere*, and the times, *la qualità dei tempi*? How, in other words, does the structure change owing to a variation in one of its internal poles?

The conclusion to be inferred from Singleton's arguments is an increasing centrality of the figure of forcing the times—the *perspective of art*, as Singleton calls it. If Machiavellian political action is chiefly making (*poiesis*, production or art) rather than acting (*praxis*, practice), such action will be external to whatever might be determined by precedent conditioning: the latter cannot affect the outcome. To assume the centrality of Machiavellian action as art, production and *poiesis* imply the move towards a theory of *riscontro* as a forcing of the times, by an activity that is not influenced by the context of origin.

Finally, the gradual emergence of an art-oriented perspective in Machiavelli's thought leads to a relatively autonomous nexus—as conceived, for example, by Louis Althusser[33]—between political action and historical conjuncture: a correlation whose presence is perhaps now clearer in the context of the *Ghiribizzi*.[34] This can be viewed as one of the alternative versions of the theory of *riscontro*, a substantial presence alongside the 'perspective of prudence' derived from Aristotle and Aquinas, sources well-known to Machiavelli, which foster a deterministic theory of *adaequatio* assuming the uniformity of human nature.

To conclude, then, the text of the *Ghiribizzi* is more rich than its deterministic surface suggests. In its denials and its marginal implications, it prefigures the main lines of Machiavelli's thought as a whole, especially his thoughts on history in relation to politics,[35] which he proceeds to explore through his entire intellectual life. The *Ghiribizzi* points at one of the main features of Machiavelli's thought: the elaboration, through the notion of *riscontro*, of an art of history, the essential correlative of an *arte dello stato*.

Notes

1. J. G. A. Pocock, *The Machiavellian Moment: Florentine Political Thought and the Atlantic Republican Tradition* (Princeton, NJ: Princeton University Press, 1975), 3.
2. See Francesco Marchesi, 'Pratica e uso della storia in Niccolò Machiavelli', in *Issues of Interpretation. Texts, Images, Rites*, ed. Carlo Altini, Philippe Hoffman, and Jörg Rupke (Stuttgart: Franz Steiner, 2018), 119–30.

3. See Franco Gaeta, 'Machiavelli storico', in *Machiavelli nel V° centenario della nascita*, ed. Raymond Aron (Bologna: Massimiliano Boni, 1972), 139–53; Carlo Dionisotti, 'Machiavelli storico', in *Machiavellerie* (Turin: Einaudi, 1980), 365–6; Gian Mario Anselmi, *Ricerche sul Machiavelli storico* (Pisa: Pacini, 1979); Felix Gilbert, 'Machiavelli's Istorie Fiorentine: An Essay in Interpretation', in *Studies on Machiavelli*, ed. Myrone P. Gilmore (Florence: Sansoni, 1972), 75–99; Felix Gilbert and Carlo Dionisotti, 'Le Istorie Fiorentine. Discussione', *Rivista storica italiana* 86, no. 4 (1974), 720–3.
4. MS. Vat. Capp. 107, 219r–220v: see *La bibliofilia* 71 (1969), 247–8.
5. See Andrea Guidi, *Un segretario militante: politica diplomazia e armi nel cancelliere Machiavelli* (Bologna: Il Mulino, 2009); Andrea Guidi, 'Esperienza e qualità dei tempi nel linguaggio cancelleresco di Machiavelli', *Laboratoire italien* 9 (2009), 233–72; Andrea Guidi, 'L'esperienza cancelleresca nella formazione politica di Niccolò Machiavelli', *Il Pensiero politico* 38, no. 1 (2005), 3–23; Robert Black, 'Florentine Political Traditions and Machiavelli's Election to the Chancery', *Italian Studies* 40, no. 1 (1985), 1–16; Robert Black, 'Machiavelli Servant of the Florentine Republic', in *Machiavelli and Republicanism*, ed. Gisela Bock, Quentin Skinner, and Maurizio Viroli (Cambridge: Cambridge University Press, 1990), 71–99; John M. Najemy, 'The Controversy Surrounding Machiavelli's Service to the Republic', in *Machiavelli and Republicanism*, 101–17.
6. '[V]edendosi con varii governi conseguire una medesima cosa et diversamente operando avere uno medesimo fine; e quello che mancava a questa opinione, le azioni di questo pontefice e li effetti loro vi hanno aggiunto': Machiavelli, *Opere*, ed. Corrado Vivanti (Turin: Einaudi, 1997–2005), vol. 2 (*Lettere; legazione e commissarie*), 135–6. All citations of *Ghiribizzi* are from this edition (henceforth *Lettere*); tr. J. B. Atkinson and David Sices in *Machiavelli and His Friends: Their Personal Correspondence* (DeKalb, IL: Northern Illinois University Press, 1996), 134–6. All translations of the *Ghiribizzi* are from this version.
7. For later expressions, see *Pr.*, ch. 25, *Edizione nazionale delle opere* (Rome: Salerno, 2001), 306: 'Di qui nasce quello ho ditto, che dua, diversamente operando, sortiscano el medesimo effetto, e dua, egualmente operando, l'uno si conduce al suo fine e l'altro no' ('From this follows what I said, that two persons working differently come out with the same effect; and of two persons working identically, one is led to his end, the other not': tr. Machiavelli, *The Prince*, tr. Harvey C. Mansfield, 2nd edn [Chicago, IL: University of Chicago Press, 1988], 99–100); and *Pr.*, ch. 25, *Ed. naz.* 307: 'Papa Iulio II procedé in ogni cosa impetuosamente, e trovò tanto e' tempi e le cose conforme a quello suo modo di procedere, che sempre sortì

felice fine' ('Pope Julius II proceeded impetuously in all his affairs, and he found the times and affairs so much in conformity with his mode of proceeding that he always achieved a happy end': tr. Mansfield, 100). See also the account of Cesare Borgia's Perugia expedition in *Disc.* 1:27. All references to the Italian texts of the principal works of Machiavelli are to the above edition (henceforth *Ed. naz.*). All translations of *The Prince* are from Mansfield.

8. See letters of 12, 13, 14, 15, 16, 19 and 21 September 1506.
9. *Pr.*, dedicatory letter, tr. Mansfield, 3.
10. 'Annibale et Scipione, oltre alla disciplina militare, che nell'uno e nell'altro eccelleva equalmente, l'uno con la crudeltà, perfidia, irreligione mantenne e suoi eserciti uniti in Italia, e fecesi admirare da popoli, che per seguirlo si ribellavano da e romani; l'altro con la pietà, fedeltà e religione, in Spagna ebbe da quelli popoli el medesimo seeguito; e l'uno et l'altro ebbe infinite vittorie': *Lettere* 136.
11. The example is discussed, with considerable differences of treatment, in *Pr.*, ch. 17, *Ed. naz.* 231–3, and *Disc.* 3: 21, *Ed. naz.* 667–8.
12. 'Questo papa, che non ha né stadera né canna in casa, a caso conseguita, e disarmato, quello che con l'ordine e con l'armi difficilmente li doveva riuscire. Sonsi veduti o veggonsi tutti e soprascripti, et infiniti altri che in simili materia si potrebbono allegare, acquistare regni o domarli o cascarne secondo li accidenti; et alle volte quello modo del procedere che acquistando era laudato, perdendo è vituperato et alle volte dopo una lunga prosperità, perdendo, non se ne incolpa cosa alcuna propria, ma se ne accusa el cielo e la disposizione de' fati': *Lettere* 137.
13. 'E perché da l'altro canto e tempi sono varii et li ordini delle cose sono diversi, a colui succedono *ad votum* e suoi desiderii, e quello è felice che riscontra el modo del procedere suo con el tempo, e quello, per opposito, è infelice che si diversifica con le sua azioni da el tempo e da l'ordine delle cose. Donde può molto bene essere che dua, diversamente operando, abbino uno medesimo fine, perché ciascuno di loro può conformarsi con el riscontro suo, perché e' sono tanti ordini di cose quanti sono province e stati': ibid. See also *Pr.*, ch. 25, *Ed. naz.* 305: '[C]redo ancora che sia felice quello che riscontra el modo del procedere suo con la qualità de' tempi, e similmente sia infelice quello che con il procedere suo si discordano e' tempi' ('I believe, further, that he is happy who adapts his mode of proceeding to the qualities of the times; and similarly, he is unhappy whose procedure is in disaccord with the times': tr. Mansfield, 99). See also *Disc.* 3:8, *Ed. naz.* 604: 'E coloro che, per cattiva elezione o per naturale inclinazione si discordono dai tempi, vivono il più delle volte infelici, ed hanno cattivo esito le azioni

loro; al contrario lo hanno quegli che si concordano col tempo' ('And those who, from an evil choice or from natural inclination, do not conform to the times in which they live, will in most instances live unhappily, and their undertakings will come to a bad end; whilst, on the contrary, success attends those who conform to the times': tr. Christian E. Detmold in Machiavelli, *The Prince and the Discourses* [New York: Random House, 1950], 439); and *Disc.* 3:9, *Ed. naz.* 607–8: 'Io ho considerato più volte come la cagione della trista e della buona fortuna degli uomini è riscontrare il modo del procedere suo con i tempi. Perché e' si vede che gli uomini nelle opere loro procedono, alcuni con impeto, alcuni con rispetto e con cauzione; e perché nell'uno e nell'altro di questi modi si passano e' termini convenienti, non si potendo osservare la vera via, nell'uno e nell'altro si erra. Ma quello viene ad errare meno e avere la fortuna prospera, che si riscontra—come ho detto—con il suo modo il tempo: e sempre mai si procede secondo ti sforza la natura' ('I have often reflected that the causes of the success or failure of men depend upon their manner of suiting their conduct to the times. We see one man proceed in his actions with passion and impetuosity; and as in both the one and the other case men are apt to exceed the proper limits, not being able always to observe the just middle course, they are apt to err in both. But he errs least and will be most favored by fortune whos suits his proceedings to the times, as I have said above, and always follows the impulses of his nature': tr. Detmold, 441).

14. '[M]a perché e tempi e le cose universalmente et particularmente si mutano spesso, e li uomini non mutono le loro fantasie né e loro modi di procedere, accade che uno ha un tempo buona fortuna et uno tempo trista. *E veramente chi fussi tanto savio, che conoscessi e' tempi et l'ordine delle cose e accomodassisi ad quelle*, arebbe sempre buona fortuna o e' si guarderebbe sempre da la trista, *et verrebbe ad essere vero che 'l savio comandassi alle stelle et a' fati*': *Lettere* 137 (emphasis added).

15. 'Ma perché di questi savi non si truova, *avendo li huomini prima la vista corta* e non potendo poi comandare alla natura loro, ne segue che la fortuna varia e comanda a li huomini, et tiegli sotto el giogo suo': ibid., 137–8 (emphasis added). For a deterministic interpretation of *riscontro*, see Miguel Saralegui Benito, *Maquiavelo y la contradicción. Un estudio sobre fortuna, virtud y teoría de la acción* (Pamplona: Eunsa, 2012), 146–65. See also Luigi Derla, 'Sulla concezione machiavelliana del tempo', in *Ideologia e scrittura nel Cinquecento* (Urbino: Argalia, 1977), 3–33; Robert Orr, 'The Time Motif in Machiavelli', in *Machiavelli and the Nature of Political Thought*, ed. M. Fleischer (New York: Atheneum, 1972), 185–208.

16. Eugenio Garin, 'Aspetti del pensiero di Machiavelli', in *Dal Rinascimento all'Illuminismo* (Pisa: Nistri-Lischi, 1970), 43–77, 57. See also Anthony J. Parel, *The Machiavellian Cosmos* (New Haven, CT: Yale University Press, 1992); Anthony J. Parel, 'Human Motions and Celestial Motions in Machiavelli's Historiography', in *Niccolò Machiavelli: politico, storico, letterato*, ed. Jean-Jacques Marchand (Rome: Salerno, 1996), 363–91, esp. 387.

17. See *Lettere* 138: 'Queste cagioni, infra le altre, apersono Italia ad Annibale e Spagna a Scipione, e così ognuno riscontrò el tempo e le cose secondo l'ordine del procedere suo. Né in quel medesimo tempo arebbe fatto tanto profitto in Italia uno simile a Scipione né uno simile ad Annibale in Spagna, quanto l'uno et l'altro fece nella provincia sua' ('These causes, among others, opened Italy up to Hannibal and Spain to Scipio, and thus each one made time and affairs consistent with his pattern of doing things. In those days a Scipio would have made less progress in Italy and a Hannibal would have made less progress in Spain than each did in his own area').

18. 'La inclusa potevo mandare sotto altre lettere, raccomandarmivi per la via di Biagio, et insomma, ciò che mi scadeva, per ora far sanza scrivervi. Ma ho voluto seguitar l'ordine del fare infinite cose sanza proposito': *Lettere* 135.

19. See Oreste Tommasini, *La vita e gli scritti di Niccolò Machiavelli nella loro relazione col machiavellismo* (Rome: Loescher, 1883); Roberto Ridolfi and Paolo Ghiglieri, 'I Ghiribizzi al Soderini', *La Bibliofilia* 72, no. 1 (1970), 53–74; M. Martelli, 'I Ghiribizzi a Giovan Battista Soderini', *Rinascimento* 9 (1971), 147–80; Roberto Ridolfi, 'Ancora sui Ghiribizzi al Soderini', *La bibliofilia* 74, no. 1 (1972), 1–7; Mario Martelli, 'Ancora sui Ghiribizzi a Giovan Battista Soderini', *Rinascimento* 10 (1972), 3–27; Gennaro Sasso, *Qualche osservazione sui Ghiribizzi al Soderini*, in *Machiavelli e gli antichi ed altri saggi*, 3 vols. (Milan: Ricciardi 1988), 2:3–56; Alessandro Fontana, 'Autour des *Ghiribizzi al Soderini* et de la volonté chez Machiavel', *La licorne* 46 (1998), 229–40; Carlo Galli, 'Riscontro', in *Enciclopedia machiavelliana*, gen. ed. Gennaro Sasso (Rome: Istituto della Enciclopedia Italiana Treccani, 2014), 427–33.

20. 'Conoscho voi et la bussola della navigazione vostra, et, quando potessi essere dannata, che non può, io non la dannerei, veggiendo ad che porti vi abbi guidato et di che speranza vi possa nutrire (onde io credo, non con lo spechio vostro, dove non si vede se non prudentia, ma per quello de' più, che si habbi nelle cose ad vedere el fine et non el mezo)': *Lettere* 136.

21. 'Insomma, se il nipote è il reale destinatario della 'responsiva', è lo zio che ne costituisce, in larga misura, l'argomento e l'occasione. E, al riguardo, converrà osservare che nessuna seria ragione obbliga a ritenere che Giovan Battista scrivesse al segretario su incarico del gonfaloniere, e che, rispondendo

al primo, Machiavelli si rivolgesse in realtà al secondo, perché, ascoltata la lezione, si risolvesse a tenerne conto': Sasso, 'Qualche osservazione sui *Ghiribizzi*', 16.

22. '[E] soprastate a tornare infino a gennaio, aren di voi in un tratto lo scoppio et il baleno; et pur si vorrebbe scendere scaglione a scaglione': *Lettere* 135.

23. See Fabio Frosini, 'La "prospettiva" del prudente. Prudenza, virtù, necessità, religione in Machiavelli', *Giornale critico della filosofia italiana* 92, no. 3 (2013), 508–43; Remo Catani, 'Astrological Polemics in the Crisis of the 1490s', in *Italy in Crisis: 1494*, ed. Jane E. Everson and Diego Zancani (Oxford: European Humanities Research Centre, 2000), 41–62.

24. 'È sufficiente che si definisca verissima la tua opinione in merito a ciò che, concordi, sostengono gli antichi: *essere il sapiente capace di mutare gli influssi degli astri. Questo infatti va inteso in riferimento non agli astri, poiché nessun mutamento può intervenire in ciò che è eterno, ma piuttosto al sapiente medesimo, il quale, passando dall'una all'altra esperienza, può mutare e cangiare sé stesso*': *Lettere* 101 (emphasis added), my translation. See Parel, 'Human Motions', in connexion with *Di fortuna*, lines 115–19; *Disc.* 1: Proemio, 39, 56; *Disc.* 2: Proemio, 29; *Istorie fiorentine* 5:1. See also Sasso, 'Qualche osservazione sui *Ghiribizzi*', 43; Gianfranco Borrelli, *Il lato oscuro del Leviathan: Hobbes contro Machiavelli* (Naples: Cronopio, 2009), 42–4.

25. '[I]nfine (non) consiglar persona né pigliar consiglo di persona, (excepto) un consiglo generale che ognun facci quello che li detta l'animo et con audacia': *Lettere* 136–7n. William J. Connell claimed that the draft of *Ghiribizzi* 'is a very sloppy draft with numerous corrections and cancellations and confusing marginalia' ('New Light on Machiavelli's Letter to Vettori, 10 December 1513', in *Europa e Italia: Studi in onore di Giorgio Chittolini* [Florence: Florence University Press, 2011, 96]). It is not clear what Connell has in mind.

26. '[T]entare la fortuna, che la (è) amica de' giovani, et mutare secondo e' tempi': *Lettere* 136–7n.

27. '[C]ome la fortuna si stracha, così si ruina l'huomo, la famiglia, la città: ogniuno ha la fortuna sua fondata sul modo di procedere suo, et ciascuna di loro si stracha et quando è stracha bisogna riacquistarla con un altro modo': ibid.

28. Sasso, 'Qualche osservazione sui *Ghiribizzi*', 52–3. See also Miguel Vatter, *Between Form and Event* (New York: Fordham University Press, 2014 [2000]), 137–43; Claude Lefort, *Le travail de l'oeuvre: Machiavel* (Paris: Gallimard, 1972), 442.

29. This is the main research path of Francesco Marchesi, *Riscontro: pratica politica e congiuntura storica in Niccolò Machiavelli* (Macerata: Quodlibet, 2017).

See also Francesco Marchesi, *Cartografia politica: spazi e soggetti del conflitto in Niccolò Machiavelli* (Florence: Olschki, 2018).
30. Machiavelli to Francesco Vettori, 10 December 1513: 'Appresso al desiderio harei che questi signori Medici mi cominciassino adoperare, se dovessino cominciare a farmi voltolare un sasso; perché, se poi io non me gli guadagnassi, io mi dorrei di me; e per questa cosa, quando la fussi letta, si vedrebbe che quindici anni che io sono stato a studio all'arte dello stato, non gl'ho né dormiti né giuocati; e doverrebbe ciascheduno aver caro servirsi di uno che alle spese di altri fussi pieno di esperienza': *Lettere* 102.
31. Carlo Ginzburg, 'Pontano, Machiavelli and Prudence: Some Further Reflections', in *From Florence to the Mediterranean and beyond: Essays in Honour of Anthony Molho*, ed. Dioga Ramada Curto, Eric R. Dursteller, Julius Kirshner, and Francesca Trivellato (Florence: Olschki, 2009), 123–5. See also Christian Lazzeri, 'Prudence, *éthique* et politique de Thomas d'Aquin à Machiavel', in *De la prudence des anciens comparée à celle des modernes :sémantique d'un concept, deplacement des problématiques*, ed. André Tosel (Paris: Les Belles Lettres, 1995), 79–128; Nancy S. Struever, *Theory as Practice: Ethical Inquiry in the Renaissance* (Chicago, IL: Chicago University Press, 1992); Klaus Held, 'Civic Prudence in Machiavelli: Toward the Paradigm Transformation in Philosophy in the Tradition of Modernity', in *The Ancients and the Moderns*, ed. Reginand Lilly (Bloomington, IN: Indiana University Press, 1996), 115–29; Eugene Garver, *Machiavelli and the History of Prudence* (Madison, WI: The University of Wisconsin Press, 1987).
32. Charles S. Singleton, 'The Perspective of Art', *Kenyon Review* 15, no. 2 (1953), 169–89, 172–3, 178. See also Alejandro Bárcenas, *Machiavelli's Art of Politics* (Leiden: Brill, 2015), especially 41–50.
33. See Louis Althusser, *Écrits philosophiques et politiques*, 2 vols. (Paris: Stock/Imec, 1994–5), 2:139; Louis Althusser, *Solitude de Machiavel et autres textes*, ed. Yves Sintomer (Paris: PUF, 1998); Louis Althusser, *Machiavelli e noi* (Rome: manifestolibri, 1999); Louis Althusser, *Sul materialismo aleatorio*, ed. V. Morfino and L. Pinzolo (Milan: Unicopli, 2000). See also Miguel Vatter, 'Machiavelli after Marx: The Self-Overcoming of Marxism in the Late Althusser', *Theory and Event* 7, no. 4 (2005), accessed on 22 August 2021 at https://muse.jhu.edu/article/244122; Filippo Del Lucchese, Fabio Frosini and Vittorio Morfino, eds., *The Radical Machiavelli* (Leiden: Brill, 2015), 393–456; Mikko Lahtinen, *Politics and Philosophy: Niccolò Machiavelli and Louis Althusser's Aleatory Materialism* (Leiden: Brill, 2009); Marie Gaille, 'What Does a "Conjuncture-Embedded" Reflection Mean? The Legacy of Althusser's Machiavelli to Contemporary Political Theory', in *Machiavelli On Liberty and Conflict*, ed. David Johnston, Nadia Urbinati, and Camila Vergara (Chicago, IL: University of Chicago Press, 2017), 399–414.

34. See Jean-Jacques Marchand, *Niccolò Machiavelli: I primi scritti politici (1499–1512): nascita di un pensiero e di uno stile* (Padua: Antenore, 1975), 388.
35. A first, crucial formulation of the *riscontro* as an internal relationship between action and the times is presented in Miguel Vatter's *Between Form and Event*. However, my interpretation differs from Vatter's (though the latter has been hugely influential for my own), for the following reasons: (*a*) Vatter overrates the option of *forcing* the times, on which he bases his entire reading of the *Ghiribizzi* and of Machiavelli's position as a whole (148); (*b*) His conclusion rests, on the one hand, on an extensive interpretation of the uniformity of human nature in the context of *riscontro* against the deterministic hypothesis (143, 164) and, on the other hand, on a reading of the contrast between Hannibal and Scipio as an example of determination of the times by political action (147); (*c*) Vatter sometimes replaces the internal relationship between modes and times with a modern, therefore, anachronistic notion of free will as executed by a typically Machiavellian historical bond (139, 164*n*); (*d*) In the last analysis, such uniformity of human nature is crucial for the text's main thesis about the social position of the actor: if that is exalted, it aims to dominate, and if popular, it wants not to be dominated. Consequently, popular action is necessarily an act of 'no-rule' in Hannah Arendt's sense, an event of pure destitution. In my view, there is in Machiavelli no such purely *évènementielle* theory of history—Arendtian, and quite Lefortian by Abensour's interpretation. Nor do we find a prevalence of the 'forcing' mode of *riscontro* until the *Florentine Histories*, and even there it is not presented from a populist angle. 'Forcing the time' is never Machiavelli's political preference, but his view of the actualization of history in a specific period.

9

'Letters as Oracles'

Machiavelli's Foresight in His Letters

Marcello Simonetta

Machiavelli's letters[1] are a fabulous field for historians and literary buffs alike. The freedom of their style, full of irony and *gravitas* at the same time, lends them to a whole range of close readings. For instance, John Najemy's book *Between Friends* focuses on the letters exchanged from 1513 to 1515 between Machiavelli and his friend Francesco Vettori, including the famous letter of 10 December 1513.[2] Najemy's book is an exercise in intertextual reading, more convincing at certain times than others but certainly calling for close attention overall. My main objection is that he sides pre-emptively with Machiavelli, presuming all through his intellectual and moral superiority to Vettori. Yet Vettori was no fool, and in his own day he was certainly more Machiavellian than Machiavelli. He managed to survive four out of five regime changes in Florence, until his death in 1540.[3] For Niccolò, one republican downfall in 1512 was enough to compromise much of his active political career, and even after he barely recovered his reputation, it did not help him much during the second republican coup in May 1527, shortly followed by his death in June. Some people, in fact, attributed his bodily demise to his bitterness at not having been hired back by the new government. Actually, things were slightly more complicated, as we will see.

The widely accepted view is that from 1513 to 1525, Machiavelli was forced to be professionally inactive, and we owe most of his major works to his joblessness during this period. However, recent discoveries indicate that Francesco's brother Paolo Vettori, on being nominated Admiral of the papal fleet in 1516, hired Machiavelli as a full-fledged secretary and involved him in a series of military and naval tasks, including at least one official mission to Cardinal Giulio de' Medici in Rome.[4] Overall, while Machiavelli's desire to serve the powers that be (that is, the Medici) may have been understated by historians, it is undeniable that Machiavelli devoted himself during this period to composing the *Discourses*, *Mandragola*, *The Art of War* (published in 1521), and the *Florentine Histories*, a commission which he received during the tenure of Cardinal Giulio de' Medici as governor of Florence. Once he had delivered the *Florentine Histories* to Pope Clement VII in May 1525, a new phase of his life began. He swung fully back into action and was entrusted with several diplomatic and military tasks. During the two last intense years, he faced hard international challenges that eventually resulted in the sack of Rome and the removal of the Medici from Florence.

The gap between his theoretical work and his practical activities at this dramatic juncture has never been studied. In this chapter, I aim to explore Machiavelli's official and private letters (designated as oracles by Bartolomeo Cavalcanti, a young humanist friend who admired him) to gauge his foresight and effectiveness in dealing with the 'effectual truth of the thing' ('verità effettuale della cosa')[5].

Machiavelli was, of course, very much in the thick of the storm during his long service as second chancellor or *Segretario* of the Florentine republic from 1498 to 1512. I will not enter into this,[6] but I would like to draw my first example from a letter written to him by Filippo Casavecchia, one of his close friends and colleagues at the chancery (with whom he often engaged in jest, even in the midst of the most serious state affairs). In June 1509, after the Florentine victory in Pisa, Casavecchia writes to Machiavelli: 'Every day that goes by, I discover you to be the best prophet that the Jews or any other people ever had.'[7]

The remark is redolent with ironic admiration, but admiration nonetheless. Needless to say, the faculty of foresight and farsightedness is not limited to Machiavelli's last years.[8] We can draw an example from December 1514, when Francesco Vettori asked his unemployed friend to provide some insight into the political situation. Machiavelli predicted that France would overcome Spain on Italian soil and strongly recommended that the Pope side with the French. Unfortunately for him, the Pope had already made a secret agreement with Spain, of which Machiavelli, having been out of the favoured circles for a while, was not aware. But his gaffe went deeper: he adamantly opposed the Medici doctrine of neutrality, thereby taking the first step to self-annihilation. His stand is expressed both in *The Prince* (Chapter 20) and the *Discourses* (2:22).

Less than a year later, the young King François I of France won the famous battle of Marignano (September 1515). Pope Leo X and his shifty nephew Lorenzo de' Medici (the undeserving dedicatee of *The Prince*, though most likely he did not even bother to read it) began to dance around the winner, and eventually managed, at a meeting in Bologna in December 1515, to align firmly with him.

Machiavelli did not gain any credit out of this; in fact, he lost most of it and was never more down on his luck than around this time. This is probably when he started actively looking for private sponsors and found chiefly two, Cosimo Rucellai and Zanobi Buondelmonti. The second was a very interesting case of *gauche caviar*, in the French phrase: a wealthy, well-meaning intellectual who wanted, somewhat naïvely, to restore the values of the Florentine republic without losing his own privileges.

I have written extensively about this character; my takeaway is that even the people who were closest to Machiavelli at this time seemed to misunderstand him. As in any situation of this sort, it took two to tango. If the spoiled brat was not imbibing Machiavelli's lesson—that a moral approach to politics would be neither effective nor significant—it was also because the instructor was being somewhat ambivalent about it:

> Machiavelli was eliciting responses that ranged from the most cynical to the most idealistic, but perhaps he would have felt less keen on the latter than on the former. Nevertheless, Buondelmonti ... affords us a glimpse into the perception of Machiavelli's works during his lifetime, in the milieu that supported him materially and made it possible for him to write them, but not necessarily to read them well.[9]

Here we hit the core problem. Ultimately, even today, debate about Machiavelli stems from the one question: *was he really mean, and did he really mean it?* Or was he, rather, denouncing the game by exposing the true nature of power to the popular gaze? Why did he open Pandora's box of politics in a totally irreversible way? These questions are still very much alive, historically and politically.

John McCormick's *Reading Machiavelli*[10] engages with the question, focusing on excerpts from *The Prince*, the *Discourses*, and the *Florentine Histories*. He is not wrong regarding the major works, but I believe that a more nuanced answer can be provided through a close reading of Machiavelli's letters. McCormick fashions Machiavelli as an unambiguous, clear-cut, almost dogmatic thinker, enamoured with the Roman republic's officers and obsessed, in particular, with the censoring role of the tribunes of the plebs. I will suggest how this one-sided approach affects his interpretation in a basic way.

Back to Work for the Medici

Machiavelli as a historian faced historiographical questions but returned from them to the political fray. The most thought-provoking scholarship in recent times has claimed that the former republican civil servant was a much less reluctant employee of the Medici than previously thought. In particular, the work of Gaetano Lettieri has produced some bold theses[11] that, while needing some fine-tuning of the details,[12] outline a new image of Machiavelli as a willing and powerful supporter of Clement VII's last attempts to preserve Italian liberty against the wave of foreign invasions.

The intrusive presence of the 'barbarians', already derided and dismissed in the last chapter of *The Prince*, was again becoming unbearable in 1525, after the French debacle in Pavia. That epochal battle had seen the King of France not only bloodily defeated but imprisoned by his arch-enemy, the King of Spain and Emperor Charles V (who celebrated his twenty-fifth birthday on that very date, 24 February). François I remained in captivity for a whole year and had to endure countless humiliations and make crippling concessions in order to regain his personal freedom. Machiavelli, ever the keen observer of politics, expressed his disbelief at Charles V's naïveté when the freeing of his regal prisoner was announced: the Emperor, he felt, must be either a fool or a madman not to realize that his foe would not keep his promises (as stated in Chapter 19 of *The Prince*, in the passage about foxes and lions).[13] He pointedly prophesied there would be 'war, and soon, in Italy'.[14]

War was indeed on its way. It was made unavoidable by the so-called Holy League of Cognac in May 1526, signed jointly by the Pope, France, Florence, and Venice, united against the Spanish imperial forces. As formidable as the alliance may have looked, the situation on the ground was actually quite dire. A huge and hungry army, mostly made up of *Landsknechte* or Lutheran mercenaries, was headed towards the rich heart of Italy, while François I, still licking his wounds and constrained by the fact that his eldest sons had been held as surety for his large promises, was unwilling to divert his military forces from his own country.

During the dramatic summer of 1526, Machiavelli feverishly corresponded with his friends Guicciardini and Vettori, rightfully worried about the worsening of the prospects for Florence and the whole peninsula. The recently deciphered letters from Vettori show in particular the failure of the papal army to subdue a defiant Siena, which pulverized the Church's besieging forces.[15] Machiavelli was the recipient of the most openly expressed concerns. A letter by Bartolomeo Cavalcanti to Machiavelli, written from Florence on 11 August 1526,[16] is a particularly meaningful testimony of the appreciation of his fellow countrymen: 'I deeply long for your letters, which hold for me the place of oracles.'[17]

The distinction between *lettere familiari* and *lettere legazioni*, especially in the last years, is an artificial one: there is an undeniable continuum between *otia* and *negotia*. The common denominator is the urgency induced by the 'qualità dei tempi' (which might imply either 'the state of the times' or 'the compulsions of the times'), as stated in the dispatch written from Bologna on 23 March 1527:

> Therefore, Magnificent Lords, if you ever thought you could save your fatherland and let it escape those dangers that now loom so huge and grave, make this last attempt through such a provision: so that whether you obtain a truce and escape the present evils to gain *time*, or (so to speak) to prolong the ruin; or whether the truce does not take effect, and you have to wage war or indeed sustain it—one way or the other, never were funds more necessary or more useful, since in either case, they will buy us *time*; and if ever the proverb was true that 'He who has *time*, has life', in this case it is most true. (Emphasis added)[18]

Without hiding any of the impending dangers, Machiavelli calls upon the Florentine powers, for one last time, to show not parsimony but generosity, and to brave the expense that might well save the country while not saving money. If the truce does not succeed, they will nonetheless have bought some vital *time*, for *time* is indeed of the essence here. (I have italicized this obsessively repeated word in the text.)

A week later, however, the situation had not greatly improved:

> as I have said, it is advisable to spend this time well, otherwise *ruin* will only be deferred, and will finally be all the greater, just as *bodies* after long illness are weaker than they were before. (Emphasis added)[19]

Machiavelli is obviously drawing here on the classic concept of the body politic, and envisaging its impending corruption.[20] But in that he was not alone. We cannot truly understand or appreciate the originality of Machiavelli's thought if we do not consider the simultaneous and parallel career of Francesco Guicciardini, who was the *Luogotenente* (Lieutenant) of the papal army from June 1526.[21] On 29 March 1527, Guicciardini wrote to Gian Matteo Giberti, Pope Clement VII's *datario* and right-hand man:

> Start right away to help yourselves in every possible way, making new Cardinals [that is, raising money on behalf of the Pope], and leaving no stone unturned; and do not think that Florence, whose *bowels* are completely empty, will support more war for you: on the contrary, you will need to wage war on behalf of Florence. (Emphasis added)[22]

The crude physiological image of the empty bowels evokes the scatological situation in which he and his fellow Florentines and Italians were steeped. By the way, his was a *real prophecy*, since only a couple of years later, during the siege of Florence in 1529–30, the city would fight for its freedom from the Medici and eventually lose its battle, finding itself completely deprived of food and starving to death.

Going back to the momentous year 1527, we find Machiavelli, writing to Vettori on 5 April, referring explicitly and approvingly to Guicciardini's letter. In another letter to Vettori on 14 April 1527 (see the full commentary in the forthcoming *Edizione nazionale*), he writes:

> We judged the war lost, as you yourself did, when I left there. This accounts for the fact that we always advised an *agreement*; but we meant an *agreement* which would be solid, not uncertain and complicated like this, made in Rome and flouted in Lombardy. We should also have a little money, to be kept in the event of this totally uncertain agreement leaving us disarmed—or in order to remain armed, make us pay the soldiers and thus be without the monies to pay for the *agreement*. Thus if a neat agreement might bring safety, a messed-up one would be wholly damaging, and lead us to our ruin. (Emphasis added)[23]

They were left with two bad options, a choice between two evils. Such was the depressing endgame of the Machiavellian either/or binary.

But politics is personal, or gets to be so. Here is the famous letter that Machiavelli wrote to Vettori on 16 April 1527:

> I love Messer Francesco Guicciardini; I love my fatherland more than my own soul; and I tell you from sixty years' experience that I do not believe that more difficult issues than these were ever contended, where peace is necessary and war cannot be abandoned; and to have on our hands a prince who is scarcely able to deal with peace alone or with war alone.[24]

I have collected, and am in the process of publishing, a new dossier of hitherto unknown and partially ciphered letters to the Otto di Pratica, the executive Florentine magistrates, from Guicciardini, who was Machiavelli's official superior and thought very much on the same wavelength. While Vettori was fearful, Guicciardini, a choleric but determined man, represented a *via di mezzo*. His virtually single-handed decision to move the papal troops towards Florence (his fatherland, as distinct from the Italian nation) when the imperial mercenary army was descending on Italy saved the city from a potential sack. However, it also made the sack of Rome inevitable.

The Guicciardinian Moment

Here we can go back to McCormick's criticism of the Cambridge School. Dismissing Pocock, he talks about the 'Guicciardini moment' with its elitist and paternalistic viewpoint.[25] While I tend to agree that overall, the approach of the Cambridge School has obscured key aspects of Machiavelli's thought, I do not altogether accept McCormick's position either. No doubt Guicciardini was a member of the Florentine 'upper caste', but extrapolating some quotes from his discourses, as if he were a character frozen in time, is an unhistorical, misleadingly synchronic way of unfocused reading. Attacking the elitism of the *ottimati* does not resolve the problem of a flawed decision-making process. Machiavelli is not uncritical of the people's fickleness. The tribunate requires a whole set of circumstances in order to be truly effective.

In one formula, Machiavelli minus Guicciardini equals Vettori. We need to include the sceptical take of Vettori, who effectively rewrote Chapter 15 of *The Prince* against utopias. Not without a hint of irony, he argued that 'according to the truth of things in this world, perhaps the utopian republics imagined by Plato or by the Englishman Thomas More were not tyrannical governments, but all the republics or principalities that I have known through history or experience all smell of tyranny'.[26] As an adjunct to this gloomy vision, one can read Guicciardini's *ricordo* 107 on the tyranny of a republic that treats all its citizens badly ('deprime tutti e [sic] sudditi'). The historical foundation of these bitter reflections was set by the virtual tyranny of the new republican government during the siege and tragic fall of Florence long after Machiavelli's death.

Vettori's complete absence from McCormick's book is very revealing. One could argue he is the 'missing link' in McCormick's argument. I would say that Guicciardini was too bold, Vettori too fearful. Did Machiavelli stay out of this fray? His personal decision to serve the Medici almost to the bitter end has often been misunderstood and understated, but it is historically undeniable.

Relying too much on the orations composed by Guicciardini or other Florentine officials, Machiavelli included, means forgetting the occasional (and sometimes opportunistic) nature of these texts, originating in a very specific set of circumstances. Hence, their theoretical and ideological value needs to be gauged with critical detachment, whereas the letters are immediate and unmediated—not unbiased, but un-(re)touchable.[27]

Even the botched attempt to liberate Florence from the Medici on 26 April 1527[28] (the 49th anniversary of the Pazzi Conspiracy,[29] the failed attempt to reverse Medici rule in 1478) was led by a small group of discontented aristocrats. Florence was saved from bloodshed, thanks to the firm action taken by the duke of Urbino, Francesco Maria della Rovere, commander of the army of the 'Holy League', and by the foreign condottiere Federico Gonzaga da Bozzolo, an old friend of Giovanni de' Medici or Giovanni delle Bande Nere, Cosimo I's father. This occurred despite Guicciardini's own spite and personal vendetta, specifically against the duke of Urbino, whose role he did not miss a chance to diminish and tarnish in his *Storia d'Italia*, while presenting himself as the saviour of his 'patria'. To his credit, Guicciardini also redeemed himself as the author of the extraordinary *Accusatoria*, the most violent self-indictment ever written by a political agent that I know of. But that explosive work remained hidden among his family papers for centuries, while his *Storia* was published in several languages throughout Europe.

The suppression of the Tumulto of Florence in 1527 was more or less the direct cause of the sack of Rome—a traumatic event that Machiavelli had indeed foreseen with great acumen. He had done so almost thirteen years earlier, on 20 December 1514, in one of those letters written to Vettori on behalf of the Medici that became the cause of his further professional isolation. There, exactly as in *The Prince*, Chapter 17, he had warned that a leader's main objective ('l'offizio principale di ogni principe') is to avoid being hated or despised, and that he cannot remain neutral:

> And to those who argue that the Pope, because of the reverence due to His person and the authority of the Church, is differently situated and will always find a refuge and save himself, I would answer that such a reply deserves some consideration, and there is some basis to it; nonetheless it is not to be relied on entirely. On the contrary, I believe that, if he is to be well advised, this factor is not to be thought of, lest such a hope leads him to a bad choice. For things that have happened once can happen again; and I know that we have seen popes flee, go into exile, be persecuted, and *suffer to the utmost* [that is, be killed] just like secular lords, and that in times when the Church enjoyed more respect in spiritual matters than it does today.[30]

The philosophy of history expressed in this letter recalls the biblical idea of the eternal return of the identical.

I would linger a little on the expression 'suffer to the utmost' ('extrema pati'), taken from Virgil's *Aeneid*:

> between hope and fear uncertain whether to deem them [Aeneas's lost companions] still alive, or bearing the final doom and hearing no more when called.[31]

Such intertextual finesse is only possible in an epistolary exchange. The euphemism speaks volumes. With powerful pagan echoes, he connects the idea of Troy's catastrophe (or apocalypse) to the fate of Catholic pontiffs. Physical death is unavoidable, but political ruin is in theory avoidable, except that denial, self-complaisance, and cowardice, together with reluctance or inability to seek long-term collective benefit over short-term individual gain, are such deeply ingrained drives in human nature that they may well contain the roots of our own doom.

In his cryptic use of Virgil, Machiavelli quietly but forcefully turns himself into a prose Dante. His ultimate foresight is on the metaphysical plane: without truly believing in the afterlife, he looks beyond death. We know that Machiavelli was rumoured to have said before dying that he would be happier in hell, as long as he could continue conversing with the great (if somewhat self-destructive) intellects of the past and the future—or just be able to correspond with them across the centuries, while the world was burning.

Notes

1. I am fortunate enough to be one of the editors of the *Edizione nazionale* of Machiavelli's *Lettere familiari*, coordinated by Francesco Bausi with Andrea Guidi, Alessio Decaria, and Carlo Varotti among others, due for publication in 2021 from Salerno Editore, Rome. In the last few years, I have made my own small contribution by finding hitherto unknown autograph letters by or to Machiavelli, and interpreting other letters in the corpus in new, subtler ways. The text of Machiavelli's letters cited in this chapter, and those of Vettori and Guicciardini, are from this forthcoming volume if not otherwise stated.
2. J. M. Najemy, *Between Friends: Discourses of Power and Desire in the Machiavelli-Vettori Letters of 1513–1515* (Princeton, NJ: Princeton University Press, 1993). See also W. J. Connell, 'Dating *The Prince*: Beginnings and Endings', *Review of Politics* 75, no. 4 (2013), 497–514.
3. All biographers state that Vettori died on 5 March 1539; but having found letters written by him later that year, I conclude that the year of his death was recorded in the Florentine style, where the calendar year started on 25 March. See my forthcoming new entry in the *Dizionario biografico degli italiani*.
4. See Andrea Guidi and Marcello Simonetta, 'I "negozi" di Niccolò nell' "ozio" di Sant'Andrea: Machiavelli e Paolo Vettori (con l'edizione di uno sconosciuto frammento autografo machiavelliano)', *Interpres* 37 (2019), 242–67.

5. *Pr.*, ch. 15.
6. On Machiavelli as a chancellor, see Andrea Guidi (co-editor of the *Lettere familiari*), *Un Segretario militante: politica, diplomazia e armi nel Cancelliere Machiavelli* (Bologna: Il Mulino, 2009).
7. 'Ogni dì vi scopro el maggior profeta che avessino mai gli Ebrei o altra generazione.' All translations from the letters are my own.
8. The instrumental use of prophecy for proceeding to battle—that is, the adoption of a prudential and providential attitude—is the subject of *Disc.* 1:14, the chapter on augurs or *pullarii*, priests who interpreted the movements of sacred fowl.
9. Marcello Simonetta, 'The Lost Discourse on Governments by Machiavelli's Friend Zanobi Buondelmonti', *Culture del testo e del documento* 18, no. 53 (2017), 165–78, 178.
10. J. P. McCormick, *Reading Machiavelli: Scandalous Books, Suspect Engagements, and the Virtue of Populist Politics* (Princeton, NJ: Princeton University Press, 2019).
11. Gaetano Lettieri, 'Nove tesi sull'ultimo Machiavelli', *Humanitas* 72, nos. 5–6 (2017), 1037–89.
12. Some minor modifications are made in Gaetano Lettieri, 'Machiavelli in gioco. Un agente segreto papale a Venezia (1525)', *Studi e materiali di storia delle religioni* 84, no. 2 (2018), 688–729. See also the article by Guidi and Simonetta cited in note 4.
13. On this passage, for the sake of convenience, I will cite only my book *Volpi e leoni: Machiavelli e la rovina d'Italia* (2014), rpt. as *Volpi e leoni: I misteri dei Medici* (Milan: Rizzoli, 2017), which contains a synthetic analysis of this crucial period, with ample bibliography and quotations from original documents, French tr. as *Les renards et les lions: Les médicis, Machiavel, et la ruine d'Italie* (Paris: Albin Michel, 2019).
14. Machiavelli to Guicciardini, Florence, 15 March 1526.
15. Vettori to Machiavelli, Florence, 5 August 1526. The ciphered passage about Siena was first published in Simonetta, *Volpi e leoni*, 277.
16. I recovered the long-lost original of this letter in the Archivio Borromeo, Isola Bella, Acquisizioni diverse, *Cavalcanti Bartolomeo*: see my article 'Lettere "in luogo di oraculi": quattro autografi dispersi di Luigi Pulci e di (e a) Niccolò Machiavelli', *Interpres* 21 (2002), 291–301.
17. '[I]o desidero sommamente le vostre lettere et che appresso di me sono in luogo di oraculi.'
18. 'Pertanto, Magnifici Signori, se voi avesti mai pensiero di potere salvare la patria vostra, e farle fuggire quelli periculi che ora tanto grandi e tanto importanti le soprastanno, fate questo ultimo conato di questa provisione,

acciò che o e' ne seguiti questa tregua e fuggasi questi presenti mali per dare *tempo*, o a dire meglio allungare la rovina, o quando pure la tregua non avesse effetto averli da potere fare la guerra, o a dire meglio sostenerla; perché nell'uno modo o nell'altro non furno mai danari piú necessarii, né piú utili, perché nell'uno modo o nell'altro ci daranno *tempo*; e se fu mai vero quel proverbio che "chi ha *tempo* ha vita", in questo caso è verissimo': Machiavelli to the Otto di Pratica, Bologna, 23 March 1527: Machiavelli, *Legazioni, Commissarie, Scritti di governo*, Edizione Nazionale, ed. Jean-Jacques Marchand, Andrea Guidi, Matteo Melera-Morettini, 7 vols. (Roma: Salerno, 2002–11), 7:213.

19. [C]onviene, come ho detto, spendere questo tempo bene, altrimenti la *rovina* si differisce, e fia tanto maggiore, quanto i *corpi* per la lunga infirmità fieno meno atti che non erano un tempo fa a sopportarla': ibid., 7:*n*134. See also Simonetta, *Volpi e leoni*, 237.

20. Recently, at a conference on the 'Three Souls', I have proposed another concept of the 'body soul', whereby the vegetative and appetitive souls seem to be taking over the rational soul, turning the *psychomachia* into a Hobbesian *polimachia* where the breakdown of orders and institutions is accelerated through the corruption of powerful and reckless individuals.

21. See Marcello Simonetta, 'Guicciardini e la "rovina d'Italia": venti lettere e un ricordo inedito del Luogotenente', *Archivio storico italiano* 177, no. 4 (2019), 773–819.

22. '[C]ominciate subito a aiutarvi con tutti i modi possibili, facendo Cardinali e non pretermettendo niente, e che non solo non pensiate che Firenze, quale è vôta insino alle *viscere*, sostenga più la guerra per voi, ma che bisogna che voi la portiate in futuro per Firenze.'

23. '[S]i giudicava la guerra perduta, come voi medesimo, quando io mi partii di costì, la giudicavi. Questo ha fatto che si è sempre consigliato lo *accordo*, ma si intendeva uno *accordo* che fosse fermo, et non dubbio et intrigato come questo, che sia fatto a Roma, et non observato in Lombardia; et che ci siano pochi danari, et quelli pochi bisogni o serbarli per un simile accordo tutto dubbio et restare disarmato; o, per restare armato, pagarli, et rimanere senza essi per lo *accordo*. Et così dove si pensava che uno accordo netto fosse salutifero, uno intrigato è al tutto pernizioso, et la rovina nostra.'

24. 'Io amo messer Francesco Guicciardini, amo la patria mia più dell'anima; et vi dico questo per quella esperienza che mi hanno data sessanta anni, che io non credo che mai si travagliassino i più difficili articuli che questi, dove la pace è necessaria, et la guerra non si puote abbandonare, et havere alle mani un principe, che con fatica può supplire o alla pace sola o alla guerra sola.'

25. See McCormick, *Reading Machiavelli*, ch. 6.

26. '[P]arlando delle cose di questo mondo sanza rispetto e secondo il vero, dico che chi facesse una di quelle repubbliche scritte e imaginate da Platone, o come una che scrive Tomma Moro inghilese essere stata trovata in Utopia, forse quelle potrebbono dire non essere governi tirannici; ma tutte quelle repubbliche o principi, de' quali io ho cognizione per istoria o che io ho veduti, mi pare che sentino di tirannide': Vettori, *Scritti storici e politici* (Rome: Laterza, 1972), 145; cf. 277–8, 281–2.
27. The *Discourses* conclude (3:49) by observing that a republic has need of new acts of foresight every day if one wishes to maintain it free, and of the *civiltà* for which Quintus Fabius 'was rightly called Maximus'. The opening word of the *Discorsi* is 'Io' ('I'), the closing word 'Massimo' ('Maximus'), as my mentor at Yale, Giuseppe Mazzotta, used to point out. Julia Conaway Bondanella and Peter Bondanella, tr. and eds. of Machiavelli, *Discourses on Livy* (Oxford: Oxford University Press, 1997), have 'new measures' for 'nuovi provvedimenti': so easy it is to overstep semantic boundaries—and so difficult to maintain the republic in a free state, as Machiavelli and Guicciardini ardently desire.
28. See Marcello Simonetta, 'Le rôle de Francesco Guicciardini dans le Tumulto del venerdì (26 avril 1527) selon certaines sources non florentines', *Laboratoire italien* 17 (2016), 287–306.
29. See Marcello Simonetta, *The Montefeltro Conspiracy. A Renaissance Mystery Decoded* (New York: Doubleday, 2008).
30. 'E chi replicasse che il papa, per la reverenza della persona e per l'autorità della Chiesa, è in un altro grado, e avrà sempre rifugio a salvarsi, risponderei che tal replica merita qualche considerazione, e che vi si può fare su qualche fondamento: nondimanco e' non è da fidarsene, anzi credo che, a volersi consigliare bene, non sia da pensarvi, perché simile speranza non facesse pigliare tristo partito; perché tutte le cose che sono state io credo che possano essere; ed io so che si sono visti dei pontefici fuggire, esiliare, perseguitare, et extrema pati, come i signori temporali, e nei tempi che la Chiesa nello spirituale aveva più riverenza che non ha oggi.'
31. '[S]pemque metumque inter dubii; seu vivere credant,/sive extrema pati, nec jam exaudire vocatos': *Aeneid* 1:218–19: text and tr. from *Virgil*, ed. H. R. Fairclough, Loeb Classical Library, vol. 1, rev. edn (Cambridge, MA: Harvard University Press, 1978).

10
Machiavelli's Lucretia and the Origins of the Roman Republic
Rape, Gender, and Founding Violence

Yves Winter

As many commentators have noted, 'founding' is a key category for Machiavelli. Both in *The Prince* and the *Discourses*, and arguably in his other works as well, Machiavelli praises the role played by founders in establishing and regenerating political institutions.[1] Founding is important because it challenges the traditional principle of heredity. In contrast to the hereditary schema, which apportions legitimacy on the basis of one's lineage, family, and pedigree, founding valorizes action. Founders create new political and social orders; in so doing, they challenge convention and exhibit a central value Machiavelli associates with free life: autonomy.[2] Founders act alone, Machiavelli insists repeatedly. They are authorized not by ancestry and tradition but by what they create. They are often outsiders, arrivistes, men of humble origin whose backgrounds do not obviously destine them to positions of power.[3] Founders pursue their political objectives with great ambition, and often by ruthless means. Lethal violence, Machiavelli intimates, is central to creating new institutions. It fulfils at least two functions: it coerces the enemies of the new order, typically powerful and wealthy elites, into submission, and it inaugurates the new order symbolically.[4]

Given the importance that Machiavelli accords to founders and to forms of founding violence in particular, it is important to inquire into the criteria for what makes an appropriate founder and appropriate forms of founding violence. At issue is the question of who can play the role of founder, and what forms of violence count as constitutively political. In this chapter, I approach this question through a reading of the legendary figure of Lucretia, the Roman woman whose rape and subsequent suicide triggered the revolution against the Etruscan kings and the establishment of the Roman republic.

Lucretia is an interesting figure. Her role in the overthrow of the Tarquins is treated extensively by Roman historians and by medieval and Renaissance authors. In this literature, she is frequently hailed as a courageous heroine, and even those who criticize her actions on moral or religious grounds (above all Augustine) treat her as one of the protagonists of the revolution that transformed Rome from a monarchy into a republic.

In his account of the Roman revolution, Machiavelli, by contrast, sidelines Lucretia and greatly diminishes her role.[5] Even though that revolution is central to Machiavelli's political theory, and notwithstanding the significance of violence in his concept of founding, Lucretia largely fades from the narrative of the upheaval in 509 BCE. While Machiavelli frequently invokes the expulsion of the Tarquins, he assigns Lucretia a peculiar and contradictory role. As I will show, this disavowal of Lucretia is surprising for historical, conceptual, and symbolic reasons.

Predictably, Machiavelli's preoccupation with founding is decisively gendered. Not only are founders generally men, but to the extent that founding is a violent process, the logics and practices of killing are embedded in hegemonic masculine discourses; they promote myths and stereotypes of militarized masculinity; and they symbolically privilege values and concerns conventionally associated with masculinity. As such, Machiavelli's work both reflects and epitomizes time-honoured patriarchal schemas prevalent in the history of Western political thought. Yet as multiple decades of feminist scholarship have shown, the gendered nature of Machiavelli's thought instantiates not merely broader trends in the history of European political thought but exhibits idiosyncratic traits.[6]

In this chapter, I explore the gendered dimension of Machiavelli's concern with violence. But unlike most of the existing scholarship on this issue, I am interested less in resolving who exercises it and to what extent women are represented as agents of violence than in the question of what forms of violence Machiavelli describes as political. What are the (gendered) norms whereby some formations of violence are recognized and celebrated as political, as having historical importance, whereas others are trivialized? Machiavelli's reception and treatment of Lucretia raise questions about the political status and meaning of sexual and gender-based violence in his work.

The Legend of Lucretia

According to legend, Rome became a republic in 509 BCE, when a popular uprising deposed the seventh king of Rome, Lucius Tarquinius Superbus (Tarquin the Proud). According to Livy (1:49), Tarquin the Proud merited his name.[7] Unlike the previous Etruscan kings, whom Livy describes as 'successive founders' ('deinceps conditores') of Rome (2:1),[8] Tarquin the Proud was a tyrant. Even though Rome at the time was an elective monarchy, Tarquin had usurped the throne, ruled by treachery, violence, and brutality, flouted political customs and traditions, and ignored the Senate. To build his ambitious construction projects, the massive temple of Jupiter on the Capitoline, the Circus, and the great sewer (cloaca maxima), he forcibly recruited large numbers of workers, who were coerced into hard labour.

Yet as Livy tells the story (1:57), it was not Tarquin's abuses of power or his merciless treatment of the working class that led to the uprising against him. Rather, the trigger was the rape and suicide of Lucretia by the king's son and confidant, Sextus. Stationed in Ardea, Sextus spent his time, between bouts of military action, in drinking with other members of the Roman elite. Amid their drinking games, the men engage in a chastity competition on behalf of their wives, squabbling over whose wife was the most virtuous. To settle the issue, they decide to mount their horses and ride to Rome to surprise their wives and see what they are up to. Whereas the other wives spend their time, much as their husbands do, at parties, drinking and amusing themselves, Lucretia is found spinning at home, surrounded by her maidservants. Sextus, at this point, becomes obsessed with Lucretia's 'beauty and proven chastity', which kindled in him 'the flame of lust, and determined him to debauch her'.[9]

A few days later, Sextus secretly returns to Lucretia's house, where he is hospitably received late at night. He then enters her chambers and rapes her at knife-point. Lucretia initially resists, but Sextus threatens to kill her and lay her next to a slave to suggest that she had been unfaithful to her husband. The prospect of such dishonour sways Lucretia, and Sextus rides away, proud of his success. Lucretia summons her father and husband, asks both to come immediately and bring a trusted friend each. Her husband brings Lucius Junius Brutus, son of the king's sister and Sextus's first cousin. She recounts the story and proclaims her innocence:

> My body only has been violated. My heart is innocent, and death will be my witness. Give me your solemn promise that the adulterer shall be punished—he is Sextus Tarquinius. He it is who last night came as my enemy disguised as my guest, and took his pleasure of me. That pleasure will be my death—and his, too, if you are men.[10]

Having dramatically conveyed her last wish, she draws a knife and plunges it into her heart.

According to Livy's narrative, Lucretia's suicide galvanizes opposition to the Tarquins. The opposition is led by Brutus, who had witnessed the suicide that left him a 'changed man', infused with a new spirit ('novum ... ingenium').[11] Brutus successfully transforms the family grief into anger at the Tarquins and goes on to deliver public speeches that impugn the royal family and demand their abdication. While the people of Rome shut the Tarquins out of the city, Brutus calls on the army to revolt and is enthusiastically received by the troops. The monarchy is abolished, and in its place, the position of the twin consuls is created. Brutus will serve as the republic's first consul, a point that is important, because it is in his capacity as consul that he will become one of Machiavelli's esteemed founder figures.

During his consulship, Brutus proves (in Livy's estimation) to be 'as zealous in guarding liberty as he had been in demanding it'.[12] Rome's republican liberty was at risk from a conspiracy of young aristocrats who 'had found life under the monarchy very agreeable'. These young members of the elite, which included Brutus's own sons, had been able to take full advantage of their privileged position under the Tarquins, giving 'a freer rein to their appetites and [living] the dissolute and irresponsible life of the court'.[13] They now found that unlike a king with whom they could negotiate and make deals, a republic governed by law was less receptive to elite influence. The young aristocrats secretly met with envoys from the Tarquins and plotted the latter's return. They were, however, overheard by a slave who promptly reported them to the consuls. The conspirators were sentenced to death. Livy writes: 'It was a memorable scene: for the consular office imposed upon a father the duty of exacting the supreme penalty from his sons, so that he who, of all men, should have been spared the sight of their suffering was the one whom fate ordained to enforce it.'[14]

Machiavelli's Version of the Roman Revolution

The expulsion of the Tarquins is a central theme in Machiavelli's *Discourses*.[15] In his rendition of Roman history, this event inaugurates the golden age of Rome, releasing the humours of the people and the nobles and giving rise to the virtuous class conflict that he regards as 'the first cause of keeping Rome free'.[16] One can call the period between the expulsion of the Tarquins and the tribuneships of the Gracchi a golden age, because during these three hundred years, the 'tumults' ('tumulti') rarely produced exile or violence ('violenza') but rather 'laws and orders in benefit of public freedom'.[17] During this period, 'freedom was never taken away by any of its citizens'.[18] The Roman people were 'hostile ... to the kingly name and a lover of the glory and common good of [their] fatherland'.[19]

Yet even though the transition from the monarchy to the republic is key to Machiavelli's account of Roman history, he actually denies that it constituted a revolution. In *Discourses* 1:9, he emphasizes rather that Romulus had already provided Rome with the orders suitable to a republic. As evidence, Machiavelli cites the fact that republican Rome did not innovate any new institutions, save replacing the king by two consuls with one-year terms. 'This testifies that all the first orders of that city were more conformable to a civil and free way of life than to an absolute and tyrannical one.'[20] For Machiavelli, Rome acquired its freedom not by revolting against the Tarquins but by '*accident ... after* the expulsion of the Tarquins' (emphasis added).[21] The 'accident' Machiavelli has in mind is Brutus's execution of his sons, which he regards as the actual moment Rome became free. New states, he insists, have enemies rather than friends. And to deal with these enemies there was 'no remedy more powerful, nor more valid, more secure, and more necessary, than to kill the sons of Brutus'.[22]

'Killing the sons of Brutus' is Machiavelli's enigmatic shorthand for the quasi-sacrificial bloodshed of the enemies of a state, especially a popular state: throughout *The Prince* and the *Discourses*, Machiavelli emphasizes the importance of a firm, uncompromising, and violent response to such enemies.[23] Brutus's execution of his sons is also listed as the first and paradigmatic item of a series of executions that 'drew the Roman republic back toward its beginning'.[24] Such returns to the beginning are important, because they are the only effective remedy against the inevitable corruption and disintegration of civic life. Accordingly, Brutus becomes, in Machiavelli's telling, the key figure and hero of the Roman revolution, or as Machiavelli puts it, 'father of Roman liberty'.[25] Brutus merits this title, not because he led a popular uprising against the monarchy but because, when confronted with the difficult choice between saving his own sons and defending the republic, he opts for the public good, even though it means sacrificing his own children.

Unlike Brutus, whom Machiavelli celebrates for his unwavering commitment to freedom and his willingness to sacrifice his own interests in the name of virtue, Machiavelli has very little to say about the other actor who similarly sacrifices her own interest in the name of virtue: Lucretia. Like Brutus, Lucretia murders her own flesh and blood in front of witnesses. Like Brutus, she sees her act as a response to a fundamental violation of the principles that regulate social and political life, a response to a most perfidious form of disloyalty and an inexcusable breach of trust. Like Brutus, who calls on the Romans to take up arms against the tyrants, Lucretia demands the Tarquins' death. Indeed, one could argue that Lucretia inaugurates the anti-tyrannical motif, turning her victimization by the tyrant into a rallying cry against the monarchy. In St. Jerome's words, Lucretia was 'the equal of Brutus, if not her superior, since Brutus learnt from [her] the impossibility of being a slave'.[26]

And yet, in the *Discourses*, Machiavelli treats Lucretia as a minor character, denying her the political and historical importance which Roman historians as well as medieval and Renaissance authors had routinely accorded her. Lucretia comes up in four chapters of the *Discourses* (3:2, 3:5, 3:7, 3:26). In the first occurrence (*Disc.* 3:2; *Opere* 197), she is already dead, and Machiavelli refers to her ('la morta Lucrezia') as the body from whom Brutus draws the bloody knife and makes the bystanders swear an oath to end the monarchy. The second time she is invoked, Machiavelli refers to her rape and suicide as a contingent event and argues that Tarquin the Proud 'was expelled not because his son Sextus had raped Lucretia but because he had broken the laws of the kingdom and governed it tyrannically … If the accident of Lucretia had not come, as soon as another had arisen, it would have brought the same effect.'[27] A couple of chapters later, Lucretia comes up again; or rather, her name does not appear, because Machiavelli doubles down on his earlier dismissal of her historical role. He now distinguishes major institutional transformations that are bloodless from ones that are bloody. The Roman revolution, he insists, is of the first kind: '[N]one other than the Tarquins were expelled, with no offense to anyone else.'[28] No offence to anyone else! Clearly, Lucretia does not count as 'qualunque altro'. Finally, Lucretia has the dubious honour of being included in the infamous chapter titled 'How a State Is Ruined Because of Women'.[29] That chapter, which focuses on state-wrecking women, suggests—in tension with the earlier claims—that 'the excess done against Lucretia took the state away from the Tarquins'.

In sum, two out of the four chapters where Lucretia appears dismiss her role in the Roman revolution entirely: in *Discourses* 3:5 and 3:7, although in the latter case it would be more accurate to say that she does not actually appear, because she is effectively erased from the narrative. In these chapters, both her rape and her suicide are trivialized and marginalized. Machiavelli seems to suggest that rape and suicide are forms of violence that do not qualify as founding events and do not count as politically relevant moments in the history of states. Not even Lucretia's injuries are recognized as politically pertinent, or indeed as morally relevant at all. The two other chapters concede Lucretia's involvement in the uprising, yet only as a passive, raped, and dead body exposed to the male gaze, an object of male desire contaminated by tyrannical power.

Machiavelli's denial in the *Discourses* of the political and historical role that other commentators routinely grant Lucretia is surprising for various reasons. First, as I briefly indicated earlier, Lucretia seems in many ways an analogue to Brutus. She is an anti-tyrannical hero who sacrifices her own flesh and blood in the name of public virtue. Why does her sacrifice not count as political, and why does she not qualify for inclusion in the pantheon of Roman founding figures? Second, Machiavelli treats the Lucretia myth at length in his comedy *Mandragola*, where he satirizes the Roman founding legend. Thus, given the importance that Livy attaches to Lucretia, Machiavelli's near-omission of Lucretia from his *Discourses on Livy* must be understood as a deliberate and calculated choice. This raises some interpretive questions. Given that most Roman historians, as well as medieval and Renaissance writers dealing with the topic, treat Lucretia as one of the protagonists of the uprising against the Tarquins, why does Machiavelli refuse to accord her such a role? What might be at stake in this deliberate disavowal of Lucretia in the *Discourses on Livy*?

Interpretive Path 1: Violence and Women's Agency

In Machiavelli's political and historical work, there is a near-systematic omission of women as perpetrators or targets of lethal violence. With a few exceptions, women neither inflict nor suffer the kind of lethal violence that Machiavelli persistently stylizes as a metonym for political action. In Machiavelli's work, violence is coded as female only in the mythic and allegorical world of the uncontrollable non-human forces *fortuna* and *necessità*, which are sometimes likened to violent actors, and where femininity serves as a prop for nature. In the politico-historical narrative, violence by or against women is marginal.

The historical record partly explains this omission. Battery and sexual assault notwithstanding, in the public world of Italian Renaissance cities, women tended to be neither perpetrators nor victims of socially recognized public forms of violence. With respect to legal violence and especially executions, Andrea Zorzi reports that in the high Renaissance, very few women were among those condemned to death.[30] (The persecution of witches did not start until the sixteenth and seventeenth centuries.[31]) Those women who were executed in the fourteenth and fifteenth centuries were primarily from the lower orders, belonging to the *popolo minuto*, and were typically executed for infanticide or for having killed their employers. And save for Caterina Sforza, the Countess of Forlì, women were rarely involved as actors in spectacular forms of political violence.

In the scholarship on Machiavelli, the absence of women as agents or patients of violence is largely addressed in terms of the categories of inclusion and exclusion. A number of feminist scholars have argued that Machiavelli explicitly or implicitly excludes women from the political space, rendering citizenship an exclusively masculine domain.[32] From this perspective, Machiavelli's rendition of the Lucretia story appears as a classic exclusion of women from political life, and a denial of their political agency. In contrast to Livy's Lucretia, who is a speaking and acting subject, and who dramatizes her suicide so as to compel her male relatives to seek justice for her death, Machiavelli's Lucretia is mute. The appropriate feminist response, then, is to recover and recuperate Lucretia's voice and agency, and to highlight her role and importance in the Roman revolution. On this reading, the critic's task is to show how Machiavelli's version of the events perpetuates a patriarchal viewpoint that has obscured the important contributions made by women to ancient and modern history. From this vantage point, Machiavelli's silence on Lucretia constitutes an erasure and incites a counter-history, one that accords representational space to Lucretia and acknowledges her importance, not just as object but as agentive subject, in igniting the Roman revolution.

Yet the interpretive claim on which such a reading is based—namely that Machiavelli shuts out women from politics—has come under significant criticism from a second strand of feminist research. These interpreters have contended that women are not simply excluded from the Machiavellian political world but selectively included on sexist terms.[33] This second group of scholars have argued that it is not *women* who are excluded from the Machiavellian political universe but *femininity*, and that women who successfully perform masculinity are, in fact, legible to Machiavelli as political agents. Scholars have pointed to various examples of women whom Machiavelli treats as skilful political actors: Dido, Caterina Sforza, Queen Giovanna of Naples, Queen Rosamund of the Longobards—all of whom are willing to kill or die in the pursuit of power.[34] Women, in other words, can be princes (or political actors); the point at issue is what is required for them to be recognized as such. From this angle, the appropriate question is not how to recover Lucretia's voice and agency, but rather to ask what the conditions are that make her unrecognizable as a political actor; or in more intentionalist language, what differentiates Lucretia from these other women—Dido, Caterina Sforza, Giovanna, Rosamund—that Machiavelli refuses to grant her the status of a female prince that he accords to the others?

Interpretive Path 2: The Economy of Male Honour

Hanna Pitkin rightly notes that it is incorrect to say that Machiavelli silences or simply bars women from the political world. She observes that Machiavelli's obvious and explicit contempt for women and femininity is accompanied by anxiety about the mysterious and dangerous powers he attributes to women.[35] Specifically, Pitkin notes that there are two archetypes of women that recur throughout his work: on the one hand, young and typically unmarried women, daughters, who are objectified as beautiful and as sexually desirable; on the other hand, older women, mothers, wives, and matrons, who are depicted as controlling access to young women and thus holding the key to promote or frustrate male pleasure and desire. Although she is married and a matron, Lucretia falls into the first category. Pitkin interprets Machiavelli's warning in *Discourses* 3:26 against women who wreck states as alluding to such women, whose mere presence makes men lose their heads.[36] Because of the seductive allure the male gaze projects onto them, they threaten masculine political actors' self-control and their mastery of their passions.[37] Pitkin further argues that Machiavelli depicts women as politically dangerous, because 'they are invested with other men's sense of honour'.[38] On this reading, women are always understood to be attached to one (or more) men: a father, husband, or brother, whose honour is invested in the woman's virtue. Circulating between men as props for male honour, women thus function as part of an economy of exchange.

Although Pitkin does not cite Lévi-Strauss, this is of course the latter's argument in *The Elementary Structures of Kinship*. According to Lévi-Strauss, the reciprocal exchange and circulation of women constitute a form of communication, in which women perform the role of signs within a heteronormative economy of male desire. But as Lévi-Strauss points out, women's bodies only become signs to the extent that the satisfaction of male sexual desire can be deferred.[39] From this perspective, the rape of Lucretia represents a breach of the protocols whereby women are exchanged; the revolt against the Tarquins seeks to re-establish the proper modalities of this exchange.

Yet if, as Pitkin suggests, Machiavelli's warning about the danger of women derives from his view of women as invested with other men's honour, the puzzle of why he sidelines the rape and suicide of Lucretia becomes even more acute: is Lucretia not the perfect manifestation of the depth and resilience of the economy of male honour that, according to Pitkin, is at the heart of Machiavelli's concerns? If Machiavelli urges his readers to beware of the political complications of desire, precisely because he is anxious about the possessive claims men make over women, then would not the story of Lucretia be the quintessential paradigm of such a situation? Why, then, would Machiavelli repudiate the significance of this 'accident' and argue that it was entirely epiphenomenal to the Roman revolution?

If Pitkin is right about the economy of male honour and the exchange of women that it presupposes, the Lucretia story becomes more problematic from the perspective of feminist criticism. Indeed, one could argue that the uprising against the Tarquins was not so much a revolution as a reaffirmation of the patriarchal protocols whereby women are exchanged. Such an interpretation dovetails with some feminist scholarship on the Lucretia myth, which has long pointed to the *limited emancipatory potential* that Lucretia represents. Simone de Beauvoir, for example, notes that Lucretia typifies the restricted political roles assigned to women in the history of Western political thought. These roles include stirring up intrigues and setting off events that are subsequently directed and managed by men. In this tradition, she argues, women have served as 'pretexts' rather than independent and active participants who make positive contributions to political life. Lucretia's suicide, she writes, 'had no more than a symbolic value'.[40]

Beauvoir's argument suggests that rejecting Machiavelli's mute Lucretia for Livy's loquacious Lucretia merely reinscribes the role of women as pretexts and does not generate a vision of women as independent agents who actively shape the political world. The literary scholar Stephanie Jed has offered a brilliant analysis of how the humanist tradition that celebrates Lucretia's rape as a prologue for republican freedom reproduces what she calls 'chaste thinking'. By 'chaste thinking', Jed means a figure of thought that ties together the narrative of Lucretia's rape and the liberation of Rome from tyranny into a logical sequence of events.[41] Specifically, 'chaste thinking' authorizes the social logic that proceeds from chastity to rape and thence through corruption, suicide, and revenge to revolution. Chaste thinking involves a nostalgic representation of past freedoms, figured in the form of uncorrupted female virtue, that are subsequently compromised by tyrannical power (aka unbridled desire leading to rape). In such a narrative, the rape is a necessary moment, because it enables and justifies the constitution of republican power and freedom. Jed's critique of the Lucretia myth thus serves as a reminder, even more forceful than Beauvoir's, that glorifying Lucretia as a republican heroine is by no means innocent or any less patriarchal than disavowing her as Machiavelli does.

Interpretive Path 3: Ambivalence

Psychoanalytically informed feminists have contended that Machiavelli's representation of women is marked by ambivalence. Pitkin, for example, argues not only that the economy of honour shapes Machiavelli's understanding of women as property but that ambivalence, specifically concerning manhood and autonomy, fundamentally structures his thought.[42] While Pitkin does not draw out the implications of her claims concerning ambivalence for the Lucretia story and its narrative of rape and suicide, other scholars have. In her examination of the dead women that litter the history of European art and literature, Elisabeth Bronfen has argued that narrative and visual images of dead women always represent more than the literal image at hand. They are cultural symptoms, and 'articulate unconscious knowledge and unconscious desires in a displaced, recoded and translated manner'.[43] Such images always contain a figurative meaning that functions allegorically for the community of survivors. Put differently, narrative and visual representations of dead women never simply inspire grief. They also inspire anxiety and desire, and these are part of what makes such representations politically effective.

For the Lucretia myth, that ambivalence is especially notable in the visual representations of the rape and suicide in European art. From Titian's late sixteenth-century painting through Gentileschi's mid-seventeenth and Tiepolo's mid-eighteenth-century works, European artists represented the rape scene in a highly eroticized manner, Lucretia's transfixed gaze suggesting both fear and desire. It is also notable that artistic representations of Lucretia's suicide, from Cranach's and Luca Cambiaso's sixteenth-century paintings to Andrea Casali's eighteenth-century version, all depict her as topless as she plunges the dagger into her heart, even though neither the textual record nor the logic of the narrative would suggest that she bares her chest prior to killing herself.

These eroticized representations suggest that the myth functions not simply as a fable for the inherent moral superiority of republics over tyrannies but that it was designed (or at least read in Early Modern Europe) to arouse desire. Melissa Matthes spells out what this means for the Lucretia myth—as told by Livy, not Machiavelli:

> Although the story of the rape of Lucretia is ostensibly an account of how the republic is founded over a woman's dead body, there is also a way in which the spectre of Lucretia's raped body continues to haunt the new republic. In the trajectory of republican history, Lucretia's story, as itself historical object, is both recalled and repeated, and then forgotten and denied. Lucretia's raped body as

well as her story remain taboo throughout the life of the republic because her sexual violation reminds her male kin of their own failed masculinity (they could not safeguard her) and of their own continued desires for sexual conquest (each would like to have the sexual and political power of the tyrant/rapist). Thus, there is in these republican renditions a recognized contagion between the recollection of the story of Lucretia's rape and the temptation that her violation represents. Indeed, although republicans do not themselves rape Lucretia, they found their citizenry on the recollection of the temptation that the spectacle of her violation recalls.[44]

For Matthes, then, Lucretia's rape and suicide is both recalled and forgotten, repeated and denied by narratives such as Livy's that extol Lucretia as a republican heroine. The Lucretia myth, Matthes suggests, both troubles republican masculinity and arouses men's unquenchable desire for sexual conquest. Matthes's provocative interpretation suggests that republican citizens derive pleasure from retelling the story of Lucretia—not the chaste pleasure of celebrating republican moral superiority, but the pleasure of reliving the temptation that the rape represents.

Interestingly, Matthes exempts Machiavelli from this charge. For Matthes, Machiavelli's refusal to participate in the Lucretia narrative on the terms set by Livy and other Roman historians is commendable. Rather than analysing what Machiavelli says about Lucretia in the *Discourses*, Matthes opts for a reading of *Mandragola* where she finds a retelling of the Lucretia story that 'return[s] agency to political actors'.[45] For Matthes, the comedic form of *Mandragola* serves to dispel some of the mythic power of the conjunction of sexual violence with political founding.

Conclusion

This chapter has explored, through the Lucretia narrative, the gendered dimension of Machiavelli's concern with violence and founding. I have shown that Machiavelli, unlike his Roman sources and Early Modern humanist contemporaries, downplays and deprecates Lucretia's role in the Roman revolution. I have argued that this trivialization of Lucretia's role is surprising for four reasons. First, Roman historians and Renaissance humanists generally glorified Lucretia's role in the overthrow of the monarchy, mythologizing Lucretia as a central founding figure. Second, Machiavelli offers conflicting accounts of Lucretia's rape in different chapters of the *Discourses*. Third, Machiavelli celebrates Brutus's execution of his sons as a key moment for founding the republic while simultaneously dismissing Lucretia's suicide, which in many ways parallels Brutus's actions. Finally, we might expect Machiavelli to treat Lucretia as exemplary of the illegitimate violence of tyranny and the uprising that ensued as a prologue to reinstating the sexual virtue that Machiavelli, following his humanist sources, associates with republican government. I thus regard Machiavelli's minimization of Lucretia as a deliberate disavowal and inquire into the meaning of this particular move.

Through engaging with the feminist literature on Machiavelli and Livy, I have reviewed a number of possible explanations for this disavowal. Machiavelli's silence on Lucretia could simply be an instance of a broader patriarchal tendency to exclude women from the political sphere, or to include them on sexist terms. Contrariwise, his refusal to engage with the myth could amount to a rejection of the moral logic whereby rape and political foundings are intertwined, such that 'rape authorizes revenge; revenge comprises revolution; revolution establishes legitimate government'.[46] Finally, Machiavelli's representation of Lucretia may be designed to interrupt the ambivalent compulsion to tell and to forget, to enact and to suppress the violence and the desire that accompanies it.

I do not propose these various interpretive approaches as possible resolutions, as I am not persuaded that any of them adequately explains the text or is consistent with Machiavelli's explicit claims elsewhere. Machiavelli seems to assign to political violence an incoherent and contradictory political value, one that cannot easily be resolved by references to conventional patriarchal norms of sexual virtue, nor to norms of representation in feminist historiography.

Notes

1. Aside from the figures named as 'most excellent' princes in Chapter 6 of *The Prince*—Moses, Cyrus, Romulus, and Theseus—the list of founders would include, at the very least, Lucius Junius Brutus, the founder of the Roman republic, whom Machiavelli exalts in the *Discourses*; the historical and mythical founders of ancient cities, such as Aeneas, Lycurgus, and Solon; the empire-builder Alexander the Great; the founder of the Roman religion, Numa Pompilius; the Greek tyrants Agathocles, Nabis, and Hiero of Syracuse; as well as the more complicated instances of contemporary princes such as Cesare Borgia, Castruccio Castracani, and Francesco Sforza.
2. See Hanna F. Pitkin, *Fortune Is a Woman: Gender and Politics in the Thought of Niccolò Machiavelli* (Berkeley, CA: University of California Press, 1999), 55.

3. See Sheldon Wolin, *Politics and Vision* (Princeton, NJ: Princeton University Press, 2004), 180.
4. See Yves Winter, *Machiavelli and the Orders of Violence* (Cambridge: Cambridge University Press, 2018).
5. See Yves Winter, 'Machiavelli and the Rape of Lucretia', *History of Political Thought* 40, no. 3 (2019), 405–32. While both the present chapter and the article cited deal with the puzzle of Machiavelli's disavowal of Lucretia, they do so from different perspectives. The present essay emphasizes the problem of founding violence, and the gendered norms whereby some forms of violence count as political whereas others are not recognized as such.
6. See Maria J. Falco, ed., *Feminist Interpretations of Niccolò Machiavelli* (University Park, PA: Pennsylvania State University Press, 2004); Michelle T. Clarke, 'On the Woman Question in Machiavelli', *Review of Politics* 67, no. 2 (2005), 229–55; Barbara Spackman, 'Machiavelli and Gender', in *The Cambridge Companion to Machiavelli*, ed. John M. Najemy (Cambridge: Cambridge University Press, 2010), 223–38.
7. My interpretation focuses on Livy's rendition, both because classicists regard his version as an artistic and dramatic masterpiece and because his history constituted Machiavelli's most significant source. See P. G. Walsh, *Livy: His Historical Aims and Methods* (Cambridge: Cambridge University Press, 1961), 214–18; R. M. Ogilvie, *A Commentary on Livy: Books 1–5* (Oxford: Clarendon Press, 1965), 219; S. N. Philippides, 'Narrative Strategies and Ideology in Livy's "Rape of Lucretia"', *Helios* 10, no. 7 (1983), 113.
8. Livy, *History of Rome* 2:1. All Latin citations are from vol. 1 of the Loeb edition, ed. Benjamin O. Foster et al. (Cambridge, MA: Harvard University Press, 1919–59); translations from Titus Livy, *The Early History of Rome*, tr. Aubrey de Sélincourt (London: Penguin, 2002).
9. Tarquinium mala libido Lucretiae per vim stuprandae capit; cum forma tum spectata castitas incitat': *History* 1:57.
10. '[C]eterum corpus est tantum violatum, animus insons; mors testis erit, sed date dexteras fidemque haud inpune adultero fore. Sextus est Tarquinius, qui hostis pro hospite priore nocte vi armatus mihi sibique, si vos viri estis, pestiferum hinc abstulit gaudium': *History* 1:58.
11. *History* 1:59.
12. '[N]on acrior vindex libertatis fuerat quam deinde custos fuit': *History* 2:1.
13. '[A]dulescentes aliquot … quorum in regno libido solutior fuerat, … adsueti more regio vivere': *History* 2:3.
14. '[C]onspectius eo quod poenae capiendae ministerium patri de liberis consulatus imposuit, et qui spectator erat amovendus, eum ipsum fortuna exactorem supplicii dedit': *History* 2:5.

15. For references to the expulsion of the Tarquins in the *Discourses*, see *Disc.* 1:3, 9, 16, 17, 25, 28, 32, 58; 3:5, 7, 26.
16. '[P]rima causa del tenere libera Roma': *Disc.* 1:4: Machiavelli, *Tutte le opere*, ed. Mario Martelli (Florence: Sansoni, 1971), 82. All citations of the *Discorsi* are from this edition (henceforth *Opere*). Translation from Machiavelli, *Discourses on Livy*, tr. Harvey C. Mansfield and Nathan Tarcov (Chicago, IL: University of Chicago Press, 1996), 16. All translations of *Discorsi* are from this version.
17. '[L]eggi e ordini in beneficio della publica libertà': ibid.
18. '[N]on fu mai tolta la libertà da alcuno suo cittadino': *Disc.* 1:28, *Opere* 110; tr. Mansfield and Tarcov, 63.
19. '[I]nimico del nome regio, ed amatore della gloria e del bene commune della sua patria': *Disc.* 1:58, *Opere* 141; tr. Mansfield and Tarcov, 117.
20. '[I]l che testifica, tutti gli ordini primi di quella città essere stati più conformi a uno vivere civile e libero, che a uno assoluto e tirannico': *Disc.* 1:9, *Opere* 91; tr. Mansfield and Tarcov, 30. The claim in *Disc.* 1:9 that the Romans did not create new institutions conflicts with the praise Machiavelli showers on the Romans in *Disc.* 1:25 for inventing the position of 'sacrificing king' ('Re Sacrificulo'): a religious official, subordinate to the high priest, who was royal only in name but could carry out the annual sacrifice that, according to custom, was reserved for the king.
21. '[P]er *alcuno accidente ... dopo* la cacciata de' Tarquinii': *Disc.* 1:16, *Opere* 99 (emphasis added); tr. Mansfield and Tarcov, 44. *Disc.* 1:17 similarly refers to Roman freedom as emerging after the Tarquins' expulsion: 'When the Tarquins were expelled, Rome could at once take and maintain its freedom' ('Roma ... cacciati i Tarquinii, poté subito prendere e mantenere quella libertà': *Opere* 101; tr. Mansfield and Tarcov, 47).
22. '[N]on ci è più potente rimedio, né più valido né più sicuro né più necessario, che ammazzare i figliuoli di Bruto': *Disc.* 1:16, *Opere* 100; tr. Mansfield and Tarcov, 45.
23. See especially *Disc.* 3:3, appropriately titled 'That It Is Necessary to Kill the Sons of Brutus If One Wishes to Maintain a Newly Acquired Freedom' ('Come egli è necessario, a volere mantenere una libertà acquistata di nuovo, ammazzare i figliuoli di Bruto': *Opere* 198; tr. Mansfield.and Tarcov, 214).
24. '[R]itirarono la Republica romana verso il suo principio': *Disc.* 3:1, *Opere* 195; tr. Mansfield and Tarcov, 210.
25. '[P]adre della romana libertà': *Disc.* 3:1, *Opere* 197; tr. Mansfield and Tarcov, 212.
26. 'Haec Lucretiam Bruto aequavit, nescias an et praetulerit: quoniam Brutus non posse servire a femina didicit': Jerome, *Adversus Jovinianum*, 1:320:

Patrologia Latina 23 (Paris: Garnier, 1883), 194; tr. from Jerome, *Letters and Select Works*, tr. W. H. Fremantle (Grand Rapids, MI: Eerdmans, 1989), 1:49.

27. 'Non fu, adunque, cacciato costui per avere Sesto suo figliuolo stuprata Lucrezia, ma per avere rotte le leggi del regno, e governatolo tirannicamente; ... E se lo accidente di Lucrezia non fosse venuto, come prima ne fosse nato un altro, arebbe partorito il medesimo effetto': *Disc.* 3:5, *Opere* 199; tr. Mansfield and Tarcov, 217.
28. '[N]on furono cacciati altri che i Tarquinii, fuora della offensione di qualunque altro': *Disc.* 3:7, *Opere* 211; tr. Mansfield and Tarcov, 236.
29. 'Come per cagione di femine si rovina uno stato': *Disc.* 3:26, *Opere* 232.
30. Andrea Zorzi, 'Le esecuzioni delle condanne a morte a Firenze nel tardo medievo tra repressione penale e ceremoniale pubblico', in *Simbolo e realtà della vita urbana nel tardo medioevo*, ed. Massimo Miglio and Giuseppe Lombardi (Rome: Vecchiarelli, 1993), 153–253, 176.
31. See Carlo Ginzburg, *The Night Battles: Witchcraft and Agrarian Cults in the Sixteenth and Seventeenth Centuries* (Baltimore, MD: Johns Hopkins University Press, 1983); Guido Ruggiero, *Binding Passions: Tales of Magic, Marriage, and Power at the End of the Renaissance* (New York: Oxford University Press, 1993).
32. See Susan Moller Okin, *Women in Western Political Thought* (Princeton, NJ: Princeton University Press, 1979), 6–7; Wendy Brown, *Manhood and Politics: A Feminist Reading in Political Theory* (Totowa, NJ: Rowman & Littlefield, 1988), 115–17; Jean Bethke Elshtain, *Women and War* (Chicago, IL: University of Chicago Press, 1995), 56–9.
33. See Arlene W. Saxonhouse, *Women in the History of Political Thought: Ancient Greece to Machiavelli* (New York: Praeger, 1985); John Juncholl Shin, 'Beyond Virtù', in *Feminist Interpretations of Niccolò Machiavelli*, 287–308.
34. See Sebastian de Grazia, *Machiavelli in Hell* (New York: Vintage, 1989), 134; Jo Ann Cavallo, 'Machiavelli and Women', in *Seeking Real Truths: Multidisciplinary Perspectives on Machiavelli*, ed. Patricia Vilches and Gerald Seaman (Leiden: Brill, 2007), 123–47; Clarke, 'On the Woman Question'.
35. Pitkin, *Fortune Is a Woman*, 110.
36. Ibid., 115.
37. Ibid., 5.
38. Ibid., 118.

39. Claude Lévi-Strauss, *The Elementary Structures of Kinship*, ed. Rodney Needham, tr. James Harle Bell and John Richard von Sturmer (Boston, MA: Beacon Press, 1969), 62–3.
40. Simone de Beauvoir, *The Second Sex*, tr. Constance Borde and Sheila Malovany-Chevallier (New York: Vintage, 2011), 150.
41. Stephanie H. Jed, *Chaste Thinking: The Rape of Lucretia and the Birth of Humanism* (Bloomington, IN: Indiana University Press, 1989), 8.
42. Pitkin, *Fortune Is a Woman*, 5.
43. Elisabeth Bronfen, *Over Her Dead Body: Death, Femininity and the Aesthetic* (Manchester: Manchester University Press, 1992), xi.
44. Melissa M. Matthes, *The Rape of Lucretia and the Founding of Republics* (University Park, PA: Pennsylvania State University Press, 2000), 6.
45. Matthes, *The Rape of Lucretia*, 174.
46. Coppélia Kahn, 'Lucrece: The Sexual Politics of Subjectivity', in *Rape and Representation*, ed. Lynn A. Higgins and Brenda R. Silver (New York: Columbia University Press, 1991), 141–59, 141.

Words and Dispositions

11

Thinking with Animals

Machiavelli's L'asino *and the Metamorphoses of Power*

Supriya Chaudhuri

> If a lion could talk, we wouldn't be able to understand it.
> —Ludwig Wittgenstein, *Philosophical Investigations*[1]

> What is man, if he is always the place—and, at the same time, the result—of ceaseless divisions and caesurae?
> —Giorgio Agamben, *The Open*[2]

Animals in Machiavelli are not really animals: they are tools he deems 'good to think with'.[3] In this he is by no means exceptional, since the same habit characterizes Western political and philosophical thought from antiquity, and the traits that Machiavelli ascribes to the animals he so frequently cites belong to a well-attested rhetorical and moral tradition. Nevertheless, as Leo Strauss pointed out in 1958, Machiavelli's insistence in the notorious eighteenth chapter of *Il Principe* that the prince should imitate the lion and the fox involves a new attention to human kinship with animals, one that can only be articulated by setting himself up as a centaur, 'a Chiron of an entirely new kind'. For Machiavelli, humanism is not enough, says Strauss: '[T]he imitation of the beast takes the place of the imitation of God.'[4] In his unfinished poem in *terza rima*, *L'asino* (begun in 1517), Machiavelli takes upon himself the more humble, but allegorically richer, garb of an ass, a creature whose importance to fifteenth- and sixteenth-century moral philosophy, iconography, and literature can scarcely be overestimated. At the same time, because the poem's incomplete state leaves the event of the speaker's own transformation unnarrated, *L'asino* as it stands covers a wide range of human–animal attributes, ending with an address by the exemplary subject of Circean enchantment, a man transformed into a pig.

Despite its brevity and incompleteness, *L'asino* is a complicated and ambitious poem, with an interesting history through the course of the sixteenth century. We first hear of it in Machiavelli's well-known letter to Lodovico Alamanni at Rome on 17 December 1517, where he expresses disappointment at being left out of Ariosto's list of poets and courtiers in the Proem to Canto 46 of *Orlando Furioso* (1516):

> These past few days I have read Ariosto's *Orlando Furioso*, and truly the poem is beautifully devised, and in many places it is wonderful. If he happens to be with you, commend me to him, and tell him that my sole complaint is that, having mentioned so many poets, he has left me hidden like a prick, and that he has treated me in his *Orlando* in a way that I will not treat him in my *Asino*.[5]

This slight (later to be compounded by Ariosto in the 1532 edition of his great poem) would, so Albert Ascoli and Victoria Kahn argue, have been felt by Machiavelli as a double failure: both as an exclusion from the community of poets and as confirming his 'exclusion from active life'.[6] Machiavelli's planned revenge is less clear than he may have intended, since Ariosto is not named in the existing fragment of *L'asino*. But Gian Mario Anselmi and Paolo Fazion note an echo of the *Orlando Furioso* in cap. 7 of the poem, and perhaps there is a mocking reference to Machiavelli's 'self-crowned' rival in the account of the burlesque coronation of a bad poet, the deluded Abate de Gaeta (Giacomo Baraballo).[7] In this lengthy *ekphrasis* (*L'asino*, cap. 6), Machiavelli mentions the trick played by Pope Leo X, who had offered the elderly poet his recently acquired elephant, Hanno, to transport him to the Capitoline Hill. Eventually, the elephant's refusal to cross a bridge led to the procession's breaking up in disorder, and the would-be poet laureate was forced to dismount. A contemporary satirical woodcut represents the scene with an ass mounted upon an elephant.[8]

But the ass remains elusive in *L'asino*. The poem commences with the poet promising to relate 'the various chances, the suffering and the grief that under an ass's form I endured'. The travails of an ass, and the poem's title, recall Apuleius, whose high reputation in the early cinquecento was founded both on Filippo Beroaldo's formidable edition of the *Asinus Aureus* (1500), its copious commentary providing an impressive model of humanist scholarship, and on Matteo Maria Boiardo's translation, the *Apulegio volgare* (completed in 1479). Boiardo's translation was eclectic, incorporating material from the Pseudo-Lucianic satire *Onos* (*The Ass*), as well as from Boccaccio, and omitting the mystical conclusion in which Lucius is converted to a follower of the goddess Isis.[9] Boiardo did, however, rely upon the *editio princeps* of 1469, which made Apuleius one of the earliest classical authors (after Cicero) to be printed in Italy, with an introduction by the humanist cleric Giovanni de Bussi.[10] Both Bussi and Beroaldo contributed to an influential tradition of moral and philosophical (mainly Neoplatonic) exegesis of Lucius's transformation into an ass, making the esoteric and magical elements, the sexual licentiousness and rhetorical flamboyance of this 'Milesian tale' simply a foil for its moral intention. In his note on the intention of the author, Beroaldo wrote:

> Truly, under the wrapping of this transmutation he wished as though in passing to describe mortal nature and human manners, so that we should be warned against becoming asses, from being men; when, having been immersed in bestial pleasures, we grow brutish with asinine stupidity and not a single spark of reason or virtue shines in us; for in this way man (as Origen teaches in his books Peri Archon) becomes a horse and a mule, and thus the human body is transformed into beastly bodies. The transformation from an ass back into a man signifies the revival of reason, after pleasures have been trodden down and corporeal delights laid aside.[11]

This allegorical reading of animal metamorphosis was by no means novel. It was based on an interpretative practice whose roots stretch back into antiquity—to Stoic allegory, to the Platonic separation of man's rational faculties from his animal nature, to Neoplatonic philosophy, and to moral readings of classical myth from the very beginnings of the Christian era (as in the pseudo-Heraclitian *Homeric Problems*) through to the *Ovide moralisé* of the medieval cleric Pierre Bersuire. Plato offers a moral explanation of the transmigration of human souls after death into the animals that best suit their natures (metempsychosis rather than metamorphosis) in both the *Timaeus* and the *Republic*, as well as an arresting image of unruly appetites as 'the beast within' the human body in the *Republic* (IX.571c, 590c). It is worth noting that the latter discussion takes place in a specific political context, that of the tyrant, who is most inclined (unlike the democrat) to give free rein to fierce and lawless desire. The Greek rhetorical tradition had always associated animals with specific virtues and vices. In his *Discourses*, the Stoic Epictetus says:

> It is because of our kinship with the flesh that those of us who incline toward it become like wolves, faithless and treacherous and hurtful, and others like lions, wild and savage and untamed, but most of us become like foxes, that is to say, rascals of the animal kingdom. For what else is a slanderous and malicious man but a fox, or something even more rascally and degraded? Take heed, therefore, that you become not one of these rascally creatures.[12]

These habits of association and interpretation persist into Renaissance moral philosophy, mythography, and humanist commentary, even into the curious human–animal physiognomies presented by Giambattista della Porta.[13] The most celebrated instance of a philosophical reading, one that Machiavelli would have known, is perhaps Giovanni Pico della Mirandola's *Oratio* (1486), where he not only describes human beings under the sway of appetite as animals but also speaks of man as having the power to choose his nature, to descend or ascend the scale of being, and to make himself either a beast or a god.[14]

What then is distinctive about Machiavelli's thinking with animals in *L'asino* or *Il Principe*? There is no doubt that, as Strauss noted, Machiavelli is proposing in the role of Chiron the centaur a new anthropology based on that 'kinship' that Plato and Epictetus had been at such pains to discipline and punish. In *L'asino*, a somewhat later work, he converts the context of transformation to fortune rather than ethics, putting at issue crucial questions of knowledge, power, and, ultimately, choice. Faced with the instability of fortune, the exercise of rational choice is in real danger of being confused with corrupted will and yet must be understood and embraced. Despite its fragmentary state and unfulfilled intention, therefore, *L'asino* remains an unusual and important contribution to what Nuccio Ordine, writing on Giordano Bruno, characterized as the sixteenth-century 'philosophy of the ass'.[15]

The poem deliberately blends an assortment of literary sources— Apuleian, Dantesque, Virgilian—with further debts to the *novella* tradition in Boccaccio and to a style of colloquial and paradoxical poetry popularized by the quattrocento poet Burchiello (Domenico di Giovanni). In the proem, the speaker declares that true to his asinine nature, he will not court the Muses. He then relates the story of a young Florentine youth addicted to running, who is attended to by a succession of doctors (*medici*: the allusion is clearly intended) but suffers a relapse: now, like an ass, he must bray his censure of the 'grudging and evil' world. In the next section, the speaker finds himself, like Dante, in a dark wood and encounters a beautiful woman, who turns out to be a handmaiden of Circe, tending her herds of fierce animals. She tells him that these beasts were once men like himself, transformed by Circe's gaze into various animal shapes. The speaker, too, already at odds with fortune, must undergo further vicissitudes through a like transformation:

> But before these stars show themselves propitious toward you, you will have to travel to explore the world, covered with a different skin,
> because that Providence which supports the human species intends you to bear this affliction for your greater good.

> Hence you must altogether lose your human semblance, and without it come with me to feed among the other beasts.
> There can be no change in this harsh star; by putting you in this place, the ill is deferred, not canceled.[16]

Crawling on all fours like one of the herd, the narrator now accompanies the lady to her chamber and enjoys her hospitality and her sexual favours, like Lucius in *The Golden Ass*.

Next day, the lady departs on her pastoral business, while the speaker, left to himself, reflects on the turns of fortune's wheel and the rise and fall of kingdoms and estates. On the one hand, these changes are inevitable, given the faults and weaknesses inherent in human nature; yet on the other hand, *virtù* (translated by Gilbert as 'energy' or 'ability') makes it possible for kingdoms to attain prosperity and peace (cap. 5, lines 79–97). Machiavelli now launches into a brief but powerful plea for human action as the principal agent of our worldly happiness: it is folly to think that kingdoms are brought down by sins like usury or lust ('l'usura, o qualche peccato carnale', 5:108), or that they can be saved by fastings, alms, and prayers ('digiuni, limosine, orazione', 5:110). Prayer is indeed useful, not so much for what it obtains from God, but because it keeps people united and in good order, and this in turn leads to good fortune.[17] Rather, it is through human endeavour that worldly goods and fortune's favour may be achieved: one who thinks that God will save him, without his own efforts, from a falling house, will perish in the ruins.

This powerful but heretical argument, in effect a secular version of the Pelagian thesis that men are saved by works, not (or not wholly) by grace, lies at the core of Machiavelli's philosophy. Since the context is not that of salvation but of earthly success, Machiavelli averts, rather narrowly, the actual danger of Pelagianism, an early but influential heresy that taught that, contrary to the explicit injunction in *Ephesians* 2:8–9 that we are saved by grace and not by works, human beings had the power to achieve salvation for themselves by doing good works and imitating Christ. Nevertheless, the argument is irreligious enough as it stands, since it relegates prayers and ceremonies ('le cerimonie e le sue divozioni') to the task of maintaining civic order and places the responsibility for earthly happiness entirely upon human beings themselves.[18]

The following chapters return to the theme of animal metamorphosis, with the narrator being taken on a tour of Circe's palace and its inhabitants, housed in separate dormitories according to their species (thus offering an opportunity for the coincidence of animal and human natures to be expounded).

Next, he sees the most prominent of them gathered together in one large chamber where, rather like Dante in the *Inferno*, he clearly recognizes many of the transformed creatures from their past lives and conduct. Most of these historical identifications escape us today, but the real climax of the episode, and the end of the poem as we have it, is in cap. 8, where a fat hog, wallowing in mud, raises his snout and addresses the narrator in familiar terms. In a discourse that rounds off the poem, the pig explains that the animal condition is far superior to the human, and totally rejects the proposition that he be changed back into his original human state. This unnamed beast seems to be identified with an acquaintance of Machiavelli's ('long before I had been known to him': 'io fui già gran tempo suo noto', 8:4). But otherwise it is clearly linked to a classical forebear, the pig Gryllus, one of Odysseus's companions transformed by Circe, who is made to defend the animal condition in Plutarch's dialogue 'Bruta animalia ratione uti' ('Beasts are Rational', *Moralia* 985–92).[19] Following Machiavelli's use of him, he re-appears in several Renaissance texts, including Erasmus's *Praise of Folly*, where Folly prefers Gryllus to Ulysses.[20] In his celebrated dialogue *Circe* (1549), Giovan Battista Gelli, one of Machiavelli's successors in the Florentine Academy, conspicuously omits the pig Gryllus but assigns his sentiments to other animal *personae*.

Plutarch's dialogue, possibly an early work, is usually read together with his much longer exercise on the intelligence of animals ('De sollertia animalium', *Moralia* 959–85), which is dated after 70 CE, around the same time that Pliny was compiling his *Natural History*, the preface to which dates from 77 CE. At the very start of Book VII of the *Natural History*, Pliny comments on the misfortune of human beings, cast naked upon the earth without hide or hair, a prey to disease, ambition, avarice, and the malice of their fellows, and inferior to animals with respect to the sharpness of their senses. Plutarch's principal satiric targets are the Stoics: the arguments he presents challenge precisely those positions that the Stoics had adopted in the classical debate on animals and humans, denying reason to the former and associating them with various vices. Not only do Plutarch's speakers, including Gryllus who refuses Odysseus's offer of restored humanity, assert that animals are rational; they also affirm that animals can form concepts, feel emotions, participate in justice, and exhibit natural virtue (especially the cardinal virtues: *Moralia* (961C–D, 962A–B, 986B–992C). As Gryllus puts it:

> the soul of beasts has a greater natural capacity and perfection for the generation of virtue; for without command or instruction, 'unsown and unploughed', as it were, it naturally brings forth and develops such virtue as is proper in each case.[21]

An inevitable consequence of the argument is the extension to animals of the Stoic notion of *oikeiôsis* (belonging), and this logic then drives Plutarch's two essays against the eating of flesh ('De esu carnium', *Moralia* 993B–999B) which Shelley said he had translated.

We must see Plutarch's choice of transformed animal as deliberate, since from the earliest phase of Stoic allegory, the conversion of Odysseus's companions to swine had invited reductive moral comment. Pigs were associated with lust and gluttony in the Greek rhetorical tradition as well as in Neoplatonic philosophy, and Christians might have recalled the fate of the Gadarene swine (an event criticized by Porphyry on the grounds of injustice to animals).[22] For Ovid, metamorphosis had posed, above all, a problem of psycho-physical identity and its loss through the violent abduction and alienation of the self by desire, grief, or fear. Ovid's account of the Circe episode powerfully evokes what it might be like to grow bristles, acquire a snout, and lose language:

> I began to grow rough with bristles, and I could speak no longer, but in place of words came only hoarse, grunting sounds, and I began to bend forward with face turned entirely to the earth. I felt my mouth hardening into a long snout, my neck swelling in brawny folds.[23]

For later readers, however, this passage, with its companion account of re-transformation, emphasizing the erectness of the human posture as against the earth-facing pig, produced not just a shudder of physical fear but also a clear object-lesson, one that did not escape Renaissance translators and commentators. For example, Arthur Golding moralizes the episode in the *Preface* to his translation of Ovid:

> So was Elpenor and his mates transformed intoo swyne,
> For followyng of their filthie lust in women and in wyne.
> Not that they lost their manly shape as too the outward showe,
> But for that in their brutish brestes most beastly lustes did growe.
> For why this lumpe of fleshe and bones this bodye is not wee,
> Wee are a thyng which earthly eyes denyed are too see.[24]

Seventy years later, Circe and her swine figure prominently in the frontispiece to George Sandys's translation of the *Metamorphoses* and are referred to in the facing explication of 'The Mind of the Frontispeece, and Argument of this Worke'.[25] Gryllus makes an unfavourable appearance in emblem-books such as Petrus Costalius's *Pegma* (1555) and Geoffrey Whitney's *A Choice of*

Emblemes (1586), where he is castigated for his recalcitrance and his choice of filth.[26] Most famously, he features in Book II of Edmund Spenser's *The Faerie Queene*, ending with the following exchange between Guyon and the Palmer:

> Said *Guyon*, See the mind of beastly man,
> That had so soone forgot the excellence
> Of his creation, when he life began,
> That now he chooseth, with vile difference,
> To be a beast, and lacke intelligence.
> To whom the Palmer thus, The dunghill kind
> Delights in filth and foule incontinence:
> Let *Grill* be *Grill*, and haue his hoggish mind,
> But let vs hence depart, whilest wether serues and wind.[27]

As Joseph Loewenstein has noted in a fine essay, Spenser is not interested in animals as such; rather, he is interested in animals *not*-as-such, in human minds in animal bodies.[28] So too, Plutarch's pig, magically gifted with human speech by Circe, is only a token beast, at once wholly identified with the animal he has become and wholly dis-identified from it. His metamorphosis is a fictional means enabling him to compare human and animal states and choose the latter. Entirely suited to the task of moral philosophy, he is unable, we might say, to articulate the problem of other minds—or, more properly, other states of being (as addressed in the celebrated question posed by Thomas Nagel in 1974, 'What Is It Like to Be a Bat?'[29]). What is it to be a non-human animal, and what kind of identity might survive the change? Plutarch does not say, though he urges an ethical and intellectual reconsideration of animal life (including humans) in terms of differing capabilities, rather than an absolute distinction of kind. Metamorphosis for him is neither a state of entrapment, where the human mind is condemned to inhabit an animal body (as often in Ovidian metamorphosis), nor is it a state of degeneration where the human becomes a 'lower' animal. Rather, he sees it as an opportunity for the exercise of choice, so that his Gryllus can freely choose the animal condition over the human one, given the natural excellence of the former. This, rather than the issue of animal reason or of human kinship with other animals, constitutes Plutarch's signal contribution to the Early Modern treatment of metamorphosis.

Machiavelli draws upon both Plutarch and Pliny in asserting animal superiority in respect of the cardinal virtues: prudence, justice, fortitude, and temperance. He repeats that animals are 'closer friends to Nature' ('a natura … maggiori amici', 8:106); that they are born 'fully clad', unlike the nakedness of men; that they have sharper faculties; and that they are free from human ills, including ambition and avarice, as well as from malice towards their own kind. If comparative knowledge about human and animal states is an important part of his hog's armoury, it is above all through his free choice of animal existence that Machiavelli's hog recalls his Plutarchan predecessor.[30] However, I am not convinced by Miguel Vatter's argument that *L'asino* exemplifies a type of 'soft primitivism' adhering to the tenets of ancient theology and that his 'animalitarianism grounds an egalitarian natural right'.[31] Vatter suggests that Machiavelli's strongly Epicurean philosophy is derived from a close study of Plutarch's *Life of Numa* and advocates a 'return' to a happier, Golden Age existence, ruled by Saturn, when human beings and animals lived alike, governed by natural order or natural right. This seems to me to miss the poem's concern with fortune—or rather, *misfortune*—and its exploration of the animal condition, not as emblematic of justice and happiness, but as a means of adapting to adversity.

For Machiavelli in *L'asino*, the fable of metamorphosis is a site where questions regarding human fortune, knowledge, and will can be posed. The pig's discourse provides an apt Plutarchan defence of the superiority of the animal condition, while the description makes comic capital of its physical details: fatness, snout, teeth, mud, muck. The speaker, who is soon to be transformed into an ass himself, is initially repelled by the creature, and we do not know whether he has changed his opinion by the close. Clearly the lady, Circe's handmaiden, is allowing her victim space to reflect upon a course that has already been presented to him as both *inevitable* and *chosen*. For this transformation, one that the narrator must accept for his own good, emblematically complements the maxim already set out in Chapter 25 of *Il Principe*: '[I]f he [the cautious man] would change his nature with the times and with affairs, his fortune would not change.'[32] This is less simple than it appears, for how are time and circumstances to be distinguished from fortune? If we adapt ourselves to changing circumstances, fortune remains unchanging, not in itself, but only to the extent that we are able to adopt, or adapt ourselves to, the form of life it assigns to us. Fortune, then, is not *what happens*, but *how we are affected by what happens*. It is in this context that we might reflect further upon the titular ass in *L'asino*, presented to us as a shape both decreed by fortune and elected—in the respect that it must be agreed to—by the speaker. As Ordine puts it:

> Machiavelli's anthropology demands movement between opposites. "Man" and "beast," "comic" and "serious" are not irreconcilable extremes, but prove to be a dignified way of coping with the "vagaries" of fortune … After the fall of

the Florentine Republic, Machiavelli's sense of isolation weighed heavily on him and *The Ass* therefore translates this state of mind, within a precise literary project, into an attempt at regaining his lost equilibrium.[33]

Given that the literary project remained unfinished, we might want to look a little more closely at Machiavelli's engagement with the question of the animal, as also at the travels/travails of the ass-human proposed in *L'asino*. Chapter 18 of *Il Principe* responds to a passage in Cicero's *De officiis* Book 1, where Cicero had said that 'there are two ways of settling a dispute: first, by discussion; second, by physical force; and since the former is characteristic of man, the latter of the brute, we must resort to force only in case we may not avail ourselves of discussion'.[34] Machiavelli advises the exact opposite:

> Thus, you must know that there are two kinds of combat: one with laws, the other with force. The first is proper to man, the second to beasts; but because the first is often not enough, one must have recourse to the second. Therefore it is necessary for a prince to know well how to use the beast and the man. This role was taught covertly to princes by ancient writers, who wrote that Achilles, and many other ancient princes, were given to Chiron the centaur to be raised, so that he would look after them with his discipline. To have as teacher a half-beast, half-man means nothing other than that a prince needs to know how to use both natures; and the one without the other is not lasting.
>
> Thus, since a prince is compelled of necessity to know well how to use the beast, he should pick the fox and the lion, because the lion does not defend itself from snares and the fox does not defend itself from wolves. So one needs to be a fox to recognize snares and a lion to frighten the wolves.[35]

Force and law, opposed to each other by the Ciceronian (and Platonic) separation of beast from man, are reconciled by the wise mythological centaur, combining in one body both man and beast.[36] The lion and the fox can then serve as symbolic animals whose natures must be 'used' by the prince as they suit his needs. The verb *usare*, so often used by Machiavelli, is significant here: does it imply the putting to use of elements in one's own nature, or does it suggest a repertory of means or styles, such as an actor might draw upon? Indeed, the advice to 'use the fox' ('usare la volpe') which concludes this paragraph is specifically in the context of dissembling, that is, of concealing one's real intentions.[37]

Cicero too, a couple of chapters later, had introduced the lion and the fox, the first in the context of force (*vis*) and the second in the context of fraud (*fraus*): 'both are unworthy of man, but fraud is the more contemptible.'

In man, this cunning is particularly reprehensible when it takes the form of hypocrisy or dissimulation:

> While wrong may be done, then, in either of two ways, that is, by force or by fraud, both are bestial: fraud seems to belong to the cunning fox, force to the lion; both are wholly unworthy of man, but fraud is the more contemptible. But of all forms of injustice, none is more flagrant than that of the hypocrite who, at the very moment when he is most false, makes it his business to appear virtuous.[38]

Most commentators have noted how deliberately Machiavelli inverts the Ciceronian recommendation to moral honesty. He places stress upon the performativity of the political, offering an influential model of politics as theatre. In an important essay, Victoria Kahn argues that the 'redefinition of representation as ruse and thus of mimesis as power is the aim of *The Prince* as a whole, but it finds a particularly forceful articulation in chapter 18'. In Kahn's reading, the binary opposition of bestial force and human law is resolved by a choice of 'bestial craft and force' alone, and mimesis—'the representational illusion'—is manipulated in the interests of power.[39]

But is mimesis, the hypocrite's or actor's ability to imitate (as Plato would say) what does not exist, specifically a human skill? In fact, both Greek treatises on animal behaviour and the rhetorical tradition upon which Cicero is drawing assigned the power of dissembling to foxes.[40] Certainly, both Cicero and Machiavelli make a distinction of degree between fraud and dissembling, so that it seems that men who use fraud (the way of the fox) must *also* know how to dissemble. Still, it is worth re-emphasizing that to 'use the fox' is by no means a form of imitation but rather a resort to inherent qualities of one's own nature (which may include dissembling). Moreover, Kahn's phrase 'mimesis as power' remains resonant, especially in the context of Machiavelli's use of the literary medium—as in *L'asino*—to test what recourse falls to the lot of the powerless, such as the poem's unfortunate narrator.

Certainly, the prince's choice of force or shrewdness, his recourse to the beast in his own nature in emulation of the ideal mentor Chiron, appears more willed and conscious than the allegorical transformations of *L'asino*, though there is a considerable substratum of allegory in *The Prince* as well.[41] There is, we must remember, some distance between the two texts: by the time Machiavelli came to write *L'asino*, fortune's changes may have weighed on his mind more heavily than the models of resourcefulness and adaptability he had used earlier. The passage in *Il Principe* draws upon numerous classical sources (such as Aesop's *Fables* and Xenophon's *Cyropaedia*), but especially on Lucretius's *De rerum natura*, a work whose influence on Machiavelli and in Renaissance Florence has drawn considerable recent attention.[42] Most signally, it appears to have influenced his understanding of passions and instincts in animals as well as men, the operation of chance in the world, and the exercise of free will. Lucretius had noted that the survival of animals depends on the transmission of characteristic qualities in the *animus*.[43] Alison Brown argues that the defiant and self-sufficient hog in *L'asino* is Lucretian as well as Plutarchan, and that a subversive morality based on Lucretian naturalism and primitivism was at work in narrowing, for Machiavelli, the gap between humans and animals: 'animal behaviour was more relevant to humans than classical moralists like Cicero suggested'.[44]

In his philosophical essay *The Open*, Giorgio Agamben attacked the false division between human and animal that constitutes a 'disjunction' in Early Modern thought:

> The division of life into vegetal and relational, organic and animal, animal and human, therefore passes first of all as a mobile border within living man, and without this intimate caesura the very decision of what is human and what is not would probably not be possible. It is possible to oppose man to other living things, and at the same time to organize the complex—and not always edifying—economy of relations between men and animals, only because something like an animal life has been separated within man ... What is man, if he is always the place—and, at the same time, the result—of ceaseless divisions and caesurae?[45]

But if Machiavelli is responding to Cicero by a resort to Lucretian naturalism, emphasizing human kinship with animals, he is also responding to the Platonic characterization of the tyrant, who fosters the 'many-headed beast and the lion' within the human body, feeding their appetites while starving the man (*Republic*, 588b–589b), and who can never experience friendship or freedom.[46] Instead of the Platonic 'beast within', needing to be disciplined by the prudent farmer, we have as tutor the humanized animal: the centaur Chiron, skilled in music, herbs, medicine, and archery. Though centaurs were violent and unruly, Chiron's noble lineage set him apart: he offered to the princes under his tutelage the secrets of both force and law. What results is, as Tania Rispoli puts it, 'a radically naturalised human being' who heals the Christian and Neoplatonic separation of body and soul, animal force and human law.[47] The new prince, not to be confused with the Platonic tyrant, is able to draw upon animal skills and strengths in aid of what Walter Benjamin might have termed the 'law-making violence' of the state.[48]

Where does this leave the ass in *L'asino*? Certainly, as Nuccio Ordine observes, there is a generic, and therefore rhetorical, difference between the seriousness of *Il Principe* and the comic ribaldry of *L'asino*. Nevertheless, the humble ass also inspires a notable vein of *serio ludere* right through the fifteenth and sixteenth centuries. Ordine draws our attention to the figure of the ass-centaur invented by Giovan Battista Pino in his *Ragionamento sovra del asino* (?1551/52), where Pino, looking back at both Apuleius and Machiavelli, and specifically mentioning the latter, substitutes his half-ass half-man for Machiavelli's Chiron.[49] Earlier than Pino, of course, was Henry Cornelius Agrippa's paradoxical encomium of the ass at the close of his *De incertitudine et vanitate scientiarum atque artium declamatio invectiva* (1526). Several other examples are cited by Ordine as background to his subtle and fascinating account of Giordano Bruno's 'asinine' philosophy, especially the satirical dialogue *Cabala del cavallo Pegaseo* (Paris [actually London], 1585), to which was added a discourse on the 'Cillenican' ass. But while Machiavelli does provide a 'paradoxical' conclusion to *L'asino* by introducing his version of Plutarch's Gryllus, it remains important that the poem, at least in its unfinished state, is less about moral philosophy or religion than about history and fortune. The narrator's fated transformation, an event to which he must be reconciled by realizing the kinship between beast and man, the preferability of the animal state, and the knowledge of the world gained by the experience of change, makes it instrumental rather than mystical. The change is in itself a mark of adversity, but like Lucius, the speaker must learn from it, putting it to use.

It is therefore worth noting that, quite apart from its mystical associations, the ass had appeared in representations of the wheel of fortune since the first half of the fifteenth century. In its best-known visualization, placing the ass on top and man at the bottom, with half-ass, half-man figures ascending and descending on both sides, it appears in a woodcut, probably by Albrecht Dürer, for the *editio princeps* of Sebastian Brant's *Das Narrenschiff*, printed at Basel in 1494. The German translation of Petrarch's *De remediis utriusque fortunae*, published at Augsburg in 1532 with woodcuts by the 'Petrarch Master' (probably Hans Weiditz the younger), has a similar illustration.[50] This reversal of the conventional understanding of fortune—making the recipient of fortune's favours an ass, while the wretched human lies at the foot of fortune's wheel—is repeated through the sixteenth century.

In his Satire VII (composed in 1523), Ariosto describes 'that painted wheel' found on playing cards (the *Tarocchi*):

> The top man on the wheel is portrayed as a donkey. Everyone understands the riddle without having to call on the Sphinx to resolve it. There one also sees that all who ascend begin to grow donkey-like in their forward parts, while what hangs behind remains human.[51]

Given the commonness of the image and the reference to playing cards popular in Ferrara, it is unlikely that Ariosto has Machiavelli's *L'asino* in mind. Later sixteenth-century Italian authors, such as Anton Francesco Doni, associate this wheel of fortune with Ariosto. Both Ordine and Stefano Pierguido cite the account in the anonymous *L'asinesca gloria dell'inasinito academica pellegrino* (1553):

> Because we see the things of the world constantly changing, hence men are now sad, now happy, according to whether Fortune is their enemy, or rather favours them at the turning of the wheel. But the Ass is always in the same condition, and in the same way is always happy, and for him the speedy wheel of Fortune never turns, on the contrary he always stays on top, and if misfortune wills him to fall he immediately becomes a man.[52]

Neither the notion that animals, unlike humans, are unaffected by fortune's whims and are therefore always happy, nor the characterization of fortune's protégé as a donkey corresponds exactly to Machiavelli's fable of misfortune in *L'asino*. In *L'asino*, the pig exalts the animal condition above the wretchedness and folly of human beings, but though his Plutarchan, and perhaps Plinian and Lucretian, links are plain, the tirade does not simply repeat the list of human ills to be found in medieval excoriations such as Lotario de' Segni's *De miseria condicionis humanae*, written at the end of the twelfth century. Rather, it adroitly cites the evils of contemporary mercantile capitalism, noting that while animals stick to one food, men journey by sea to Eastern kingdoms to glut their changing appetites (8:97–102). Moreover, the lady has already told the narrator that his impending change, however necessary and useful, is an affliction ('disagio', 3:120), caused by the failure to purge 'adverse' and 'hostile' humours.[53] In fact, the poem adheres fairly closely to the classical identification of human temperaments, or 'humours,' with animal prototypes. Thus, in the sixth chapter, we learn that men filled with excessive fury and rage are converted to bears, the idle and indolent are goats, and the noble and magnanimous are lions—but 'few of them are from your city'

(6: 56: 'ma pochi ce ne son del tuo paese'). In the seventh chapter there is a 'malicious and annoying' (7: 31: 'maligna e'mportuna') fox, who has yet to find a net capable of trapping him. Whether in *Il Principe* or in *L'asino*, Machiavelli is not attempting to overturn a classical way of describing character or *ethos*. Nor does his thinking with animals follow the pattern of paradox that we find in some representations of fortune's wheel, or in the encomiastic 'philosophy of the ass'. Rather, we find in both works an agile and thoughtful engagement with the animal (both natural and symbolic) as the repository of human qualities that we fail to recognize in ourselves or of possibilities of being that extend the scope of the human beyond the narrow Neoplatonic model.

The importance of this way of thinking is evident if we look at a work often compared with Machiavelli's poem, Giovan Battista Gelli's *Circe* (1549), a set of ten dialogues with a series of animals metamorphosed by Circe. In a hierarchical scale from the oyster to the elephant, all the creatures refuse re-conversion except the last, formerly a philosopher, who is persuaded that man can attain divinity.[54] Gelli's dialogues were published the same year as Machiavelli's fragment, which saw print only twenty-two years after its author's death.[55] Although Gelli obviously draws on Plutarch, and perhaps on Machiavelli, the pig is absent from his list of animals. Chiara Cassiani argues for an iconological, even hieroglyphical reading of Gelli's dialogue, examining the symbolic significances of his animal speakers in terms of Cinquecento enthusiasms. As she notes:

> In *Circe*, Gelli does not follow Dante's conception of metamorphosis as a descent into sin, but interprets the Ovidian *motif* in the manner of sixteenth-century mythographers and iconologists, for whom the images of animals are moral allegories of Platonic and Pythagorean theories of the soul.[56]

In Cassiani's reading, Gelli's animals, with their sustained and eloquent defences of the animal condition and their repudiation of their wretched past existences as fisherman, farmer, or woman, articulate social and moral debates in the Florentine Academy. They suggest Gelli's own humble origins and his ambitious intellectual and linguistic projects, which found favour with Cosimo's efforts to reform the institution. Gelli became a member in January 1541, with Carlo Lenzoni and shortly after Pierfrancesco Giambullari, as Cosimo sought to pack the Academy with his protégés. Gelli's social status was both fluid and vulnerable; his feminism, perhaps drawing on Plutarch and expressed through the discourses of the hare, the hind, and Circe herself, has drawn sustained attention.[57]

However, Gelli's theriophily may be less radical than it seems. His metamorphosed animals, embracing change and repudiating human identity, manifest an uncategorizable selfhood that can freely choose its mode of being. In the end, the elephant chooses humanity in order to become more than human: to know the divine. It is impossible not to regard this selfhood as that mode of being that Pico della Mirandola, in a passage Gelli cites in his dedicatory letter to Cosimo de' Medici, assigns to man:

> In the power of man has been freely placed the ability to choose the way in which he likes best to live, and, as if he were a new Prometheus, to transform himself into everything he wishes, taking on like a chameleon the colour of all those things to which he comes closest in his affections; and finally, to make himself either earthly or divine, and cross over to that state which is most pleasing to the choice of his free will.[58]

Gelli substitutes the more controversial and tragic figure of Prometheus for Proteus in Pico's celebrated encomium of the human capacity for self-making. In the interests of her argument, Cassiani accepts the judgement of some editors who emend to 'Proteo', though both Roberto Tissoni and Brigitte Urbani retain the original (and several times repeated) reading of 'Prometeo'. But, in fact, the substitution draws attention, like a *lapsus Freudianus*, or like the missing pig, to Gelli's attempt to escape some of the contradictions in Pico's model of freedom, by recalling the Promethean maker, rather than the Protean shape-shifter.

Pico's *Oratio* itself offers, we may recall, a curious sleight of hand, accommodating moral determinism to prelapsarian free will and contrasting existential hierarchy with human mobility up and down the scale of being. Humanity itself is located in difference, or possibly *différance*: that is, in an endless capacity for movement, without fixed location. The hierarchy of creation is an order in which every place is taken, so that any choice of life is effectively to become something else. The human, by this schema, is what cannot be identical with itself: it can only be identical with what it desires, yet it can only achieve this identity in self-loss.[59] Circe's swine would be placed at the lower end of the scale, the allegorical result of persistence in corrupt moral habit, but also, perhaps, kin to the human through shared appetites. By excluding the pig, Gelli evades both the moral question and the argument from Lucretian naturalism, choosing the unfixed metamorphic identity that Pico proposes but aligning it to the heroic Prometheus rather than the slippery Proteus. His metamorphosed animals are no more than alternative life-choices, his Circe an embodiment, as one of his lectures on Petrarch suggested, of free will.[60] Unlike Machiavelli, he never really confronts the issue of the human *as* animal.

Gelli's dialogue achieved instant European success, with numerous Italian editions; it was translated into French the following year and into English in 1558. His work was later claimed for Renaissance 'theriophily', a term proposed by George Boas for a strain of pro-animal, often neo-Plutarchan thought that extends through and after Montaigne.[61] The more recent scholarly field of animal studies, however, focuses on actual animals and their treatment in Early Modern culture. Neither Machiavelli nor Gelli offers promising material for such investigation. If Machiavelli prefers to speak of fortune and the need to adopt the way of the animal, Gelli is more inclined towards philosophical allegory. But the figure of Circe, the fable of metamorphosis, and allegorized beasts continue to haunt the later sixteenth century. In Giordano Bruno's magical treatise *Cantus Circaeus* (1582), the muddy, ferocious, and defiling pig is placed at the very entrance to Circe's house, and Bruno actually refers to the 'wheel of metamorphoses' ('la ruota di metamorfosi') in his philosophical dialogue, *De gl' heroici furori* ('The Heroic Frenzies', 1585):

> Now this conversion and vicissitude is figured in the wheel of metamorphosis, in which a man is placed at the top, and a beast at the bottom, a half-man, half-beast descends from the left, and a half-beast, half-man ascends from the right ... [T]he heroic lover, raising himself by his conception of the species of divine beauty and goodness upon the wings of his intellect and intellectual will, elevates himself towards divinity, relinquishing the form of more base subjects.[62]

Despite his paradoxical defence of 'asinine philosophy' in the *Cabala del cavallo Pegaseo* (1585), Bruno does not endorse Machiavelli's assertion of human kinship with animals, nor does he focus upon the changes wrought by fortune. Instead, as we see in the earlier passage, he brings the wheel of fortune back full circle to the wheel of metamorphosis, offering the more conventional, hierarchical image where man is placed at the top and the animal at the bottom, with human reason elevated over the 'baseness' of the beastly condition.

Let me close, however, by noting another coincidence of print. Between 1584 and 1588, five editions of Machiavelli's works, including *L'asino* and *Il Principe*, were printed in London, with false Italian imprints, by the publisher John Wolfe. These publications overlapped with the first editions of six of Giordano Bruno's dialogues, including *Cabala del cavallo Pegaseo* and *De gl' heroici furori*, brought out in 1584 and 1585, also with fake continental imprints, by the London publisher John Charlewood.[63] While Machiavellian politics and Brunian philosophy were alike important for the influence they exerted on English thought around the close of the sixteenth century, their treatment of the myth of metamorphosis may seem peripheral to those concerns. But what survives of Machiavelli's unfinished *L'asino* represents, I would suggest, a considerable ambition. It sought to place the transformed, 'animalized', human at the centre of an enquiry into power, knowledge, and freedom, and to seek a fuller understanding of what it might mean to be human in the extended sense of an animal life.

Notes

1. Ludwig Wittgenstein, *Philosophical Investigations*, German text with English tr. by G. E. M. Anscombe, P. M. S. Hacker, and Joachim Schulte, rev. 4th edn (Oxford: Wiley-Blackwell, 2009), Part II, p. 235e, § 327.
2. Giorgio Agamben, *The Open: Man and Animal*, tr. Kevin Attell (Stanford, CA: Stanford University Press, 2003), 16.
3. It was Claude Lévi-Strauss who in 1962 applied the term 'bonnes à penser', translated as 'good to think with', to animals: see *Le totémisme aujourd'hui* (Paris: PUF, 1962), 128, tr. R. Needham, *Totemism* (Boston, MA: Beacon, 1963), 89.
4. Leo Strauss, *Thoughts on Machiavelli* (Glencoe, IL: The Free Press, 1958), 78.
5. 'Io ho letto ad questi dì *Orlando Furioso* dello Ariosto, et veramente el poema è bello tucto, et in di molti luoghi è mirabile. Se si truova costì, raccomandatemi ad lui, et ditegli che io mi dolgo solo che, havendo ricordato tanti poeti, che m'habbi lasciato indreto come un cazo, et ch'egli ha facto ad me quello in sul suo *Orlando*, che io non farò a lui in sul mio *Asino*': Niccolò Machiavelli, *Tutte le opere*, ed. Mario Martelli (Florence: Sansoni, 1971), 1194–5 (henceforth *Opere*). Translations of all texts are mine unless otherwise indicated.
6. Albert Russell Ascoli and Victoria Kahn, 'Introduction', in *Machiavelli and the Discourse of Literature*, ed. Albert Russell Ascoli and Victoria Kahn (Ithaca, NY: Cornell University Press, 1993), 1–15, 15; see also 3–4.
7. See Gian Mario Anselmi and Paolo Fazion, *Machiavelli, L'asino e le bestie* (Bologna: CLUEB, 1984), 90–3. All citations of *L'asino* are from this edition. Anselmi and Fazion further note (90) how the *ekphrastic* description of the sculptured frieze above the arch leading into Circe's palace, where the Abate de Gaeta is shown, recalls the *Hypnerotomachia Poliphili*, a work that had also drawn on Apuleian material, like Machiavelli's *L'asino*.
8. See Silvio A. Bedini, *The Pope's Elephant* (Harmondsworth: Penguin, 2000), 93.

9. See *Apulegio Volgare, tradotto per el conte Mattheo Maria Boiardo* (Venice: Nicola daristotele da Ferrara & Vincenzo de Polo, 1518). Poggio Bracciolini's Latin translation of the Pseudo-Lucianic *Ass* probably dates from 1450; it was printed by Ludwig Hohenwang at Augsburg c. 1477. For details, see Alexander Scobie, *More Essays on the Ancient Romance and Its Heritage* (Beitrage zur Klassischen Philologie, Band 46; Meisenheim am Glan: Verlag Anton Hain, 1973), 49–52. The cultural context is explored in Carlo Dionisotti, *Gli umanisti e il volgare fra quattro e cinquecento* (Florence: Felice le Monnier, 1968). There are references to an earlier translation, perhaps by Boiardo's grandfather Feltrino, but this is lost. In manuscript, Apuleius provided material both for Giovanni Boccaccio's *Decamerone* (completed 1353: Boccaccio made his own autograph copy of *The Golden Ass*), and for Francesco Colonna's arcane romance, the *Hypnerotomachia Poliphili* (printed 1499; Colonna used both manuscripts and Bussi's edition). See Julia Haig Gaisser, *The Fortunes of Apuleius and the* Golden Ass: *A Study in Transmission and Reception* (Princeton, NJ: Princeton University Press, 2008), 173–7. For a full discussion, see Supriya Chaudhuri, 'Lucius, thou art translated: Adlington's Apuleius', *Renaissance Studies* 22, no. 5 (2008), 678–85.

10. *Lucii Apuleii platonici madaurensis philosophi metamorphoseos liber: ac nonnulla alia opuscula eiusdem: necnon epitoma Alcinoi in disciplinarum Platonis desinunt* (Rome: Pietro de Maximo [Conradus Sweynheym and Arnoldus Pannartz], 1469).

11. 'Verum sub hoc transmutationis inuolucro, naturam mortalium & mores humanos quasi transeunter designare uoluisse. ut admoneremur ex hominibus Asinos fieri, quando uoluptatibus belluinis immersi Asinali stoliditate brutescimus, nec ulla rationis uirtutisque scintilla in nobis elucescitsic enim homo ut docet origenes in libris periarchon, fit equus et mullus, sic transmutatur humanum corpus in corpora pecuina: Rursus ex Asino in hominem reformatio significat calcatis uoluptatibus exutisque corporalibus deliciis rationem resipiscere': *Commentarii a Philippo Beroaldo conditi in Asinum Aureum Lucii Apuleii* (Bologna: Benedictus Hector, 1500), fol. 2v, 'Scriptoris intentio'.

12. Epictetus, *Discourses* 1:3:7–9, ed. and tr. W. A. Oldfather, 2 vols., Loeb Classical Library (Cambridge, MA: Harvard University Press, 1956). The vigour of this denunciation, in a style continued by popular moralists, depends on Epictetus's ignoring a point that he himself makes later (*Discourses* 2:8:6 ff): that animals cannot really be vicious, because they lack understanding.

13. Giambattista della Porta, *De humana physiognomonia* (Vico Equense: Giuseppe Cacchi, 1586).
14. Giovanni Pico della Mirandola, *Oratio*, in *Pluralità delle vie: alle origini del Discorso sulla dignità umana di Pico della Mirandola*, ed. Pier Cesare Bori and Saverio Marchignoli (Milan: Feltrinelli, 2000), 104: 'Quis hunc nostrum chamaeleonta non admiretur? Aut omnino quis aliud quicquam admiretur magis? Quem non immerito Asclepius Atheniensis versipellis huius et se ipsam transformantis naturae argumento per Protheum in mysteriis significari dixit' ('Who then will not look with awe upon this our chameleon, or who, at least, will look with greater admiration on any other being? This creature, man, whom Asclepius the Athenian, by reason of this very mutability, this nature capable of transforming itself, quite rightly said was symbolized in the mysteries by the figure of Proteus'). Also *Pluralità delle vie*, 106: 'Si quem enim videris deditum ventri, humi serpentem hominem, frutex est, non homo, quem vides; si quem in fantasiae quasi Calipsus vanis praestigiis cecucientem et subscalpenti delinitum illecebra sensibus mancipatum, brutum est, non homo, quem vides' ('For example, if you see a man given over to his belly and crawling upon the ground, it is a plant and not a man that you see. If you see anyone blinded by the illusions of his empty and Calypso-like imagination, and seduced by these empty wiles into becoming slave to his own senses, it is a brute not a man that you see').
15. Nuccio Ordine, *Giordano Bruno and the Philosophy of the Ass*, tr. Henryk Baranski (New Haven, CT: Yale University Press, 1996). Machiavelli is discussed in 126–33.
16. 'Ma prima che si mostrin queste stelle/liete verso di te, gir ti conviene/cercando il mondo sotto nuova pelle;/ché quella Provvidenza che mantiene/l'umana spezie, vuol che tu sostenga/questo disagio per tuo maggior bene./Di qui conviene al tutto che si spenga/in te l'umana effigie, e, senza quella,/meco tra l'altre bestie a pascer venga./Né può mutarsi questa dura stella;/e, per averti in questo luogo messo,/si differisce il mal, non si cancella': *L'Asino*, ed. Anselmi and Fazion, 145–6; tr. as in *Machiavelli: The Chief Works and Others*, tr. Allan Gilbert, 3 vols. (Durham, NC: Duke University Press, 1965), 2:758. All translations from *L'Asino* are from this version.
17. 'Perché da quelle in ver par che si mieta/unione e buono ordine; e da quello/buona fortuna poi dipende e lieta': *L'asino*, 5:121–3.
18. On Machiavelli and religion, see Victoria Kahn, *The Future of Illusion: Political Theology and Early Modern Texts* (Chicago, IL: University of Chicago Press, 2014), 83–113. Note especially her discussion of Lucretius, 95–102, in the context of Lucretian naturalism later in this chapter.

19. On Plutarch's dialogue, see, among much else, Lucas Herchenroeder, 'Τί γὰρ τοῦτο πρὸς τὸν λόγον; Plutarch's "Gryllus" and So-Called "Grylloi"', *American Journal of Philology* 129, no. 3 (2008), 347–79; Alain Billaut, 'Le Modèle animal dans le traité de Plutarque', and Christophe Brechet, 'La Philosophie de Gryllos', both in *Les Grecs de l'antiquité et les animaux: Le cas remarquable de Plutarque*, ed. Jacques Boulogne (Lille: Université Charles de Gaulle, 2005), 33–42 and 43–61; Giovanni Indelli, 'Plutarco, bruta animalia ratione uti: qualche riflessione', in *Plutarco e le scienze*, ed. Italo Gallo (Genoa: SAGEP Editrice, 1992), 317–15; and generally, Richard Sorabji, *Animal Minds and Human Morals* (Ithaca, NY: Cornell University Press, 1993) and Marcel Detienne, 'Between Beasts and Gods', in *Myth, Religion and Society: Structuralist Essays by M. Detienne, L. Gernet, J.-P. Vernant and P. Vidal-Nacquet*, ed. R. L. Gordon (Cambridge: Cambridge University Press, 2009), 219–30.
20. Desiderius Erasmus, *The Praise of Folly and other Writings*, ed. and tr. Robert M. Adams (New York: W. W. Norton, 1989), 35.
21. Plutarch, *Moralia*, 987b: *Moralia*, ed. and tr. Harold Cherniss and William C. Helmbold, Loeb Classical Library, 15 vols. (Cambridge, MA: Harvard University Press, 1957), 12:501.
22. Porphyry, *Against the Christians*, fr. 49, on Matthew 8:28–34, Mark 5:117, and Luke 8:32–3. See also Plotinus, *Enneads*, tr. S. MacKenna (London: Faber, 1969), 1:6:6: '[T]he unclean loves filth for its very filthiness, and swine foul of body find their joy in foulness'; 2 Peter 2:22 (Geneva Bible): 'But it is come unto them, according to the true proverbe, the dogge is returned to his owne vomit: and the sowe that was washed, to the wallowing in the myer.'
23. '[S]aetis horrescere coepi,/nec iam posse loqui, pro verbis edere raucum/ murmur et in terram toto procumbere vultu,/osque meum sensi pando occallescere rostro,/colla tumere toris': Ovid, *Metamorphoses*, 14:279–83, ed. and tr. Frank Justus Miller, Loeb Classical Library, 2 vols. (Cambridge, MA: Harvard University Press, 1958).
24. *The Fyrst fovver bookes of P. Ouidius Nasos worke, intitled Metamorphosis*, tr. Arthur Golding (London: Willyam Seres, 1565), sig. *ii r.
25. *Ovid's Metamorphosis Englished, Mythologiz'd, and Represented in Figures by G.S.*, tr. George Sandys (Oxford: John Lichfield, 1632).
26. See Petrus Costalius, *Pegma, cum narrationibus philosophicis* (Lyon: Matthias Bonhomme, 1555), 176, 'In Grillum: Voluptatem immanissimus quisque sequitur lubens'; Geoffrey Whitney, *A Choice of Emblemes, and other Devises* (Leyden: Christopher Plantyn, 1586), 82, 'Homines voluptatibus

transformantur'. Whitney does not name Gryllus, but clearly recalls Plutarch's story.
27. Edmund Spenser, *The Faerie Queene*, II.xii.87: Spenser, *Poetical Works*, ed. J. C. Smith and E. de Selincourt (London: Oxford University Press, 1912, rpt. 1970). On Spenser's Grill, see the entry by Supriya Chaudhuri in *The Spenser Encyclopedia*, ed. A. C. Hamilton (Toronto: University of Toronto Press, 1990).
28. See Joseph Loewenstein, 'Gryll's Hoggish Mind', *Spenser Studies* 22 (2007), 243–56, 246.
29. Thomas Nagel, 'What Is It Like to Be a Bat?', *Philosophical Review* 83, no. 4 (1974), 435–50.
30. Alison Brown, in her chapter 'Lucretian Naturalism and the Evolution of Machiavelli's Ethics' in *Lucretius and the Early Modern*, ed. David Norbrook, Stephen Harrison, and Philip Hardie (Oxford: Oxford University Press, 2015), 69–89, 82, suggests that the pig's free will is Lucretian rather than Plutarchan.
31. Miguel Vatter, 'Of Asses and Nymphs: Machiavelli, Platonic Theology and Epicureanism in Florence', *Intellectual History Review* 29 (2019), 101–27, 120.
32. '[S]e si mutassi di natura con li tempi e con le cose, non si muterebbe fortuna': *Opere* 296; tr. from *The Prince*, tr. Harvey C. Mansfield (Chicago, IL: University of Chicago Press, 1998), 100. All translations from *The Prince* are from this version. On this matter, see J. G. A. Pocock, *The Machiavellian Moment* (Princeton, NJ: Princeton University Press, 1975), 178–82.
33. Ordine, *Giordano Bruno*, 127.
34. 'Nam cum sint duo genera decertandi, unum per disceptationem, alterum per vim, cumque illud proprium sit hominis, hoc beluarum, confugiendum est ad posterius, si uti non licet superiore': Cicero, *De officiis*, ed. and tr. Walter Miller, Loeb Classical Library (Cambridge, MA: Harvard University Press, 1975), I.xi.34. On Machiavelli's inversion of Cicero, see Ezio Raimondi, 'The Politician and the Centaur', in Ascoli and Kahn, *Machiavelli and the Discourse of Literature*, 146–7; Machiavelli, *Il Principe*, ed. Mario Martelli and Nicoletta Marcelli (Rome: Salerno, 2006), 236.
35. 'Dovete, adunque, sapere come sono dua generazioni di combattere: l'uno con le leggi, l'altro con la forza: quel primo è proprio dello uomo, quel secondo è delle bestie: ma perché el primo molte volte non basta, conviene ricorrere al secondo. Pertanto, a uno principe è necessario sapere bene usare la bestia e l'uomo. Questa parte è suta insegnata a' principi copertamente dagli antichi scrittori; li quali scrivono come Achille e molti altri di quelli principi antichi furono dati a nutrire a Chirone centauro, che sotto la sua disciplina li custodissi. Il che non vuole dire altro, avere per precettore uno mezzo bestia e mezzo uomo, se non che bisogna a uno principe sapere usare l'una e l'altra natura; e l'una sanza l'altra non è durabile.

Sendo, dunque, uno principe necessitato sapere bene usare la bestia, debbe di quelle pigliare la golpe e il lione; perché il lione non si defende da' lacci, la golpe non si defende da' lupi. Bisogna, adunque, essere golpe a conoscere e' lacci, e lione a sbigottire e' lupi': *Pr.*, ch. 18, *Opere* 283; tr. Mansfield, 69.

36. On the centaur, see Ed King, 'Machiavelli's "L'Asino": Troubled Centaur into Conscious Ass', *Canadian Journal of Political Science/Revue canadienne de science politique* 41, no. 2 (2008), 279–301.

37. '[E] quello che ha saputo meglio usare la golpe, è meglio capitato. Ma è necessario questa natura saperla bene colorire, ed essere gran simulatore e dissimulatore' ('and the one who has known best how to use the fox has come out best. But it is necessary to know well how to color this nature, and to be a great pretender and dissembler'): *Pr.*, ch. 18, *Opere* 283; tr. Mansfield, 70.

38. 'Cum autem duobus modis, id est aut vi aut fraude, fiat iniuria, fraus quasi vulpeculae, vis leonis videtur; utrumque homine alienissimum, sed fraus odio digna maiore. Totius autem iniustitiae nulla capitalior quam eorum, qui tum, cum maxime fallunt, id agunt, ut viri boni esse videantur': Cicero, *De officiis*, I.xiii.41. No equivalent for the Loeb translator's 'hypocrite' appears in the original.

39. Victoria Kahn, 'Virtù and the Example of Agathocles in Machiavelli's *Prince*', *Representations* 13 (1986), 63–83, 65. See also Victoria Kahn, 'Revisiting Agathocles', *Review of Politics* 75, no. 4 (2013), 557–72.

40. For example, see Oppian, *Halieutica*, 2:107–19, in *Oppian, Colluthus, Tryphiodorus*, ed. and tr. A. W. Mair, Loeb Classical Library (Cambridge, MA: Harvard University Press, 1987).

41. On this, see Kahn, 'Virtù and the Example of Agathocles', 76–9.

42. Machiavelli does not cite Lucretius, but he made his own transcription of *De rerum natura*, in a manuscript preserved in the Vatican Library. See Brown, 'Lucretian Naturalism', 69–89, and the same author's *The Return of Lucretius to Renaissance Florence* (Cambridge, MA: Harvard University Press, 2010). See also Tania Rispoli, 'Imitation and Animality: On the Relationship between Nature and History in Chapter XVIII of The Prince', in *The Radical Machiavelli: Politics, Philosophy, and Language*, ed. Filippo Del Lucchese, Fabio Frosini, and Vittorio Morfino (Leiden: Brill, 2015), 190–203.

43. 'Principio genus acre leonum saevaque saecla/tutatast virtus, volpes dolus et fuga cervos' ('In the first place, the fierce breed of savage lions owes its preservation to its courage, the fox to its cunning, the deer to its speed in flight'): Lucretius, *De rerum natura*, ed. and tr. W. H. D. Rouse, rev. Martin Ferguson Smith, Loeb Classical Library (Cambridge, MA: Harvard University Press, 1975), 5:862–3; see also 3:741–53.

44. Brown, 'Lucretian Naturalism', 81.

45. Agamben, *The Open*, '*Mysterium disiunctionis*', 15–16.
46. On Machiavelli's lion, see Timothy J. Lukes, 'Lionizing Machiavelli', *American Political Science Review* 95, no. 3 (2001), 561–75.
47. Rispoli, 'Imitation and Animality', 196. Rispoli quotes the adage attributed to Marsilio Ficino, 'bestia nostra, id est sensus; homo vero noster, id est ratio' ('our beast, that is sense; our man, however, is reason') and notes that Machiavelli is closer to the Aristotelian, anti-transcendental position advocated by Pietro Pomponazzi (ibid., 197–8).
48. Walter Benjamin, 'Critique of Violence', in *Reflections: Essays, Aphorisms, Autobiographical Writings*, tr. Edmund Jephcott, ed. Peter Demetz (New York: Schocken Books, 1986), 283–4.
49. See Ordine, *Giordano Bruno*, 119–26; also Nuccio Ordine, 'Asinus portans mysteria: le *Ragionamento sovra de l'Asino* de Giovan Battista Pino', in *Le monde animal au temps de la Renaissance*, ed. M. T. Jones-Davies (Paris: Jean Touzot, 1990), 180–92; Nuccio Ordine, 'Simbologia dell'asino. A proposito di due recenti edizioni', *Giornale storico della letteratura italiana* 161, no. 513 (1984), 116–30.
50. Among much else, see Alfred J. Doren, 'Fortuna im Mittelalter und in der Renaissance', *Vorträge der Bibliothek Warburg* B.II, 1 Teil, ed. Ernst Cassirer and Fritz Saxl (Leipzig: Teubner, 1922–3), 71–145; and Michael Schilling, 'Rota Fortunae: Beziehungen zwischen Bild und Text in Mittelalterlichen Handschriften', in *Deutsche Literatur des späten Mittelalters, Hamburger Colloquium 1973*, ed. Wolfgang Harms and L. Peter Johnson (Berlin: Erich Schmidt Verlag, 1975), 293–313.
51. 'Quel che le siede in cima si dipinge/uno asinello: ognun lo enigma intende,/ senza che chiami a interpretarlo Sfinge./Vi si vede anco che ciascun che scende/comincia a inasinir le prime membra,/e resta umano quel che a dietro pende.' Text and tr. from P. D. Wiggins, *The Satires of Ludovico Ariosto. A Renaissance Autobiography* (Athens, OH: Ohio University Press, 1976), 178–9.
52. 'Perche vediamo noi le cose del mondo mutarsi del continuo, onde sono gli huomini hor tristi, hor lieti secondo che la fortuna e loro nimica, overo favorevole al voltare della ruota. Ma l'Asino nel medesimo stato si trova sempre, ad un medesimo modo e sempre lieto, ne per lui si volge mai la veloce ruota della Fortuna, anzi vi sta egli sempre su la cima, e se la disgrazia pur vuole ch'ei ne cada diventa subito un'huomo': *L'asinesca gloria dell'inasinito academica pellegrino* (Venice: Marcolini, 1553), 33. Text and translation from Stefano Pierguido, '"Gigantomachia" and the Wheel of Fortune in Giulio Romano, Vincenzo Cartari and Anton Francesco Doni, and the Authorship

of the "Asinesca Gloria"', *Journal of the Warburg and Courtauld Institutes* 67 (2004), 275–84, 280–1. *L'asinesca gloria* has been attributed to Anton Francesco Doni, but Pierguido argues convincingly for Vincenzo Cartari as its author. However, Doni referred to Ariosto's wheel of fortune in at least two places, including his *La Zucca* (Venice: Francesco Marcolini, 1551): see Pierguido, 'Gigantomachia', 282, and Ordine, *Giordano Bruno*, 139.

53. 'E quelli umori i quai ti sono stati/cotanto avversi e cotanto nimici,/non sono ancor, non sono ancor purgati': cap. 3:103–5.

54. *La Circe di Giovanbatista Gelli, Accademico fiorentino* (Florence: Lorenzo Torrentino, 1549). I have used the following edition: Giovan Battista Gelli, *La Circé*, ed. Brigitte Urbani (Paris: Classiques Garnier, 2015). See also Brigitte Urbani, 'Jeux de la métamorphose dans deux textes du *Cinquecento* Florentin: *L'Âne d'or* de Machiavel et *La Circé* de Gelli', *Studii di știința și cultura* 10, no.3 (2014), 15–28.

55. *L'asino doro di Nicolo Machiauelli, con alcuni altri cap. & nouelle del medesimo, nuouamente metti in luce, & non più stampati* (Florence: Bernardo Giunta, 1549).

56. 'Nella *Circe*, Gelli non segue la concezione dantesca della metamorfosi come caduta nel peccato, ma interpreta il motivo ovidiano alla maniera dei mitografi e degli iconologi cinquecenteschi, per i quali le immagini degli animali sono allegorie morali delle teorie platoniche e pitagoriche sull'anima': Chiara Cassiani, *Metamorfosi e conoscenza: i dialoghi e le commedie di Giovan Battista Gelli* (Rome: Bulzoni, 2006), 113.

57. See Marilyn Migiel, 'The Dignity of Man: A Feminist Perspective', in *Refiguring Woman: Perspectives on Gender and the Italian Renaissance*, ed. Marilyn Migiel and Juliana Schiesari (Ithaca, NY: Cornell University Press, 1991), 211–32.

58. 'In potestà de l'uomo è stato liberamento posto il potersi eleggere quel modo nel quale più gli piace vivere, e, quasi come un nuovo Prometeo, trasformarsi in tutto quello che egli vuole, prendendo, a guisa di cameleonte, il color di tutte quelle cose a le quali egli più si avvicina con l'affetto; e finalmente, farsi o terreno o divino, e a quello stato trapassare che a la elezione de il libero voler suo piacerà più': G. B. Gelli, *Dialoghi*, ed. Roberto Tissoni (Bari: Laterza, 1967), 145. See also Gelli, *La Circé*, ed. Urbani, 62.

59. Giorgio Agamben, *The Open*, 30, comments: 'the humanist discovery of man is the discovery that he lacks himself, the discovery of his irremediable lack of *dignitas*' (which Agamben glosses as 'rank').

60. See Cassiani, 110.

61. See George Boas, *The Happy Beast in French Thought of the Seventeenth Century* (1933; rpt. New York: Octagon Books, 1966). A work sometimes

cited in this context is the papal nuncio Girolamo Rorario's two part treatise, *Quod animalia bruta ratione utantur melius homine* (1544, but printed only in 1648).

62. 'Hor questa conversion et vicissitudine è figurate nella ruota delle metamorfosi, dove siede l'huomo nella parte eminente, giace una bestia al fondo, un mezzo huomo et mezzo bestia descende dalla sinistra, et un mezzo bestia et mezzo huomo ascende da la destra ... il furioso heroic inalzandosi per la conceputa specie della divina beltá et bontade, con l'ali de l'intelletto et volontade intellettiva s'inalza alla divinitade lasciando la forma de suggetto piu basso': *De gl' heroici furori* 1:3: Giordano Bruno, *Des Fureurs Héroïques*, ed. Paul-Henri Michel (Paris: Les Belles Lettres, 1954), 197. See also *Cantus Circaeus*, in *Jordani Bruni Opere Latine Conscripta*, ed. V. Imbriani and C. M. Tallarigo, vol. 2 (Naples: D. Morano, 1886; facs. Stuttgart-bad Cannstatt: Friedrich Fromann Verlag, 1961), 184.

63. See A. Gerber, 'All of the Five Fictitious Italian Editions of Writings of Machiavelli and Three of Those of Pietro Aretino Printed by John Wolfe of London (1584–1588)', *Modern Language Notes* 22, nos. 1, 5, 7 (1907), 2–6, 129–35, 201–6; Harry R. Hoppe, 'John Wolfe, Printer and Publisher', *The Library*, 4th Ser. 4 (1933), 241–74; Joseph Loewenstein, 'For a History of Literary Property: John Wolfe's Reformation', *English Literary Renaissance* 18, no. 3 (1988), 389–412; Harry Sellers, 'Italian Books Printed in England before 1640', *The Library*, 4th Ser. 5, no. 2 (1924), 105–28, 122–8; A. M. Pellegrini, 'Giordano Bruno and Oxford', *Huntington Library Quarterly* 5, no. 3 (1942), 303–16; Mordechai Feingold, 'Giordano Bruno in England, Revisited', *Huntington Library Quarterly* 67, no. 3 (2004), 329–46; Tiziana Provvidera, 'John Charlewood, Printer of Giordano Bruno's Italian Dialogues, and his Book Production', in *Giordano Bruno, Philosopher of the Renaissance*, ed. Hilary Gatti (Abingdon: Routledge, 2016), ch. 7, 167–86; Hilary Gatti, *The Renaissance Drama of Knowledge: Giordano Bruno in England* (London: Routledge, 1989).

12

Machiavellian Rhetoric Revisited

Victoria Kahn

In this chapter, I want to use our present political moment to think about why we are still reading Machiavelli. To put this in a more pointed way, I want to ask: what is the interest of reading Machiavelli now, when in the United States, in Europe, and in other parts of the world, we see a rise of nationalism and nativism, an undermining of democratic institutions, and an increasing authoritarianism on the part of democratically elected rulers? I am thinking of Donald Trump in the United States, Recep Tayyip Erdoğan in Turkey, and movements like the Alternativ für Deutschland in Germany. By way of addressing our contemporary moment, I want to begin with an earlier, similarly charged moment in the reception of Machiavelli, the years immediately after the end of the Second World War.

At the end of his life, the philosopher Ernst Cassirer wrote a controversial history of political thought entitled *The Myth of the State*, in which, as we will see, Machiavelli plays a central role. In one way, the title was a misnomer, since one of Cassirer's main points was that political thought in the West has historically set itself against myth, in favour of philosophical or scientific analysis. In another way, however, the title was apt since the book was composed in response to Cassirer's experience in Nazi Germany, in particular his experience of the artificial or manufactured myth of the Nazi state. Earlier in his life, Cassirer had published a three-volume *Philosophy of Symbolic Forms*, in which myth featured as both an early stage of symbolic thinking and a permanent feature of human culture. This conception of myth, he now felt, could not completely account for the form myth took in the twentieth century. In particular, it could not account for the role of technology in producing myth and for the use of such manufactured myths to manipulate opinion and belief in the fascist state.

In an eloquent passage in the last chapter of *The Myth of the State*, Cassirer spoke of his dawning realization that the technological manipulation of myth could fundamentally transform human nature:

Of all the sad experiences of these last twelve years this is perhaps the most dreadful one. It may be compared to the experience of Odysseus on the island of Circe. But it is even worse. Circe had transformed the friends and companions of Odysseus into various animal shapes. But here are men, men of education and intelligence, honest and upright men who suddenly give up the highest human privilege. They have ceased to be free and personal agents ... They act like marionettes in a puppet show—and they do not even know that the strings of this show, and of man's whole individual and social life, are henceforward pulled by the political leaders.

Cassirer went on to argue that 'the usual means of political oppression would not have sufficed to produce this effect'. It was technology, understood as a series of techniques for producing, and as the new twentieth-century media for amplifying, the myth of the state: the systematic degradation of language, the introduction of new rites, the unifying myth of a master race, and the mythic view of time and history as fate.[1]

Machiavelli plays a central if odd role in Cassirer's analysis. In three short chapters at the centre of the book, Cassirer develops the argument that Machiavelli is 'the founder of a new science of politics', comparable in its radical innovation to Galileo's new science of nature.[2] Particularly striking, Cassirer argued, was Machiavelli's lack of interest in hereditary principalities and republics, in traditional forms of political rule and legitimation, and his preoccupation with the structure of the new de facto state.[3] Machiavelli's analysis of this new world of power politics is characterized by a certain dispassionate preoccupation with technique or strategy:

Machiavelli looked at political combats as if they were a game of chess. He had studied the rules of the game very thoroughly. But he had not the slightest intention of changing or criticizing these rules. His political experience had taught him that the political game never had been played without fraud, deception, treachery, and felony. He neither blamed nor recommended these things. His only concern was to find the best move—the move that wins the game.[4]

Only in the last hortatory chapter of *The Prince* does Machiavelli abandon his pose of cool analysis and become 'rhetorical'.[5]

Repeatedly throughout these chapters, Cassirer stresses that Machiavelli the man was principled, honest, and naturally loath to recommend treachery;[6] at the same time, Cassirer insists that this is irrelevant to our understanding of *The Prince*. In this work, Machiavelli is able to put aside his republican convictions (of which we know from the *Discourses* and Machiavelli's own correspondence) and present politics as a matter of realistic evaluation and dispassionate technique. Although Cassirer does not use the language of means and ends, we could say that his Machiavelli does not argue that the end justifies the means; instead, he simply gives us the means without regard to ends.

At the same time that Cassirer represents Machiavelli as 'a scientist and technician of political life', he tells us that Machiavelli could not help but notice that this scientific approach often failed to master political realities.[7] In a passage that reads as Cassirer's own covert personal confession, he writes:

> Machiavelli saw this antinomy very clearly, but he could not solve it and he could not even express it in a scientific way. His logical and rational method deserted him at this point. He had to admit that human things are not governed by reason, and that, therefore, they are not entirely describable in terms of reason.[8]

Hence Machiavelli's recourse to the 'half-mythical' figure of Fortune in Chapter 25 of *The Prince*. Although Machiavelli expresses himself mythically and metaphorically, the real message of this chapter is that Fortune only half controls our fates, while it is up to us to do the rest, and to be as flexible as we can in responding to its changes. The point, Cassirer argues, is that material weapons are not enough; we also need a 'new *type* of strategy—a strategy based upon mental weapons instead of physical weapons' (emphasis in the original).[9]

It is against this putatively scientific backdrop that the Romantic reception of Machiavelli and the modern fascist myth of the state emerge as declines or deviations from the forward march of history and reason. Machiavelli is one thing, Machiavellism is another, according to Cassirer. Machiavelli himself was working in the circumscribed arena of 'small Italian tyrannies of the Cinquecento'[10] and could certainly not have predicted what later centuries would make of his scientific approach to politics. While in the centuries immediately after Machiavelli, his insights into power politics were counterbalanced by the natural rights theory of the state, this was not always the case. Romantic writers destroyed this bulwark of rights theory and in so doing, unleashed 'the most uncouth and uncompromising materialism in political life'.[11]

In his anatomy of the nineteenth-century figures who contributed to the modern myth of the state, Cassirer singles out Hegel's theory of the state, which he links to Hegel's acceptance of Machiavelli's notion of *virtù*. Cassirer quotes a passage from *The Philosophy of History*, where Hegel writes:

> We assert then that nothing has been accomplished without interest on the part of the actors and if interest be called passion we may affirm absolutely that nothing in the world has been accomplished without *passion*. (Emphasis in the original)

Cassirer then comments: '[H]ere too Hegel accepts Machiavelli's conception of *virtù*. "Virtue" means strength; and there is no stronger and more powerful motive in human life than the great passions. The Idea itself would not actualize itself without engaging all human passions.'[12] He then draws the conclusion that Hegel's theory of the state anticipates the fascist myth of the state:

> [I]t was the tragic fate of Hegel that he unconsciously unchained the most irrational powers that have ever appeared in man's social and political life. No other philosophical system has done so much for the preparation of fascism and imperialism as Hegel's doctrine of the state—[which Hegel calls] this 'divine Idea as it exists on earth'.[13]

In short, Cassirer believes that 'Machiavellism showed its true face and its real danger when its principles were later applied to a larger scene and to entirely new political consequences. In this sense we may say that the consequences of Machiavelli's theory were not brought to light until our own age' and 'our modern forms of dictatorship'.[14]

In the conclusion to *The Myth of the State*, Cassirer raises the question of how and why fascism arose and what resources we have to resist it, should it recur. Fascism arises not only for economic, social, and political reasons but because the cultural resources of art, religion, and poetry have become weak. (This, needless to say, is not so much an explanation as a tautology.) But, Cassirer insists, philosophy can provide ethical resources for resisting fascism.

> It is beyond the power of philosophy to destroy the political myths. A myth is in a sense invulnerable. It is impervious to rational arguments; it cannot be refuted by syllogisms. But philosophy can do us another important service. It can make us understand the adversary... When we first heard of the political myths we found them so absurd and incongruous, so fantastic and ludicrous that we could hardly be prevailed upon to take them seriously. By now it has become clear to

all of us that this was a great mistake. We should not commit the same error a second time. We should carefully study the origin, the structure, the methods, and the technique of the political myths. We should see the adversary face to face in order to know how to combat him.[15]

From a contemporary perspective, at least in the United States, these comments seem utterly, painfully relevant. When we first heard of Trump as a candidate for president, it too seemed to many Americans 'so fantastic and ludicrous that we could hardly be prevailed upon to take [him] seriously'. But 'by now, it has become clear to all of us that this was a great mistake'. I will return to this issue at the end of this chapter.

Despite its clear-sighted analysis, Cassirer's book was not well received. In an early review of *The Myth of the State*, Eric Voegelin accused Cassirer of subscribing to an idea of historical progress, whereby myth was superseded by rationalism. Only someone who subscribed to this view could be surprised by the upsurge of myth in modernity. He also faulted Cassirer for failing to explain why such myths arose and for failing to see that 'the new myth emerges because the old myth has disintegrated'. At the same time, Voegelin noted the difference between Cassirer's last book and some of his earlier work: in *The Myth of the State*, Voegelin found 'no awareness that the myth is an indispensable forming element of social order though, curiously enough, in his earlier work on the philosophy of the myth Cassirer, under the influence of Schelling, had seen this problem quite clearly'.[16]

Leo Strauss, who had written his dissertation with Cassirer, was also critical of *The Myth of the State*. He noted that in Cassirer's historical narrative the achievements of the Enlightenment were called into question by Romanticism, with its '"deep wish to go back to the sources of poetry" … The political insufficiency of romantic aestheticism, in its turn, paved the way for the "realistic" political use of myth in the twentieth century'.[17] (Cassirer had made something of the same connection in *The Myth of the State*.[18]) But Strauss then turned this characterization against Cassirer himself, asking: '[I]s not aestheticism the essence of his own doctrine?' By this, Strauss seemed to have in mind Cassirer's failure to elaborate an ethical philosophy that would provide the grounds for a critique of the Nazi state. Strauss quotes Cassirer's observation about Plato: 'No modern writer would ever think of inserting his objections to poetry and art into a work dealing with politics. We see no connection between the two problems.' Strauss then objects: 'But is not the obvious connection between politics and "art", according to Plato as well as other philosophers, that both must be subservient to morality?'[19]

In Strauss's view, Cassirer implicitly raises the question of the relationship between political technique and ethics, but offers no satisfactory answer. Strauss noted further that if Cassirer was right in his defence of Enlightenment values, including the social contract doctrine of the period,

> an adequate answer to the challenge raised by the doctrines favoring the political myths of our time—for example, those of Spengler and Heidegger—would have been not an inconclusive discussion of the myth of the state, but a radical transformation of the philosophy of symbolic forms into a teaching whose center is moral philosophy.[20]

A decade later, Strauss composed *On Tyranny* and *Thoughts on Machiavelli*, both of which traced the modern inability to recognize and condemn Nazi and Soviet tyranny to Machiavelli's conflation of the prince and the tyrant in *The Prince*.[21] I will return to this problem as well.

From a contemporary perspective, two things are striking about Cassirer's *The Myth of the State*. The first is Cassirer's failure to see the implications of his own analysis. He sees a contrast between Machiavelli the scientific analyst of power politics and Machiavelli the myth-maker, or between Machiavelli the dispassionate technician and Machiavelli as read by Romantic critics of the Enlightenment. But as Cassirer himself shows with respect to the modern period, scientific technique and myth need not be opposed. What Cassirer fails to see, in other words, is that part of Machiavelli's scientific approach to politics involves just that artificial production or manufacture of myth that Cassirer condemns in the twentieth century. This in turn raises the question of the difference, if any, between Machiavelli's technical approach to politics and those modern techniques of the myth of the state that Cassirer condemns.

The second thing to note is Cassirer's inadequate historical analysis. It is not Galileo's technical interest in the laws of nature that helps to explain Machiavelli's approach but rather the chief technical resource available to Machiavelli, the art of rhetoric. This art, as I will argue more fully later, has from antiquity onwards been fundamentally concerned with the relationship between means and ends, technique and ethics, the *utile* and the *honestum*: which is to say, it has always been interested in the question of how the same techniques that serve the republic could also be used to defend tyranny, and vice versa. In contrasting Machiavelli's putatively neutral, scientific, or technical approach to politics with the fascist manipulation of the myth of the state, Cassirer unwittingly enacts the problem that is central to Machiavelli's work as well as to his reception, both in the Renaissance and in later centuries.

In what follows, I will argue that the art of rhetoric does a better job of accounting for all those features of Machiavelli's work noted by Cassirer. At the same time, it also helps us make sense of the question, not fully acknowledged by Cassirer, of the difference between Machiavelli and modern proponents of the myth of the state. As we shall see, rhetoric lies behind several of the techniques that Cassirer sees in the modern myth of the state: the manipulation of language, the introduction of new rites, and the unifying role of myth. But the rhetorical technique of argument on both sides of a question also provides a tool for critical thinking, not least of all the critique of myth—what we might call 'ideology'—that is fully on display in Machiavelli, and that Cassirer ignores.[22]

It is well known that rhetoric was the discipline at the heart of the Renaissance humanist curriculum and the essential qualification for anyone, like Machiavelli, working in the Florentine chancellery. The more important question is: what does Machiavelli's work look like through the lens of rhetorical technique? Here I agree with the analysis of John Tinkler, who argued long ago that *The Prince* was fundamentally shaped not by the techniques of epideictic rhetoric, the rhetoric of praise and blame, typical of the 'mirror of princes' genre. Instead, *The Prince* is a work of deliberative rhetoric—the rhetoric of the forum, in which issues of safety and justice are debated. As Tinkler reminds us, the topics of deliberative rhetoric are the honourable, the useful, and the necessary (*honestas, utilitas, necessitas*). The honourable includes what the author of the *Ad Herennium* calls *animus* or character, while the useful includes fortune.[23] Tinkler argues that, whereas an author like Thomas More asserts the compatibility of *fortuna* and virtue in his *Utopia*, Machiavelli makes the problem of their relation central to *The Prince*.[24] In fact, it seems fair to say that it is just this relationship between the useful, which Tinkler claims was the goal of deliberative rhetoric for Cicero, and the honourable, the goal of deliberative rhetoric for Quintilian, that is the subject of deliberation in *The Prince*.

In short, the technique of arguing on both sides of a question informs the structure of *The Prince* as a highly self-reflexive work of deliberative rhetoric, in which the recurrent topic of deliberation is the relative value of the *honestum* and the *utile*. Argument on both sides of a question is also the skill that allows Machiavelli to defend one-man rule in *The Prince* and republicanism in the *Discourses*, even as he recommends the same techniques of force and fraud in both works.

Virginia Cox has qualified Tinkler's argument in order to bring out the novelty of Machiavelli's interpretation of the rhetorical tradition.

She claims, against Tinkler, that Cicero saw both the honourable and the useful as the goals of deliberative rhetoric, and that Machiavelli distanced himself from this Ciceronian tradition in seeing the end of deliberative rhetoric as the useful. In doing so, he drew near to the far more pragmatic, pseudo-Ciceronian *Ad Herennium*, where the honourable or praiseworthy is a subset of the useful, rather than being an independent value.[25] Here, in other words, the focus of analysis is not weighing the relative claims of *honestas* and *utilitas*, but the consideration of the *tutum*, that which contributes to security, and the *laudabile*, that which contributes to one's reputation. As Cox notes, the praiseworthy stands in an ambivalent relation to the morally right, and is instead dependent on 'a "right" filtered through the manipulable vagaries of public perception'. In this way, Machiavelli's reliance on *Ad Herennium* allows him to convert 'what was conventionally treated as a moral question—how a prince should behave—into one of political technique'.[26]

One of the things that this attention to rhetoric affords us is a different view of technique from what we find in Cassirer. This is because Machiavelli's repertoire of political technique includes those rhetorical features of his work which, as even Cassirer recognized, were at odds with his view of Machiavelli as a scientist. These include Machiavelli's abuse of language, or what rhetoricians called *paradiastole* or rhetorical redescription.[27] The most obvious example occurs in Chapter 15 of *The Prince*, where Machiavelli attributes such redescription to the force of circumstance. Thus, he advises the prince that something that appears to be virtuous may turn out in practice to be vice, and something that appears vice will prove to be the source of security and well-being. Machiavelli's political technique also includes a rhetorical appeal to the passions, a central feature of all of Machiavelli's work. Machiavelli famously writes that it is better to be feared than loved, and offers numerous examples of how a prince can instil such fear in his subjects and rivals. Both in *The Prince* and the *Discourses*, Machiavelli is particularly attentive to the uses of spectacle and ritual to stir up the passions of the viewers.[28] Finally, Machiavelli's repertoire includes the creation of myth at the founding of the state, as when Numa feigns conversation with a nymph in order to convince the Romans that his new laws were divinely inspired. It also upholds the role of religion in preserving the state, as when he describes the Roman practices of auspices and of swearing oaths.[29]

I would suggest that we can develop the rhetorical analysis of Machiavelli still further. While Tinkler and Cox argue that Machiavelli commonly sides with utility over honour, I think it more accurate to say that Machiavelli makes us question what this distinction means in the realm of politics.

Here I agree with Maurizio Viroli that to read *The Prince* as a work of rhetoric is to be mindful that its goal is to persuade, and that part of what Machiavelli wants to persuade us to see is a kind of honour peculiar to the realm of politics, which includes establishing 'new laws and new practices', or founding and preserving one's state.[30] Machiavelli does not simply affirm the autonomy of politics from ethics, as Croce once claimed. Rather, in Viroli's words:

> What Machiavelli was in fact doing in the central chapters of *The Prince* was to restate and refine a view on conflicts between security and virtue which did not affirm or vindicate the autonomy of politics from ethics, but was in fact considered to be the view which a *good* man should offer on political matters. When he stresses that, when the safety of the state is at stake, moral considerations are to be postponed, or when he redescribes virtues and vices, he was doing what a *vir bonus dicendi peritus* as defined by Roman masters of eloquence was supposed to do.[31]

We can press this argument even further. It is not just that Machiavelli sees the honourable as emerging from within the realm of politics; his deliberative rhetoric actually fosters a dialectical mode of analysis that produces an immanent critique both of humanism and of the rule of the prince. In the Renaissance, some of Machiavelli's critics perceived amoral argument on both sides of a question as immoral. His admirers, however, perceived Machiavelli's rhetoric as a method that was exemplary in its flexible response to contingency and a dialectical mode of analysis that was at once descriptive and subversive. For these admirers, Machiavelli offered a rhetoric not only for constituting the state but also for challenging the status quo: rhetorical politics could fuel a critique of the existing state of affairs. Specifically, Machiavelli invites us to consider whether what appears to be virtuous at first sight ends up being so in practice or in the long run. And part of Machiavelli's argument, both in *The Prince* and the *Discourses*, is that in the long run, republics are more lasting than principalities and capable of accommodating greater *virtù*.

In my earlier work, I have discussed some of the ways in which Machiavelli insinuates a dialectical critique of the status quo in his work.[32] To cite just one example, in the transition between chapters 8 and 9 of *The Prince*, Machiavelli appears to be arguing *in utramque partem*, on both sides of the question. In chapter 8 he defends the tyrannical rule of Agathocles; in chapter 9 he defends the civil principality. But if one reads these chapters closely, one comes to the conclusion that the example of Agathocles is designed to help us see that the prince who wants to succeed must, in the long run, take into account the opinions of his subjects. He does this by playing on the dual meaning of *virtù*.

Thus, he writes of Agathocles both that he had *virtù* and that it cannot really be called *virtù* to murder one's fellow citizens; and later, that one can get power (*imperio*) in this way, but not glory. *Virtù* is clearly not the same as Christian virtue, but it is also not equivalent to glory, which is a higher term of praise for Machiavelli than mere *virtù*. Later in the same chapter, he notes that Agathocles survived because he changed his ways and began to attend to the interests of his subjects. In so doing, he looks towards the civil principality of chapter 9 as the more effective mode of politics.

Let me clarify my point by distinguishing it from the interpretation of Strauss, one of the most tenacious readers of Machiavelli. Strauss notes Machiavelli's play with *virtù* in the description of Agathocles[33] and glosses Machiavelli's message as follows: the prince

> need not possess and exercise moral virtue proper, although the reputation for possessing some of the moral virtues is indispensable for him. The prince need not even possess virtue in the sense of such dedication to the common good as excludes ambition. But he must possess that virtue which consists of 'brain', or 'greatness of mind', and manliness combined—the kind of virtue praised by Callicles in Plato's *Gorgias* and possessed by the criminals Agathocles and Severus.[34]

So far, so good. But Strauss then goes on to claim that the ground of such *virtù* 'is not the common good but the natural desire of each to acquire wealth and glory'.[35] As we have seen, however, Machiavelli nowhere ascribes such a desire for glory to Agathocles. And he does not do so, I suggest, precisely because he is observing that rhetorical tact for which Strauss elsewhere praises the author of *The Prince*.[36] Ultimately, I would argue, Machiavelli's rhetorical task is not only to instruct the prince how to hold on to power but also how to let go of it. Agathocles illustrates one argument for ceding some power to one's subjects, which we might call the argument from greater longevity: Agathocles retained his position for his entire life because he curbed his violent deeds and catered to the interests of his subjects. Machiavelli implicitly and tactfully suggests the Medici might do so as well.

I now want to return to Cassirer's claim that Machiavelli offers a merely technical analysis of politics, and Strauss's complaint that Cassirer fails to address the central ethical issue posed by Machiavelli's technique. As long as Cassirer thinks of Machiavelli as a technical analyst of politics, he is unable to see Machiavelli the rhetorician, including the dialectical and critical dimension of Machiavelli's rhetoric. And as long as he sees him as the founder of a new political science, he is unable to see the central role that myth and the imagination play in Machiavelli's work. These techniques can be used to support both tyrants and republics. But they also give us a critical purchase on tyranny that makes the case for republicanism. In *The Myth of the State*, Cassirer writes, against Hegel, that

> [t]he great thinkers of the past were not only 'their own times apprehended in thought'. Very often they had to think beyond and against their times. Without this intellectual and moral courage, philosophy could not fulfil its task in man's cultural and social life.[37]

In Machiavelli's day, this thinking beyond and against one's time was the function of rhetoric. Moreover, while Cassirer asserts that philosophy makes us know the techniques of the adversary, he does not see philosophy as a power to change the world.[38] By contrast, knowing the techniques of the adversary and using them precisely to effect change was, in Machiavelli's time and our own, the task of the orator. *Pace* Cassirer, Machiavelli helps us to see that politics is not a science, and that, as Claude Lefort argued many years ago, Cassirer's own notion that it could be is itself a myth, the myth of scientific objectivity, divorced from human interests and human agency.[39]

This, I suggest, is the relevance of Machiavelli to the present moment. In Machiavelli's *The Art of War*, the general Fabrizio Colonna says:

> It is easy to persuade a few men of something, or to dissuade them from it, for, if words are not sufficient, you can use authority or force. The difficulty lies in removing a dangerous opinion … from a multitude, where words are the only means available.[40]

And yet Machiavelli was also convinced that one cannot maintain one's power or challenge the status quo with eloquence alone. Savanarola failed because he was an unarmed prophet. In Trump's America, these observations have a new urgency, where so many people have been persuaded by his nativist and nationalist rhetoric, aided and abetted by the new technological advances that magnify the power of such rhetoric. We have only to think of Twitter, Facebook, or the internet generally. There are also new conduits for money, 'the sinews of war', facilitated by the US Supreme Court's decision deregulating campaign finance in its judgement on the Citizens United case. So what comfort, if any, can we take from Machiavelli?

Here I think there are two answers: the first having to do with rhetoric as the manipulation of myth and the second with rhetoric as a vehicle of political critique. Let me begin with the first point. Here it is important to see that myth, or the work of the imagination, is not simply an add-on in Machiavelli's work, as Cassirer implies. On the contrary, Machiavelli shows us that men are more often persuaded by rhetoric than by reason, by powerful images than by logic. Whereas Cassirer held out the hope that philosophy would gain the upper hand by analysing and exposing the techniques of the adversary,[41] Machiavelli points the way to the necessary creation of counter-myths to the fascist myth of the state. These counter-myths would use the same tools, the same technologies, as fascist leaders, but to different ends. They would attempt to redirect the passions of the multitude so that they become a powerful political force for good.

Let me now turn to the second related point concerning rhetoric as a vehicle of political critique. Here it is useful to see that the terms of abuse applied to rhetoric in the Renaissance—in particular, its association with force and fraud—suggest that it was viewed in the way critics now view ideology. Paul Ricoeur once defined ideology as the distortion of the symbolic structure of social life in the service of class interest. Ideology involves both the impact of violence in discourse, and a dissimulation whose key eludes consciousness. But Ricoeur went on to argue that ideology and what he describes as utopian critique are two sides of the same coin: both presuppose a pre-existing symbolic relationship to the world. Distortion could not occur if we were not already operating within a symbolic system. But if distortion is possible, so are other forms of interpretation, other reformulations of our imaginative relation to the world. It is this that also allows for us to take our distance on ideology and to offer a utopian critique of the status quo.[42]

Something similar could be said of Renaissance rhetoric. Rhetoric was accused of being an instrument of deception, an expression of particular interests, or a potentially coercive system of symbolic interaction. Yet Renaissance writers were also aware of the power of rhetoric to undermine existing forms of authority and to create new ones. Machiavelli was associated with rhetoric in the Renaissance precisely because both were perceived to be subversive in just this way. Machiavelli invites us to take rhetoric seriously, both because it does not take the relationship between the honourable and the useful for granted but instead makes it subject to debate; and because it encourages a dialectical mode of thinking that provides a critical purchase on authoritarian rule. But the rhetorical tradition also teaches us that this dialectical mode of thinking needs to be linked to the practical formulation of counter-myths, myths of enlightenment, and democratic engagement to counteract the ones promulgated by the authoritarian ruler. *The Myth of the State* falls short of this pragmatic insight, which Machiavelli's rhetoric did so much to foster.

Notes

1. See Ernst Cassirer, *The Myth of the State* (New Haven, CT: Yale University Press, 1946), 286, see also 282–96 generally; and John Michael Krois, *Cassirer: Symbolic Forms and History* (New Haven, CT: Yale University Press, 1987), 193–5. The current chapter is part of a diptych on Cassirer's *Myth of the State*: in 'Art, Judaism, and the Critique of Fascism in the Work of Ernst Cassirer' (*Representations* 148 [2019], 114–35), I explore Cassirer's contrasting of myth with the critical power of art and Jewish ethical traditions.
2. Cassirer, *The Myth of the State*, 128; see also 130.
3. Ibid., 134.
4. Ibid., 143.
5. Ibid., 144.
6. Ibid., 120.
7. Ibid., 156.
8. Ibid., 157.
9. Ibid., 162.
10. Ibid., 140.
11. Ibid., 141.
12. Ibid., 268.
13. Ibid., 273.
14. Ibid., 140–1.
15. Ibid., 296.
16. Eric Voegelin, review of Ernst Cassirer's *The Myth of the State*, in *Journal of Politics* 9, no. 3, (1947) 445–7, 446.
17. Leo Strauss, review of Ernst Cassirer's *The Myth of the State*, in *What Is Political Philosophy? and Other Studies* (Chicago, IL: University of Chicago Press, 1988 [1959]), 294. Strauss noted further that if Cassirer was right in his defence of Enlightenment values, including the social contract doctrine of the period, 'an adequate answer to the challenge raised by the doctrines favoring the political myths of our time—for example, those of Spengler and Heidegger—would have been not an inconclusive discussion of the myth of the state, but a radical transformation of the philosophy of symbolic forms into a teaching whose center is moral philosophy'. (Strauss, review, 295).

18. See Cassirer, *The Myth of the State*, 180–6.
19. Strauss, review, 296.
20. Ibid., 295.
21. I discuss Strauss on tyranny in my book *The Future of Illusion: Political Theology and Early Modern Texts* (Chicago, IL: University of Chicago Press, 2014), see esp. 87.
22. Hans Blumenberg took issue with Cassirer's interpretation of Machiavelli in 'The Concept of Reality and Theory of the State', arguing that Machiavelli's divorce of politics from ethics made room for the use of rhetoric, and for a politics of words that in certain situations could supplant a politics of violence. See also Blumenberg's 'An Anthropological Approach to the Continuing Significance of Rhetoric', in *After Philosophy: End or Transformation?* ed. Kenneth Baynes, James Bohman, and Thomas McCarthy (Cambridge, MA: MIT Press, 1987), 429–57. However, Blumenberg does not provide the relevant historical contextualization in terms of the reception of classical rhetoric in Machiavelli's time. On this debate, see Angus Nicholls, 'Hans Blumenberg on Political Myth: Recent Publications from the *Nachlass*', *Iyyun: The Jerusalem Philosophical Quarterly* 65, no. 1 (2016), esp. 16–17.
23. See John F. Tinkler, 'Praise and Advice: Rhetorical Approaches in More's *Utopia* and Machiavelli's *The Prince*', *The Sixteenth Century Journal* 19, no. 2 (1988), 187–207, 190: 'In both genera, the topoi of *honestas* or *animus* on the one hand, and of *fortuna* or *utilitas* on the other, are often seen as opposed: fortune thwarts men's actions, and considerations of honor can easily be at odds with considerations of advantage. However, there were also obvious rhetorical advantages to bringing the two into unison. A course of action that satisfied both honor and utility was obviously better than one that sacrificed either. Similarly, it was easier to praise a man who was both fortunate and virtuous than one who lacked either fortune or virtue.'
24. Ibid., 196.
25. Virginia Cox, 'Machiavelli and the *Rhetorica ad Herennium*: Deliberative Rhetoric in *The Prince*', *The Sixteenth Century Journal* 28, no. 4 (1997), 1109–41, 1120. Cox also discusses Machiavelli's rhetoric in 'Rhetoric and Ethics in Machiavelli', in *The Cambridge Companion to Machiavelli*, ed. John M. Najemy (Cambridge: Cambridge University Press, 2010), 173–89. See also Maurizio Viroli, *Machiavelli* (Oxford: Oxford University Press, 2011), arguing that the author of *Ad Herennium* 'divides advantage ("utilitas") into security ("tuta") and honour ("honestas") and subdivides security into might and craft ("Vim et dolum") and honour in the right and the praiseworthy ("rectum et laudabile")' (85).

26. Cox, 'Machiavelli and the *Rhetorica ad Herennium*', 1130, 1128. See also Viroli, *Machiavelli*: 'Machiavelli's allegiance to the teaching of the *For Gaius Herennius* emerges from the analysis of the *dispositio* of the arguments. As we have seen, under the heading of security, the adviser on matters of state has to be able to offer suggestions on issues that pertain more specifically to might—that is, armies, manpower, and the like—and to craft—that is, money, promises, and dissimulation—while under the heading of honour he shall speak of what is right—that is, of virtues, and of what is laudable. In the first part of *The Prince* he in fact discusses matters pertaining to the security of principalities; in the second he offers his advice concerning the qualities that make a prince laudable or blameworthy, and virtue—which are the two subheadings of honour' (86–7).

27. The modern scholar who has done the most to revive interest in the political uses of *paradiastole* is Quentin Skinner. See his *Reason and Rhetoric in the Philosophy of Hobbes* (Cambridge: Cambridge University Press, 1996), 170–1; 'Paradiastole: Redescribing the Vices as Virtues', in *Renaissance Figures of Speech*, ed. Sylvia Adamson, Gavin Alexander, and Katrin Ettenhuber (Cambridge: Cambridge University Press, 2007), 147–63; 'Machiavelli and the Misunderstanding of Princely Virtù', in *Machiavelli on Liberty and Conflict*, ed. David Johnston, Nadia Urbinati, and Camila Vergara (Chicago, IL: University of Chicago Press, 2017), 139–63; and 'Rhetorical Redescription and Its Uses in Shakespeare', in *From Humanism to Hobbes: Studies in Rhetoric and Politics* (Cambridge: Cambridge University Press, 2018), 89–117.

28. Cox, 'Rhetoric and Ethics', 183–4.

29. I have discussed these examples in *The Future of Illusion*, ch. 3.

30. Viroli, *Machiavelli*, 85.

31. Ibid., 95.

32. See my *Machiavellian Rhetoric: From the Counter-Reformation to Milton* (Princeton, NJ: Princeton University Press, 1994), esp. chs. 1 and 2; and my 'Revisiting Agathocles' in *The Review of Politics* 75, no. 4 (2013), 557–72.

33. Leo Strauss, *Thoughts on Machiavelli* (Glencoe, IL: The Free Press, 1958), 47.

34. Ibid., 269.

35. Ibid.

36. Strauss claims that '[i]n the *Prince*, [Machiavelli] omits, within the limits of the possible, everything which it would not be proper to mention in the presence of a prince. He dedicated the *Prince* to a prince because he desired to find honorable employment; the book therefore exhibits and is meant to exhibit its author as a perfect courtier, a man of the most delicate sense of propriety' (ibid., 26).

37. Cassirer, *The Myth of the State*, 296.
38. See Donald Philip Verene, 'Cassirer's Political Philosophy', in *Cassirers Weg zur Philosophie der Politik*, ed. Enno Rudolph (Hamburg: Felix Meiner Verlag, 1999): 'Cassirer does not regard philosophy as a power to correct actively the ills of social life' (28).
39. As Claude Lefort points out, Machiavelli subscribes to his own myth of an objective political science, the myth of the absolute distinction between myth and science. See Claude Lefort, *Le travail de l'oeuvre Machiavel* (Paris: Gallimard, 1986), 190–205.
40. 'A persuadere o a dissuadere a' pochi una cosa, è molto facile, perché, se non bastano le parole, tu vi puoi usare l'autorità e la forza; ma la difficultà è rimuovere da una moltitudine una sinistra opinione e che sia contraria o al bene comune o all'opinione tua; dove non si può usare se non le parole …': *L'arte della guerra*, Book 4: Machiavelli, *Tutte le opere*, ed. Mario Martelli (Florence: Sansoni, 1971), 354; tr. from Cox, 'Rhetoric and Ethics', 176.
41. Cassirer, *The Myth of the State*, 296.
42. Paul Ricoeur, *Lectures on Ideology and Utopia* (New York: Columbia University Press, 1986), 8–10. I discuss Ricoeur in the Coda to *Machiavellian Rhetoric* (238–9).

13

Machiavelli Reading

Swapan Chakravorty

Reading, Presence, and Representation

The act of reading almost always involves a vanishing trick. It is an escape from our self-evident identity, or, to put it in a tautological gloss, from what we identify as evidence of our so-called self. Writing on the problem of the self in connection with literature, especially as it appears in the existentialist psychology of Ludwig Binswanger, Paul de Man distinguishes between four possibilities that make it difficult to find a ground on which 'selves' may meet the unity of the literary consciousness. Of these, two are 'the self that reads' and the 'the self that reads itself'. Straying from the arguments of Binswanger examined by de Man, one could say that in the first, the reader felt that she was other than *she* at the time of reading, and that in the second, the author's self shifted with contingent interpretations of her work. Whichever way we look at the distinctions—and de Man has four, not two—they seem designed to scramble the reader's fragile ontological co-ordinates at the moment of reading.[1] The 'I' who reads is not always the 'I' accessible to us as a sturdily cognizable *object*, although we are conscious of the undeniable *subjective* experience we go through as readers.

Readers of Wolfgang Iser may recall his adaptation of Ernst Cassirer's idea of the concept as a model of symbol usage involved in reading fiction—fiction being that species of speech that lacks a situational reference. Cassirer thought of the concept as a way of moving its object to an ideal distance so that it might be understood (one might also say, 'so that it may be *read*')—a process in which *presence* needs to make way for *representation*.[2] Cassirer's phenomenology of knowledge was not the only idea Iser drew on. Roman Ingarden was not an idealist like Cassirer, but his phenomenological realism served Iser well. Iser agrees with Ingarden that one who reads a text is the source of 'concretization'. The reader, instead of merely contemplating a finished object, generates significance by fleshing out the indeterminacies of the text.[3] The reader of fiction translates the world into something it is not: into symbols that are independent of the visible, making it possible for the reader, in principle at least, to see an invisible world.[4] 'Fictional language represents such an arrangement of symbols, for in Ingarden's terms it is not anchored in reality, and in Austin's terms it has no situational context.'[5] Seeing an 'invisible world' is to make representation visible. This too is a disappearing trick, one in which the reader and her world both disappear to clear the stage for representation.

There are less taxing ways of speaking of the disappearing act involved in reading, if not of the more general idea of the escape from one's consciously experienced identity. In a short meditation titled 'On Reading: Words and Images', Orhan Pamuk writes: 'To carry a book in your pocket or in your bag, particularly in times of sadness, is to be in possession of another world, a world that can bring you happiness.' This is a form of 'escapism', concedes Pamuk, but 'it is still good to escape'.[6] But the Pamuk who 'read' the novel was not the Pamuk who wrote the essay. In a closely linked piece titled 'The Pleasures of Reading', Pamuk speaks of the intimacy he felt with Stendhal's *The Charterhouse of Parma*. Yet he is certain that, unlike the heroes in Proust, he 'never assumed the identities of other characters or believed these events were happening to me'. Pamuk makes no mention of Cervantes's sad knight who almost ingested romances until they were part of him. Unlike him, Pamuk 'was not present in the novel'. Nevertheless, he enjoyed the excitement of entering a strange terrain. His eyes would pull back from the old copy of *The Charterhouse of Parma* in his hand to gaze at its yellowing pages from a distance, just as he would interrupt his drinking to gaze lovingly at the bottle of soft drink in his hand: he 'studied the interior world of the novel in much the same way as I once studied the liquid inside my soft-drink bottle'.[7]

Absorption and aloofness—insistence on the simultaneity of the two processes involved in reading fiction would have pleased Cassirer, who saw in the concept the means of moving the world to an ideal distance to allow for representation, which, in its turn, would enable the act of reading. It would have also gladdened Abhinavagupta, the tenth-century philosopher from Kashmir who believed that the sensitive reader or viewer might feel one with the subject of poetry only if she cleared the mind's mirror by observing the way poetry worked. Poetic speculation is in need of the clarity which the speculum of the attuned consciousness provides.[8]

These discussions pertain to the reading of fiction and poetry. Are they relevant to the reading of other species of texts, especially when the focus of our attention is such a writer as Machiavelli, who commented on anterior texts to present his views on politics and history in terms of the conventions of reading he unsettled?[9] Moreover, Machiavelli was also a writer of fiction and plays, and an avid reader of all forms of classical and more recent literature.

The question of immersion and distance, however, seems more than obliquely relevant to the ways in which Machiavelli read and interpreted non-fiction, although one is looking here at matters that do have a contextual reference. We notice the same slide of layers as in the reader of fiction—the reader as sovereign self and the reader as other-than-self, the reader as sole witness to a silent trace and the reader who conducts a conversation with a spectre that needs to be absent so that it may be re-imagined as a living voice. The perplexities of the situation may turn out to be an advantage, placing the reader in dialogue with a physically unheard voice, and hence legitimizing deviant and polemical readings of texts that apparently deal with historical events and records. Machiavelli, a reader trained in the humanist tradition, is thus able to read texts as Machiavelli the writer of urgent, and admittedly partisan, polemics. One could look at such reading in another way. Like Faustus in the play by his English reader Christopher Marlowe, Machiavelli turns the act of reading into *performance*, into the staged enactment of a decision by the thorough actor (or the pitiable actor, depending on whether you believe Mephostophiles when he says he had turned the pages as Faustus read).[10]

A good Renaissance instance of the escape through books from an oppressive world is Montaigne's willing suspension of common sense when he describes himself as the sovereign prince in his library in *Essais*, 3:3. In the library he is seated on his throne, assured of 'la domination pure': 'I try to make my authority over it absolute, and so withdraw to this one corner from all society, conjugal, filial, and civil.'[11] This is at odds with the picture of the study as the spiritual theatre that may decide the destiny of the Christian soul. I have cited the instance of *Doctor Faustus*. One could think of other telling examples. The many visual images of Saint Jerome in his study created during the Renaissance provide a good source. Two depictions that come to mind are the painting by Antonello da Messina (c. 1475; currently in the National Gallery, London) and the 1514 engraving by Albrecht Dürer (currently in the National Galleries of Scotland). The latter shows the saint writing with a crucifix placed at the corner of the table, with a skull on the window sill behind the cross in the left foreground serving as *memento mori*. Alternatively, one could think of Sandro Botticelli's portrait of Saint Augustine in the Ognissanti Church in Florence (c. 1480). The fresco has the saint reading in his cell, right hand on his chest close to the heart, writing materials resting on his left hand, his eyes lifted from the book held open in front of him. At the other end, one gets images of the tranquil self-possession of the humanist scholar, the kind of reader that Montaigne wished to be in his study, which had its walls and ceiling inscribed with excerpts and images from the key texts of classical and Christian culture. An instance of the desired tranquility is Hans Holbein the Younger's 1523 portrait of Erasmus (now in the National Gallery, London), seemingly collected, with contemplative eyes gazing into the distance, hands resting quietly on a closed tome.[12]

I write 'seemingly' since such contemplation may conceal a spiritual tempest raging below the surface. Reading, even fortuitous reading with the angels instead of the devil turning the pages, was a motif in Christian conversion narratives from Saint Augustine to Petrarch.[13] Found images and texts speak with a different tone of urgency, causing turbulence rather than withdrawal into a region of Stoic indifference, insulated from incursions of the contingent. They may induce a withdrawal nonetheless, although one which, paradoxically, may determine absolute consequences for the Christian reader.

In any case, there is the pretence of presence even as one escapes from the everyday world. Petrarch corresponded with dead authors such as Cicero, and Machiavelli summoned Dante for a conversation in *A Dialogue on Language* (c. 1515), making it plain that he would employ speech prefixes as in a play rather than persist with the tedious tags indicating speakers in prose fiction: 'But I should like to have a word with Dante, and to get away from "he said" and "I replied", I will indicate the speakers ...'[14] The physical absence of the interlocutor is the pre-condition of such dialogue, and writing makes such absences and spectral conversations conceivable. One could adapt Cassirer's observation and say that one had to escape presence in order to make representation possible.[15]

In spite of the convergence of interests between evangelism and print capitalism that brought Catholic and Protestant printers together in their enthusiasm for the new technology of print, habits of oral and scribal cultures needed reassurance as a tide of printed materials flooded Early Modern Europe. The literary evidence seems to suggest that one anxiety which was sought to be assuaged was that print (manuscripts were too confined to the lettered elite to cause equal anxiety) should not necessarily dislodge a text from the continuum of dialogue and spoken discourse found, for instance, in heard sermons.[16] We are reminded of Milton's famed observation that books contained 'a potency of life in them to be as active as that soul was whose progeny they are'.[17]

One may also call to mind Donne's testy dismissal of the 'fondling motley humorist' in *Satire I*. The study could also be a 'wooden chest', which is a coffin, confining like a prison, yet liberating since one might converse with past authors:

> Leave mee, and in this standing woodden chest,
> Consorted with these few bookes, let me lye
> In prison, and here be coffin'd, when I dye ...[18]

Donne lists among his interlocutors 'Gods conduits, grave Divines', 'Natures Secretary, the Philosopher', 'jolly Statesmen', 'Chroniclers', and 'Giddie fantastique Poëts of each land' (lines 5–10). Born a recusant Catholic (his mother Elizabeth Heywood was great niece of the Catholic martyr Thomas More) and converted to the Church of England, Donne certainly knew of Machiavelli, and had probably read him. Machiavelli fits his label of 'jolly Statesm[a]n, which teach how to tie / The sinewes of a cities mistique bodie' (lines 7–8). Machiavelli figures along with Ignatius Loyola in his satire *Ignatius His Conclave* (1611) as attending on the devil in hell. Scholars have more often than not taken the satire as rehearsing the clichés of Tudor and Stuart England concerning the 'Machiavel', a figure largely derived from *Contre Machiavel* (1576), Innocent Gentillet's Calvinist tract published in Geneva.[19] However, Stefania Tutino has persuasively argued that Donne's Machiavelli was not the stereotypical Machiavel, nor was his Machiavelli 'a predecessor for Ignatius'. While Ignatius was using religion to argue in favour of the Pope's 'spiritual monarchy', 'the Florentine was concerned with politics, and was trying to advance the cause of the princes'. Donne, therefore, examines 'Machiavelli's doctrine from a political point of view and with respect to the relationship between politics and religion'—a compelling indication of a more than casual acquaintance with Machiavelli's writing.[20]

Donne takes to his wooden chest texts of multiple genres. While treating them as material embodiments of their authors' voices, he, even if unwittingly, dramatizes a different strain in the ambivalence inherent in reading as an encounter with a trace, a communion with the mark of an absence. The reader does not immerse herself in a parley as Donne claims he does as reader, although the pretence of live colloquy demands the fantasy of such an immersion. The text one reads is able to speak by virtue of being a silent voice, a voice in a coffin, a series of sounds encoded in ciphers. The deciphering reader maintains a critical distance, which is inalienable from her engagement with the written text. Time helps in creating the distance, and not just because the serious reader had better keep away from the opinion of the multitude. Nagasawa, the boastful but attractive student in Haruki Murakami's novel

Norwegian Wood, never read any author who had not been dead for at least thirty years (except Scott Fitzgerald who had missed the thirty-year bar by only two years). 'If you only read the books that everyone else is reading, you can only think what everyone else is thinking. That's the world of hicks and slobs.'[21] This may sound like an odd reason for not reading recent literature, but distance is crucial. Walter Savage Landor was a writer who took apartments in the Medici Palace in 1821 and was, like Machiavelli, briefly exiled from the city. In Florence he started writing the *Imaginary Conversations*, where the dialogue involves historical figures and not reader and author. However, the exchanges between Pericles and Sophocles are certainly richer in abstract reflections than those between Pitt and Canning, irrespective of one's opinion of the comparative literary worth of the two dialogues.[22]

Pamuk is entirely credible when he claims that he absents himself from the novel of Stendhal that he loves to read. Readers wish to speak to the dead, like epic characters who visit the underworld and meet past authors. If the reader also happens to be an author, the act of reading may be inextricable from the act of writing. The writer would then be analogous to Dante, writing his *Comedy* as he is guided by Virgil through a rite of passage, in course of which he meets dead poets and philosophers in the fourth canto of *Inferno*. The distance, hence, is an enabling condition for the intimacy with past writers. It allows the reader to correspond with dead authors, ask questions that one's vantage in the present enables one to do. Cognition of a text, as Hans-Georg Gadamer famously observed, is at the same time re-cognition.[23]

Humanist Reading: Action and Performance

Was Machiavelli a reader like Donne or Milton? Or was he more of a performative reader, like Montaigne or the fictional Faustus? Renaissance manuals of instruction encouraged readers to *act*. William Sherman, in his discussion of Renaissance readers' scribbles on the margins of texts, reminds us that the 'actual' reader was at the same time the reader linked to *action*.[24] Sherman cites Lisa Jardine and Anthony Grafton's essay '"Studied for Action": How Gabriel Harvey Read His Livy'. Jardine and Grafton show that Early Modern scholarly readers did not passively receive texts but were active interpreters. The authors of the essay employed the word 'activity' in a strong sense: 'not just the energy which must be acknowledged as accompanying the intervention of the scholar/reader with his text, nor the cerebral effort involved in making the text the reader's own, but reading as intended to give rise to something else.' This would partially support Antonio Gramsci's claim, discussed later in this chapter, that Machiavelli wrote like the author of a party manifesto. At the same time, the scholar/reader could conduct 'a variety of goal-directed readings, depending on the initial brief'.[25] One might add that 'action' could include the function of the *actor*, the role one played in the act of reading.

There are apparent difficulties in considering Machiavelli the reader through the prism of Gramscian Marxism. Machiavelli certainly echoed humanist premises concerning the aims of learning.[26] In addition, he seems to have believed in some steady human traits through history identifiable as 'human nature'. In the *Discourses*, he even bases lessons to be drawn from history on such immutability: 'all cities and all peoples are and ever have been animated by the same desires and the same passions' (1:39).[27] Quentin Skinner justifiably maintains that Machiavelli often sounded pessimistic about one's ability to change 'human nature', 'of transforming our natural selfishness into a willing and virtuoso concern for the common good'.[28] This does not rule out a belief in action as the fruit of reading history, in the capacity to guard against swings in fortune and alter circumstances in one's favour. The humanist intellectual of the Renaissance could often betray unsteady faith in this human capability and be guilty of indifference to this goal of reading past authors. Not every humanist was a 'civic humanist': many preferred the docility of inert appreciation of texts at a safe distance from the burden of political action. His purpose in the *Discourses*, says Machiavelli, was to draw men out of the errors of fetishized learning, so that 'those who read my remarks may derive those advantages which should be the aim of all study of history'.[29]

Machiavelli's iteration of humanist instructions to readers is compatible with his creative reinterpretation of such instructions, or his 'reading' of them. In fact, it has been suggested that it is the immutability of the human condition, if not of human nature, that enables Machiavelli's 'cross-temporal' programme of reading 'to breathe new life into the present'.[30] Even if he were one of the first readers of Christian Europe to read the Bible through secular eyes, to the extent of considering Moses's humility as political weakness, and of imagining his mentor Yahweh to be a warrior god who trained Moses in the *virtù* of the liberator, he did treat the Old Testament as humanists had treated Greco-Roman history, as a source of models for history-writing, kingship, governance, and military strategy.[31] Jacob Soll writes that Machiavelli was one of the first moderns to create political theory out of textual criticism, and to select historical instances relevant to the present—a choice driven by considerations of political prudence.[32] I believe that Machiavelli's 'intention' is not always germane to the way he read history, or to the ways in which we might read him. The projective emphasis in Machiavelli's writings is seldom as straightforward as it is, for instance, in the final *adhortatio* in *The Prince*. Yet thinkers of substance have found Machiavelli speaking to their times because of such a projective strain. In *Machiavelli and Us*, Althusser points out that Machiavelli spoke to Hegel not in the past tense but in the present; in particular, he spoke 'of the German political situation'. As for Gramsci, Althusser believes that Machiavelli spoke to him in the present tense, or 'better still, in the future'.[33]

What kind of reader, then, was Machiavelli? To put the question differently, how do we as readers read Machiavelli's reading or his *action* as reader? On 10 December 1513, Machiavelli wrote a craftily worded letter to Francesco Vettori, the Florentine ambassador to Rome.[34] The letter is justly renowned as crucial to any study of the genesis of *The Prince*. Exiled in 1512 from Florence, where he had been Secretary to the Second Chancery, Machiavelli was living in Sant'Andrea in Percussina, located in a *frazione* of San Casciano Val di Pesa. Machiavelli mentions his work in progress, provisionally titled *De principatibus*. It is probable that he hoped that Vettori would plead with Giuliano de' Medici, the proposed dedicatee, to rescind the order of *relegatio* or exile passed on him. He boasts of having learnt to snare thrushes through September—an unlikely month, since the fowling season started in October— and proceeds to give a vivid account of his life in the country. The routine involves getting up with the sun, and surveying the work of clearing a thicket from which neighbours plotted to carry away firewood free. Next comes the time he spends with books. Leaving the wood he goes to a spring with a book under his arm—Dante, Petrarch, or a 'minor' poet such as Tibullus or Ovid. Machiavelli does not 'absent himself' from the texts at this point, not at least by a significant distance. 'I read of their amorous passions and their loves; I remember my own—and for a while these reflections make me happy.'[35] There may have been more than a reference to past amours: salacious details in many letters were probably suppressed when the manuscript volume was being copied.[36] Such lightly immersive reading is followed by observation of life in the country—along the road, in the tavern, talking to strangers and picking up gossip. After lunch, he returns to the inn and 'acts' ('m'ingaglioffo') the rustic with the landlord, butcher, miller, and a couple of bakers. He joins in games and squabbles. 'So, trapped among this vermin, I rub the mould from my wits and work off the sense of being so cruelly treated by Fate—content to be driven on along this road if only to watch for her to show some sign of shame.'[37] Machiavelli is *acting* with the vermin, but he is also *acting* the wronged victim with Vettori. He is actor and sufferer, observer of manners and observed of Fate. More importantly, like the consummate player, he is true to decorum. He has one set of costumes to read Dante, Petrarch, Tibullus, and Ovid; a finer set when he takes his seat, much like Montaigne in his library, among the courtly greats from antiquity.

> When evening comes, I return home and go into my study. On the threshold I strip off my muddy, sweaty, workday clothes, and put on the robes of court and palace, and in this graver dress I enter the antique courts of the ancients and am welcomed by them, and there I taste the food that alone is mine, and for which I was born. And there I make bold to speak to them and ask the motives of their actions, and they, in their humanity, reply to me. And for the space of four hours I forget the world, remember no vexation, fear poverty no more, tremble no more at death: I pass indeed into their world.[38]

Machiavelli the costumed reader–actor recalls not only Montaigne, but H. G. Wells's protagonist Richard Remington in *The New Machiavelli* (1911) and his theatrical reverie. Remington describes a figment of his version of Machiavelli:

> At the entrance, he says, he pulled off his peasant clothes covered with the dust and dirt of that immediate life, washed himself, put on his 'noble court dress,' closed the door on the world of toiling and getting, private loving, private hating and personal regrets, sat down with a sigh of contentment to those wider dreams.[39]

The retreat from 'immediate life' is readerly escape, a performance. At the same time, it is the play-actor's *action*: the act of reading and interpretation is inseparable from the act of writing. Machiavelli says hard on the heels of the quoted sentence:

> And as Dante says that there can be no understanding without the memory retaining what it has heard, I have written down what I have gained from their conversation, and composed a small work *De principatibus*, where I dive as deep as I can into ideas about this subject, discussing the nature of princely rule, what forms it takes, how these are acquired, how they are maintained, why they are lost.[40]

Machiavelli's study is also the scene of his writing, 'mio scrittoio'. This may be usefully compared with the fictional Remington's fashioning the figure of

Machiavelli the reader through his own act of writing, as represented through the first-person narrative:

> I like to think of him so, with brown books before him lit by the light of candles in silver candlesticks, or heading some new chapter of 'The Prince,' with a grey quill in his clean fine hand.[41]

Dressed for his role in the hall of past masters, the dead authors whom Robert Burton had described as *mortuis magistris* in *The Anatomy of Melancholy*,[42] he calls them back to life, although what we really get to 'hear' from them are not answers to his questions, but Machiavelli's own 'reading', the answers to questions that only Machiavelli could ask of the dead masters from his moment in history, a 'reading' that issues in the form of *De principatibus*. One could say the same of Machiavelli the reader–author of the *Discourses*.

Reading as Conversation with the Dead

The trope of the conversation with dead authors recalls the opening line in Stephen Greenblatt's *Shakespearean Negotiations*: 'I began with the desire to speak with the dead.'[43] In his book *Speaking with the Dead*, Jurgen Pieters argues against the protocols of dialogical reading proposed by Greenblatt and those influenced by his brand of New Historicist poetics. Pieters believes that as far as Machiavelli is concerned, the conversation need not be so much *with* the dead as *among* them. The scholar or historian should pay more attention to what the text says than to the questions we put to it. The text does address the present, but in a much more direct way than Greenblatt believes. The historian need not have any questions ready beforehand: listening intently to the conversation in the text should suffice.[44] One need hardly be partial to New Historicist habits of reading to see that Machiavelli would have been less of an 'unsettled question' if he had read anterior texts in this way. At least, he would have far fewer provocative answers to the questions that one might ask five centuries after his death. The question of Machiavelli, as Croce had guessed, is hardly 'closed'.[45] Pieters's approach to Machiavelli seems untenable for a broader reason. He pays scarce attention to the difficult problem of the temporal rift that often separates the genesis of a text from the moment of its reception. Gadamer is far more convincing on this matter: what the text says, must be what it says *to us*. 'To understand a text is to come to understand oneself in a kind of dialogue.'[46]

Machiavelli, admittedly, was a reader in the humanist tradition. Even if one were none too sure of a single protocol of reading in the age of humanism, one could hardly doubt the prevalence of such a thing as a humanist training in reading for young pupils. In the letter to Vettori written on 10 December 1513, Machiavelli invokes Dante to declare that reading must result in *action*, or else memory fails to retain what is read (although one might substitute 'heard' for 'read', since the reading of classics is imagined as an audience with the dead masters). Reading was primarily for use, as John Brinsley the Elder, a schoolmaster in Leicestershire trained at Cambridge, wrote in his 1612 work *Ludus literarius: Or, the Grammar Schoole*: 'To read and not to vnderstande what wee read, or not to know how to make vse of it, is nothing else but a neglect of all good learning; and a meere abuse of the means & helps to attaine the same.'[47] The best way to use one's reading was to write about what one has read and learnt: writing was a potent form of action. Brinsley was writing almost exactly a century after Machiavelli had drafted his letter to Vettori. However, his activist precept to young learners was not too distant from what fourteenth- or fifteenth-century humanist educators such as Guarino Guarini of Verona (1374–1460) or Rudolph Agricola (1444–85) had written. Here is a passage from Agricola's *Lucubrationes* published in Cologne in 1539:

> We ourselves must compose and publish something from all that we have learned so that our studies do not lie sluggish and sterile in our minds … If we are not able to hand anything on to our successors or if we put forward to our contemporaries nothing beyond what we have learned, what is the difference between us and a book?[48]

It is easy to lose sight of the crucial differences below the apparent conformity of Machiavelli's declarations with the discipline of reading instilled in pupils by humanist teachers. Some scholars have discerned in Machiavelli's way of reading ancient texts a radical core in humanism which he bravely pursued. In line with the civic humanism of the Renaissance, Machiavelli walked the extra mile of treating social and political reality as a human artefact, not as a non-transcendent object of knowledge. In this, he was the first to voice a certain ambivalence of modernity, manifest in the necessarily multiple goals of ethics.[49] On the other hand, Michael Sherberg argued in 1991, drawing on Maria-Elisabeth Conta's notion of textual *deixis* explained in *Deissi testuale ed anafora* (1981),[50] that Machiavelli's *Discourses* use metatextual signposts that look forward and backward, combining proleptic with analeptic functions. The signposts guide readers to other places in the text, and retard, if not resist, linear readings. The technique, according to Sherberg, enables Machiavelli to teach readers 'how to read and think about history, or more precisely, how to read and think his way'. He is able to control the apparent disarray by keeping to a plan keyed to textual units such as the chapter. But the oscillating movement through textual sequences helps create an 'internal temporality' in which the past may speak to the present. Although Sherberg speaks of 'plan' and 'control', he is careful to mention Machiavelli's 'associative mental processes', in which his address to the implied reader can at times melt into a monologue, into words directed at himself as author.[51]

There have been further contributions to the debate centred on the alleged conformity of Machiavelli's interpretation of texts to the standard techniques of humanist reading. Ronald J. Schmidt Jr., for instance, has recently suggested that by reading Machiavelli anachronistically, one could find in *The Prince* and the *Discourses* a 'new life for the democratic imagination'.[52] Schmidt looks at 'anachrony' in a Derridean sense. Jacques Derrida had spoken of the necessity of the present to be non-contemporaneous with itself to make responsible reading possible—a reading aware of the justice we owe to victims of wars, capitalist imperialism, or other forms of violence, and also to those yet unborn:

> Without this *non-contemporaneity of itself with the living present*, without that which secretly unhinges it, without this responsibility and this respect for justice concerning those who *are not there*, of those who are no longer or who are not yet *present and living*, what sense would there be to ask the question, 'where?' 'where tomorrow?' 'whither?' (Emphases in the original)[53]

Such non-contemporaneity of the present with itself is a useful way of looking at Machiavelli's responsive and responsible conversations with past authors. It is in this specific Derridean spirit that Schmidt examines 'anachrony'. Further, the anachronous is the point from which a spectral authority sees us as not seeing it. This, according to Schmidt, is close to Althusser's treatment of Machiavelli as an 'uncanny companion for reading and thinking'. Schmidt considers this way of reading not distant from Machiavelli's own way of reading and writing.[54] Victoria Kahn had shown that Counter-Reformation Europe read Machiavelli as a source from which one could gather historical instances to suit themes and *topoi*. Schmidt supplements Kahn's argument by arguing that Machiavelli's communion with past masters went beyond that objective: he used anachronistic scholarship, as Schmidt himself intends doing against the neo-liberal consensus of his time, 'to produce exhortations to enact democratic alternatives'.[55]

Does Sherberg's astute view, or Schmidt's, entirely account for the unsettling effect Machiavelli's polemics still has on us? I say this keeping in view the apparent difference between targeted readers of *The Prince* and the *Discourses*. Reading directed toward action, performative reading, dialogue with the dead, polemical engagement with anterior texts, metatextual signposting, anachronous reading—all such elements contribute to our understanding of Machiavelli's practice as reader and commentator. At the same time, an eclectic mix of these strategies might increase the perplexities of present-day readers of Machiavelli instead of dispelling them. I would like to suggest that we could extend Gramsci's insight into Machiavelli's objectives as writer to follow the way he might have approached past texts.

Symptomatic Reading

Gramsci was a keen reader of Machiavelli's texts since at least the time when he was a university student in Turin, where his teacher of literature Umberto Cosmo advised him in 1922 to start working on a book on Machiavelli.[56] Gramsci wished to read Machiavelli historically, as a creation of the circumstances of his time.[57] Yet he provides a point of departure for reading Machiavelli as an intellectual mediator in shaping history by writing on historical texts, as a participant in the future. In this, there was a deep resemblance between Machiavelli's aims and Gramsci's. Like the latter, Machiavelli was a man of action writing as a political historian. Unlike the Neoplatonic philosophers and several humanists of his time, Machiavelli was not exclusively committed to a contemplative life. Nor was he willing to accept passivity in the name of *ragione*, an acceptance of facts unmediated by desire. Machiavelli held that genuine *virtù* was tempered by the sort of reasonableness that enabled one to plan ahead should fortune turn hostile, and even change the situation. As one commentator studying Gramsci's reading of Machiavelli wrote of the latter's activist ethic: 'A *datum* was merely a *factum*, what men made.'[58] Hence, Gramsci's reading of Machiavelli differed substantially from those of Croce and Cassirer, who saw him as a dispassionate political scientist.[59]

Gramsci believed that Machiavelli's ideas were not 'bookish', the 'monopoly of isolated thinkers, a secret memorandum circulating among the initiated'. Rather, he wrote like the author of a party manifesto.[60] He did not write political history to persuade a learned coterie. What Gramsci wrote about the author who writes the history of a political party may more generally be applied to the activist historian: 'The historian, though giving everything its due importance in the overall picture, will emphasise above all the real effectiveness of the party, its determining force, positive and negative, in having contributed to bringing certain events about and in having prevented other events from taking place.'[61] It is not hard to see that Gramsci is extrapolating Marxist prescriptive notions, or what he termed the 'philosophy of praxis', using Machiavelli as a credible alibi. Gramsci may have overstated his case in thinking of Machiavelli as the writer of a political manifesto, and in thinking that in that manifesto, Machiavelli becomes the people. A manifesto is not addressed to an individual as *The Prince* seemingly was. 'Under the guise of the Prince,' wrote Althusser, 'it is in fact the people [Machiavelli] is addressing.' But a manifesto is written to organize the people, not to a non-existent individual, even though in the concluding invocation to the prince, Machiavelli brings the rescue fantasy centred on an absolute ruler to a concrete climax by merging with the people: he 'becomes the people'.[62]

In the letter to Francesco Vettori, Machiavelli describes his reading as an encounter with a spectral voice, the mark of an absence which, as we argued, makes representation possible. I would like to believe that the trace allowed readers to construct a *symptomatic reading* of the text, and it is in this direction that I would like to extend Gramsci's and Althusser's insights into the way Machiavelli read history and the way we may read him. Machiavelli was inaugurating a version of political commentary that read historical texts and commentaries symptomatically. I think that the notion of *symptomatic reading* may be useful in making sense of the way Machiavelli *wished* to write. Intention was important to Gramsci: the authorial motive, the activist intent, was his point of departure in the discussion of Machiavelli in *The Modern Prince*.

I am thinking of symptomatic reading not in the strict Freudian sense, but in the way Althusser used it in *Reading Capital*. Althusser claimed that his was an attempt to read the works of Marx *symptomatically*, that is, read them with 'the progressive and systematic reflection of the problematic on its objects such as to make them *visible*'. This is because the apparent and specific answers we read in Marx, according to Althusser, are to questions that are not immediately visible. Lenin's interpretation of the Russian explosion of 1917 was an answer, but not to a proximate question. It was an answer to the absent question: in what way did Marx 'invert' the Hegelian dialectic?

> [I]t was only possible to pose to the practical political analyses Lenin gives us of the conditions for the revolutionary explosion of 1917 the question of the *specificity* of the Marxist dialectic on the basis of an *answer* which lacked the proximity of its *question*, an answer situated *at another place* in the Marxist works at our disposal.[63]

Ben Brewster glosses the word 'reading' in *Reading Capital* as symptomatic reading, *lecture symptomale*. It is not extracting the essence from the shell of characters and sounds, but constructing the unconscious of the text, its problematic 'centred on the absence of problems and concepts within the problematic as much as their presence'. 'Both Hegel and empiricist readings are attempts to return to the myth of direct communication, to the *logos*, and they therefore have a religious inspiration. Marx's own reading of the classics provides an example of symptomatic reading.'[64] One could say the same of the readings of anterior texts cited in this chapter by Petrarch, Montaigne, Donne, Milton, and, apparently, Machiavelli as he presents himself as an appropriately attired courtier-reader in his letter to Vettori. I would like to think that Machiavelli's reading of Livy was symptomatic for comparable reasons, although Althusser, oddly, did not himself employ his symptomatic method in reading Machiavelli.[65] Nonetheless, one is forced to relate questions and answers in Machiavelli's writing that are not always contiguous, or even evident. One turns to the 'elsewheres' of his reading and commentary on past texts for the links. We are reminded of Althusser's use of a comparison from Book 3 of Machiavelli's *The Art of War*. Althusser's trope may be put to good use, although in this instance he is warning readers against enlisting Machiavelli in their political cause. Machiavelli is like cannons in the line of the march. Cannons mounted on carriages cannot be kept within the ranks of marching troops since they face the direction opposite to that in which they ought to fire. We often are unable to guess which way Machiavelli is firing: his cannons face the wrong direction.

Machiavelli as Symptomatic Reader

I conclude with two examples. The first is from *The Prince* and the second from the *Discourses*. It has often been noticed that in *The Prince*, Machiavelli signals the coincidence of compatibility with, and difference from, the conventions in manual-for-princes literature by using Latin chapter-titles alongside the Tuscan prose of Florence in the body of the text. The chapter headings recall the standard themes of manuals for princes, while the main document arrives at startling variations on those themes. On a few occasions, Machiavelli craftily draws the reader's attention to the differences through such strategies as textual *deixis*. Gramsci, schooled in the canny hermeneutics of censorship, would have seen these ploys as indication of Machiavelli's political agenda. At the start of the fifteenth chapter of *The Prince*, for instance, Machiavelli writes:

> It now remains to be seen what are the methods and rules for a prince as regards his subjects and friends. And as I know that many have written of this, I fear that my writing about it may be deemed presumptuous, differing as I do, especially in this matter, from the opinions of others.[66]

Machiavelli provides a convincing reason for the departure in the repetition. Political prescriptions ought to be anchored in experience, and follow from premises other than moral and theological ones:

> But my intention being to write something of use to those who understand, it appears to me more proper to go to the real truth of the matter than to its imagination; and many have imagined republics and principalities which have never been seen or known to exist in reality; for how we live is so far removed from how we ought to live, that he who abandons what is done for what ought to be done, will rather learn to bring about his own ruin than his preservation.[67]

However, Machiavelli's ancient Roman republic in the *Discourses* reads more like an 'imagined republic', against which he outlines the way forward for an Italy that lacks unity and freedom from external aggression. In the second and fourth chapters of the *Discourses*, to cite one instance, he argues that the Roman republic may not have had a wise law-giver such as Lycurgus of Sparta, but the disunity between the people and the Senate in Rome secured for it, almost fortuitously, long-lasting power and freedom (115–16, 118–21, 211). The unity of Italy is the ostensible aim in *The Prince*; but the *Discourses* concludes that the Roman republic gained in force and liberty by assimilating disunity and social conflict into the system of governance. Machiavelli, once again, is firing 'elsewhere'.

But let me return to the passage quoted from the fifteenth chapter of *The Prince*. The passage echoes a similar instance from the eighteenth chapter, where Machiavelli praises integrity and respect for the law, as advised by the ancients such as Cicero.[68] But in the same chapter, he finds these to be risky virtues in a man entrusted with governing a state. Machiavelli looks for and finds suitable examples in the 'elsewheres' of ancient texts: for instance, when they tell us that Achilles and other princes were trained by Chiron the centaur—a hint that monarchs must combine the human with the beastly in their approach to rule. Although Natale Conti echoes him, Machiavelli seems to have been inventive in allegorizing Chiron in this way.[69]

The second example comes from the *Discourses*. The thirty-seventh chapter of the first book of the *Discourses* is well known for its observations on the reasons of the decline of the Roman republic. It dwells on Livy's discussion of how the land reforms sought to be enforced by the tribunes of the plebs, Tiberius Sempronius Gracchus and, later, his brother Gaius Sempronius Gracchus, failed because of the squabbling nobles. The laws were intended to redistribute excess holdings among the urban poor, who were idle and whose landlessness rendered them ineligible for military service, which in its turn weakened the army. The agrarian land laws had deep-rooted flaws.[70] The flouting of the laws was made possible by the commission appointed to implement them, and their failure ultimately led to civil war and the tyranny of Caesar. As has been noticed, Machiavelli shifts in this chapter from social conflict centred on honours to that centred on possessions, the latter being far more ruinous for a republic.[71] Machiavelli commences his examination of the two kinds of social conflict with a remarkable passage:

> It was a saying of ancient writers, that men afflict themselves in evil, and become weary of the good, and that both these dispositions produce the same effects. For when men are no longer obliged to fight from necessity, they fight from ambition, which passion is so powerful in the hearts of men that it never leaves them, no matter to what height they may rise. The reason for this is that nature has created men so that they desire everything, but are unable to attain it; desire being thus being always greater than the faculty of acquiring, discontent with what they have and dissatisfaction with themselves result from it. This causes the changes in their fortunes; for as some men desire to have more, whilst others fear to lose what they have, enmities and war are the consequences; and this brings about the ruin of one province and the elevation of another.[72]

The translation suggests that Machiavelli is speaking here not of *fortuna* in the abstract nor of Fortuna the goddess, but of individual fortune. However, the word he uses in Italian is still *fortuna*: 'Da questo nasce il variare della fortuna loro.' More importantly, he traces the effects of fortune to human nature and the social instability inherent in the disproportion between desire and gratification. Elsewhere in the text, Fortuna the goddess appears like a supra-social being that humans and republics must learn to contend with. The thirty-first chapter of the third book of the *Discourses*, for example, starts with Livy's praise of Camillus, who remained unmoved by the extreme changes in his fortune. Livy makes Camillus say: 'My courage has neither been inflated by the dictatorship nor abated by exile.'[73] Machiavelli quotes the words to demonstrate that 'fortune has no power over him'.[74] This need not necessarily contradict what he had said in the thirty-seventh chapter of the first book. But there is a crucial difference. In the thirty-seventh chapter of the first book, fortune is clearly a function of human nature and of the conflicting interests of social orders. By reviving the agrarian reforms, the Gracchi disturbed the fragile balance between ambition and need that the disunity between the Senate and the people had maintained. The conflict that was institutionalized in the polity was thus given free rein to focus on the fight for material possessions, thereby hastening the collapse of the republic. The answer that the celebrated opening of the thirty-seventh chapter of Book 1 was providing was to a question that was not proximate in Machiavelli: it was excavated from the source text and reproduced in the thirty-first chapter of Book 3.

Machiavelli and the 'Unconscious' of His Text

The 'unconscious' of Machiavelli's text is more appropriately applied to his reading. The symptomatic reading of ancients manifests itself in a complex figure in the carpet, of which Machiavelli was acutely aware. Machiavelli was more of a performer as conscious political writer, and at the same time more than a costumed reader conversing with the dead. Like the reader of fiction, he was aware of the distance between the text, its embedded codes directing interpretation, and the reader-self, estranged from the text being read and leading it, through a staged enactment, towards a politically inflected reception by readers of his own interpretation of that text. He was anticipating and participating in the political interpretation of pre-Christian texts conducted by Christian authors such as Giovanni Botero (1544–1617), the philosopher–poet who wrote *Della ragion di stato* (1589) against Machiavelli, and the neo-Stoic philosopher Justus Lipsius (1547–1606), whose reading of Tacitus could be usefully contrasted to Machiavelli's reading of Livy. However, the answers in Botero and Lipsius's discussions of past writers, or those in the moral manuals for princes that Machiavelli rejects in the fifteenth chapter of *The Prince*, were to proximate questions; those in Machiavelli lay in questions to be found in the 'elsewheres' of Livy's text, or simply in the absences, or in what constituted the unconscious in Livy's *Ab urbe condita*.

In his collection of *terza rima* poems known as *I Capitoli*, Machiavelli had installed a new pantheon by ousting the old gods of, among other things, politics. One could argue, as one critic at least has done, that Machiavelli does something similar in his non-fiction, creating a new theogony by reading old gods out of his political cosmology.[75] That objective was achieved, not simply by interpreting classical texts in accordance with humanist principles of reading, but by training his guns at strategic moments at what we least expect him to. Machiavelli the reader 'always fires elsewhere'.[76]

Notes

1. Paul de Man, *Blindness and Insight: Essays in the Rhetoric of Contemporary Criticism*, 2nd rev. edn (London: Methuen, 1983 [1971]), 39. The other two possible selves de Man speaks of are 'the self that judges' and 'the self that writes'.
2. Ernst Cassirer, *The Philosophy of Symbolic Forms*, tr. Ralph Manheim, 3 vols. (New Haven, CT: Yale University Press, 1953), 3:307.
3. Roman Ingarden's views are set out at length in *The Literary Work of Art: An Investigation on the Borderlines of Ontology, Logic, and Theory of Literature*, tr. George G. Grabowicz (Evanston, IL: Northwestern University Press, 1973). On the difference between Ingarden and Iser's views, see Menachem Brinker, 'Two Phenomenologies of Reading: Ingarden and Iser on Textual Indeterminacy', *Poetics Today* 1, no. 4 (1980), 203–12.
4. Wolfgang Iser, *The Act of Reading: A Theory of Aesthetic Response* (Baltimore: Johns Hopkins University Press, 1978), 64. See my discussion of the issue in '*Hypocrite Lecteur*: Reading on the Early Modern Stage', in *Renaissance Themes: Essays Presented to Arun Kumar Das Gupta*, ed. Sukanta Chaudhuri (New Delhi: Anthem Press, 2009), 38–9.
5. Iser, *Act of Reading*, 64.
6. Orhan Pamuk, 'On Reading: Words or Images', in *Other Colours: Essays and a Story*, tr. Maureen Freely (London: Faber, 2007), 110–12, 110.
7. Orhan Pamuk, 'The Pleasures of Reading', in *Other Colours*, 114.
8. See Swapan Chakravorty, 'Being Staged: Unconcealment through Reading and Performance in Marlowe's *Doctor Faustus* and Bharata's *Nāṭyśāstra*', *Philosophy East and West* 66, no. 1 (2016), 40–59, 50. See also J. L. Masson and M. V. Patwardhan, *Aesthetic Rapture: The Rasādhyāya of the Nāṭyasāstra* (Pune. Deccan College, 1970), 6.
9. See Janet Coleman, 'Machiavelli's *Via Moderna*: Medieval and Renaissance Attitudes to History', in *Niccolò Machiavelli's The Prince: New Interdisciplinary Essays*, ed. Martin Coyle (Manchester: Manchester University Press, 1995), 40–64. This chapter differs from Coleman's opinion (41) that Machiavelli simply followed established protocols of reading history which may then be applied to contemporary problems. I consider this to be at best a partial view.
10. See Christopher Marlowe, *The Complete Works*, vol. 2: *Doctor Faustus*, ed. Roma Gill (Oxford: Clarendon Press, 1990), Appendix B (B-text), 13.94–6. I have written elsewhere that Faustus in his study may be regarded as living and *acting* in the Sartrean mode of 'being-what-he-is-not': see my 'Being Staged', 45.

11. 'J'essaie à m'en rendre la domination pure, e à sous traire ce seul coin à la communauté et conjugale, et filiale, et civile': Michel de Montaigne, *Essais*, 2 vols., ed. Maurice Rat (Paris: Garnier, 1962), 2:249; tr. from Montaigne, *Complete Essays*, tr. Donald M. Frame (1957; Stanford, CA: Stanford University Press, 1986 [1965]), 629.
12. Antonello da Messina, *Saint Jerome in His Study* (c. 1475), oil on lime, National Gallery, London, Room 55, NG1418; Albrecht Dürer, *Saint Jerome in His Study* (1514), engraving on paper, National Galleries of Scotland, Edinburgh, Print Room, P2690; Sandro Botticelli, *Saint Augustine in His Study* (c. 1480), fresco, Chiesa di Ognissanti, Firenze (Florence); Hans Holbein the Younger, *Erasmus* (1523), oil on wood, National Gallery, London, Room 2, L658.
13. See Saint Augustine, *Confessions*, 8.12.29, ed. and tr. William Watts, Loeb Classical Library, 2 vols. (London: William Heinemann, 1912), 1:464–5; Petrarch, *Familiares* 4:1, in *Prose*, ed. G. Martellotti, P. G. Ricci, E. Carrara, and E. Bianchi (Milan: Riccardo Ricciardi, 1955), 840–1; tr. by Hans Nachodas in *The Ascent of Mont Ventoux*, in *The Renaissance Philosophy of Man*, ed. Ernst Cassirer, Paul Oskar Kristeller, and John Herman Randall Jr. (Chicago, IL: University of Chicago Press, 1948), 44. Saint Augustine followed a child's voice in a neighbouring house urging him to pick up the Bible; the first passage that hit the eye was Saint Paul's Epistle to the Romans 13:14, which converted him from his dissolute ways and dispelled all doubts concerning Christ. Petrarch, in turn, chanced upon a passage in the tenth book of *Confessions*.
14. 'Ma perché io voglio parlare un poco con Dante, per fuggire "egli disse" ed "io risposi", noterò gl'interlocutori davanti': Machiavelli, *Discorso o dialogo intorno alla nostra lingua*, as in *Tutte le opere*, ed. Mario Martelli (Florence: Sansoni, 1971), 926; tr. Machiavelli, *The Literary Works with Selections from the Private Correspondence*, ed. J. R. Hale (London: Oxford University Press, 1961), 181.
15. The theme has been dealt with at length in Jurgen Pieters, *Speaking with the Dead: Explorations in Literature and History* (Edinburgh: Edinburgh University Press, 2005): on Machiavelli, see 19–23.
16. See Elizabeth L. Eisenstein, 'In the Wake of the Printing Press', *Quarterly Journal of the Library of Congress* 35, no. 3 (1978), 183–97, 186, 189, 191.
17. John Milton, *Areopagitica* (1644), ed. Richard C. Jebb (Cambridge: Cambridge University Press, 1918), 6.
18. John Donne, 'Satyre I', in *Complete Poetry and Selected Prose*, ed. John Hayward (London: Nonesuch Press, 1929, rpt. 1962), lines 1–4.

19. On Gentillet, see Edmond M. Beame, 'The Use and Abuse of Machiavelli: The Sixteenth-Century French Adaptation', *Journal of the History of Ideas* 43, no. 1 (1982), 33–54, esp. 41–5.
20. Stefania Tutino, 'Notes on Machiavelli and Ignatius Loyola in John Donne's *Ignatius His Conclave* and *Pseudo Martyr*', *English Historical Review* 119, no. 484 (2004), 1308–21, see esp. 1310, 1317. Donne seems to have known William Fowler, made secretary to Queen Anne in 1593, and one of the earliest English translators of Machiavelli's *The Prince*: see R. C. Bald, *John Donne: A Life* (London: Oxford University Press, 1970), 141. Donne wrote a letter to Henry Goodyer requesting him to plead with William Fowler for a court position for him: see Edmond Gosse, *The Life and Letters of John Donne*, 2 vols. (Gloucester, MA: Peter Smith, 1959 [1891]), 1:13–31; and Deborah Aldrich Larson, 'John Donne and the Astons', *Huntington Library Quarterly* 55, no. 4 (1992), 635–41, 641. See also Alessandra Petrina, *Machiavelli in the British Isles: Two Early Modern Translations of The Prince* (London: Routledge, 2016 [2009]), 69–86. Petrina thinks that the translation was completed in the 1590s: see Alessandra Petrina, 'The Travels of Ideology: Niccolò Machavelli at the Court of James VI', *Modern Language Review* 102, no. 4 (2007), 947–59, 950. For the stereotypical view, see Mario Praz, 'Machiavelli and the Elizabethans', *Proceedings of the British Academy* 14 (1928), 1–49, esp. 44–5; and A. F. Marotti, 'John Donne's Conflicted Anti-Catholicism', *Journal of English and Germanic Philology* 101, no. 3 (2002), 358–79, esp. 374.
21. Haruki Murakami, *Norwegian Wood* (1987), tr. Jay Rubin (London: Vintage, 2003 [2000]), 39.
22. See Walter Savage Landor, *Imaginary Conversations* (1824–46), ed. Charles G. Crump, 6 vols. (London: J. M. Dent, 1891), 1:59–67, 2:335–52.
23. See Hans-Georg Gadamer, *Philosophical Hermeneutics*, tr. and ed. David E. Linge (Berkeley, CA: University of California Press, 1976), 100–1.
24. William H. Sherman, 'What Did Renaissance Readers Write in Their Books?', in *Books and Readers in Early Modern England: Material Studies*, ed. Jennifer Andersen and Elizabeth Sauer (Philadelphia, PA: University of Pennsylvania Press, 2002), 119–37, 127.
25. Lisa Jardine and Anthony Grafton, '"Studied for Action": How Gabriel Harvey Read His Livy', *Past and Present* 129 (1990), 30–78, 30–1. Sherman, in citing the essay, stresses the variety of the reader's roles suggested by Jardine and Grafton: see Sherman, 'What Did Renaissance Readers Write in Their Books?', 127.
26. On the compatibility of Machiavelli's practice with humanist rhetorical principles, see Maurizio Viroli, *Machiavelli's God* (Princeton, NJ: Princeton University Press, 2010), 89–153.

27. '[I]n tutte le città ed in tutti i popoli sono quegli medesimi desiderii e quelli medesimi omori': Niccolò Machiavelli, *Le grandi opere politiche*, ed. Gian Mario Anselmi and Carlo Varotti (Turin: Bollati Boringhieri, 1993), 2:155; tr. Christian E. Detmold in Machiavelli, *The Prince and the Discourses* (New York: Random House, 1950), 216. All citations from the *Discorsi* are from this edition and translation; reference by book, chapter and page.
28. Quentin Skinner, 'Machiavelli on the Maintenance of Liberty', *Politics* 18, no. 2 (1983), 3–15. On 'human nature' in Machiavelli and Marx, see Antonio Gramsci, *Selections from the Prison Notebooks*, tr. and ed. Quintin Hoare and Geoffrey Nowell-Smith (Delhi: Aakar, 2015 [1971]), 134–5.
29. '[C]he coloro che leggeranno queste mia declarazioni, possino più facilmente trarne quella utilità per la quale si debbe cercare la cognizione delle istorie': *Disc.* 1: Proemio, *Le grandi opere* 2:21; tr. Detmold, 105. See Michael Sherberg, 'The Problematics of Reading in Machiavelli's *Discourses*', *Modern Philology* 89, no. 2 (1991), 175–95, 179–80.
30. Ronald J. Schmidt Jr., *Reading Politics with Machiavelli* (New York: Oxford University Press, 2018), 8.
31. *Pr.*, ch. 6. Machiavelli claimed that Christianity privileged contemplative and humble men over active men with leadership qualities: see *Disc.* 2:2. Moses as the destined liberator of his people violently conquered other territories, as he did in the part of Syria he named Judea: see *Disc.* 2:8, *Le grandi opere* 2:261; tr. Detmold, 304. See Steven Marx, 'Moses and Machiavellism', *Journal of the American Academy of Religion* 65, no. 3 (1997), 551–71, especially 553. Ronald J. Schmidt Jr. has recently argued that Machiavelli saw Moses as a messianic founder-prophet unlike others such as Romulus and Numa Pompilius. Moses focused on social and political issues, such as corruption, slavery, and foreigners, which plagued Machiavelli's own time—another aspect of Machiavelli's dialogical reading. See Schmidt Jr., *Reading Politics*, 50–78.
32. See Jacob Soll, *Publishing* The Prince: *Reading, History, and the Birth of Political Criticism* (Ann Arbor, MI: University of Michigan Press, 2008), 89–114.
33. Louis Althusser, *Machiavelli and Us* (French original 1995), ed. François Matheron, tr. Gregory Eliot (London: Verso, 1999), 9, 10.
34. First published in A. Ridolfi, *Pensieri intorno allo scopo di Nicolò* [sic] *Machiavelli nel libro "Il Principe"* (Milan: G.G. Destefanis, 1810), 61–6, the text of the letter was based on a copy ordered by Machiavelli's grandson Giuliano de' Ricci (1543–1606). Subsequent editors have emended the text. On the textual history, see William J. Connell, 'New Light on Machiavelli's Letter to Vettori, 10 December 1513', in *Europa e Italia: Studi in honore di*

Giorgio Chittolini; Europe and Italy: Studies in Honour of Giorgio Chittolini, RetiMedievali E-Book 15 (Florence: Florence University Press, 2011), 104–8, accessed on 3 June 2019 at https://archive.org/details/EuropaEItalia. StudiInOnoreDiGiorgioChittolini.EuropeAndItaly.

35. '[L]eggo quelle loro amorose passioni e quelli loro amori, ricordomi de' mia, gòdomi un pezzo in questo pensiero': *Tutte le opere* 1159, tr. *Literary Works* 138.
36. Ricci admitted that he had suppressed material in the manuscript volume of letters deemed indecent: Connell, 'New Light', 97–8.
37. 'Così rinvolto entra questi pidocchi traggo el cervello di muffa, et sfogo questa malignità di questa mia sorta, sendo contento mi calpesti per questa via, per vedere se la se ne vergognassi': *Tutte le opere* 1159–60; tr. *Literary Works* 139.
38. 'Venuta la sera, mi ritorno a casa, et entro nel mio scrittoio; e in su l'uscio mi spoglio quella veste cotidiana, piena di fango e di loto, e mi metto panni reali e curiali; e rivestito condecentemente entro nelle antique corti delli antiqui huomini, dove, da loro ricevuto amorevolmente, mi pasco di quel cibo, che solum è mio, et che io nacqui per lui; dove io non mi vergogno parlare con loro, e domandarli della ragione delle loro actioni; e quelli per loro humanità mi rispondono; e non sento per quattro hore di tempo alcuna noia, sdimenticho ogni affanno, non temo la povertà, non mi sbigottiscie la morte: tutto mi transferisco in loro': *Tutte le opere* 1160; tr. *Literary Works* 139.
39. H. G. Wells, *The New Machiavelli* (London: John Lane the Bodley Head, 1911), 5–6.
40. 'E perché Dante dice che non fa scienza sanza lo ritenere lo havere inteso, io ho notato quello di che per la loro conversatione ho fatto capitale, e composto uno opusculo *De principatibus*, dove io mi profondo quanto io posso nelle cogitationi di questo subbietto, disputando che cosa è principato, di quale spetie sono, come e' si acquistono, come e' si mantengono, perché e' si perdono': *Tutte le opere* 1160; tr. *Literary Works* 139.
41. Wells, *The New Machiavelli*, 6.
42. Robert Burton, *The Anatomy of Melancholy* (1621), ed. Holbrook Jackson (London: J. M. Dent, 1932, rpt. 1972), part 2, section 2, member 4, p. 91. Burton's account of reading in this section echoes the dialogue with the dead that one finds in Montaigne, Donne, and Machiavelli. The passage from a letter that Burton quotes in translation from the Dutch scholar Daniel Heinsius, professor and librarian of Leiden University, sounds especially close to Montaigne and Machiavelli: 'I no sooner … come into the library, but I bolt the door to me, excluding lust, ambition, avarice,

and all such vices ... and in the very lap of eternity, amongst so many divine souls, I take my seat, with so lofty a spirit and sweet content that I pity all our great ones and rich men that know not this happiness' (ibid.).
43. Stephen Greenblatt, *Shakespearean Negotiations: The Circulation of Social Energy in Renaissance England* (Berkeley, CA: University of California Press, 1988), 1.
44. See Pieters, *Speaking with the Dead*, 17–24, especially 22.
45. Croce wrote that Machiavelli was 'a question that perhaps will never be closed'. See Benedetto Croce, 'Una questione che forse non sichiuderàmai: La questione del Machiavelli', *Quadreni della Critica* 14 (1949), 1–9, rpt. *Indaginisu Hegel e schiarimenti filosofici*, ed. A. Savorelli (Bari: Laterza, 1952), 164–76.
46. Gadamer, *Philosophical Hermeneutics*, 57; see also 101.
47. John Brinsley, *Ludus literarius: or, the Grammar Schoole* (1612), 42, accessed on 25 November 2018 at https://quod.lib.umich.edu/e/eebo/A16865.0001.001/1:9?rgn=div1;view=fulltext. On Brinsley's method of instruction, see Peter Mack, 'Renaissance Habits of Reading', in *Renaissance Essays for Kitty Scoular Datta*, ed. Sukanta Chaudhuri (Kolkata: Oxford University Press, 1995), 1–6.
48. 'Ipsi excudere aliquid proferreque valeamus, neve studia nostra apud animum segnia et (ut ita dicam) sterilia reponantur ... quod si nihil ad posteros mandare poterimus, nihil extra ea quae didicimus ad praesentes proferre, quid tandem inter librum et nos intererit?': Rodolphus Agricola, *Lucubrationes aliquot lectu dignissimae* (Nieuwkoop: De Graaf, 1967 [1539]), 198, as cited in Mack, 'Renaissance Habits of Reading', 6.
49. See Hanan Yoran, 'Machiavelli's Critique of Humanism and the Ambivalences of Modernity', *History of Political Thought* 31, no. 2 (2010), 247–82, 251.
50. Maria-Elisabeth Conta, *Deissi testuale ed anafora* (Pavia: Istituto di storia della lingua italiana, Università di Pavia, 1981), cited in Sherberg, 'Problematics of Reading', 180*n*14.
51. Sherberg, 'Problematics of Reading', 180–1, 186–7, 192.
52. Schmidt Jr., *Reading Politics with Machiavelli*, 23. See also John P. McCormick, *Machiavellian Democracy* (Cambridge: Cambridge University Press, 2011). McCormick argues that Machiavelli reconstructs a hypothetical Roman republic that is democratic and inclusive, unlike the aristocratic republics of Sparta and Venice, in order to devise strategies to moderate the behaviour of 'the people's eternal oppressors' (37): see 21–35. McCormick strains his thesis of Machiavelli as a supporter of armed

populism and 'democracy', by which he means the 'tribunate' and 'assembly' of popular government' (7). Elsewhere, he sees Machiavelli as advocating 'the salutary effect of institutionalized social conflict': see John P. McCormick, *Reading Machiavelli: Scandalous Books, Suspect Engagements, and the Virtue of Populist Politics* (Princeton, NJ: Princeton University Press, 2018), 14. On McCormick's analysis of the implications of Machiavelli's comments on Sparta and Athens, *see Reading Machiavelli*, 47–52. McCormick's thesis hinges on the belief that the people, although different from the nobles, are less inclined to oppress if given the power: see ibid., 78–82, 95–6, 129.

53. Jacques Derrida, *Specters of Marx: The State of the Debt, the Work of Mourning, and the New International*, tr. Peggy Kamuf (French original 1993; English tr. 1994, rpt. New York: Routledge, 2006), xviii.
54. Schmidt Jr, *Reading Politics with Machiavelli*, 2, 4. See Derrida, *Specters of Marx*, 1–60; Althusser, 'Machiavelli's Solitude', tr. Ben Brewster, *Machiavelli and Us*, 116–17.
55. Schmidt Jr, *Reading Politics with Machiavelli*, 27. See Victoria Kahn, *Machiavellian Rhetoric: From the Counter-Reformation to Milton* (Princeton, NJ: Princeton University Press, 1994), 61.
56. See letter from Gramsci to Tatiana Schucht dated 23 February 1931, in Antonio Gramsci, *Lettere dal carcere* (Turin: Einaudi, 1965), 411, cited in A. B. Davidson, 'Gramsci and Reading Machiavelli', *Science and Society* 37, no. 1 (1973), 56–80, 58n8. The original can be found at https://www.iperteca.it/download.php?id=1661, accessed on 12 June 2019.
57. See Gramsci, *Selections from the Prison Notebooks*, 140.
58. Davidson, 'Gramsci and Reading Machiavelli', 73.
59. See Benedetto Croce, 'Machiavelli and Vico', in Benedetto Croce, *Philosophy, Poetry, History: An Anthology of Essays*, tr. and ed. C. Sprigge (London: Oxford University Press, 1966), 655–60; and Ernst Cassirer, *The Myth of the State* (New Haven, CT.: Yale University Press, 1946), 128 (see 116–32). Davidson, 'Gramsci and Reading Machiavelli', 80n91, also takes issue with the obliquely moral view of Machiavelli held by Leo Strauss, who is willing to concede the autonomy of political science, but considers Machiavelli, though at odds with Christian ethics, among the 'wise of the world': see Leo Strauss, *Thoughts on Machiavelli* (Glencoe, MA: Free Press, 1958), 175–6. On Croce's and Gramsci's approaches to Machiavelli, see also Benedetto Fontana, *Hegemony and Power: On the Relation between Gramsci and Machiavelli* (Minneapolis, MN: University of Minnesota Press, 1993), 14–34.

60. Gramsci, *Selections from the Prison Notebooks*, 134. My sources for Gramsci's observations on Machiavelli are the English translations in this volume. Gramsci's notes on Machiavelli are to be found in *Note sul Machiavelli, sulla politica e sullo stato moderno* (Turin: Einaudi, 1949) and in his other *Prison Notebooks*. See Davidson, 'Gramsci and Reading Machiavelli', 56.
61. Gramsci, *Selections from the Prison Notebooks*, 151.
62. Ibid., 126. See Althusser, *Machiavelli and Us*, 25.
63. Louis Althusser, Étienne Balibar, Roger Establet, Pierre Macherey, and Jacques Rancière, *Reading Capital: The Complete Edition*, tr. Ben Brewster and David Fernbach (French originals 1965–96; English translations 1970–2015; London: Verso, 2016), 32.
64. Ibid., 540, 542.
65. See Warren Montag, 'Uno Mero Esecutore: Moses, *Fortuna*, and *Occasione* in *The Prince*', in *The Radical Machiavelli: Politics, Philosophy, and Language*, ed. Filippo Del Lucchese, Fabio Frosini and Vittorio Morfino (Leiden: Brill, 2015), 237–49, 240.
66. 'Resta ora a vedere quali debbano essere e' modi e governi di uno principe con sudditi o con gli amici. E perché io so che molti di questo hanno scritto, dubito, scrivendone ancora io, non essere tenuto prosuntuoso, partendomi massime, nel disputare questa materia, dagli ordini degli altri': *Pr.*, ch. 15, *Le grandi opere* 1:91; tr. Luigi Ricci and E. R. P. Vincent, in Machiavelli, *The Prince and The Discourses* 56 (see note 27). All references to *Il Principe* are to this text and translation.
67. 'Ma sendo l'intento mio scrivere cosa utile a chi la intende, mi è parso più conveniente andare drieto alla verità effettuale della cosa, che alla imaginazione di essa. E molti si sono imaginati republiche e principati che non si sono mai visti né conosciuti essere in vero; perché egli è tanto discosto da come si vive a come si doverrebbe vivere, che colui che lascia quello che si fa per quello che si doverrebbe fare impara piuttosto la ruina che la perservazione sua': ibid.
68. See Cicero, *De Officiis*, tr. Walter Miller, Loeb Classical Library (Cambridge, MA: Harvard University Press, 1913), 14–16 (Book 1:4), 79 (Book 1:23). The idea is common in manual-for-princes literature. Erasmus, for example, held that *dominium*, *imperium* and *regnum* were pagan notions. Christian authority implied *administratio* (administration), *beneficentia* (benefaction), and *custodia* (guardianship). See Desiderius Erasmus, *The Education of a Christian Prince*, tr. A. H. T. Levi, in *Collected Works of Erasmus*, vol. 27: *Literary and Educational Writings* (Toronto: University of Toronto Press, 1986), 217.

69. Natale Conti, *Mythologiae* (1568), tr. John Mulryan and Steven Brown, Volume 316 of Medieval and Renaissance Texts and Studies, 2 vols. (Tempe, AZ: Arizona Center for Medieval and Renaissance Studies, 2006), 2:860. See also Machiavelli, *The Prince*, tr. and ed. Robert M. Adams, Norton Critical Edition, 2nd rev. edn (New York: W. W. Norton, 1992 [1977]), 48*n*3.
70. See R. A. Bauman, 'The Gracchan Agrarian Commission: Four Questions', *Historia: Zeitschrift für Alte Geschichte* 28, no. 4 (1979), 385–408.
71. See Filippo Del Lucchese, 'Crisis and Power: Economics, Politics and Conflict in Machiavelli's Political Thought', *History of Political Thought* 30, no. 1 (2009), 78–9.
72. 'Egli è sentenzia degli antichi scrittori, come gli uomini sogliono affliggersi nel male e stuccarsi nel bene; e come dall'una e dall'altra di queste due passioni nascano i medesimi effetti. Perché, qualunque volta è tolto agli uomini il combattere per necessità, combattono per ambizione; la quale è tanto potente ne' petti umani, che mai, a qualunque grado si salgano, gli abbandona. La cagione è, perché la natura ha creati gli uomini in modo, che possono desiderare ogni cosa, e non possono conseguire ogni cosa: talché, essendo sempre maggiore il desiderio che la potenza dello acquistare, ne risulta la mala contentezza di quello che si possiede, e la poca sodisfazione d'esso. Da questo nasce il variare della fortuna loro: perché, disiderando gli uomini, parte di avere più, parte temendo di non perdere lo acquistato, si viene alle inimicizie ed alla guerra; dalla quale nasce la rovina di quella provincia e la esaltazione di quell'altra': *Disc.* 1:37, *Le grandi opere* 2:146; tr. Detmold 208 (see note 27).
73. 'Nec mihi dictatura animos fecit, nec exilium ademit': Livy, *History*, 6:7, as quoted by Machiavelli, *Disc.* 3:31, *Le grandi opere* 2:492; tr. Detmold, 500.
74. '[L]a fortuna non avere potenza sopra di loro': ibid.
75. See Haig Patapan, '"I Capitoli": Machiavelli's New Theogony', *The Review of Politics* 65, no. 2 (2003), 185–207.
76. Althusser, *Machiavelli and Us*, 5.

14

A Language for Politics and a Language of Politics

Words as a Tool of Understanding and of Action in Machiavelli

Jean-Louis Fournel[*]

Towards a Semantic History of Politics: A Proposal for a Political Philology

Machiavelli employs a language that is at once unique and embedded in a particular 'quality of the times' ('le qualità de' tempi', in his own phrase[1]). This language originates in the interaction of heterogeneous cultural and semantic traditions: the legal, the medical, the scientific, as also the languages of commerce, of the Chancery, and of the new politics of the time. For this reason, I plan to dwell on the *time* to which the words belong, and on the *uses* to which Machiavelli puts them, rejecting all aprioristic methods.

I will base my study on a simple historical factor: Machiavelli—to start with the obvious—is, above all, someone who speaks and writes in order to do politics.[2] Hence, the language I will consider is a *language conceived for politics*: a language that *is* politics in the first place, and then, only secondarily, a language *of* politics, *from* politics, and, eventually, a language *about* politics. My aim is to examine the effects of Machiavelli's choice of words in order to assign them a precise status: a status that is strictly and eminently political, and dependent on a political situation. The linguistic, rhetorical, or gnoseological status of words is obviously present and operative as well, but eventually subsidiary.

On a larger scale, for the Florentine people belonging to the 'war generation',[3] words no longer hold a central place in individual and collective thought. Facts and their effects are what matter in the first instance; the only relevant question about words concerns their efficacy in representing those facts and reporting or inducing those effects. These are the two fundamental conditions for words to become political. We are encountering an unprecedented rhetorical approach, though to grasp this, we must depart from the teachings of mainstream humanism in the fifteenth century. In particular, we should no longer think in terms of a value or privilege accorded to a re-invented language that directly imitates both the words (signs) and the things (referents) derived from the Ancients.

Rather, we should focus on the understanding of modern issues and the adaptation of language to aid that understanding. When literature is left out of the picture, when philology is made to serve a historiographical critique and philosophy bends before experience, the new 'rhetoric of the emergency' (that is to say, a language calling for immediate action in a context of political and military crisis) can of course call up some elements of the humanistic heritage such as dialogism, or the view of philology as a historical approach to language; but the question now arises whether such considerations are any longer fruitful. Instead, the revolutionary 'rhetoric of emergency' moves to the foreground and turns out to be an instrument to understand and represent conflict and power by exploiting new categories and forms.

This allows for a type of critical humanism that clearly departs from the practices of the immediate civic past. The rhetoric of war is now made integral to the history of the present times. The lesson derived from good humanistic methods has been profitable, but it has migrated from historical texts to the words and objects of contemporary reality while retaining its own procedures: comparing sources (as humanists compare the sources of information to publish the ancient texts), insisting on the temporality of language, using conjecture not to analyse events but to establish accurate texts as humanists did. The rhetoric of war offers itself as a potential philology for the present time. In other words, we might speak of an incipient affirmation of the *autonomy of political language*, perhaps more convincing than the autonomy of politics defended by Croce and by a long critical tradition.

To claim this does not entail a return to the figure of 'Machiavelli the man of letters'.[4] The most crucial element in Machiavelli's text is neither the audience, nor the public, nor the recipient of the utterance, but the function and effects of the utterance itself. The ambition to 'write something useful for whoever understands it'[5] is intended not so much to exalt the recipient as to emphasize the efficacy of the writing. Such efficacy has a double value: on the one hand, it is connected with a political action; on the other, inextricably linked to the former, it is involved in the constitution of a new knowledge that aims at being historically active. Such knowledge is evoked in the preface to Book 1 of the *Discourses on Livy*, where Machiavelli criticizes the approach of the modern denizens of the Italian peninsula towards the art and texts of the Ancients.[6] Hence, we may speak of an 'effectual truth' (*verità effettuale*) of language, on the model of the Machiavellian hapax 'verità effettuale della cosa' (effectual truth of the thing),[7] as language proves to be the foundation of a possible *political philology*. We may thereby develop a semantic history of politics.

What, then, do we mean by 'political philology'?[8]
- A slow and close reading of texts, focusing on the identification of words whose relevance depends on the fact that they are living and fluid forms. This is not only a matter of establishing a text and fixing it, as in the logic of ecdotics, and the words so identified are not always well-known concepts.
- A study of words that does not only consider their theoretical function, but reconnects them to their pragmatic and, above all, strategic stakes as a language of effects, a language conceived to understand the effectual or pragmatic truth, built on the effects of truth (*verità effettuale*).
- The unceasing confrontation of words with a particular 'quality of the times' (*qualità dei tempi*) or 'of the moment'—a quality triggered by a specific historical conjuncture, and extant only during that conjuncture.

A major consequence of this methodological choice is that it adds nuance to discourses normally presuming on the stability in transmission of the language of politics. In the history of ideas, many terms lead back to a single logic of transmission: *tradition, canon, legacy, heritage, lesson, teaching, influence, restitution, translatio, renovatio, fortune*. These various—but, in our view, unsatisfying—processes are all rooted in the notion that the historian's first task should be to determine the lexical permanence of the texts, and thus to restore the perennial dialogue of the *auctores*, who remain exclusive holders of the legitimate word. But the language of politics entails more than such simple transmission. We cannot assert both the singular historicity of every political society (hence its distinctive verbal confrontations, reflecting its power relations, struggles, and varied forms of conflict) and, at the same time, the permanence of its discursive legacy, and particularly of its lexicon. Undoubtedly, political language undergoes transmission. But if we postulate that the words of politics are handed down from one era to another, one historical moment to another, we should also grant that such transmission is not peaceful; on the contrary, it admits semantic fluidity—that is, the resilience or adaptability of words and the evolution of their meaning. The semantic history of politics is based precisely on the study of these changes, migrations, and shifts in meaning.

What is the 'story' of Machiavellian words? On the one hand, it is a long and exogenous story, a story of already available words, touching what Machiavelli, in the dedicatory epistle of *The Prince*, calls 'the constant reading of ancient things'.[9] Such words are inscribed in a precise field of thought, be it political, philosophical–political, political–military, or any other. We are dealing here with a rich semantic spectrum with its own tradition, its specific recurrences, and a store of material to draw from, which Machiavelli exploits. But we also need to conceive of an external, collective, and contemporary story which is not authorial or, at least, not only authorial. Here lies the importance of, for instance, the official registers of the Florentine *pratiche*, or the working documents of the Chancery.[10] Such sources define the borders of a shared lexical domain. This second story has its roots in the long experience of modern things:[11] the point here is to consider the specific uses of words at precise conjunctures.

To illustrate the first story (the external one), I will consider Machiavelli's relationship with the Latin or Latin-based tradition, and the variegated Latinisms in his work. Later on, to illustrate the second story, I will look at an extremely contemporary 'Florentine' lexicon that includes a technical vocabulary (*scoppietto* instead of *archibugio*, or *zuffa* in place of *giornata* or *fatto d'arme*).[12] Besides these two stories, I will discuss the associated use of hapaxes in Machiavelli's discourse, such as *l'arte dello stato*, *principato civile*, or *verità effettuale*.[13] The importance of these semantic events is striking, because they are used up as soon as created, and disappear in the text.

Despite the obvious presence of a strong Tuscan vernacular tradition, the use of the language of politics during the period of permanent war, starting in the autumn of 1494 and continuing for more than half a century, produces an unprecedented radicalism—what we may call a semantic crisis. There is a new call to signify and interpret a dramatic situation by using original forms and categories, because the old ones are not 'effectual' any more: neither the old Thomistic and the republican city-states' reading grids nor the more recent humanistic ones. In order to describe the new war, a quicker and crueller war with more disruptive effects—a war that can blow out entire states—it was necessary to generate new discourses, built with words that may not be entirely new but whose meaning can be adjusted and, to some extent, re-invented. The expressive and cognitive logic of such utterance depends on a precise and, even more crucially, *necessary* political action. To produce the precise effect required, the language must be straightforward, clear, univocal, and immediate, free from any mediations that might obscure their purpose. Stable, traditional sources of language prove inadequate owing to the melding of the immediate past, bearing its own linguistic heritage, and the tumultuous present—that is to say, the contingent state of war. This explains the importance of tracking down all evidence of indeterminacy, transfers and contradictions, taking into account the plurality of the languages involved in the discourses of war and of state. Obviously, this semantic revolution has an impact on translating procedures, as translation must be understood not only as a testimony of influences and legacies but also of changes and adaptations.[14]

The need to ponder the *present* of the political language compels us to take into account the circulation of people, texts, and ideas, not in line with categories such as 'influence' or *fortuna* but according to the logic and criteria of *exchange* (and occasionally conflict), of *hybridization*, and of *stratification*. The language of politics is a functional language: open, fragile, polysemic, bound to the external constraints of military threat and of conjecture, along with the internal tension of hypotheses that constitutes political action in the uncertain times of war: at such times, political action is inseparable from the formulation of hypotheses characterized by internal tension. The rhetoric of war (both civil and external) is imbued with a specific rationale that can be unfolded through lexical analysis. This language obviously clashes with words that blur the events from a gnoseological point of view, and threaten liberty[15] and justice[16] from a praxeological point of view. To be more precise, the following languages are rejected: the language of demagoguery and conservatism; the language of sophistry; and, above all, the language of tyranny. We should remember, for example, that the struggle of Savonarola, reliant on an anti-tyrannical logic, is at the same time a linguistic struggle. It is not surprising that the Friar calls for a return to a sober apostolic rhetoric.[17]

From this perspective, speech is interesting not only as an act, to be studied in terms of pragmatic and performative logic,[18] but as a set of tools—that is, words belonging to the new lexicon of politics and war. It enables us to understand and to act *at the same time*, above all to understand *in order to* act. It incorporates a linguistic experience of politics, a verbalization of politics using words that are structurally unstable, bound to the present historical conjuncture.

My aim is to contribute to a semantic history of the modern state. This implies, however, that the Machiavellian *stato*[19] must be examined from a non-teleological perspective: not simply as an anticipation of the laic Westphalian State, but rather as a complex, ambivalent, polymorphic entity. To understand this kind of state, it is fundamental to consider the panoply of words that are constitutive of the state as a device or a 'system'—which, in turn, is hard to understand without the system of warfare. Hence, the Florentine political lexicon appears more and more as a crucial field of investigation.

For my study focused on political philology and the 'effectual truth of language', seeking to illuminate the effects of Machiavelli's words, I should ideally clarify my purpose by drawing the distinctions between the language of war, the language of state, the language of history, and the language of the political time(s). Owing to space constraints, I will restrict my analysis to an example from the language of war. But first, as a short intermezzo, I will try to summarize in tabular form the origins, the elements, and the effects of Machiavelli's language.

Interlude

Forms, process, and necessity

- The rhythm of inscription in Chancery documents produces a language that is direct and immediate. This explains why in the Dedication to *The Prince*, Machiavelli refuses to adorn his language. We can therefore speak of *a language of immediacy*.
- The writing process of individual Florentine authors as well as public institutions involves a blend of collective and individual meanings: law and *consulte e pratiche* against authorial liberty, a shared vocabulary against individual *inventio*. Collective and individual languages coexist and interact.
- Spoken language, natural language (the language of the people, not the language of rhetoric and literature), and technical language occur side by side in the same texts, creating the twofold phenomenon of a *mixture of styles* and a *mixture of levels*.
- The function of 'discerning from afar' ('vedere discosto', in Machiavelli's phrase[20]): understanding before anyone else what is new and what will be effectual, hence attaching the appropriate words to those external factors and determining the new course of action.[21]
- The postulation of aporias and hapaxes: these are the Gordian nodes, manifestations of the condensation of meaning and the situation-specific temporality of the language.

The moments and the genres

On examining different moments of Machiavelli's writing, we can observe some peculiar features of each moment:

- In the Chancery period, the experience of functional and professional writing. In this period, two modalities of discourse coexist: the expression of command and the expression of opinion.
- In *The Prince*, polysemy and dialogism.
- In the *Discorsi*, construction of knowledge and an open form of writing.

- In *The Art of War*, the time of origin of the words—whether Latinisms like *deletto*, words from everyday life like *zuffa*, or technicalities relating to weapons—as new material for a classic dialogue.
- In the *Florentine Histories*, the linearity of a 'national' history, defined on the basis of social conflicts and classes.

The Language of War as the Language of State

Machiavelli teaches us that one cannot replicate the specific logic inherent in words: we cannot use that traditional content to understand what they mean with respect to contemporary history, to what is happening just now. We can look for various things in words, but in his political works, Machiavelli is interested only in one thing—how words feed political action. He is struck by the fact (this is where recent humanist doctrine intervenes) that words can *die*, when what they say no longer corresponds to any reality. When that happens, they become illusions, images or, even worse, mere traces, of interest only to those antique dealers mentioned in the preface to the *Discourses* who view the heritage of ancient Rome as fragments of statuary. But words can also *be generated* through neologisms, by re-semantization of old worn-out words, or by original hapaxes—syntagms that die as soon as they appear but that play a significant part in readings of Machiavelli.

Moving on to the second part of my chapter, I will now propose—maybe too briefly, but pointing out more demonstrations and examples in the footnotes[22]—a specific illustration of the somewhat general considerations laid out earlier. I will focus on the gap between the language of war and the language of state.

In Machiavelli's military vocabulary, it is often hard to find corresponding words for the full vocabulary of the ancient tradition. He also points out the invalid calques introduced by the moderns. This does not mean that Machiavelli ignores the vocabulary of the past; in fact, there is a real tension, and sometimes contradiction, between his love of the Ancients and his awareness of the obsolete status of some of their words. In *The Art of War*—that is to say, at the theoretical pinnacle of his discourse on war—Machiavelli does not usually draw on the contemporary lexicon: in fact, he constantly remarks on the military inferiority of the Moderns compared to the Ancients. He also leaves a lot of room both for the simplification of contemporary terminology (concerning, for instance, the semantic field relating to artillery) and for the ancient lexicon even when it appears opaque (like the terms of ancient siege warfare entirely drawn from Vitruvius, or the orders of soldiers in the Greek and Roman armies). To further complicate matters, at times he also chooses terms that are not just strictly contemporary but strictly local or Florentine: *scoppietto*, for instance, which he consistently prefers to *archibugio*.[23] In terms of the same logic (here departing from the practice of the Chancery years), in *The Art of War*, Machiavelli refuses to enter into the lexical proliferation signifying modern military tools: he simply adopts the word *artiglieria* (artillery) to refer to firearms in general.

The polymorphic language of war thus becomes a language that blends the different time-periods of the military lexicon:

- One part comes from the distant past. It is ennobled, but also sometimes dimmed, by its ancient origin.
- A second part belongs to a more recent tradition, often local. It is linked to everyday life in the city, and to a specific political space.
- A third part arises from contemporary military practice and reflects the confusions of a still unstable technical language, evolving with new inventions in artillery and engineering.

In Machiavelli's vocabulary, the temporal stratification is much more prominent than the spatial: the most fecund dialectic is that between Latin and the vernacular, rather than between the various Italian and European vernaculars. The major issues in his language of war are the distinctions between the Latin lexical heritage, the lively contemporary scene, and the inputs from military innovation, along with the porosity of the border between internal conflict and external war.[24]

The composite language forged by Machiavelli has its own inbuilt variable factor, for two reasons: first, the art of warfare evolves continuously at the technical level and, second, the language of war does not only involve the battlefield but affects other human actions, especially the discourses of politics and history. It is not fortuitous that a work like *The Prince* expends few words, all in all, on the strictly technical component of military practices. Actual warfare in the field is only discussed in contexts like the employment of mercenary troops (as opposed to one's own armies, *arme proprie*[25]) or to demonstrate the permanent presence of war in politics—whether to denounce the 'sins' of the Italian princes of the time or in the final invocation in Chapter 26 of a redeemer supported by a new 'third order' (*ordine terzo*) of infantry.

Rather than the technology of warfare, *The Prince* focuses on a range of other issues: the organization and discipline of the army; the structuring antagonism of politico-military relations, of neutrality versus a system of alliances (one must learn to be a true friend or a true enemy: ch. 20); the necessity of a minimum military force (ch. 10); the power of religion (ch. 11); the *virtù* and fortune of captains and princes; the knowledge of military sites; the soldiers' love for their leader; and the lack of martial *virtù* in 'such corrupt times as ours'. On the other hand, Machiavelli does not dwell for long on, inter alia, recruitment (the famous *deletto* in *The Art of War* which was the crucial point of the *ordinanza* of 1506); artillery and firearms; the naming of weapons; the disposition of troops before the battle; fortifications; or the funding of mercenaries. *The Prince* is indeed the principal site of the generic language that characterizes all Machiavelli's texts, because in this treatise weapons are always implicit in the discussion, the heart of its argument. Nonetheless, *The Prince* turns on four major questions, none of which draws upon a predominantly technical lexicon. These are the use of mercenaries as a political–moral issue; the military prowess of a new prince; the relation between laws and weapons; and, finally, the triumph of foreign policy over internal, with the emergence of soldiers as a third factor in governance.[26]

The language of war is indeed, to some extent, the language of state and not always the language of the army. The permanent tension between those two poles of the political order, war and statecraft, is remarkably illustrated in the acrimonious exchange between the Cardinal of Rouen and the still young *segredario* Machiavelli, reported at the end of Chapter 3 of *The Prince*.[27] Here, the Secretary censures the French for their ignorance of affairs of 'the state', in a riposte to Rouen's remark that the Italians did not understand war.[28] The exchange raises a crucial question: what is the nature of the semantic bond between war, a clear and distinct historical reality, and the state, a polysemic notion difficult to negotiate but central to the political thought of the times, and not only in the peninsula? Searching for a possible answer, Machiavelli makes one of his major methodological choices, clearly reflecting his critical humanism: a spatio-temporal comparatism.

Machiavelli forges a language of his own, a political language that is open and somewhat fluid, as undefined as some of his references to contemporary space set in historical time. The French position, as exemplified by Rouen, is useful in order to read the Italian position, and vice versa; but above all, the combination of the two perspectives allows a line of thought that plays with words, constantly reconnecting with both today's 'quality of the times' and the history that lies behind it. It is unlikely that the Cardinal of Rouen would speak to Machiavelli in the Tuscan vernacular (especially as the meeting takes place in the French court), but the fact that they do not use the same language is secondary in this case: had they done so, it is not at all sure that they would have ascribed the same meaning to the words. Even among people who speak the same language, the terms used to express 'the state' may not be homogeneous. For instance, in *The Prince* the stable language of the state is intersected by lexical hapaxes, which disappear as soon as they are created. These hapaxes signal the need to overcome the internal aporias of reasoning, the apparent contradictions, and the oxymorons that the historian needs to solve. The 'civil principality' (*principato civile*), for instance, presents the hypothesis of a princely power that is not absolute in law but is supported by the people; the 'effectual truth' (*verità effettuale*) indicates the epistemological need to pay attention to the effects; the 'art of the state' (*l'arte dello stato*) shows how politics is also a real trade with its own techniques, its body of knowledge, and its singular devices. The quasi-hapax 'the extraordinary' (*estraordinario*) suggests a possible way to conceive of a specific historical moment that defies regularity and definition in more general terms.

A logic analogous to that of the hapax operates in the use of apparent calques, derived from Latin, at specific crucial moments. The word *deletto* (*dilectus* in Latin, with respect to the recruitment of troops) in *The Art of War* is an example: a remarkable dynamic recovery of an apposite word that cannot be rendered by a plain translation. In order to ensure its maximum force and meaning, the word is even 'burnt' after being used in a very limited number of cases: after about thirty occurrences, mostly in Book I of *The Art of War*, which discusses the political question of using one's own weapons, the word occurs only once more in the dialogue and twice in the *Discourses* (3:30 and 3:33).[29] It does not occur in any of Machiavelli's other writings, nor in any other military works of the time that I could consult.

We can ascribe to the same rationale the exactly opposite procedure: the expansion, and thereby reduction, of a series of precise terms to a single generic term.[30] This appears in Machiavelli's authoritative treatment of siege warfare and the use of missiles in such warfare. In *The Art of War*, he writes:

> The tools whereby the Ancients defended their lands were many, such as ballistas, onagers, scorpions, crossbows, fustibals, and slings, and many too were those that they used in assault, such as battering rams, siege towers, muscles (*musculi*), *plutei*, mantlets, scythes and tortoises (*testudini*). In place of such things, there is nowadays the artillery, which serves the purpose of both offence and defence, but I will not discuss this matter further.[31]

The list of ancient weaponry replicates word for word that in Vegezio's fifth-century *De re militari* (4:22, 4:13–17), but Machiavelli mentions these machines only to prove that he knows about them, not to adapt them to the modern world. This particular ancient lexicon is dead, of interest only to antique dealers. In the modern context, he uses the single word *artiglieria* (artillery), which would equally have sufficed to subsume the thirteen ancient terms. Machiavelli never goes back to this list: in fact, he explicitly abandons this lexicon for good, adding, 'I will not discuss this matter further.' Nonetheless, these authentic 'semantic events' impart a characteristic tension to the language of politics, making it at once strong and fragile: strong in its ability to overcome the *topoi* and the heritage of set rules, fragile owing to the disappearance of the author's theoretical solutions once their specific moment is past.

Conclusion: The Art of Language as the Art of Statecraft; the Art of Statecraft as the Art of Language

The rhetoric of the state of emergency and the state of war leads Machiavelli back to the methodological heritage of the humanists, as a way to question words critically and to understand language in conjunction with history. Nonetheless, he puts this heritage at the service of a work in which words exist only as objects and events. He has imbibed the good historicist method of humanist philology, but it is no longer applied to texts to be emended and stabilized with *castigationes*—instead, to the changing life of words and to politics as a dynamic practice.

In my study of the language of politics, I set out to define a complex logic that admits an inadequacy in the resources of language—hence the need for renovation, a call to expose the gaps and illusions of the inherited language and, thereby, demand greater verbal efficiency: that is to say, a direct and appropriate language, immediately proximate to the specific circumstance, to suit the needs of modern politics. The temporal stratifications of the vocabulary are considered in this light. The energy and the timing of the words are also important, because the effect of the utterance in that specific situation is uniquely significant. This factor calls sometimes for a language that is not strictly military but more generic, putting to best use the vagueness of the adopted vocabulary, be it technical, Latin, or any other—at other times, a language that is purely that of the state, understanding the *stato* as a space where politics is articulated in terms of conflict.

From this perspective, Machiavelli's solutions differ according to the specific moment and the specific text, but they always offer a subtle balance between the various lexicons. The only criterion for judging the efficacy of the language is how well it serves the art of statecraft. The situation of emergency and permanent war does not entail the victory of *res* over *verba* (contrary to what a hasty judgement may at times suggest); rather, it demands a new way of bonding *res* and *verba*. The fundamental choice of *arme proprie* means resorting not only to non-mercenary troops but also to weapons that meet the needs of the republican order, of a certain type of political community. *Arme proprie* are also 'proper weapons' in the sense of weapons 'proper' to one, one's own weapons: 'proper words' has a similar syntax, being the words befitting that particular subject and situation. It is perhaps for this reason that Jacques Gohory observes, in the preface to the 1571 reprint of his French translation of the *Discourses*, that Machiavelli was the first to 'merge natural language with the language of the state'.[32]

Notes

* This chapter has been translated by Alessia Loiacono.
1. *Pr.*, ch. 25: Machiavelli, *Tutte le opere*, ed. Mario Martelli (Florence: Sansoni, 1971), 295. All citations from Machiavelli, unless otherwise mentioned, are from this edition (henceforth *Opere*). Translations from *Il principe* as in *The Prince: With Related Documents*, ed. and tr. William J. Connell (Boston, MA: Bedford/St. Martins, 2005).
2. See Jean-Louis Fournel and Jean-Claude Zancarini, 'Des mots pour comprendre et pour agir', in Machiavel, *Le Prince/De Principatibus*, ed. Jean-Louis Fournel and Jean-Claude Zancarini (Paris: Presses universitaires de France, 2000), 545–610. The present chapter results from my work, carried out with Jean-Claude Zancarini, in preparing translations and comments relating to Florentine political thought (Guicciardini, Machiavelli, Savonarola, Giannotti, Vettori) at the time of the so-called Italian Wars. See Jean-Louis Fournel and Jean-Claude Zancarini, *La grammaire de la république* (Geneva: Droz, 2008). For further suggestions on this topic, see, for instance, Jean-Louis Fournel and Jean-Claude Zancarini, 'Che cosa il lessico dice della politica nella Firenze delle guerre d'Italia', in *Lingua e politica*, ed. Rita Librandi and Rosa Piro, Associazione degli storici della lingua italiana (ASLI) (Florence: Cesati, 2016), 71–84.
3. By this term I mean people born between 1460 and 1480, who reached adulthood and began to write and participate in Florentine politics from c. 1494, that is, the start of the Italian Wars. See Jean-Louis Fournel, 'Retorica della guerra, retorica dell'emergenza nella Firenze repubblicana', *Giornale critico della filosofia italiana* 85, no. 3 (2006), 389–41; and on the Italian Wars, Michael Mallet and Christine Shaw, *The Italian Wars (1494–1559)* (Harlow: Pearson, 2012).

4. See Carlo Dionisotti, 'Machiavelli, Man of Letters', in *Machiavelli and the Discourse of Literature*, ed. A. Russell Ascoli and Victoria Kahn (Ithaca, NY: Cornell University Press, 1993), 17–52. Dionisotti also deals elsewhere with this subject, as in 'Machiavelli letterato', in *Machiavellerie* (Turin: Einaudi, 1980), 227–66. See also Franco Fido, 'The Politician as Writer', in *The Comedy and Tragedy of Machiavelli: Essays on the Literary Works*, ed. Vickie B. Sullivan (New Haven, CT: Yale University Press, 2007), 138–58.
5. '[S]crivere cosa utile a chi la intende': *Pr.*, ch. 15, *Opere* 280.
6. Here Machiavelli points out the particular relationship of his contemporaries to the Ancients: '[U]n frammento d'una antiqua statua sia suto comperato gran prezzo, per averlo appresso di sé, onorarne la sua casa e poterlo fare imitare a coloro che di quella arte si dilettono; ... da l'altro canto, le virtuosissime operazioni che le storie ci mostrono ... essere più presto ammirate che imitate': *Opere* 76. ('[A] fragment of an old statue has been bought at a high price because someone wants to have it near oneself to honour his house with it and to be able to have it imitated by those who delight in that art ... [O]n the other hand ... the most virtuous works the histories show us ... are now rather admired than imitated': tr. from *Discourses on Livy*, tr. Harvey C. Mansfield and Nathan Tarcov [Chicago, IL: University of Chicago Press, 1996]).
7. *Pr.*, ch. 15, *Opere* 280.
8. See Jean-Claude Zancarini, 'Une philologie politique: Les temps et les enjeux des mots (Florence, 1494-1530)', *Laboratoire italien* 7 (2007), 61–74, accessed on 3 June 2019 at https://journals.openedition.org/laboratoireitalien/132.
9. '[U]na continua lezione delle antique': *Opere* 257.
10. See *Consulte e pratiche della repubblica fiorentina*, ed. Denis Fachard, 4 vols. (Geneva: Droz, 1988–93). My focus on the context surrounding our author—and thus not strictly authorial—might recall Skinner's premise of the 'linguistic context'. But my conception differs slightly from Skinner's, as the 'linguistic context' depends profoundly on the particular political circumstances, as well as on the strategies and tactics developed in a specific and unique quality of the times, and not merely on general rules. (See the critical analysis of the 'linguistic context' by Igor Mineo, 'La repubblica come categoria storica', *Storica* 43-44-45 [2009], 125–67). On 'linguistic context', see Quentin Skinner, *Visions of Politics* (Cambridge: Cambridge University Press, 2002), vol. 1: *Regarding Method*; and three articles by J. G. A. Pocock: 'The History of Political Thought: A Methodological Enquiry', in *Philosophy, Politics and Society*, 2nd ser., ed. Peter Laslett and W. G. Runciman (Chicago, IL: University of Chicago Press, 1962), 183–202;

'The Concept of a Language and the *Métier d'historien*: Some Considerations on Practice', in *The Languages of Political Theory in Early-Modern Europe*, ed. Anthony Pagden (Cambridge: Cambridge University Press, 1987), 19–38; 'The Machiavellian Moment Revisited: A Study in History and Ideology', *Journal of Modern History* 53, no. 1 (1981), 49–72.

11. '[U]na lunga esperienzia delle cose moderne': *Pr.*, dedicatory epistle, *Opere* 257.

12. See Jean-Louis Fournel, 'Il genere e il tempo delle parole: dire la guerra nei testi machiavelliani', in *The Radical Machiavelli: Politics, Philosophy and Language*, ed. Filippo Del Lucchese, Fabio Frosini, and Vittorio Morfino (Boston, MA, and Leiden: Brill, 2015), 23–38.

13. *L'arte dello stato* appears at the end of the famous letter to Vettori, 10 December 1513 (*Opere* 1160); *principato civile* in *Pr.*, ch. 9 (*Opere* 271); *verità effettuale* in *Pr.*, ch. 15 (*Opere* 280). On the subject of hapaxes, see Jean-Louis Fournel, 'I tempi delle parole nella prosa machiavelliana: considerazioni su tre storie incrociate', in *Lessico ed etica nella tradizione italiana di primo cinquecento*, ed. Raffaele Ruggiero (Lecce: Pensa, 2016), 123–38.

14. See Elisa Gregori, ed., *Fedeli, diligenti, chiari e dotti. Traduttori e traduzioni nel Rinascimento* (Padua: CLEUP, 2016).

15. The concept of liberty offers the most emblematic illustration of the semantic battles and continuous transformations of meaning that we referred to earlier. Evidence of this can be found in the formidable line of studies, by Rubinstein, Skinner, and many others, on the semantic weight of the word 'liberty' in republican culture. See Nicolai Rubinstein, 'Florentine Constitutionalism and Medici Ascendancy in the Fifteenth Century', in *Florentine Studies: Politics and Society in Renaissance Florence*, ed. Nicolai Rubinstein (London: Faber, 1968), 442–62, and Nicolai Rubinstein, 'Florentina libertas', *Rinascimento* 2 (1986), 3–26, rpt. in Nicolai Rubinstein, *Studies in Italian History in the Middle Ages and the Renaissance*, vol. 1, *Political Thought and the Language of Politics: Art and Politics*, ed. Giovanni Ciappelli (Rome: Edizioni di storia e letteratura, 2004), 273–94. See also the new analysis proposed by Igor Mineo in 'La repubblica come categoria storica'. On the tension between tradition and innovation, see Laurent Baggioni and Jean-Claude Zancarini, 'Dulcedo libertatis: Liberté et identité florentine chez Bruni, Machiavel et Guichardin', in *Libertés et Libéralismes*, ed. Jean-Pierre Potier, Jean-Louis Fournel, and Jacques Guilhaumou (Lyon: ENS Editions, 2012), 21–43.

16. On the question of justice, see Diego Quaglioni, 'From Medieval Jurists to Machiavelli', in *European Political Thought 1450–1700*, ed. Howell A. Lloyd, Glenn Burgess, and Simon Hodson (New Haven, CT:

Yale University Press, 2007), 55–74; Diego Quaglioni, *Machiavelli e la lingua della giurisprudenza: Una letteratura della crisi* (Bologna: Il Mulino, 2011). According to Quaglioni, law is still a major component of Machiavelli's innovative synthesis: juridical language, as a language of the experience of power, is heavily present in his texts. This view should be supplemented from Erica Benner, who wisely points out that Machiavelli 'does not speak directly of *giustizia* or *iniustizia*, he often uses paraphrases or related words that signal a concern for justice, especially *leggi, respetto, obligo,* or *termini*': *Machiavelli's Ethics* (Princeton, NJ: Princeton University Press, 2009), 290.

17. See Savonarola's text on poetry, *Apologeticus de ratione poeticae artis*: Edizione nazionale delle opere di Girolamo Savonarola, *Scritti filosofici*, ed. Giancarlo Garfagnini and Eugenio Garin (Rome: Belardetti, 1982), 209–72.

18. See J. L. Austin, *How to Do Things with Words* (Cambridge, MA: Harvard University Press, 1962).

19. See Quentin Skinner, 'From the State of Prince to the Person of the State', in *Visions of Politics*, vol. 2: *Renaissance Virtue*, 368–413; Alison M. Ardito, *Machiavelli and the Modern State: The Prince, the Discourses on Livy, and the Extended Territorial Republic* (Cambridge: Cambridge University Press, 2015). For a logic closer to mine, see Romain Descendre, 'Le cose di stato: sémantique de l'État et relations internationales chez Machiavel', *Il pensiero politico: rivista di storia delle idee politiche e sociali* 41, no. 1 (2008), 3–18, and the entry 'Stato' (with bibliography) in the *Enciclopedia Machiavelli* (2014).

20. Found twice, for instance, in variant forms in *Pr.*, ch. 3 (*Opere* 260).

21. See *Pr.*, ch. 15; *Disc.*, 'Proemio'.

22. See esp. Jean-Louis Fournel and Jean-Claude Zancarini, 'La langue du conflit dans la Florence des guerres d'Italie', in *Les mots de la guerre dans l'Europe de la Renaissance,* ed. M. M. Fontaine and J.-L. Fournel (Geneva: Droz, 2015), 259–84.

23. The use of *scoppietto* in *The Art of War* illustrates the use of a remarkably 'Florentine' contemporary lexicon that even serves as a substitute for the technical lexicon that one might expect: *scoppietto* is used in the place of *archibugio*, in the same way that *zuffa* substitutes for *giornata* or *fatto d'arme*. Interestingly, the French translation by Jean Charrier restores the 'non-Florentine' logic, translating *scoppietto* by *arquebuse*.

24. The most outstanding demonstration of the specificity of military language in *The Art of War*, the *Discorsi* or *Il Principe*—where military Latinisms prevail—rests, *a contrario*, on the analysis of military vocabulary in the official correspondence of the Florentine Chancery: for instance, whereas in *The Art of War* he uses only the generic world *artigleria*, in *Letters from Chancery* he names the specific types of guns current in his day: *archibuso*,

A Language for Politics and a Language of Politics 277

    bombarde grosse, *bombardelle*, *cannone*, *cortaldo*, *falconetto*, *passavolante*, *spingarda*. The vocabulary of the *condotta* is understandably frequent in the Chancery correspondence: *condotta/condottiere* appears only once in *Il Principe* and about fifteen times in the *Florentine Histories*, but over 300 times in the official letters. The same applies to words such as *lancia*, *rivellino*, *tagliata*, *ripari*, *bastione*. On the other hand, in the official letters Machiavelli never uses Latin loan-words like *dardo*, *pilo*, and *sarissa* from the technical lexicon, which predominates in *The Art of War*. In the official letters *asta* occurs only once, *caterva* and *legione* never.

25. The phrase is used repeatedly in *Pr.*, ch. 13 (*Opere* 278).
26. It is no accident that the 'third difficulty' a prince might face, from the greed and cruelty of his soldiers, is introduced rather late in *Il Principe*, in Chapter 19. This is a major sign of the internally generative power of *Il Principe*—that is, the capacity of the author to generate *from the text itself* new steps of the argument that were not initially envisaged, and that do not appear in the original plan of the work.
27. For a full discussion of this episode, see Jean-Louis Fournel, 'La Guerre et l'État: Statuts et histoires d'un micro-texte machiavélien (*Le Prince*, III, 48)', *Exercices de rhétorique* 3 (2014), accessed on 30 October 2019 at http://rhetorique.revues.org/258.
28. '[D]icendomi el cardinale di Roano che gli Italiani non si intendevano della guerra, io gli risposi che e' Franzesi non si intendevano dello stato; perché, se se n'intendessono, non lascerebbono venire la Chiesa in tanta grandezza': *Pr.*, ch. 3, *Opere* 262. 'For when the Cardinal of Rouen told me that the Italians did not understand war, I replied to him that the French did not understand states [singular *stato* in Italian], since, if they understood them, they would not allow the Church to come into such greatness.'
29. *Opere* 236, 240.
30. We should nonetheless grant that rather than expressing approximations, a generic lexicon might allow one to generate and apply words, usages, and techniques with more precision. From this perspective, Machiavelli does not neglect verbal precision when required; he simply does not treat it as a binding condition in all circumstances. If the soldier and the civilian are inseparable (as argued in *The Prince*, chs. 12–14 and in the prologue to *The Art of War*), this does not mean that they should be confused; in fact, the *exercise* of war must not be an 'art', that is to say a business, for the citizens and the subjects.
31. 'Gli instrumenti co' quali gli antichi difendevano le terre erano molti, come baliste, onagri, scorpioni, arcubaliste, fustibali, funde; ed ancora erano molti quegli co' quali le assaltavano, come arieti, torri, musculi, plutei, vinee, falci, testudini.

In cambio delle quali cose sono oggi l'artiglierie, le quali servono a chi offende e a chi si difende; e però io non ne parlerò altrimenti' : *The Art of War* 7:75–6, *Opere* 381; my translation. It is worth revisiting the imprecise but enlightening solution in an old translation: 'The engines which the Ancients made use of in the defence of a town were many; the chief of which were such as threw darts and huge stones to a great distance, and with astonishing force: they made use of several likewise in besieging towns, as the battering ram, the tortoise, and many others: instead of which great guns are now used both by besiegers and those that are besieged': *Works of Nicholas Machiavel Secretary of State to the Republic of Florence, newly translated from the originals ... by Ellis Farneworth* (London: Thomas Davies, 1762), 2:148.

32. *Les discours de* Nic. Macchiavel *citoyen et secrétaire de Florence, sur la première décade de Tite-Live dez l'édification de la ville. Traduitz d'Italien en François et de nouveau reveuz et augmentez par Iacques Gohory Parisien* (Paris: Robert le Mangnier, 1571), sig. C3v.

Afterlife

15

Machiavelli and Gandhi

Sukanta Chaudhuri

This chapter looks at two of the most radical political thinkers in human history, but their radicalism is on such dramatically opposite lines that any meaningful comparison seems unrealistic. Mohandas Karamchand Gandhi heads the list of iconic apostles of non-violence. Four centuries earlier, Niccolò Machiavelli had proposed violence in many guises, from open warfare to covert assassination, as the default mode of successful political strategy. For Gandhi, politics was inseparable from ethics, while Machiavelli placed the two in uneasy tandem at best. Gandhi never mentions Machiavelli in his writings, even to oppose or dismiss him. Nonetheless, I would like to explore a deeper paradigm where both might find a place.

When the Boer War broke out, Gandhi and his associates were faced with a political choice that was also a moral choice. Should the Indian community seize this opportunity to have their own back on the British by siding with the Boers? Many thought so, but Gandhi argued for supporting the British, and that actively by setting up an ambulance corps. In his words:

> Our existence in South Africa is only in our capacity as British subjects. … And if we desire to win our freedom and achieve our welfare as members of the British Empire, here is a golden opportunity for us to do so… It must largely be conceded that justice is on the side of the Boers. But every single subject of a state must not hope to enforce his private opinion in all cases. The authorities may not always be right, but … it is [the subjects'] clear duty generally to accommodate themselves, and to accord their support, to acts of the state.[1]

We have here an extraordinary mix of moral and political arguments, principles and pragmatism. Moreover, the moral factors are conflicting, as Gandhi believes the Boers to have justice on their side. Yet he would support the British, not only out of 'clear duty' but to serve the Indians' own long-term interest. Of two moral alternatives, he chooses the one (arguably the less moral) that happens also to be the better tactical strategy. He was to advance the same justification for Indian participation in the First World War.[2] Needless to say, he later rejected these arguments during India's independence movement, by which time he had challenged the identity of Indians as British subjects. But the underlying design, the synthesis of moral principle and strategic advantage, persists, binding together a far more complex, changing, and inconsistent set of premises.

In *Discourses* 1:47, Machiavelli cites several broadly parallel instances where an aggrieved population had the opportunity to remove or harm hated rulers but refrained from doing so. In one such instance, the population of Capua, threatened by Hannibal, was persuaded by the magistrate Pacovius Calanus to retain the much-detested senators as there were no others who could feasibly take charge of the state; hence, said Calanus, they should resist the temptation to 'subdue the pride of the nobles and revenge themselves for the injuries received at their hands'.[3] Meanwhile, Calanus had talked to the senators as well, urging them to mend their ways, which they did. Gandhi was less successful in South Africa, but his initiative with the ambulance corps found favour among the whites: '[T]he knowledge that the Indians, forgetful of their wrongs, were out to help them in the hour of their need, had melted their hearts for the time being.'[4]

Machiavelli does not define the Capuans' dilemma in moral terms, but at the bottom it is precisely that of the South African Indians: the tactical decision masks a moral choice. Most of the conflicts cited in *The Prince* and the *Discourses* between the moral and the pragmatic prove, on examination, to be a choice between two goods rather than between good and bad. As he declares most famously in Chapter 15 of *The Prince*, it is good to reconcile the opposites when one can; where this is not possible, the political good must prevail. In *The Prince*, the good sought by the autarchic ruler is, primarily and often solely, his own continuation in power. But *The Prince* is addressed to a particular ruler, Lorenzo de' Medici (from whom Machiavelli had obtained no particular favour, indeed who had imprisoned, persecuted, and exiled him), exhorting him to unite Italy, expel the foreign forces, and restore the land to its former glory. In the republican context of the *Discourses*, the common weal is markedly more foregrounded, and ethical factors urged as politically valid—in which case, of course, they are to be preferred even by the criteria of *The Prince*, where it is thought better, if feasible, to base the appearance of goodness on reality. Thus, Machiavelli can assert that virtuous rulers achieve security as well as glory in a world replete with peace and justice;[5] that humanity in governance is better than violence and ferocity;[6] that envy is silenced by a ruler's virtue and goodness;[7] and that love of one's country makes a citizen forget his private wrongs.[8] Some of these assertions contradict others in the same text, whether *The Prince* or the *Discourses*.

One may see this, in Wilbur Sanders's grudging phrase, as Machiavelli's 'final failure to exclude the moral order'.[9] But it seems more correct to accept it, like Isaiah Berlin, as admitting a devastating duality in human values:

> an insoluble dilemma, ... a permanent question mark in the path of posterity. It stems from his *de facto* recognition that ends equally ultimate, equally sacred, may contradict each other, that entire systems of value may come into collision without possibility of rational arbitration.[10]

Gandhi is among those who set out to meet the challenge of that 'permanent question mark', but first let me follow Berlin on Machiavelli a little farther:

> Anyone whose thought revolves round central concepts such as the good and the bad, the corrupt and the pure, has an ethical scale in mind in terms of which he gives moral praise and blame.[11]

This 'ethical scale' encompasses the full truth of the human condition, not 'the fairy tales of shallow moralists'[12] that pervade the extensive literature of 'advice to princes' preceding Machiavelli. Machiavelli's radical importance lies in that he compels all subsequent political thought, and hence political practice, to consider the ethicality of rule and governance. If the hasty judgement of critics from Gentillet down sees him as divorcing ethics from politics, it is because he has brought them into contact in the first place.

One prominent line of development, among professed Machiavellians like Francis Bacon, has indeed attempted this divorce. But another current, intermittently visible and rarely operative, has met the challenge head-on, seeking to unite the two competing value-systems. One such line, embracing violence, runs through the motley history of anarchism and far-left activism. Another line, rejecting violence, emanates from Rousseau and continues through Thoreau and Tolstoy, not to mention cultures of disengagement and non-violent anarchy like the Bohemian and Hippie movements. But this line shares some of its DNA with the epoch-making, totally activist, real-life, real-time political engagement nodally modelled on Gandhi and exemplified by Abdul Ghaffar Khan, Martin Luther King Jr., and Nelson Mandela. Viewed in this light, I would propose that Gandhi is Machiavelli's heir, in the extended and subversive sense in which Einstein is Newton's heir. When Gandhi writes 'what is true of families and communities is true of nations. There is no reason to believe that there is one law for families and another for nations',[13] he is simultaneously rejecting and extending Machiavelli's postulation of these two spheres.

The paradox may be less acute than appears at first sight. A prominent difference between Machiavelli's approach and Gandhi's is that the latter's public agenda is an article of his private spiritual quest. As he writes in the preface to his Autobiography:

> What I want to achieve ... is self-realization, to see God face to face, to attain *Moksha* [spiritual liberation] ... All that I do by way of speaking and writing, and all my ventures in the political field, are directed to this same end.[14]

Machiavelli has no religious or spiritual end in his writings; he looks at such matters externally and dispassionately. Religious faith is for him one major political instrument among others. What he almost studiedly conceals, however, except in rare outbursts like the last chapter of *The Prince*, is his deep personal commitment to the freedom and welfare of Italy in general and Florence in particular. It is also an ideological commitment drawing its sustenance from the model of ancient Rome. But in his writing, he does not link either his emotional life or (except for the occasional reminiscence) his own public career with his political discourse. This disengagement is no less noteworthy than the alleged divorce between private and public, the ethical and the pragmatic, in the terms of his discourse.

The contrast with Gandhi is striking and fundamental, but perhaps not entirely so. Gandhi frequently asserts that his political work is an adjunct to his spiritual life. 'My bent is not political but religious,' he writes to G. S. Arundale in 1919.[15] When Edwin Montagu, the Secretary of State for India, remarked to him, 'I am surprised to find you taking part in the political life of the country!', Gandhi replied, 'I am in it because without it I cannot do my religious and social work.'[16] But for all such statements about his personal role, and his stress on the organic role of religion in Indian society, his central political mission is totally and strikingly secular. As he writes in the crucial tenth chapter of *Hind Swaraj*:

> In reality, there are as many religions as there are individuals; but those who are conscious of the spirit of nationality do not interfere with one another's religion. If they do, they are not fit to be considered a nation. If the Hindus believe that India should be peopled only by Hindus, they are living in dream-land. The Hindus, the Mahomedans, the Parsis and the Christians who have made India their country are fellow countrymen, and they will have to live in unity, if only for their own interest.[17]

Hence, his political programme must be non-religious, although (or therefore) compatible with all religions. That is why it is possible, on whatever terms, to compare Gandhi with Machiavelli, but quite impossible to compare him with Savonarola.

Interestingly, it is Machiavelli who sees religion—if only in a disengaged, external perspective—as a politically binding force. Its articles of faith might be the concern of individual citizens, but its potential as a tool of governance concerns the polity:

> It is therefore the duty of princes and heads of republics to uphold the foundations of the religion of their countries, for then it is easy to keep their people religious, and consequently well conducted and united. And therefore everything that tends to favor religion (even though it were believed to be false) should be received and availed of to strengthen it.[18]

Machiavelli's community had only one religion, Gandhi's had many. He is all too aware of the dangers of division, conflict, and hatred in such a situation. In *Hind Swaraj* and later works, he always defines the energizing power of *satyagraha* as a non-doctrinal 'soul-force'; if the name of God is evoked at all, it is in a passing, non-sectarian context. Soul-force has a political and economic dimension as well; most crucially, it engages the power of mass psychology:

> [W]here they [the common people] learn soul-force, the commands of the rulers do not go beyond the point of their swords, for true men disregard unjust commands. Peasants have never been subdued by the sword, and never will be. They do not know the use of the sword, and they are not frightened by the use of it by others. That nation is great which rests its head upon death as its pillow.[19]

Ultimately, I see Gandhi as viewing the public role of organized religion in a light not unlike Machiavelli's, as a socially binding force lending unmatched emotive energy, credibility, and popular commitment to a political programme without forming an intrinsic part of the programme itself. He can even apply social and political criteria to religious doctrines and practices, including those of Hinduism:

> Thus if I could not accept Christianity either as a perfect, or the greatest religion, neither was I then convinced of Hinduism being such. Hindu defects were pressingly visible to me. If untouchability could be a part of Hinduism, it could but be a rotten part or an excrescence. I could not understand the *raison d'être* of a multitude of sects and castes. What was the meaning of saying that

the Vedas were the inspired Word of God? If they were inspired, why not also the Bible and the Koran?[20]

There is a clear element of the relative, partial, or contingent, even the external or objective, in Gandhi's engagement with the spiritual and philosophic premises that he declares to be absolute in nature and organic in operation. It is an intellectual or epistemological engagement no less than a spiritual or ethical one, on different and independent terms.

The same feature can be traced in Machiavelli. In Chapter 15 of *The Prince*, he says, 'it has appeared to me more fitting to go directly to the effectual truth of the thing than to the imagination of it.'[21] He continually insists that his political discourse is empirical, not theoretical or a priori, hence governed by circumstance or contingency. The celebrated discourse on fortune in Chapter 25 turns on this point:

> I believe, further, that he is happy [*felice*] who adapts his mode of proceeding to the qualities of the times; and similarly, he is unhappy whose procedure is in disaccord with the times ... [I]f the times and affairs change, [a ruler] is ruined because he does not change his mode of proceeding.[22]

A very similar account in *Discourses* 3:8–9 adds a major corollary:

> But he errs least and will be most favored by fortune who suits his proceedings to the times, ... and always follows the compulsion of his nature [*sforza di natura*: Detmold has 'the impulses of his nature'].[23]

Both prescriptions in this sentence ally Machiavelli's discourse to a general epistemic current of the time, an expansive and multifaceted skepticism. Skepticism is the philosophical position of consistently doubting any cognitive premise. In classical philosophy, it is chiefly of cautionary value, one might almost say nuisance value, in appraising more constructive philosophical systems; but in the Renaissance, it acquires its own constructive dimension where current methodologies and knowledge-systems are questioned in order to generate new ones. Among other crucial results, the new skepticism leads to an epistemology of the contingent, where truth is a dynamic, evolving entity generated by experience. Experience is, of its nature, singular, the product of a unique set of circumstances encountered at a particular intersection of time and place. The synthesis it embodies is uniquely authentic but also uniquely unstable and unrepeatable. Machiavelli's political empiricism adopts this basic epistemological position.

Later in the century, the existential quality worked into the very fabric of experience is inspiredly defined by Montaigne in his *Essays* 3:2, 'Du repentir':

> The world is but a perennial movement ... I do not portray being: I portray passing. Not the passing from one age to another, ... but from day to day, from minute to minute ... This is a record of various and changeable occurrences, ... and, when it so befalls, contradictory ideas: whether I am different myself, or whether I take hold of my subjects in different circumstances and aspects. So, all in all, I may indeed contradict myself now and then; but truth, as Demades said, I do not contradict.[24]

There is no evidence that Gandhi had read Montaigne, but these words of Montaigne are uncannily reflected in a passage that appeared in *Harijan* on 29 April 1933:

> I am not at all concerned with appearing to be consistent. In my search after Truth I have discarded many ideas and learnt many new things. Old as I am in age, I have no feeling that I have ceased to grow inwardly or that my growth will stop at the dissolution of the flesh. What I am concerned with is my readiness to obey the call of Truth, my God, from moment to moment.[25]

The only new element added to Montaigne are the allusions to God and the afterlife, and even those are equivocal. Does 'Truth, my God' imply belief in a greater God synonymous with truth, or in truth itself as his god? Either way, the investigative, experimental, variable nature of his endeavour is plain, as enshrined in the title of his autobiography, *The Story of my Experiments with Truth*. Its Introduction anticipates the 1933 piece in *Harijan*: truth is absolute, but

> as long as I have not realized this Absolute Truth, so long must I hold by the relative truth as I have conceived it...
>
> I hope and pray that no one will regard the advice interspersed in the following chapters as authoritative. The experiments narrated should be regarded as illustrations, in the light of which everyone may carry on his own experiments according to his own inclinations and capacity.[26]

Like Montaigne, he is making 'essays', not reaching conclusions.

But his use of 'experiments', *prayogo*, is interesting too. It is scientists that make experiments: 'My purpose is to describe experiments in the science of Satyagraha, not to say how good I am.'[27] The process is analogous to the development of scientific method out of Early Modern skepticism by what Francis Bacon, one of its leading exponents, termed the 'probative' approach. It is generally granted that Bacon applied this inductive method of acquiring knowledge not only to the natural sciences but, in his *Essays*, to the study of politics, society, and individual behaviour. Gopalkrishna Gandhi points out something even more telling: 'The Gujarati part-title, *Satyana prayogo* translates itself literally to "Truth's Experiments" or "Experiments *of* Truth" rather than "Experiments *with* Truth".'[28] It is truth that is experimenting with Gandhi, not Gandhi with truth. The end is not the development of the man Mohandas; it is the gradual revelation of the nature and power of truth.

We may be reminded of some lines from Rabindranath Tagore's last poem, written on his deathbed. A beguiling mistress of illusions has spread the path of her creation with many wiles; but by this deceit, she has provided a means to mark out the noble of heart:

> The path that your stars light up for him is the path within him, ever clear, ever bright, made so by his simple faith. He may be cunning on the outside but is straight within: there is his glory. He finds truth in the heart of his own being, bathed in his own light.[29]

I have not seen it documented or even suggested anywhere, but I would venture the speculation that Tagore had Gandhi in mind while writing these lines. His man of great soul (*mahatva*) matches Gandhi's description of the ideal *satyagrahi*:

> Satyagraha is based on self-help, self-sacrifice and faith in God. ... [A]s a Satyagrahi I hold to the faith, that all activity pursued with a pure heart is bound to bear fruit ... [through] adherence to Truth and Truth alone.[30]

Now for a really long shot. To compare Machiavelli and Gandhi as political thinkers may be admissible; to compare Gandhi the political practitioner with, say, Cesare Borgia seems beyond the pale of sanity or decency.[31] Unsurprisingly, the passages cited earlier from Gandhi and Tagore have no close parallel in Machiavelli's accounts of the man of *virtù*. The closest, perhaps, is the citing of Livy's report of Camillus's declaration: 'My courage has neither been inflated by the dictatorship nor abated by exile.'[32] Machiavelli's own comment follows:

> These words show that a truly great man is ever the same under all circumstances; and if his fortune varies, exalting him at one moment and oppressing him

at another, he himself never varies, but always preserves an unwavering soul [*lo animo fermo*], which is so closely interwoven with the way he conducts his life [*il modo del vivere loro*] that every one can readily see that the fickleness of fortune has no power over him. (Translation modified from Detmold)[33]

The reference to fortune links this ideal figure to the aggressively virile man of *virtù* (pun on *vir* intended) in Chapter 25 of *The Prince*, who controls the goddess Fortuna like the female she is by beating and ill-using her—that is to say, by adapting circumstance rather than adapting himself to it—a very different take on the heroic ideal than Camillus's model of endurance and equanimity. What the Machiavellian man of *virtù* has in common with the *satyagrahi* is their shared sense of an intrinsic humanity—call it the power of personality, a moral force in the broadest sense—as the source of their strength, rather than any externally induced spiritual motivation. The secular power of *satyagraha* takes on the deeper sense of a force engendered by the unaided human faculties, deeply ethical but not extra-rational or spiritual, perhaps not even ideological if that word implies a theoretical rationale. We may be reminded of Hannah Arendt's 'revolutionary spirit', the wellspring of a freedom that resists the founding—that is, the formulaic delimitation—of its own order, that seeks 'a source of political authority that is not transcendent, absolute, or extrapolitical'.[34] Machiavelli's innovation is demonstrably 'revolutionary' in this sense, Gandhi's vastly more so in its direct impact.

A last hurdle remains. For Machiavelli, military strength was the chief instrument of political strength: hence his stress on a state having an army of its own citizens. How can such a thinker be equated with the world's most celebrated exponent of non-violence? The attempt would be absurd if the criterion were to be the actual power of arms. But this patent disparity is countered by another factor: Gandhi clearly views *satyagraha* as an instrument of battle. Over and over, he uses the imagery of war to explain the efficacy of *satyagraha*. In his celebrated open letter of 1920, he tells 'Every Englishman in India':

> you have ensured our incapacity to fight in open and honourable battle. Bravery on the battlefield is thus impossible for us. Bravery of the soul still remains open to us.[35]

In Chapter 38 of *Satyagraha in South Africa*, he calls the continuation of a £3 tax on Indians in Natal 'a cause of "war"', putting the word in quotation marks.[36] He writes in the same context:

> In a pure fight the fighters would never go beyond the objective fixed when the fight began even if they received an accession to their strength in the course of fighting, and on the other hand they could not give up their objective if they found their strength dwindling away.[37]

As borne out by Gandhi's lifelong practice, *satyagraha* has to be strategized: the leader must know when to advance or to retreat, when to compound with the adversary, on which flank to extend battle. In countless passages, the metaphoric use of military terms almost acquires the flavour of the literal. As with the notion of truth, the tactical unfolding of *satyagraha* problematizes, without ever dissolving, the idea of *satyagraha* as an expression of love.

One of Gandhi's most constant themes is the difference between passive resistance and *satyagraha*. Mere passive resistance, he explains, is the resort of those without the means of active resistance. *Satyagraha*, on the contrary, is an 'intensely active force'.[38] On 29 November 1947, he writes to Madame Edmond Privat in Switzerland of his and the nation's error in pursuing merely passive resistance, which was enough to ensure India's political freedom, but not *satyagraha*—or, as he now calls it, 'Non-violent Resistance', which would have made for genuine reform of the nation.[39] Two months and a day later, he proved his point with his life.

Yet he admits that the Indians of South Africa may not have 'taken to Satyagraha ... if they had possessed arms or the franchise'.[40] It is *because* they do not have these strengths, *because* their colonial bondage is a permanent cause of weakness, that they have to seek for strength elsewhere: by his inspired innovation, in turning that very weakness into strength. In Chapter 6 of *The Prince*, while considering rulers who introduce 'new orders and modes', Machiavelli wryly comments:

> It is however necessary ... to examine whether these innovators stand by themselves or depend on others; that is, whether to carry out their deed they must beg or indeed can use force. In the first case they always come to ill and never accomplish anything; but when they depend on their own and are able to use force, then it is that they are rarely in peril. From this it arises that all the armed prophets conquered and the unarmed ones were ruined.[41]

Gandhi's political genius lay in working out the means whereby an unarmed prophet could conquer resoundingly by exploiting his very absence of arms. It is a piquant fancy to imagine Winston Churchill on his deathbed saying, in imitation of Julian the Apostate's dying words to Christ, 'You have conquered, O Gujarati!'

In fact, Julian's Galilean is part of the picture. In *Discourses* 2:2, Machiavelli attributes the supineness of Italy in good part to the tolerance and passivity of the Christian religion:

> Our religion, moreover, places the supreme happiness in humility, lowliness, and a contempt for worldly objects ... These principles seem to me to have made men feeble, and caused them to become an easy prey to evil-minded men.[42]

Ancient paganism, on the contrary, 'places the supreme good in greatness [*grandezza*] of soul, strength of body, and all such other qualities as render men most strong' (*fortissimi*: translation modified from Detmold).[43] Gandhi was impressed by the message of renunciation in the New Testament and attempted to unite the Sermon on the Mount with the *Bhagavadgita* and the teachings of the Buddha.[44] He goes so far as to assimilate truly Christian conduct with true *satyagraha*, not just passive resistance:

> Jesus Christ indeed has been acclaimed as the prince of passive resisters but I submit in that case passive resistance must mean Satyagraha and Satyagraha alone ... The phrase passive resistance was not employed to denote the patient suffering of oppression by thousands of devout Christians in the early days of Christianity. I would therefore class them as Satyagrahis.[45]

Unlike Machiavelli, Gandhi regards the apparent weakness of Christianity as a strength. But as I said earlier, he consistently declines to see religion, and still less religious doctrine or ritual, as an integral element of *satyagraha*. At most, it can be an influence to strengthen a person's own moral fibre:

> Of the thing that sustains him through trials man has no inkling, much less knowledge, at the time. If an unbeliever, he will attribute his safety to chance. If a believer, he will say God saved him. He will conclude, as well he may, that his religious study or spiritual discipline was at the back of the state of grace within him. But in the hour of his deliverance he does not know whether his spiritual discipline or something else saves him.[46]

We return to the essential secularism of *satyagraha* as a political ideal or strategy, however it might be sustained or even generated in particular individuals (or a community at large) by religious faith. We also return to the idea of an intrinsically human moral force as the motive power of *satyagraha*, a Gandhian *virtù* balancing the Machiavellian.

Gandhi never mentions Machiavelli, but there is a notable overlap in their central concerns. From his intensive engagement with *Realpolitik*, he extends the line of empirical political analysis established by Machiavelli. His genius lies in applying this insight to a diametrically opposite practical agenda, validating the Machiavellian paradigm on a plane where it might be thought fantastically inapplicable. The resemblance may be fortuitous, but it allows for telling insights.

There is an interesting angle on Machiavelli's take on Christianity that seems to have escaped notice. If, according to him, true Christianity enfeebled the Italian spirit, a naïve logic might have enjoined that the decline of Christianity would strengthen it. Machiavelli, however, does not find any value in the unbroken line of warfare, manipulation, and acquisition running through the Christian era in European history. Rather, he views it as no less an enfeebling and degenerating force, as testified by his scathing account of the Catholic Church in *Discourses* 1.12: '[T]he evil example of the court of Rome has destroyed all piety and religion in Italy, which brings in its train infinite improprieties and disorders'.[47] Machiavellian relativism demands that any order must be true to its own foundational premises. It must engage, or at least experiment, with what it sees as truth. The Catholic Church has emphatically failed to do so in his view.

The direction of time's arrow precludes an analysis of Gandhi by Machiavelli, and the lack of cultural contact the Florentine's analysis of the Emperor Ashok. A committed realist like Machiavelli would not have ignored those examples. He would surely have accommodated both within his political vision, perhaps reshaping its contours. The end result, I suspect, would not have overthrown the Machiavellian design we know but given it a wiser and more total shape within an essentially similar view of the human condition.

Notes

1. Mohandas Karamchand Gandhi, *Satyagraha in South Africa*, tr. Valji Govindji Desai (1928): *The Selected Works of Mahatma Gandhi*, vol. 3 (Ahmedabad: Navajivan Publishing House, 1968, rpt. 1995), ch. 9, 97–8.
2. Mohandas Karamchand Gandhi, *An Autobiography or the Story of My Experiments with Truth*, tr. Mahadev Desai (1927; rpt. Ahmedabad: Navajivan Publishing House, 2015), 4:38–9, 320–5 (references by part, chapter, and page).
3. '[D]omare la superbia della Nobilità, e vendicarsi delle ingiurie ricevute da quella': Machiavelli, *Le grandi opere politiche*, 2 vols., ed. Gian Mario Anselmi and Carlo Varotti (Turin: Bollati Boringhieri, 1993), 2:179; tr. Christian E. Detmold in Machiavelli, *The Prince and the Discourses*, intr. Max Lerner

(New York: Random House, 1950), 235. All citations from the *Discorsi* are from this edition and translation.
4. Gandhi, *Satyagraha*, ch. 9, 106.
5. *Disc.* 1:10.
6. Ibid., 3:19–20.
7. Ibid., 3:30.
8. Ibid., 3:47.
9. Wilbur Sanders, *The Dramatist and the Received Idea* (Cambridge: Cambridge University Press, 1968), 64.
10. Isaiah Berlin, 'The Originality of Machiavelli', in *Against the Current*, 25–79 (Oxford: Oxford University Press, 1981 [1979]), 74.
11. Ibid., 55.
12. Ibid., 49.
13. Mohandas Karamchand Gandhi, *Hind Swaraj or Indian Home Rule*, new edn (Ahmedabad: Navajivan Publishing House, 1938 [1909], rpt. 1946), ch. 17, 57.
14. Gandhi, *Autobiography*, xii.
15. Letter of 4 August 1919: *The Collected Works of Mahatma Gandhi* (henceforth *CWMG*), 98 vols. (Sevagram: Gandhi Sevagram Ashram/Publications Division, Govt. of India, 1999), 18:255, accessed on 17 March 2020 at https://www.gandhiashramsevagram.org/gandhi-literature/collected-works-of-mahatma-gandhi-volume-1-to-98.php.
16. Letter to C. F. Andrews, 6 July 1918: Mohandas Karamchand Gandhi, *Selected Letters: The Selected Works of Mahatma Gandhi*, vol. 5 (Ahmedabad: Navajivan Publishing House, 1995 [1968]), 56 (henceforth *Letters*).
17. Gandhi, *Hind Swaraj*, ch. 10, 35. See also letter to Anne Marie Petersen, 13 January 1920, *CWMG* 19:317; letter to Hakim Ajmal Khan, 12 March 1922, *Letters* 138.
18. 'Debbono, adunque, i principi d'una republica o d'uno regno, i fondamenti della religione che loro tengono, mantenergli; e fatto questo, sarà loro facil cosa mantenere la loro republica religiosa, e, per conseguente, buona e unita. E debbono, tutte le cose che nascano in favore di quella, come che le giudicassono false, favorirle e accrescerle ...': *Disc.* 1:12, *Le grandi opere* 2:74–5; tr. Detmold, 150.
19. Gandhi, *Hind Swaraj*, ch. 17, 60–1.
20. Gandhi, *Autobiography*, 2:15, 127.
21. '[M]i è parso più conveniente andare drieto alla verità effettuale della cosa, che alla imaginazione di essa': *Le grandi opere* 1:91; tr. as in Machiavelli, *The Prince*, tr. Harvey C. Mansfield, 2nd edn (Chicago, IL: University of Chicago Press, 1998), 61.

22. 'Credo, ancora, che sia felice quello che riscontra el modo del procedere suo con le qualità de' tempi, e similmente sia infelice quello che con il procedere suo si discordano e' tempi … [S]e li tempi e le cose si mutano, e' rovina, perché non muta moo di procedere': *Le grandi opere* 1:134–5; tr. Mansfield, 99–100.
23. 'Ma quello viene ad errare meno, ed avere la fortuna prospera, che riscontra … con il suo modo il tempo, e sempre mai si procede, secondo ti sforza la natura': *Disc.* 3:9, *Le grandi opere* 2:419; tr. Detmold, 441.
24. 'Le monde n'est qu'une branloire perenne … Je ne peints pas l'estre. Je peints le passage: non un passage d'aage en autre, … mais de jour en jour, de minute en minute … C'est un contrerolle de divers et muables accidens et d'imaginations irresoluës, et, quand il y eschet, contraires; soit que je sois autre moymesme, soit que je saisisse les subjects par autres circonstances et considerations. Tant y a que je me contredits bien à l'adventure, mais le vérité, comme disoit Demades, je ne la contredy point': Montaigne, *Essais*, ed. Maurice Rat, 2 vols. (Paris: Garnier, 1962), 2:222; tr. from Montaigne, *Essays*, tr. Donald M. Frame (Stanford, CA: Stanford University Press, 1957, rpt. 1968), 610–11.
25. 'Notes: Inconsistencies?', *CWMG* 61:23–4.
26. Gandhi, *Autobiography*, xiii–xiv.
27. Ibid., xiv.
28. Gopalkrishna Gandhi, 'Gandhi's Autobiography: The Story of Translators' Experiments with the Text', lecture, Jadavpur University, 2008, 5, accessed 17 March 2020 at http://rajbhavankolkata.nic.in/writereaddata/PDF/Speech/autobiography.pdf.
29. Rabindranath Tagore, *Shesh lekha*, poem 15; my translation.
30. Gandhi, *Satyagraha*, ch. 23, 249–50.
31. In fact, there are many points of contact between Machiavelli's depiction of Cesare Borgia or Duke Valentino and Gandhi's of General Smuts, a man with whom he seems to have had a sneaking empathy. See *Satyagraha*, ch. 25, 269: 'I am however sure of two things. First, he [Smuts] has some principles in politics, which are not quite immoral. Secondly, there is room in his politics for cunning and on occasions for perversion of truth.'
32. 'Nec mihi dictatura animos fecit, nec exilum ademit': *Disc.* 3:31, *Le grandi opere* 2:492; tr. Detmold, 500.
33. 'Per le quali si vede, come gli uomini grandi sono sempre in ogni fortuna quelli medesimi; e se la varia, ora con esaltarli, ora con opprimerli, quegli non variano, ma tengono sempre lo animo fermo, ed in tale modo congiunto con il modo del vivere loro, che facilmente si conosce, per ciascuno, la fortuna non avere potenza sopra di loro': ibid.

34. See Paul A. Kottman, '*Novus ordo saeclorum*: Hannah Arendt on Revolutionary Spirit', in *Political Theory and Early Modernity*, ed. Graham Hammill and Julia Reinhard Lupton (Chicago: University of Chicago Press, 2012), 143–58, 146.
35. *Young India*, 27 October 1920: *Letters* 101.
36. Gandhi, *Satyagraha*, ch. 38, 372. Cf. 'The battle of Civil Disobedience', letter to Carl Heath, 25 January 1941, *Letters* 228.
37. Gandhi, *Satyagraha*, ch. 38, 370–1.
38. Gandhi, letter to the Viceroy, 2 March 1930, *Letters* 187.
39. *Letters* 322.
40. Gandhi, *Satyagraha*, ch. 13, 154.
41. 'È necessario pertanto … esaminare se questi innovatori stanno per loro medesimi o se dependano da altri; cioè, se per condurre l'opera loro bisogna che preghino, ovvero possono forzare. Nel primo caso capitano sempre male e non conducano cosa alcuna; ma, quando dependono da loro proprii e possono forzare, allora è che rare volte periclitano': *Le grandi opere* 1:51; tr. Mansfield, 24.
42. 'La nostra religione … [h]a dipoi posto il sommo bene nella umiltà, abienzione, e nel dispregio delle cose umane: … Questo modo di vivere, adunque, pare che abbi renduto il mondo debole, e datolo i preda agli uomini scelerati': *Le grandi opere* 2:236; tr. Detmold, 285.
43. '[L]'altra lo [il sommo bene] poneva nella grandezza dello animo, nella fortezza del corpo, ed in tutte altre cose atte a fare gli uomini fortissimi': ibid.
44. Gandhi, *Autobiography*, 1:20, 65–6.
45. Gandhi, *Satyagraha*, ch. 13, 157. See also letter to Madame Edmond Privat, 29 November 1947, *Letters* 322.
46. Gandhi, *Autobiography*, 1:21, 67.
47. '[P]er gli esempli rei di quella corte [*sc.* di Roma], questa provincia ha perduto ogni divozione e ogni religione: il che si tira dietro infiniti inconvenienti e infiniti disordini…': *Le grandi opere* 2:76; tr. Detmold, 151.

16

The Prince between Gramsci and Althusser

Vittorio Morfino[*]

I began preparing this chapter with the idea of putting two opposing interpretative models of Machiavelli, and particularly of *The Prince*, into tension: Gramsci's absolute historicism and Althusser's theoretical anti-humanism. These approaches appear to be opposites, even if both are expressions of the Marxist tradition—in the twentieth century, perhaps even the highest expressions. My work on the texts has largely subverted this initial idea.

But let us begin from the materiality of the texts. In the first place, it should be noted that neither Gramsci nor Althusser devoted a work to Machiavelli, if we understand by 'work' an effort that was completed and published as such.

Gramsci's reading of Machiavelli is contained for the most part in the 1949 volume *Note sul Machiavelli*,[1] edited by Palmiro Togliatti and Felice Platone, which has well-known philological limitations. Both Valentino Gerratana's 1975 edition[2] and the *Edizione Nazionale* directed by Gianni Francioni for the Fondazione Gramsci[3] restore historical depth to Gramsci's work and enable us to situate each of Gramsci's reflections on Machiavelli in the context of the development of his thought. As for Althusser, throughout the work published during his lifetime, Machiavelli's name appears only rarely.[4] However, this scarcity is offset by the large quantity of texts dedicated to Machiavelli contained in the archives at the Institut Mémoires de l'édition contemporaine (IMEC), which have now been published, at least in part:

- the manuscript of a course held in 1962[5]
- the manuscript of a course held in 1971–2, of which there is a second version with numerous modifications presumably made in 1975–6, with the title *Machiavelli et nous* (*Machiavelli and Us*)—a version that Althusser continued to correct until the 1980s[6]
- an article with the title 'La solitude de Machiavel' ('Machiavelli's Solitude'), from 1977[7]
- a note on Machiavelli and Gramsci, from 1977[8]

- a text with the title *Que faire?* (*What Is to Be Done?*) with a long digression on Machiavelli, from 1978[9]
- the part dedicated to Machiavelli in *The Underground Current of the Materialism of the Encounter*, from 1982[10]
- two excerpts from an autobiography, given the title *The Only Materialist Tradition* by its editors, from 1985[11]
- a manuscript text from 1986 entitled *Machiavelli philosophe*[12]

Gramsci's Reading of Machiavelli

Let us begin with Gramsci's reading. A historicist reading, indeed! But what exactly does this adjective mean in this instance? It is well known that in *Reading Capital*, Althusser projects onto Gramsci the fundamental categories of the Hegelian conception of history: the homogeneous continuity of time, and contemporaneity or the category of the historical present. This means that a thinker, a philosopher, or an ideologist is the child of an epoch, and that no one can leap beyond their own time.

Indeed, we find this reflection at Q13, §13:

> The habit of considering Machiavelli too much as a 'politician in general', as a 'political scientist', is present in all times. Machiavelli must be considered as the necessary expression of his own time and as strictly linked to the conditions and demands of his time which follow: 1) from the internal struggles of the Florentine republic and from the particular structure of the State that did not know how to liberate itself from communal-municipal residues, i.e., from a form of feudalism that had become paralyzing; 2) from the struggles among Italian States for balance within the Italian framework, which was hindered by the existence of the papacy and by other feudal, municipal residues of the city-state and non-territorial forms of the state; 3) from the struggles of the Italian States more or less supportive for a European balance, i.e., the contradictions between the needs of an internal Italian equilibrium and the exigencies of European States in a struggle for hegemony.[13]

A few lines later, Gramsci again writes that 'Machiavelli is a man entirely of his epoch, and his political science represents the philosophy of his time'.[14]

Machiavelli is thus for Gramsci an 'expression' of his time, a man of his 'epoch'. We seem to be operating within the fundamental grammar of Hegelian historicism that Althusser attributes to Gramsci, in which the category of contemporaneity or the historical present dominates. But the historical present or contemporaneity is immediately complicated in the relationship between the national and the international, citing the influence on Machiavelli of the examples of 'France and Spain, which have achieved a strong unity of the territorial state'.[15] The philosophy of Machiavelli's time is not the direct expression of its immediate causes; rather, it represents a historical tendency, which is the tension 'in the organization of absolute national monarchies, the political form that allows and facilitates an ulterior development of the bourgeois productive forces'.[16]

In a brief note in Notebook 6, Gramsci had already expressed this problem synthetically in a historicist key:

> Machiavelli really serves the absolute states in their formation, because he was the expression of the European 'philosophy of the epoch' more than the Italian.[17]

The idea is very clearly expressed in a letter to his sister-in-law Tania dated 14 November 1927:

> Machiavelli was the theorist of the nation-states ruled by absolute monarchy ... [H]e, in Italy, theorized what in England was energetically accomplished by Elizabeth, in Spain by Ferdinand the Catholic, in France by Louis XI and in Russia by Ivan the Terrible, even if he did not know and could not know some of these national experiences, which actually represented the historical problem of the epoch that Machiavelli had the genius to intuit and systematically express.[18]

From this perspective, Gramsci could oppose the interpretation of Paolo Treves, who held that Guicciardini, and not Machiavelli, is the true politician. The true politician, says Gramsci, does not take actual reality as a given, as 'something static and immobile', but as a 'relation of forces in continuous movement and shifting equilibrium', to which it is possible to apply the will by creating a new equilibrium, 'founding it on that determinate force that is considered progressive'.[19] In the notebook, we find a precise reflection on this point:

> Guicciardini signals a step backwards in political science from Machiavelli. The greater 'pessimism' of Guicciardini means only this: Guicciardini returns to a purely Italian political thought, while Machiavelli had risen to a European thought. Machiavelli is not understood if we do not consider that he overcomes the Italian experience in the European experience (international in that epoch): his 'will' would be utopian without that European experience. The same conception of 'human nature' becomes different in the two thinkers for this reason. Machiavelli's notion of 'human nature' presupposes 'European man', who in France and Spain has effectually overcome the feudal phase [which dissolved] into absolute monarchy. Therefore, it is not 'human nature' that is opposed to

what in Italy arises as an absolute unitary monarchy, but transitory conditions that the will can overcome.[20]

Up to this point, the framework of historicism can hold: Machiavelli is the expression of the most advanced thought of his epoch, going beyond the immediate expression of the surrounding reality, the Italy of his time, which is entirely immersed in the economic-corporative situation that Gramsci considers the worst form of feudal society, the least progressive, and the most stagnant.[21] But Machiavelli's anachronism is not confined to the contemporary situation of Italy and Europe. In Notebook 13, criticizing the abstract character of Sorel's conception of myth, which appears in his aversion to Jacobinism, Gramsci claims:

> the Jacobins ... certainly were a 'categorical incarnation' of Machiavelli's *The Prince*. The modern Prince must have a part dedicated to Jacobinism (in the integral meaning that this notion has had historically and must have conceptually), exemplifying how it was formed concretely and how it has carried out a collective will that, at least in some aspects, was creation *ex novo*, original.[22]

What makes the Jacobin an incarnation of Machiavelli's prince is 'the capacity to radically pose the problem of the peasant revolution'[23] and appeal to popular support in order to establish a new type of state with exceptional means.

This first anachronism refers immediately to another, with which it is directly connected. Gramsci establishes a strict link between Jacobinism and physiocratic culture:

> French Jacobinism would be inexplicable without the presupposition of physiocratic culture, with its demonstration of the social and economic importance of the direct cultivator.[24]

This raises a question that Gramsci posed to Piero Sraffa through Tania in a letter dated 21 March 1932. The question is posed in the terms of a possible research perspective for Notebook 13:

> Machiavelli's economic theories were studied by Gino Arias (in the 'Annali di Economia' of the University of Bocconi) but it should be asked whether Machiavelli had economic theories: it will be a question of whether the essentially political language of Machiavelli can be translated into economic terms, and to which economic system it can be reduced. See if Machiavelli, who lived in the mercantilist period, was politically in advance of his times and anticipated some needs of which he then found expression in the physiocrats.[25]

We know that Sraffa responded to Tania by suggesting an analogy with William Petty.[26]

However, Machiavelli's anachronism is not limited to his contemporaneity with the political and economic ideas of the eighteenth century. In a critical passage in Notebook 5, which discusses a text by Azzolini, Gramsci goes as far as labelling Machiavelli's work a 'philosophy of praxis':

> In his discussion, his critique of the present, he expressed some general concepts which are presented in aphoristic and non-systematic form, which could even be called a 'philosophy of praxis' or a 'neo-humanism' insofar as he does not recognize transcendental or immanentist elements (in the metaphysical sense), but rather bases himself entirely on the concrete action of mankind that, through its historical compulsions, works upon reality and transforms it.[27]

Gramsci does not say that Machiavelli anticipates Marx and Engels's historical materialism but that Machiavelli's conception of the world can be defined as a philosophy of praxis in the sense of the 'absolute this-sidedness' of Notebook 10.[28]

Finally, there is an anachronism that is not expressed *apertis verbis*, even though it is easily identifiable. It is strictly linked to Gramsci's interpretation of Jacobinism, which is strongly influenced by his reading of Albert Mathiez's *Bolshevism and Jacobinism* (1920, translated in instalments in *L'ordine nuovo*, 1921). Mathiez's work fascinated Gramsci. 'It is clear,' writes Rita Medici, 'that Gramsci was receptive to the French historian's interpretation, which held that Jacobinism and Bolshevism constitute a single myth.'[29] Behind the incarnation of *The Prince* in Jacobinism, its incarnation in Bolshevism and Leninism is thus apparent, although never openly expressed. If we are dealing here with a historicist reading, we must recognize that it is not dominated by the category of contemporaneity but rather by a complex play of different temporalities whose *décalage* with respect to the path of history is measured in terms of anticipation and delay.[30]

We can now turn to Gramsci's reading of *The Prince*. It is not a close reading. The letter of Machiavelli's text never, or almost never, appears. Gramsci's reading is instead a sketch that outlines an encounter with the great traditions of reading *The Prince* on the one hand, and on the other, with Gramsci's own contemporaries, particularly Croce, Russo, and a few others. Gramsci offers a series of observations on *The Prince* which can be synthesized into three points:

- the relation with the interpretative tradition
- the relation of *The Prince* to Machiavelli's overall work
- the internal structure of *The Prince*

In terms of the first point, Gramsci excludes as inadequate the readings of *The Prince* both in terms of Machiavellianism and in terms of democracy. In particular, with respect to the latter interpretative thread, Gramsci writes:

> It seems that Machiavelli's intentions in writing *The Prince* were more complex and even more 'democratic' than they would be according to the 'democratic' interpretation.[31]

The second point concerns the way in which *The Prince* must be read in the context of Machiavelli's total corpus. The *Florentine Histories* must be read as 'an analysis of the real Italian and European conditions from which arises the immediate needs contained in *The Prince*'.[32] As for *The Art of War*, Gramsci agrees with Russo that this work compliments *The Prince*. He also shares with Russo the following view on the relation between *The Prince* and the *Discourses on Livy*:

> In the *Prolegomena*, Russo makes *The Prince* the treatise of dictatorship (a moment of authority and the individual), and the *Discourses*, the [treatise of] hegemony or consensus alongside authority and force. This observation is certainly correct. So is the observation that there is no opposition in principle between principality and republic, which are rather the hypostasis of two moments of authority and universality.[33]

Finally, Gramsci makes extremely precise comments on the internal structure of *The Prince*. Just as he emphasizes the deep connection between *The Prince* and Machiavelli's other key works, he also underscores the link between the analytic chapters and the rhetorical conclusion. There is no discontinuity between the 'logical rigour' and the 'scientific detachment' of the first twenty-five chapters and the final conclusion:

> It seems that all the 'logical' labour is nothing but the self-reflection of the people, an internal reasoning, which is done in the popular consciousness and has its conclusion in an immediate, passionate cry. That is why the epilogue of *The Prince* is not something extrinsic, something 'applied' from the outside, something rhetorical, but something that must be explained as a necessary element of the work, or rather as the element that allows its true light to reverberate over the entire work.[34]

We now come to Gramsci's reading of *The Prince*. The heart of his reading consists in the interpretive thesis that *The Prince* is an intervention in the Italian conjuncture ('in the politics and history of his country') in order to affirm the necessity of founding a nation-state that could only have the characteristics of absolute monarchy. Its utopian character derives from the fact that 'the "prince" does not exist in historical reality', but was 'a pure doctrinal abstraction'.[35] However, Machiavelli did not present the 'utopia' of 'an already constituted state ['uno stato già costituito'] ... with all its functions and constituted elements',[36] but instead, a text capable of arousing action, which describes the necessary means for reaching a determinate end. In this sense, according to Gramsci, *The Prince* has the characteristics of a political manifesto: its style aims to push the revolutionary class of the time into action.

In this way, it is a democratic intervention. Machiavelli's ferocity is turned against the feudal elements, the nobles, and the clergy, against the feudal anarchy that prevents the foundation of a nation-state. It is in this sense that Gramsci reads the example of the Duke Valentino (Cesare Borgia): 'The Prince must put an end to feudal anarchy: this is what the Duke Valentino has done in Romagna, relying on the productive classes of merchants and peasants.'[37] As a democratic intervention, *The Prince* should also be understood as advocating a reform of the militia, which must provide the prince with the military instrument for setting up the new state:

> Given the military-dictatorial character of the head of State, as is required in a period of struggle for the foundation and consolidation of a new power, the indication of class contained in *The Art of War* should also be understood for the general state structure: if the urban classes want to put an end to internal disorder and external anarchy, they must rely on the peasants as a mass, constituting a secure and loyal armed force of an absolutely different kind from mercenary armies.[38]

Even errors of a military nature, such as undervaluing the importance of artillery, are due to the fact that Machiavelli's centre of interest, even in *The Art of War*, is political and not technical-militaristic: '[H]e thinks especially about infantry, whose masses can be enlisted with a political action.'[39]

Hence, the intervention in the Italian conjuncture is a democratic intervention but deeper and more complex than what the democratic (*democraticistiche*) interpreters of Machiavelli want. And this complexity is due to the 'double perspective of political and state action':

> Different degrees in which the double perspective can be presented, from the most elementary to the most complex, corresponding to the double nature of the Machiavellian centaur, beast and man, force and consent, authority and

hegemony, violence and civility, the individual and universal moment ('Church' and 'State', agitation and propaganda, tactics and strategy, etc.).[40]

In the few pages that Gramsci devotes to Machiavelli, the famous 'Machiavelli puzzle' postulated by Croce, of finding the true Machiavelli among an endless succession of 'new' ones, seems to have been completely solved. He identifies a precise unity in Machiavelli's work in general, and in *The Prince* in particular: they constitute a democratic intervention in Italian history and politics, where 'democratic' means the construction of a unitary State, an absolute monarchy[41] that, with force and the consent of the popular masses, destroys the feudal elements of Italian society at the time. The book is written 'for everyone and no one':

> It is written for a hypothetical 'man of providence' who could manifest himself, as Valentine or other *condottieri* manifested themselves, from nothing, without dynastic tradition, by their exceptional military qualities.[42]

Althusser's Reading of Machiavelli

We now can take up Althusser's reading of Machiavelli. I think its main phases are the following:
- the 1962 course
- *Machiavelli and Us* (1972–5)
- Althusser's new confrontation with Gramsci (1977–8)
- the writings of the 1980s

For reasons of space, it will not be possible for me to follow the historical evolution of Althusser's reading. I will limit myself to *Machiavelli and Us*, the most extensive and self-contained text treating of the Florentine secretary, referring only where necessary to the other texts.

The reading Althusser presents in this text is not limited to *The Prince*, as in the 1962 course, but is an interpretation of the unity of *The Prince* and the *Discourses*. The reading of Gramsci, which in the 1962 course was simply recalled in passing,[43] becomes the explicit starting point and occupies the entire first chapter. Here we find Althusser's reflections on the 'gripping, but elusive' ('saissant mais insaisissable'),[44] character of Machiavelli, which pertains to both politics and philosophy. On the philosophical plane, it is owing to the fact that Machiavelli is a theorist of the beginning: 'the beginning [that] is ... rooted in the essence of a thing, since it is the beginning of *this* thing. It affects all its determinations, and does not fade with the moment, but *endures* with the thing itself [emphasis in the original].' However, Althusser adds, before the thing begins, 'there was something else, but nothing of it'.[45] The beginning is symbolized by the formula of the *verità effettuale* (effectual truth)[46] that pushes the earlier discourses into the sphere of the imaginary. In this sense, Machiavelli's silence concerning the political theories of Aristotle, Cicero, and Christianity is tantamount to a declared rupture, according to Althusser: 'It was enough for Machiavelli to speak differently to denounce the imaginary character of the reigning ideology in political matters.'[47]

But it is in the political field that Machiavelli provides the greatest surprise. In order to illustrate the point in all its force, Althusser returns to Gramsci. Machiavelli is not simply the thinker who introduced the question of the state, as Hegel thought:

> The state that Machiavelli expects from The Prince ... is not the state in general (corresponding 'to its concept') but a historically determinate type of state, required by the conditions and exigencies of nascent capitalism: a *national* state.[48]

Thus, Machiavelli becomes the thinker who poses the political problem of the constitution of the nation-state. This is constituted neither spontaneously nor by decree but is the outcome of a class struggle determined by a series of pre-existing economic, geographical, historical, linguistic, and cultural factors, as also by international relations of force. Gramsci claims that *The Prince* is a revolutionary-utopian text because we are dealing with 'a theoretical text ... affected in its modality and dispositive by political practice'.[49] In this sense, Althusser can say that Machiavelli is the first theorist of the conjuncture: he does not generally think about the question of national unity but starts from the existing determinants and circumstances, not simply in order to enumerate them but rather to transform them into forces. As Gramsci argued, the effectual reality is not a static reality but the operation of relations between forces that change the meaning of a project. The problem then becomes to determine which political practice can serve to group together the positive forces of the Italian conjuncture.

According to Althusser, this interpretation implies a 'vacillation' in the status of the theoretical propositions undermined by political practice. In fact, the theoretical space has no subject, while the space of political practice has no meaning except in terms of its subject, the new prince. The theoretical analysis of the conjuncture thus carries meaning if it allows the identification of an 'empty place' in which the action of the 'subject' (*sujet*) can be inserted.

(Owing to the ambiguity of the term *sujet*, Althusser proposes to replace it with *agent*. Gramsci had designated it as 'will', *volontà*.) Althusser adds:

> I say empty, to mark the vacillation of *theory* at this point: because it is necessary for this place to be *filled*—in other words, for the individual or party to have the capacity to become sufficiently strong to count among the forces, and strong enough again to rally the allied forces, to become the principal force and overcome the others. (Emphasis in the original)[50]

However, there is not only one empty space but two, as Gramsci's definition of *The Prince* as a manifesto indicates: the second empty space is the one through which the text stages this political practice. In order to be politically effective, the text *'must be inscribed somewhere in the space of this political practice'* (emphasis in the original).[51] The manifesto must declare itself to be partisan and gain more partisans: in other words, Machiavelli treats his text as a means of transferring political practice into the realm of ideology. In order to do this, he constructs a topological space and fixes the viewpoint of the people as the viewpoint from which he writes his text. In this sense, we can claim that Machiavelli is a theorist neither of tyranny nor of the state in general but rather of the popular state. However, if the viewpoint is that of the people, the text is addressed to the prince. This implies the rejection of the democratic reading that identifies the viewpoint of the text with the addressee: the reflection of the people on itself, to which Gramsci refers, does not transform the consciousness of the people into a political force but prepares for the advent of the prince.

Turning to an analysis of the *Discourses on Livy*, Althusser maintains some distance from a republican reading of this work. Machiavelli's main interest in the *Discourses* is Rome, but not insofar as it is a model of a republic: 'Rome is *par excellence* the observable objective experience of the foundation of a state that endured.'[52] What interests him about Rome is its foundation, a republic founded by a king:

> Machiavelli's utopianism does not consist in resort to Rome as the prop for a moral ideology that is required in the present. It consists in recourse to Rome as *guarantee* or *rehearsal* for a *necessary* task, whose concrete conditions of possibility are, however, *impossible* to define. (Emphasis in the original)[53]

It is not an ideological or political utopia but a theoretical one, insofar as it attempts to think out the conditions of possibility of an 'impossible task, to think the unthinkable'.[54] In this effort, Machiavelli found himself 'engaged in forms of thought without any precedent' ('engagé dans des formes de pensée à peuprès sans précedent').[55]

In his third chapter, 'The Theory of the "New Prince"', Althusser shows the profound unity of *The Prince* and the *Discourses on Livy*. They are united by the common project of considering the constitution of a nation-state: by Althusser's interpretation, Rome, in Machiavelli, outlines à la cantonade a theory of the foundation and duration of a new state. In particular, Roman history is instructive as regards the relation between laws and conflict:

> In his theory of the class struggle as the origin of the laws that limit it, Machiavelli adopts the viewpoint of the people.[56]

From this premise, Althusser derives the following thesis: in the conflict between the people and the nobles, 'the king takes the people's side by decreeing laws'.[57]

This does not mean, however, that one must be alone in order to found a state. Gramsci had spoken of the unity of *The Prince* and the *Discourses* by thinking of them under the categories of dictatorship (on the individual plane) and hegemony (on the universal plane). Althusser thinks of them through the categories of absolute beginning and duration—that is, the moment of the 'settlement of laws' and 'emergence from solitude', to which the metaphors of foundation and of taking root correspond: 'So long as their distinctiveness is borne in mind, these two moments can help us to think the difference between *The Prince* and the *Discourses*—in other words, their non-difference, their profound unity.'[58] Machiavelli is thus neither a monarchist nor a republican. His only aim is to define the theoretical space of the object of *The Prince*.

Turning to *The Prince*, Althusser more or less repeats the analysis of his 1962 course,[59] this time explicitly citing Gramsci:

> Machiavelli can set up his political problem only on condition of *making a clean sweep of existing feudal forms as incompatible with the objective of Italian unity.* (Emphasis in the original)[60]

In other words, the account of principalities in the first eleven chapters of *The Prince* is not neutral but rather excludes several types of principalities—tyrannies, hereditary principalities, ecclesiastical principalities—as not being functional for his project. Republics are not included in Machiavelli's list because they are urban forms of feudalism. All of these are excluded as possible foundations of the project; however, they are not excluded 'from the political field in which this unity must be accomplished', given that the body of the nation is not fixed in advance, is in part aleatory—the stake of a struggle whose borders are not assigned [*arrêtées*]—and because it is ultimately necessary to envisage annexation of territories with different languages and customs in order to embody the nation.[61]

To define the new principality is Machiavelli's point of departure. It is reliant on a double passage, of a man 'from private citizen to ruler' and of a region from 'geographical expression' to nation-state:[62] a double venture related to the encounter or non-encounter of *virtù* and *fortuna*. This is the crucial point of the theory, where, according to Althusser, politics presents itself in the form of a determinate absence, because Machiavelli 'leaves the names of the protagonists in this encounter *completely blank* [*laisse complètement en blanc*]; he provides them with no *identity*' (emphasis in the original).[63]

Therefore, the geographical space and individual are by definition unknown; hence, national unity cannot be accomplished by starting from the existing principalities. To Althusser, however, this seems to be a positive silence: the encounter will take place but outside of the existing principalities and states. The example of Cesare Borgia shows precisely that this 'starting from nothing' is attainable. There is in it a 'discrepancy [*décalage*] between the definite and indefinite, the necessary and the unforeseeable. This discrepancy, thought and unresolved by thought, is the presence of history and political practice in theory itself'.[64]

We can now examine Althusser's Chapter 4, 'The Political Practice of the New Prince', which treats of Machiavelli's discussion in Chapters 11–23 of *The Prince*. In this chapter, Althusser partially recasts and partially develops his 1962 course.[65] According to Althusser, at this point Machiavelli leaves aside the problem of pure beginning as 'inassignable' and assumes that things—the process of becoming the prince and becoming the state—have already begun. Althusser's argument focuses on two elements: the army and ideology. As for the army, Althusser claims that Machiavelli's theses are impressive in their consistency, incisiveness, and political acuteness. Like Gramsci, he maintains that these theses anticipate the Jacobins, as well as Clausewitz and Mao.[66] First, Machiavelli maintains that the army is the state apparatus par excellence: that is, he affirms the primacy of force over ideology and laws. Second, the army must be thought *sub specie politica*: in other words, Machiavelli maintains the primacy of politics over military technique. Third, the aforementioned primacy of force must be thought of under the aegis of the primacy of politics, 'the prince's popular and national politics'.[67] And finally, the prince must rely on his own army.

Here, Gramsci is again the fundamental point of reference for Althusser's interpretation. Althusser broadly repeats his analysis from the 1962 course of different types of troops as well as Gramsci's conclusions on the popular army, founded first on recruitment from the popular strata of town and country ('the blending of town and country'[68]) and secondly on reorganization based on the primacy of infantry over cavalry. These are profoundly revolutionary ideas: on the one hand, the armed campaign carries a political message against the feudal lords; on the other, the primacy of infantry over cavalry reverses the social hierarchies of the time. Here Althusser refers extensively to Gramsci in order to conclude that 'the men of the towns and countryside begin to become—learn to become—one and the same people'.[69] Thus, the army is necessary for the construction of the nation-state but not as a simple means to an external end. Recruitment makes the goal internal to the medium. 'The army', writes Althusser, 'can serve as a means to a political end only if it is already the realized form of the relevant politics.'[70] In other words, the army is not only a force available to the prince to reach national unity, it also creates consensus by acting on the minds of the soldiers: 'The military apparatus simultaneously exercises an ideological function.'[71]

Turning to the analysis of consensus in the Gramscian sense—that is, as ideology—Althusser divides the field of Machiavelli's treatment into religion and the image of the prince. The former, as Gramsci emphasized, is a dominant ideology of the masses ('without the support of ideology, no popular consent to the state'[72]), which the latter—that is, the representation of the prince—stands upon as a very particular ideological form. Althusser distances himself from Gramsci on this point by emphasizing, in the figure of the centaur, the splitting of the beast into force and fraud. The latter

> possesses no objective existence: it does not exist. If fraud is a way of governing, given that it has no existence, it can be employed only when it is based on laws or force ['en prenant appui sur les lois ou sur la force']. Fraud, then, is not a third form of government; it is government to the second degree, a manner of governing the other two forms of government: force and laws.[73]

However, this ideological politics must be subjected to the primacy of politics per se: that is, the prince must compose and control his image politically not by conforming to the spontaneous popular ideology in a demagogic way but by inserting himself, with his own political project, into that spontaneous ideology. In this sense, the thematization of fear without hate has a clear class meaning according to Althusser, because this hate is the hatred of the people against the nobles:

> The theory of fear without hatred is the theory of the political precondition for 'popular goodwill' towards the Prince. It is also, factually, an acknowledgement of the popular state's double function: the unity of coercion and popular consent that so struck Gramsci in Machiavelli.[74]

Machiavelli is therefore not a utopian thinker. Rather, in the way in which he thinks of the conditions of class and existence characterizing absolute monarchy, he thinks of the particular conjuncture and goes directly to the truth of the matter, with concepts that make him 'the greatest materialist philosopher in history'.[75]

Conclusion

At the end of my account, it should be clear that the starting point suggested by my title, to think of *The Prince* as being in tension between different or even opposed interpretations, is completely inadequate. Not only is there no opposition between Gramsci's and Althusser's readings; we can discern a strong continuity. Several years ago, Filippo Del Lucchese wrote that Althusser's true encounter with Machiavelli takes place in his writings on aleatory materialism, whereas in the earlier writings (above all in the 1962 course and *Machiavelli and Us*), we are confronted with a non-original reading that Del Lucchese, playing with Althusser's late terminology, calls 'the void of an encounter'.[76] As for Althusser's 'non-original' reading, Del Lucchese still has the merit of emphasizing Gramsci's importance, just as other authors have done in passing.

But by putting the problem in these terms, we lose a crucial perspective, namely that Althusser's encounter with Machiavelli takes place entirely through Gramsci:[77] if we find something new in his reading of Machiavelli, this *novum* must be sought within his work on Gramsci.[78] In one of the two autobiographical writings dedicated to Machiavelli in 1985, and published in the journal *Lignes* with the title 'The Only Materialist Tradition', Althusser recognizes this debt. After observing that Machiavelli's thought must be read as the project of the 'historical realization of Italian national unity',[79] he adds: 'Gramsci has seen this extremely well, although he has blundered in everything else.'[80] Here, Althusser acknowledges one important debt but dismisses the rest, which in my view leads critics astray. Actually, Althusser's debt to Gramsci is much larger, although certainly animated by this key point.

The 1970s course, as well as the 1962 course, has as its fundamental interpretative framework the question of the unitary nation-state. This allows Althusser, on the basis of Gramsci, to reject the opposition between monarchy and republicanism for a much deeper and more complex democratic reading: the absolute monarchy that is allied to the people against the feudal elements of society. And yet Althusser fully accepts the designation of *The Prince* as a manifesto and a utopia in Gramsci's sense: that is, not as a yearning for an ideal state but as a project of political intervention. Moreover, the entire reading that Althusser proposes of the principalities, armies, and the political practice of the prince is nothing but the full development of what Gramsci had only sketched out with reference to the analytic chapters and rhetorical conclusion of *The Prince*: the entire analysis is geared to constructing the strategy of the new prince in the Italian conjuncture. Althusser also accepts Gramsci's key reflection on the army and on the primacy of politics over the military element, and the anticipation of Jacobinism in the merging of city and country, just as he extends the logic of Gramsci's argument regarding the political value of infantry over cavalry. Moreover, he accepts Gramsci's interpretation of the political practice of the prince and of religion as an all-pervasive ideological factor of the times, as well as the two levels of force and consent on which the prince must act, and the theory of violence directed against the feudal world.

Even that is not all. If Gramsci's suggestion of the deep unity of *The Art of War* and *The Prince* is indeed taken up by Althusser, he also reads the unity of *The Prince* and the *Discourses* with the help of hints from Gramsci, as I have indicated earlier. In the 1977 text 'Machiavelli's Solitude', Althusser uses the Gramscian term 'dictatorship', making the debt explicit even from a terminological point of view.[81] There is thus no contradiction between a monarchic and a republican Machiavelli but rather a unity: in the *Discourses*, Machiavelli searches for the example of a state that lasts, a state founded by kings but capable of becoming popular.

Is Althusser's reading, then, a simple repetition of Gramsci's? Such a claim would probably be unjust because Gramsci's reading, while being extremely powerful, consists largely of hints. It would be more accurate to claim that Althusser grasps the profound internal logic of Gramsci's interpretation and develops it as far as possible. In a certain sense, it could be said that Althusser, in his course from the 1970s, wrote the book on Machiavelli that Gramsci could not have written, drawing out all the analytic and synthetic conclusions that, certainly to us in retrospect, appear ineluctable: that does not mean they were such before they were drawn.

Having said that, some elements of originality in Althusser's reading should also be outlined. First of these is the encounter between *virtù* and *fortuna*: the occasion, the conjuncture, the element that in the 1962 course will come to be identified as an 'insoluble contradiction'[82] of Machiavelli's thought. In the 1970s course, and even more emphatically in the writings on aleatory materialism, it is precisely the impossibility of assigning a name and space to this beginning that constitutes one of the points of force in Machiavelli's political thought and what Althusser calls his philosophy. From the viewpoint of political theory, this point marks Machiavelli's alterity to subsequent political philosophy, with its theory of the accomplished fact, and to the state. He conceives of the fact in its unfolding ('compiersi'); he can also admit the violence of the birth of the state and the radically aleatory character of its boundaries, what Althusser in 'Machiavelli's Solitude' calls 'primitive political accumulation'.[83]

This element of the aleatory has some implications for the concept of the modern prince, which was clearly the guiding force behind both Gramsci's and Althusser's readings. If for Gramsci the modern prince is a historical given,[84] a factor necessary in order to think strategy, for Althusser it is subjected to the same contingency that characterizes the birth of the state: he cannot renounce the figure of the fox, which introduces the element of fear and cunning. Here Althusser reverts to Machiavelli's originary formulation in *The Prince*, with epistemological consequences. Gramsci claims that *The Prince* is 'a self-reflection of the people':[85] 'Machiavelli himself becomes the people, is confused with the people: not with a people "generically" understood, but with the people that Machiavelli has convinced by his earlier discussion, of which he becomes and experiences the consciousness and expression, feels himself.'[86]

What Gramsci thinks through the categories of 'myth' and 'concrete fantasy',[87] the fusion of ideology and science on the one hand and the prince and people on the other, Althusser thinks through the category of the gap: the gap between science and ideology and between the prince and the people.[88] The gap means that the theory must be inscribed in both the political and the ideological conjunctures but cannot enter the popular consciousness, transparent to itself. So too the prince must implement a popular politics but cannot identify himself with the people; rather, the people will be made such by the political practice of the prince: 'in the army common to them, the men of the towns and countryside begin to become—learn to become—one and the same people'.[89] It is here, in the definition of these 'gaps', that Althusser finds his Machiavelli, the Machiavelli of the material encounter and of the 'fox': the Machiavelli Althusser will insist on in his writings of the 1980s.[90]

I want to emphasize forcefully, one last time, that this unorthodox reading cannot be unearthed simply from Machiavelli's text. In other words, what Althusser says at the beginning of the 1970s course is not true, namely that he reads Machiavelli as if he were contemporary to Machiavelli's first readers. Althusser's Machiavelli is the Machiavelli of Gramsci. If one wants to see Althusser's work in the correct light, one must start from the work internal to this reading: work that perhaps allows us today to read Gramsci in a different way, reactivating the force suppressed, by reading Gramsci after Althusser.[91]

Notes

* This chapter has been translated by Dave Mesing.
1. Antonio Gramsci, *Note sul Machiavelli: sulla politica e sullo stato moderno*, ed. Palmiro Togliatti and Felice Platone (Turin: Einaudi, 1949).
2. Antonio Gramsci, *Quaderni del carcere*, ed. Valentino Gerratana, 4 vols. (Turin: Einaudi, 1975).
3. Antonio Gramsci, *Quaderni del carcere*, ed. Giuseppe Cospito, Gianni Francioni, and Fabio Frosini (Rome: Fondazione Gramsci, 2007).
4. See also Louis Althusser, *Montesquieu: La politique et l'histoire* (Paris: PUF, 1959), 12, and especially Louis Althusser, 'Soutenance d'Amiens', in *La solitude de Machiavel*, ed. Yves Sintomer (Paris: PUF, 1998), 199–232, 205.
5. Louis Althusser, 'Machiavel' (1962), in *Politique et histoire de Machiavel à Marx* (Paris: Seuil, 2006), 207–54.
6. Louis Althusser, *Machiavel et nous*, in Althusser, *Écrits philosophiques et politiques*, 2 vols., ed. François Matheron (Paris: Stock/IMEC, 1994–5), 2:42–168.
7. Louis Althusser, 'La solitude de Machiavel', in *La solitude de Machiavel*, 311–24.
8. MS. ALT2.A57-01.09, Althusser Archive, IMEC.
9. MS. ALT2.A26-05.06/07, Althusser Archive, IMEC.
10. Louis Althusser, 'Le courant souterrain du matérialisme de la rencontre', in *Écrits philosophiques et politiques*, 1:539–79.
11. Louis Althusser, 'L'unique tradition matérialiste', *Lignes* 18 (1993), 71–119.
12. MS. ALT2.A29-06-07, Althusser Archive, IMEC.
13. Gramsci, *Quaderni*, ed. Gerratana, Notebook 13, §13, 1572. All references to this edition are by notebook, section, and page number: for example, Q6, §50, 723. Passages cited in translation only. All Gramsci translations are by Dave Mesing for this article.
14. Ibid.
15. Ibid.

16. Ibid.
17. Q6, §50, 723.
18. Antonio Gramsci, *Lettere dal carcere 1926–1937*, ed. A. Santucci (Palermo: Sellerio, 1996), 133.
19. Q13, §16, 1578; earlier in Q8, §84, 990.
20. Q3, §16, 760.
21. Q13, §1, 1559.
22. Ibid.
23. G. Liguoiri and P. Voza, eds., *Dizionario 1926–1937* (Rome: Carrocci, 2009), 352.
24. Q13, §13, 1575.
25. Ibid.
26. Letter of 21 April 1932: Gramsci, *Lettere dal carcere*, 571.
27. Q5, §127, 657.
28. Q10, §30, 1271.
29. Liguori and Voza, eds., *Dizionario*, 351.
30. Louis Althusser, 'L'objet du *Capital*', in Louis Althusser, Jacques Rancière, Pierre Macherey, Étienne Balibar and Roger Establet, *Lire le Capital*, 245–418 (Paris: PUF, 1996 [1965]), 291.
31. Q14, §33, 1691.
32. Q13, §13, 1573.
33. Q8, §48, 970.
34. Q13, §1, 1556.
35. Ibid. Cf. Q25, §7, 2292: '[E]ven Machiavelli's *Prince* was, in its own way, a utopia.'
36. Q5, §127, 657.
37. Q13, §13, 1572; earlier in Q1, §10, 9.
38. Q13, §13, 1572–3; earlier in Q1, §10, 9.
39. Ibid.; earlier in Q1, §10, 9.
40. Q13, §14, p.1576; earlier in Q8, §84, 990.
41. '[F]orm of popular regiment ... that ... supported the bourgeoisie against the nobles and against the clergy': Q13, §25, 1618.
42. Ibid.
43. Althusser, 'Machiavel', 196.
44. Louis Althusser, *Machiavel et nous* (Paris: Tallandier, 2009), 38; Louis Althusser, *Machiavelli and Us*, ed. François Matheron, tr. Gregory Elliott (London: Verso, 1999), 6.
45. Althusser, *Machiavelli and Us*, 6; *Machiavel et nous*, 39.
46. *Pr.*, ch. 15: Machiavelli, *Tutte le opere*, ed. Mario Martelli (Florence: Sansoni, 1971), 280.

47. Althusser, *Machiavelli and Us*, 8; *Machiavel et nous*, 41.
48. Althusser, *Machiavelli and Us*, 10 (translation modified); *Machiavel et nous*, 44.
49. Althusser, *Machiavelli and Us*, 17 (translation modified); *Machiavel et nous*, 54.
50. Althusser, *Machiavelli and Us*, 20; *Machiavel et nous*, 58.
51. Althusser, *Machiavelli and Us*, 22; *Machiavel et nous*, 60.
52. Althusser, *Machiavelli and Us*, 48; *Machiavel et nous*, 99.
53. Althusser, *Machiavelli and Us*, 51; *Machiavel et nous*, 104.
54. Althusser, *Machiavelli and Us*, 52; *Machiavel et nous*, 104.
55. Ibid.
56. Althusser, *Machiavelli and Us*, 59; *Machiavel et nous*, 114.
57. Ibid.
58. Althusser, *Machiavelli and Us*, 65; *Machiavel et nous*, 122.
59. Cf. Althusser, 'Machiavel', ch. 1 ('Le point de départ: la revue des principautés'), 207–16.
60. Althusser, *Machiavelli and Us*, 70; *Machiavel et nous*, 121.
61. Althusser, *Machiavelli and Us*, 72–3; *Machiavel et nous*, 132.
62. Althusser, *Machiavelli and Us*, 73; *Machiavel et nous*, 133.
63. Althusser, *Machiavelli and Us*, 76; *Machiavel et nous*, 137.
64. Althusser, *Machiavelli and Us*, 80; *Machiavel et nous*, 143.
65. See also Althusser, 'Machiavel', ch. 2 ('L'armée et la politique'), 217–20.
66. Here it is interesting to compare the 1962 course, where we find the name of Lenin instead of Mao (219).
67. Althusser, *Machiavelli and Us*, 84; *Machiavel et nous*, 149.
68. Althusser, *Machiavelli and Us*, 87; *Machiavel et nous*, 153.
69. Althusser, *Machiavelli and Us*, 87; *Machiavel et nous*, 154.
70. Althusser, *Machiavelli and Us*, 89; *Machiavel et nous*, 156.
71. Ibid.
72. Althusser, *Machiavelli and Us*, 91; *Machiavel et nous*, 158.
73. Althusser, *Machiavelli and Us*, 95; *Machiavel et nous*, 165.
74. Althusser, *Machiavelli and Us*, 101; *Machiavel et nous*, 173.
75. Althusser, *Machiavelli and Us*, 103; *Machiavel et nous*, 176.
76. Filippo Del Lucchese, 'Sul vuoto di un incontro: Althusser lettore di Machiavelli', in *Rileggere il Capitale. La lezione di Louis Althusser*, Part 2, ed. Maria Turchetto (Milan: Mimesis, 2007), 31–49.
77. This point was also emphasized by Emmanuel Terray: 'It seems to me that two roads could have led Althusser to Machiavelli: the study of the relationships between politics and philosophy of the eighteenth century in France, which Althusser had considered making the subject of a thesis,

and his reading of Gramsci.' Emmanuel Terray, 'An Encounter: Althusser and Machiavelli', tr. Antonio Callari and David Ruccio, in *Postmodern Materialism and the Future of Marxist Theory*, ed. Antonio Callari and David Ruccio (Hanover, NH: Wesleyan University Press, 1997), 255–77, 258.
78. In this sense, the claim by Adam Holden and Stuart Elden seems to be important. They refer to Althusser's 'neo-Gramscian' reading: '"It Cannot Be a Real Person, a Concrete Individual": Althusser and Foucault on Machiavelli's Political Technique', *Borderlands* 4, no. 2 (2005), 2.
79. Althusser, 'L'unique tradition matérialiste', 101.
80. Ibid.
81. '[T]he first moment of the State ... is ... the monarchic, or dictatorial moment': Althusser, *Machiavelli and Us*, 120; 'La solitude de Machiavel', 316.
82. Althusser, 'Machiavel', 233.
83. Althusser, *Machiavelli and Us*, 125; 'La solitude de Machiavel', 320.
84. 'This organism is already given from historical development and the political party': Q13, §1, 1558.
85. Q13, §1, 1556.
86. Ibid.
87. Q13, §1, 1555–6.
88. See Terray, 'An Encounter: Althusser and Machiavelli', 257–7.
89. Althusser, *Machiavelli and Us*, 87; *Machiavel et nous*, 154.
90. See my chapter 'La storia come "revoca permanente del fatto compiuto"', in *La varia natura, le molte cagioni: studi su Machiavelli*, ed. Riccardo Caporali (Cesena: Il Ponte vecchio, 2007), 125–40.
91. Frosini's recently proposed reading of Gramsci moves in this direction: Fabio Frosini, *Da Gramsci a Marx: ideologia, verità, politica* (Rome: Derive Approdi, 2009).

The Contributors

Thomas Berns teaches political philosophy and Renaissance philosophy at the Université Libre de Bruxelles. A philosopher of politics, laws, and norms in the broad sense, he is the author of (among other volumes) *Violence de la loi à la Renaissance* (2000), *Souveraineté, droit et gouvernementalité* (2005), *Gouverner sans gouverner: Une archéologie politique de la statistique* (2009), *Du courage: Une histoire philosophique* (co-authored, 2010), and *La guerre des philosophes* (2019). His current work focuses on new forms of normativity.

Guido Cappelli has a PhD from the University of Messina and Milan 'Sacro Cuore'. He is Associate Professor of Italian Studies at the University of Naples 'L'Orientale'. He has previously worked at the Autonomous University of Barcelona, the Carlos III University of Madrid, and the University of Extremadura. Besides several papers in academic reviews, his publications include, among others, a critical annotated edition of Giovanni Pontano's *De principe* (2003) and the monograph *Maiestas: Politica e pensiero politico nella Napoli aragonese* (2016).

Prasanta Chakravarty is Associate Professor of English, University of Delhi, and editor of the web journal *Humanities Underground*. His most recent work is *The Creature: In Power and Pain* (2021). His other works include *Like Parchment in the Fire: Literature and Radicalism in the English Civil War* (2006), a monograph on Early Modern radical heretic culture; *The Opulence of Existence: Essays on Aesthetics and Politics* (2016), a collection of essays on literary forms and our political predicament; and *Time, Doubt and Wonder in the Humanities: Between the Tick and the Tock* (2019). He has edited two critical anthologies: *Shrapnel Minima, Writings from Humanities Underground* (2014); and *Populism and Its Limits: After Articulation* (2020). Another edited volume, *Assured Self, Restive Self: Encounters with Crisis* (2022) is forthcoming.

Swapan Chakravorty (1954–2021) was the first Kabiguru Rabindranath Tagore Distinguished Professor in the Humanities at Presidency University, Kolkata. He was previously Professor of English, Jadavpur University; Director General of the National Library of India, Kolkata; and Secretary and Curator of Victoria Memorial

Hall, Kolkata. He has contributed significantly to the fields of book history and Early Modern literature and culture. His publications include *Society and Politics in the Plays of Thomas Middleton* (1996) and the co-edited volumes *Print Areas: Book History in India* (2004), *Moveable Type: Book History in India* (2008), *New Word Order: Transnational Themes in Book History* (2011), and *Founts of Knowledge* (2015).

Sukanta Chaudhuri is Professor Emeritus in the Department of English, Jadavpur University, where he was founding Director of the School of Cultural Texts and Records. He is a Corresponding Fellow of the British Academy. His monographs include *Renaissance Pastoral and Its English Developments* (1989), *Translation and Understanding* (1999), and *The Metaphysics of Text* (2010). Among his edited volumes are the Third Arden edition of *A Midsummer Night's Dream* (2017), *Pastoral Poetry of the English Renaissance* (2 vols., 2016–18), and *The Cambridge Companion to Rabindranath Tagore* (Cambridge University Press, 2020). He was Chief Co-Ordinator of the Tagore online variorum *Bichitra* and has translated widely between English, Bengali and Italian. He also works in the fields of urban studies and digital humanities.

Supriya Chaudhuri is Professor of English (Emerita) at Jadavpur University. She writes and researches on Renaissance literature, cultural history, modernism, and the history of ideas. Her recent publications include *Religion and the City in India* (edited, 2022), *Commodities and Culture in the Colonial World* (co-edited, 2018) and chapters in *Blind Spots of Knowledge in Shakespeare and His World*, ed. S. Mukherji (2019); *The Cambridge History of Travel Writing*, ed. N. Das and T. Youngs (Cambridge University Press, 2019); *Eastern Resonances in Early Modern England*, ed. C. Gallien and L. Niayesh (2019); and *The Cambridge Companion to Rabindranath Tagore*, ed. Sukanta Chaudhuri (2020).

Jean-Louis Fournel is Professor of Italian Renaissance History and Culture at the Université Paris 8 and former Dean of the Nouveau Collège d'Études Politiques. He has published several papers on the political thought of the Italian Renaissance, the history of Italian republics, and the history of rhetoric. With Jean-Claude Zancarini, he has published French translations with commentary of texts by Savonarola (*Sermons, écrits politiques et pièces du procès*, 1993), Machiavelli (*Le Prince/De principatibus*, 2000 and 2014), and Guicciardini (*Ricordi/Avertissements politiques*, 1988; *Histoire d'Italie*, 2 vols., 1996; *Écrits politiques*, 1997). His more recent books are, with J.-C. Zancarini, *La politique de l'expérience: Savonarole, Guicciardini et le républicanisme florentin* (2002), *La Grammaire de la république: langages de la politique chez Francesco Guicciardini (1483–1540)* (2009), and *Machiavel: Une vie en guerres* (2020); also *Idées d'empire* *en Espagne et en Italie du XIVe au XVIIe siècles* (ed. with Françoise Crémoux, 2011) and *La cité du soleil et les territoires des hommes. Le savoir du monde chez Campanella* (2012).

Victoria Kahn is Katharine Bixby Hotchkis Professor of English and Professor of Comparative Literature at the University of California, Berkeley. She is the author of *Rhetoric, Prudence and Skepticism in the Renaissance* (1985), *Machiavellian Rhetoric: From the Counter-Reformation to Milton* (1994), *Wayward Contracts: The Crisis of Political Obligation in England, 1640–1674* (2004), *The Future of Illusion: Political Theology and Early Modern Texts* (2014), and *The Trouble with Literature* (2020), based on her Clarendon Lectures.

Christopher Lynch is Professor Emeritus of Political Science at Carthage College. He earned his BA from St. John's College, Annapolis, and his MA and PhD degrees from the University of Chicago's Committee on Social Thought. He has held visiting appointments at Boston College, the University of Dallas Rome campus, and the University of Chicago. His translation and interpretation of Machiavelli's *The Art of War* was published in 2003. He has co-edited (with Jonathan Marks) *Principle and Prudence in Western Political Thought* (2016), and has recently completed *Machiavelli on War*, a book on war and foreign affairs in Machiavelli's writings. He is currently preparing (with Nathan Tarcov) a translation of Machiavelli's fiction and poetry. He has published numerous articles and served as a senior advisor at the United States Department of State.

Doyeeta Majumder completed her first two degrees from Jadavpur University and her PhD from the University of St Andrews. After teaching at the University of Edinburgh and then at Shiv Nadar University, Delhi, she is now Assistant Professor of English at Jadavpur University. Her monograph *Tyranny and Usurpation: The New Prince and Lawmaking Violence in Early Modern England* appeared in 2019. She has translated *Il Principe* into Bengali (2012). Her research interests include Early Modern law and literature, political and juridical theory, and intellectual history.

Francesco Marchesi is research fellow and contract professor at the University of Pisa. He has been a postdoctoral fellow at the Fondazione Luigi Einaudi di Torino and the Scuola Normale Superiore di Pisa. He is the author of *Riscontro: Pratica politica e congiuntura storica in Niccolò Machiavelli* (2017), *Cartografia politica: Spazi e soggetti del conflitto in Niccolò Machiavelli* (2018), *Geometria del conflitto: Un esercizio di materialismo* (2020), and *Machiavellian Ontology* (forthcoming).

Vittorio Morfino is Full Professor of the History of Philosophy at the University of Milan-Bicocca, Director of the Master's Programme in the Critical Theory of Society, and Directeur de Programme at the Collège International de Philosophie.

He has been a visiting professor at the Universidade de São Paulo, the Université Paris 1 Panthéon-Sorbonne, the Université Bordeaux-Montaigne, and the Universidad Nacional de Cordoba. He is the author of *Il tempo e l'occasione: L'incontro Spinoza Machiavelli* (Milan, 2002, Paris, 2012), *Incursioni spinoziste* (2002), *Il tempo della moltitudine* (Rome, 2005, Paris, 2010, Madrid, 2013, Santiago, 2015), *Plural Temporality: Transindividuality and the Aleatory between Spinoza and Althusser* (2014), and *Genealogia di un pregiudizio. L'immagine di Spinoza in Germania da Leibniz a Marx* (2016). He is an editor of *Quaderni materialisti* and *Décalages. An Althusserian Journal*.

Christopher Nadon teaches at Claremont McKenna College, having previously been at the University of Chicago, the University of Kiev-Mohyla Academy, and Trinity College, Hartford, CT. He is the author of *Xenophon's Prince* (2001) and editor of *Secularism and Enlightenment: Essays on the Mobilization of Reason* (2013). He has published articles on religion and politics in Sarpi, Hobbes, Locke, Montesquieu, and Tocqueville, and on the theologico-political problem in the thought of Leo Strauss.

Paul A. Rahe holds the Charles O. Lee and Louise K. Lee Chair in the Western Heritage at Hillsdale College, and is Robert S. Mertz Visiting Scholar at Stanford University's Hoover Institution. He majored in History, the Arts and Letters at Yale University; read *Litterae Humaniores* at Wadham College, Oxford, on a Rhodes Scholarship; and returned to Yale to do his PhD in Ancient Greek History. He is the author of *Republics Ancient and Modern: Classical Republicanism and the American Revolution*, 2 vols. (1992), *Against Throne and Altar: Machiavelli and Political Theory under the English Republic* (Cambridge University Press, 2008), *Montesquieu and the Logic of Liberty* (2009), *Soft Despotism, Democracy's Drift: Montesquieu, Rousseau, Tocqueville, and the Modern Prospect* (2009), and four books on ancient Lacedaemon: *The Grand Strategy of Classical Sparta: The Persian Challenge* (2015), *The Spartan Regime: Its Character, Origins, and Grand Strategy* (2016), *Sparta's First Attic War: The Grand Strategy of Classical Sparta, 478–446 B. C.* (2019), and *Sparta's Second Attic War: The Grand Strategy of Classical Sparta, 446–418 B. C.* (2020).

Marcello Simonetta graduated from Roma La Sapienza and has a PhD from Yale University. He has taught in the US and in France. He currently lives in Florence, where he is a senior scholar with the Medici Archive project. He is the author of, among other books, a trilogy on the Medici family (translated into several languages) and most recently of *Tutti gli uomini di Machiavelli: Amici, nemici (e un'amante)* (2020). He is one of the editors of the forthcoming national edition of Machiavelli's Letters.

Yves Winter is Associate Professor of Political Science at McGill University, where he teaches the history of political thought and contemporary social and political theory. His research interests include Machiavelli, the history of Marxism, and critical theory. Thematically, his work focuses on questions of violence, political order, and the collective imagination, including the historical and discursive conditions that rationalize practices of violence and render them imaginable and justifiable. Most recently, he has published *Machiavelli and the Orders of Violence* (Cambridge University Press, 2018).

Index

Abensour, Miguel, 161*n*35
Abhinavagupta, 236
Achilles, 84, 202, 250
adaequatio, 5, 146, 149–54
Aeneas, 169, 186*n*1
Aesop, 204
Agamben, Giorgio, 16*n*7, 193, 204, 217*n*59
Agathocles, 58, 186*n*1, 227–8
Agricola, Rudolph, 245
Agrippa, Henry Cornelius, 205
Alamanni, Lodovico, 193
aleatory, the, 10, 307, 309, 311
Alexander, 59, 84–5, 186*n*1
Alternativ für Deutschland, 219
Althusser, Louis, 5–6, 15, 29, 30*n*19, 116, 1609*n*33, 242, 246, 248–9, 259*n*54, 260*n*62, 296–7, 303–12, 314*n*77, 315*n*78
Ammirato, Scipione, 86–7
Andrews, C. F., 293*n*16
Anglo, Sydney, 16*n*6, 55
animals and animal nature, 14, 100–3, 106–7, 113–16, 193–210, 210*n*3, 211*n*12, 216*n*47, 220, 250, 302–3, 308
Anselmi, Gian Mario, 155*n*3, 194, 210*n*7
Apuleius, 194, 196, 205, 211*n*9
Aquinas, Thomas, 153–4

Aragonesi, 129
Ardito, Alissa M., 46*n*4, 276*n*19
Arendt, Hannah, 17*n*16, 161*n*35, 289
Argelati, Filippo, 89*n*6
Argyropoulus, 79
Arias, Gino, 299
Ariosto, 14, 18*n*26, 194, 206, 217*n*52
aristocracy/nobility/*ottimi*, 37, 39, 97–9, 102–3, 114, 126–8, 131, 133, 168, 177, 251, 259*n*52, 282, 302, 306, 309, 313*n*41. See also *grandi*
Aristotle and Aristotelianism, 15, 22, 28, 31, 38, 60–1, 73, 78–9, 81–3, 91*n*26, 130, 135*n*16, 153–4, 216*n*47, 304
arms, one's own (*armi proprie*), 35, 43, 48*n*27, 49*n*32, 52*n*62, 83, 147, 269, 273. See also militia, citizens'
Armstrong, W. A., 67
Arundale, G. S., 284
Ascoli, Albert, 194
Ashok, Emperor, 292
astuzio fortunata, 127, 130
Athens, 77, 86, 259*n*52
Augsburg, 205
Augustine, 30*n*15, 78, 175, 237–8, 254*n*13
Aurelio, Diogo Pires, 138*n*38
Aurelius, Marcus, 65–6, 72*n*40, 76
Aurispa, Giovanni, 74, 88*n*2

Ausonius, 22
Austin, J. L., 236, 276*n*18
authority, 2, 5, 12, 58–61, 64–7, 87, 88*n*1, 110, 123, 128, 130, 169, 229–30, 237, 260*n*68, 289, 301–2
Azzolini, Giulio, 300

Bacon, Francis, 283, 288
Baggioni, Laurent, 275*n*15
Baglioni, Giampaolo, 151
Balestrieri, Giovanni G., 135*n*13
Baraballo, Giacomo, 194
Bárcenas, Alejandro, 160*n*32
Baron, Hans, 9, 31, 45*n*3, 62, 88*n*2
Barthas, Jérémie, 41–2, 51*n*54
Bartholomew's Day massacre, 55
Bartolus of Sassoferrato, 56–7, 128, 141*n*76
Bauman, R. A., 261*n*70
Bausi, Francesco, 134*nn*1–2, *n*6, 136*n*24, 137*n*31, 138*n*46, 170*n*1
Bayley, Charles Calvert, 45*n*2
Beame, Edmond M., 17*n*21, 255*n*19
Beauvoir, Simone de, 183
Becchi, Ricciardo, 25
Benito, Miguel Saralegui, 157*n*15
Benjamin, Walter, 205
Benner, Erica, 45*n*4, 92*n*37, 276*n*16
Bentivoglio family, 129
Berlin, Isaiah, 1, 283
Berns, Thomas, 5, 29*n*6, 30*n*15, *n*18
Beroaldo, Filippo, 194–5
Bessarion, Basilios, Cardinal, 74
Bhagavadgita, 291
Bible, 76, 169, 241, 254*n*13, 285–6, 291; Ezra, 75; Isaiah, 75, 78; Matthew, 213*n*22, 291 (Sermon on the Mount); Mark, 213*n*22; Luke, 213*n*22; Ephesians, 197; Romans, 254*n*13; 2 Peter, 213*n*22

Billaut, Alain, 213*n*19
Binswanger, Ludwig, 235
Birago, Lampugnino, 74
Black, Robert, 50*n*48, 155*n*5
Blumenberg, Hans, 232*n*22
Boas, George, 209
Boccaccio, Giovanni, 89*n*9, 194, 196, 211*n*9
Boccanegra, Simon, 129
Bock, Gisella, 17*n*21
Bodin, Jean, 8
Boer War, 281–2
Bohemianism, 283
Boiardo, Feltrino, 211*n*9
Boiardo, Matteo Maria, 194, 211*n*9
Bologna, 129, 163, 166, 172*n*18
Bolshevism, 300
Bonapartism, 10, 44
Bondanella, Julia Conaway and Peter, 173*n*27
Borgia, Cesare (Duke Valentino), 39, 50*n*45, 58, 139*n*60, 156*n*7, 186*n*1, 288, 294*n*31, 302, 307
Borrelli, Gianfranco, 159*n*24
Botero, Giovanni, 252
Botticelli, Sandro, 237
Bracciolini, Jacopo, 74
Bracciolini, Poggio, 62, 74, 88*n*5, 211*n*9
Brant, Sebastian, 205
Brechet, Christophe, 213*n*19
Brewster, Ben, 249
Briguglia, Gianluca, 135*n*16
Brinsley, John, 245
Bronfen, Elisabeth, 184
Brown, Alison, 204, 214*n*30, 215*n*42
Brown, Wendy, 189*n*32
Brunello, Anthony, 9
Bruni, Leonardo, 31, 38, 62, 73, 77–8, 90*n*22

Index

Bruno, Giordano, 196, 205, 209–10, 218*n*63
Brutus, Lucius Junius, 176–80, 186, 186*n*1
Brutus, Marcus Junius, 63
Buchanan, George, 61
Buddha, the, 291
Buondelmonti, Zanobi, 164
Burchiello (Domenico di Giovanni), 196
Burns, J. H., 66
Burton, Robert, 244, 257*n*42
Bussi, Giovanni de, 194, 211*n*9
Butler, Samuel, 48*n*23
Butters, Humphrey, 18*n*25, 47*n*13

Cadoni, Giorgio, 135*n*11, 136*n*24, 140*n*64, 141*n*78
Caesar. *See* Julius Caesar
Caferro, William P., 37, 49*n*38
Calanus, Pacovius, 282
calques, 268, 271
Cambiaso, Luca, 184
Cambridge School, 4, 9, 11, 64, 168
Cambyses, 85
Camillus, 251, 288–9
Cancellario/Chancery, Florentine, 31, 37, 42, 153, 163, 225, 242, 262, 265, 267, 269, 276*n*24
Canning, George, 240
Cappelli, Guido, 12, 135*n*20, 136*n*25, 138*n*41, *n*45
Capponi, Niccolò, 46*n*4
Cartari, Vincenzo, 217*n*52
Carthage/Carthaginians, 35
Casali, Andrea, 184
Casavecchia, Filippo, 163
Cassiani, Chiara, 207–8, 217*n*60
Cassirer, Ernst, 13, 15, 54, 68*n*3, 120*n*44, 219–26, 228–30, 231*n*17, 232*n*22, 234*n*38, 235–6, 238, 247, 259*n*59

Cassius, 63
Castiglione, Baldassare, 13
Castracani, Castruccio, 99, 186*n*1
Catani, Remo, 159*n*23
Catherine of France, Queen of England, 36
Cavalcanti, Bartolomeo, 163, 165
Cavallo, Jo Ann, 189*n*34
centaurs, 193, 196, 202, 204–5, 215*n*36, 250, 302–3, 308. *See also* Chiron
Cervantes, Miguel de, 235
Chakravarty, Prasanta, 3
Chakravorty, Swapan, 8, 17*n*19, 253*n*8, *n*10
Chamayou, Grégoire, 109, 114
Chancery. *See* Cancellario
Charles the Bold, 36–7
Charles V, Emperor, 87, 165
Charles VII of France, 36
Charles VIII of France, 34
Chaudhuri, Sukanta, 12
Chaudhuri, Supriya, 14, 211*n*9, 214*n*27
Chiron, 193, 196, 202–5, 250. *See also* centaurs
Christ, Jesus, 109, 197, 254*n*13, 290–1. *See also* Bible, Christianity
Christianity, 6, 15, 25, 44, 67, 76–9, 81, 197, 204, 237–8, 252, 256*n*31, 259*n*59, 260*n*68, 285, 291–2, 304
Chrysoloras, Manuel, 73
Church, Catholic, 34, 77, 165, 169, 277*n*28, 292, 303. *See also* Christianity, Pope/papacy
Churchill, Winston, 290
Cicero, 63, 74, 88*n*1, 124, 136*n*21, 194, 202–4, 214*n*34, 225–6, 238, 250, 304
Ciompi revolt, 32

Circe, 193, 196, 198–201, 207–9, 210n7, 220
cities/city-states, 10, 32–4, 39–40, 44, 47n15, 123–4, 265, 297, 308, 310
citizens/citizenship, 1–4, 12, 31–4, 37, 40, 43–4, 76, 100, 104, 110–12, 129–31, 133, 137n31, 181, 185. *See also* militia, citizens'
civic humanism, 31, 35, 37–8, 44
civil princes/principalities, 121, 125–33, 135n13, 136n22, 139*58, n*60, 140n64, 227–8, 271
civil war, 113, 123, 251
civitas, 23, 103–4, 110, 123, 128, 131
Clarke, Michelle T., 187n6, 189n34
Clarke, Paula C., 47n13
Claudius, Appius, 123
Clausewitz, Carl von, 307
clemency, 63, 103–5
Clement VII, Pope (Giulio de' Medici), 80, 87, 162–3, 165–6
clergy, 302, 313n41. *See also* Church, Pope/papacy
Clough, Cecil H., 31, 47n15
Coby, J. Patrick, 52n70
Cognac. *See* Holy League
Coleman, Janet, 253n9
Colonna, Fabrizio, 32–3, 42–3, 52n64, 229
Colonna, Francesco, 210n7, 211n9
Commodus, 57, 66
condottieri, 39, 169, 277n24, 303
Connell, William, 38, 50n46, 53n71, 159n25, 170n2, 256n34, n36
consensus, 126, 128, 130–3, 141n78, 301, 308
Conta, Maria-Elisabeth, 245
contado/contadini, 32–6, 39–41, 43–4, 47n15, 48n28, 302, 308, 310
Conti, Natale, 250

Cooper, Roslyn Pesman, 47n13, 50n50, 51n52, 52n68
Corella, Don Miguel de, 39, 50n45
Cornarius, Jonas, 74
Cosmo, Umberto, 247
Costalius, Petrus, 199
countrymen/countryside. *See contado/contadini*
Cox, Virginia, 225–6
Cranach, Lucas, 184
Croce, Benedetto, 15, 227, 244, 247, 258n45, 260n59, 263, 300, 303
Cuppano, Lucantonio, 86
Cyaxares, 85–7
Cyrus, 21, 73–6, 83–7, 186n1
da Bozzolo, Federico Gonzaga, 169

Dainotto, R., 134n5
Dante Alighieri, 62, 89n9, 96, 112, 170, 196, 198, 207, 238, 240, 242–3, 245
Davidson, A. B., 259n56, n59
de Grazia, Sebastian, 17n14, 189n34
De Keyser, Jeroen, 88n3
de Man, Paul, 235
de Sanctis, Francesco, 116
de Seyssel, Claude, 8
Decemviri, 123, 135n12
Del Lucchese, Filippo, 261n71, 309
Deleuze, Gilles, 30n19
della Porta, Giovanni, 196
della Rovere, Francesco Maria, 169
Derla, Luigi, 157n15
Derrida, Jacques, 16n7, 24, 246, 259n53
Descendre, Romain, 134n9, 136n22, n26, 137n31, 139n58, n60, 276n19
determinism, 3, 5, 21, 146, 148–9, 151–4, 157n15, 161n35, 208
Detienne, Marcel, 213n19

Index

Detmold, Christian E., 291
Di Rienzo, Eugenio, 140*n*67
Dido, 181
Dieci di Balia, 146–7
Dionisotti, Carlo, 50*n*50, 155*n*3, 211*n*9, 274*n*4
Dollimore, Jonathan, 58
Domenichi, Lodovico, 86
Domitian, 57
Doni, Francesco, 206, 217*n*52
Donne, John, 238–40, 255*n*20, 257*n*42
Donzelli, Carmine, 141*n*74
Doren, Alfred J., 216*n*50
Dostoevsky, Fyodor, 2
Dürer, Albrecht, 205, 237
dynastic rule. *See* hereditary rule

Eighty, Council of, 40
Einstein, Albert, 283
Eisenstein, Elizabeth L., 254*n*16
Elden, Stuart, 315*n*78
Elias, Norbert, 13, 119*n*35
Elshtain, Jean Bethke, 189*n*32
Emerton, Ephraim, 56
Engels, Friedrich, 15, 300
Enlightenment, 7, 14, 15, 223–4, 230, 231*n*17
Epictetus, 195, 211*n*12
Epicurus, 201. *See also* Lucretius
Erasmus, Desiderius, 13, 198, 238, 260*n*68
Erdoğan, Recep Tayyip, 219
Erwin, Séan, 48*n*22
Estensi, 129
ethics, 7, 12, 15, 68*n*3, 98–105, 110, 113–16, 196, 200, 222–4, 227–8, 231*n*1, 232*n*22, 245, 259*n*59, 281–4, 286, 289
Eugene IV, Pope, 77

experience, 1, 5, 24–8, 93*n*51, 145, 147–8, 151, 235–6, 250, 263, 265, 286–7, 298, 305

Facebook, 229
fascism, 7, 55, 219, 221–2, 224, 230
Fazion, Paolo, 194, 210*n*7
fear, political, 6, 13, 60, 82, 100, 107, 111–12, 126–7, 129, 226, 308–9, 311
Feingold, Mordechai, 218*n*63
Femia, Joseph V., 18*n*27
Ferdinand of Aragon, 34, 36, 298
Ferrara, 129, 206
feudalism, 11, 40, 69*n*17, 128, 297–9, 302–3, 306, 308, 310
Fichte, Johann Gottlieb, 15
Ficino, Marsilio, 78–82, 91*n*26, 216*n*47
Fido, Franco, 274*n*4
Figgis, John Neville, 72*n*43
Filelfo, Francesco, 74, 76, 88*n*5
Fitzgerald, F. Scott, 240
Florence/Florentines, 4, 12, 14, 18*n*25, 31–3, 36–44, 48*n*20, 50*n*45, 57, 51*n*52, 59, 62, 69*n*17, 73–4, 79–80, 82, 87, 99, 111, 116, 121, 123, 129, 134*n*4, 139*n*56, 146–7, 153, 162–4, 165–9, 201–2, 204, 240, 242, 276*n*23, 284, 297
Florence, Siege of, 87
Florentine Academy, 198, 207
Fontana, Alessandro, 158*n*19
Fontana, Benedetto, 259*n*59
force and forcing (*forzare/sforzare*), 1, 2, 5, 24–6, 28, 40, 85, 129, 151, 202–4, 225, 229–30, 289–90, 301–4, 307–8, 310
fortune/*fortuna*, 5–7, 15, 21–2, 24, 27–8, 34, 42, 73, 83, 86, 98–9, 103–4, 116, 127, 140*n*64, 146,

148–53, 180, 196–7, 201, 203, 205–7, 209, 216*n*52, 221, 225, 232*n*23, 241, 247, 251, 264, 266, 270, 286, 288–9, 307, 311
Foucauld, Michel, 30*n*19
founding a state, 2, 4, 21, 23, 25, 27, 38, 64–5, 82, 111, 116, 131, 138*n*48, 174–5, 177, 179–80, 185–6, 186*n*1, 226–7, 302, 305–6
Fournel, Jean-Louis, 13, 139*nn*55–56, 273*nn*2–3, 275*nn*12–13, 276*n*22, 277*n*27
Fowler, William, 255*n*20
France, 298
Francioni, Gianni, 296
François I of France, 35, 163, 165
freedom, 2–6, 10–12, 15, 30*n*18, 112, 131, 140*n*68, 141*n*77, 177–8, 183, 188*nn*21–22, 204, 208, 210, 250, 289–90. *See also* liberty
Frosini, Fabio, 140*n*61, *n*64, *n*68, 315*n*91

Gadamer, Hans-Georg, 240, 244
Gaeta, Franco, 155*n*3
Gaille, Marie, 16*n*9, 160*n*33
Gaisser, Julia Haig, 211*n*9
Galilei, Galileo, 220, 224
Gandhi, Gopalkrishna, 288
Gandhi, Mohandas Karamchand, 12, 281–5, 287–9, 291–2, 294*n*31
Gandini, Antonio, 86
Garin, Eugenio, 149, 151
Garver, Eugene, 18*n*23, 160*n*31
Gatti, Hilary, 218*n*63
Gelli, Giovan Battista, 198, 207–9
generosity (*generosità*), 102, 105, 166
Genoa, 129
Gentileschi, 184
Gentillet, Innocent, 8, 55, 239, 255*n*19, 283

Gerber, A., 218*n*63
Germany, 219
Gerratana, Valentino, 296
Geuna, Marco, 135*n*12
Ghibellines, 34, 81
Ghiglieri, Paolo, 158*n*19
Giambullari, Pierfrancesco, 207
Giberti, Gian Matteo, 166
Gilbert, Allan H., 36, 134*n*7, 135*n*16, 197
Gilbert, Felix, 49*n*40, 155*n*3
Ginzburg, Carlo, 153–4, 189*n*31
Giovanna, Queen of Naples, 181
Giovanni, Domenico di. *See* Burchiello
Gohory, Jacques Gohory, 2, 8, 273
Golding, Arthur, 199
Gombrich, Ernst, 120*n*44
Goodyer, Henry, 255*n*20
Gosse, Edmond, 255*n*20
governo popolare, 37–40, 51*n*52
Gracchi, 177, 251–2
Grafton, Anthony, 240
Gramsci, Antonio, 1, 10, 15, 40, 41, 43, 44, 240–2, 247–9, 256*n*28, 259*nn*56–59, 260*nn*59–60, 296–312, 315*n*91
grandezza, 91*n*31, 94*n*62, 291
grandi (primi cittadini), 37–41, 43, 123–4, 128, 131, 133. *See also* aristocracy/nobility
Greece/Greeks, 37, 59, 61, 74, 186, 268
Greek language and letters, 38, 56, 73, 88*n*1, 195, 199, 203
Greenblatt, Stephen, 244
Gregory I, Pope, 57
Grill (in Spenser), 200, 214*n*27. *See also* Gryllus
Grisolia, Michelangelo, 88*n*5
Gryllus, 198–200, 205, 214. *See also* Grill

Guarini, Guarino, 62, 245
Guelfs, 34, 81
Guicciardini, Francesco, 13, 37–41, 165–9, 173*n*27, 298
Guidi, Andrea, 46*n*7, 47*n*11, *n*15, 49*n*33, *n*40, 50*n*45, 51*n*52–53, 155*n*5, 170*n*1, *n*4, 171*n*6, *n*12

Hankins, James, 45*n*2, 50*n*43, 77–8, 137*n*26, *n*36, 138*n*45, 140*n*69
Hannibal, 147, 161*n*35, 282
hapaxes, 153, 263, 265, 267–8, 271, 275*n*13
Harrington, James, 8
hate in politics, 60, 84, 111, 169, 282, 308–9
Heath, Carl, 295*n*36
Hegel, Georg Wilhelm Friedrich, 5, 15, 113, 221–2, 229, 242, 248–9, 297, 304
Heidegger, Martin, 224, 231*n*17
Heinsius, Daniel, 257*n*42
Held, Klaus, 160*n*31
Henry V of England, 36
Henry VI of England, 36
Henry VIII of England, 35, 54–5, 68*n*5
Herchenroeder, Lucas, 213*n*19
Herder, Johann Gottfried von, 15
hereditary rule, 11, 57–62, 65–7, 69*n*17, 174, 220, 303, 306
Herodotus, 75
Heywood, Elizabeth, 239
Hiero of Syracuse, 186*n*1
Hippie movement, 283
Hobbes, Thomas, 73, 87
Hohenwang, Ludwig, 211*n*9
Holbein, Hans, the Younger, 238
Holden, Adam, 315*n*78
Holy League, 95n, 165, 169
Hoppe, Harry R., 218*n*63

Hörnqvist, Mikael, 12, 46*n*7, 47*n*12, 49*n*40, 50*n*45, 51*n*52, 53*n*71, 98, 118*n*12
Huguenots, 8, 55
humanism, 7–9, 11, 13–14, 50*n*43, 60–1, 64, 73–4, 76–8, 83–4, 92*n*37, 121–2, 126–30, 132, 135*n*20, 138*n*41, 183, 185–6, 193–5, 217*n*59, 225, 227, 237–8, 240–1, 245–7, 252, 255*n*26, 262–3, 265, 268, 270, 272, 296, 300. *See also* civic humanism
humanity, 75, 84, 86, 104, 114, 198, 208, 243, 282, 289
hunting, 3, 83–4, 96–110, 113–16

Indelli, Giovanni, 213*n*19
Ingarden, Roman, 235
Inglese, Giorgio, 134*n*1, 140*n*60
internet, the, 229
Isabella of Castile, 34
Iser, Wolfgang, 235
Italian Wars, 273*nn*2–3, 262

Jacobs and Jacobinism, 10, 40, 44, 299–300, 307
Jardine, Lisa, 240
Jed, Stephanie, 183
Jerome, Saint, 179, 237
Joan of Arc, 36
Johnstone, Steven, 11*n*14
Jones, Philip J., 47*n*11
Judas, 62
Julian, Emperor (the Apostate), 290–1
Julius Caesar, 62–6, 84–5, 251
Julius II, Pope, 146–7, 151
Jurdjevic, Mark, 18*n*25, 105
justice, 75, 101, 104, 109–10, 125, 198, 200–1, 225, 246, 275*n*16, 281–2

Kahn, Coppélia, 190*n*46
Kahn, Victoria, 7–8, 13, 194, 203, 212*n*18, 214, 215*n*41, 233*n*29, *n*32, 234*n*42, 246, 259*n*55
Kelly, Donald R., 17*n*21
Kelsen, Hans, 5
Kent, F. W., 50*n*46
Khan, Abdul Ghaffar, 283
Khan, Hakim Ajmal, 293*n*17
King, Ed, 215*n*36
King, Martin Luther, Jr., 283
Koselleck, Reinhart, 122
Kottman, Paul A., 295
Krois, John Michael, 231

Lacedaemonia. *See* Sparta
Laclau, Ernesto, 132, 140*n*66, *n*68
Lahtinen, Mikko, 16*n*9, 160*n*33
Landor, Walter Savage, 240
language, 13–14, 90*n*22, 122, 127–8, 145, 169, 181, 220–1, 225–6, 236, 262–73, 276*n*16, *n*24, 299
Larivaille, Paul, 130, 135*n*14, 139*n*59, 141*n*72
Larner, John, 50*n*44
Larson, Deborah Aldrich, 255*n*20
law/laws, 2, 3–4, 6, 10, 11, 32–3, 43, 56–7, 62–5, 76, 82–3, 85, 104, 112, 126, 136*n*26, 137*n*31, 177, 202–4, 226, 250–1, 267, 270, 276*n*16, 283, 306–8
law, natural, 14, 103
law, rule of, 3, 6, 63, 110, 126
lawgivers, 2, 6, 23, 27, 64–5, 79, 82, 226–7, 250
lawmaking violence, 58, 62, 65, 67, 205
Lazzeri, Christian, 160*n*31
le Bon, Gustav, 112–13
Lee, Alexander, 46*n*4
Lefort, Claude, 15, 16*n*9, 161*n*35, 229, 173*n*161, 234*n*39

legislators. *See* lawgivers
Leisi, Ernst, 48*n*23
leisure (*otia, ozio*), 1, 97, 100, 166
Lenin, Vladimir/Leninism, 248, 300, 314*n*66
Lenzoni, Carlo, 207
Leo X, Pope (Giovanni di Lorenzo de' Medici), 80, 82, 163, 194
Leroy, Louis, 8
letters, man of, 12–14, 79, 263
Lettieri, Gaetano, 165, 171*n*12
Lévi-Strauss, Claude, 182, 210*n*3
Levvenklaius, Johannes, 74
liberal democracy, 44, 108–9
liberality, 9, 75, 79, 84–5, 105
liberty, 2–4, 28, 30*n*19, 43, 88*n*1, 101, 124, 177–8, 250, 266–7, 275*n*15. *See also* freedom
libido/licence, 88*n*1, 124, 195
linguistic context, 274*n*10
Lipsius, Justus, 15, 252
Livy, 12, 38, 175–7, 180–1, 183–6, 187*n*7, 250–2, 288. *See also* Machiavelli, *Discorsi*
Locke, John, 87
Loewenstein, Joseph, 200, 214*n*28, 218*n*63
Louis XI of France, 298
Louis XII of France, 34, 36
Love, Jeff, 16*n*7
love, political, 6, 13, 63, 75, 112, 126–9, 226
Lowe, K. J. P., 47*n*13
Loyola, Ignatius, 239
Lucian/pseudo-Lucian, 42, 194, 211*n*9
Lucretia, 174–86
Lucretius, 204, 206, 208, 212*n*18, 215*n*42
Lukes, Timothy J., 51*n*53, 216*n*46
Lycurgus, 23, 27, 64, 82, 186*n*1, 250

Lynch, Christopher, 3, 91*n*32
lynching, 102, 108–11, 113

Macaulay, Thomas Babington, 15
Machiavelli, Niccolò, works
  Arte della guerra, Dell' (*The Art of War*), 22, 29*n*3, 32–3, 35–6, 38–9, 41–3, 46*n*10, 47*n*15, 48*n*22, *n*28, *n*30, 49*nn*34–35, 50*n*47, 51*n*52, 52*nn*56–58, *nn*60–61, *n*64, 71*n*32, 63, 99, 130, 162, 229, 234*n*40, 249, 268–71, 276*nn*23–24, 277*nn*30–31, 301–2, 310
  L'Asino, 3, 14, 114, 193–4, 196–8, 200–7, 209–10, 210*n*7
  Belfagor, 3
  Capitoli, 22, 252
  Discorsi (*Discourses*), 2, 4, 8, 21, 23, 26–8, 29*nn*12–18, 34, 37–8, 41, 44, 48*n*22, *n*24, *nn*28–29, 49*n*32, *nn*35–36, 50*n*49, 52*n*58, *n*61, *nn*65–66, *n*69, 53*nn*72–74, 54, 56, 59–60, 62–63, 65–66, 71*n*30, *n*34, *nn*36–37, 72*nn*39–41, 79, 81, 85–6, 91*n*26, 92*n*35, 94*n*55, *n*61, *n*63, 95*nn*64–65, *nn*68–69, 110–12, 119*nn*33–34, 123–4, 127, 134*n*6, *n*10, 135*nn*11–12, 16, 136*nn*23–24, 137*n*31, 138*n*48, 139*n*54, n56,153, 156*n*7, n11, *n*13, 159*n*24, 162–4, 171*n*8, 173*n*27, 174, 177–80, 182, 185, 186*n*1, 188*nn*15–16, *nn*18–25, 189*nn*27–29, 221, 225–7, 241, 244–7, 249–51, 256*n*29, *n*31, 261*nn*72–73, 263, 267–8, 271, 273, 276*n*21, *n*24, 282–3, 286, 291–2, 293*n*5, *n*18, 294*n*23, *n*32, 301, 303, 305–6, 310

Discursus florentinarum rerum post mortem iunioris Laurentii Medices, 82, 93*n*41
Ghiribizzi, 145–6, 149–54, 159*n*25, 161*n*35
Istorie fiorentine (*Florentine Histories*), 41, 48*n*22, 78–80, 91*n*26–28, *nn*31–32, 92*nn*33–34, 105, 153, 159*n*24, 161*n*35, 162–4, 268, 277*n*24, 301
Letters, 25, 46*n*6, 49*n*35, 52*n*59, 96, 146–7, 150, 156*n*8, 159*n*25, 162–9, 170*n*1, 171*n*7, 172*nn*18–19, *nn*23–24, 173*n*30, 193–4, 242–3, 245, 248–9, 257*nn*34–38, *n*40, 275*n*13, 276*n*24. See also *Ghiribizzi*, Letters from the Chancery. *For recipients, see under the person's name.*
Letters from the Chancery, 147–9, 163, 166 276*n*24
Mandragola, 106–8, 162, 180, 185
Principe, Il (*The Prince*), 1, 8–12, 14, 21–5, 28, 29*nn*1–2, *n*7, *n*11, 32–8, 41, 46*n*9, 47*n*16, 48*n*22, 49*n*35, *n*37, 51*n*54, 54, 56, 58, 62, 66, 69*n*15, *nn*18–19, 73–4, 83–4, 86, 92*nn*39–40, 93*nn*44–52, 94*nn*54–57, *n*59, *n*63, 96–7, 105, 108, 122–3, 126–7, 130–1, 134*n*3, 135*n*14, *n*17, 136*n*24, 137*nn*31–36, 138*n*38, *n*40, *nn*42–44, *n*47, 139*n*50, *n*52, 139*n*58, 140*n*62, 65, 141*n*73, *nn*75–76, *n*78, 155*n*7, 156*n*9, n11, *n*13, 163–5, 168–9, 171*n*5, 174, 178, 186*n*1, 193, 196, 201–3, 205, 207, 209, 215*n*35, *n*37, 220–21, 224–8, 242, 244, 246–50, 252, 256*n*31, 260*n*66,

264, 267, 269–71, 273*n*1, 274*n*4, *n*7, 275*n*11, *n*13, 276*n*20–21, 277*nn*25–26, *n*28, *n*30, 282–4, 286, 289–90, 296, 300–7, 309–11, 313*n*46
Mack, Peter, 258*n*47
Majumder, Doyeeta, 11
Mallet, Michael, 273*n*3
Mandela, Nelson, 283
Mansfield, Harvey C., 18*n*22
manuals for princes, 249, 252, 260*n*68
Mao Zedong, 307
Marchand, Jean-Jacques, 47*n*12, 146, 161*n*34
Marchesi, Francesco, 5, 159*n*29
Marignano, Battle of, 163
Marks, Louis, 41
Marlowe, Christopher, 8, 237
Marotti, A. F., 255*n*20
Marsh, David, 88*n*3
Marsiglio of Padua, 66
Martelli, Mario, 134*n*1, *n*4, 138*n*47, 139*n*56, *n*58, 141*n*74, 158*n*19
Marx, Karl, 15, 248–9, 256*n*28, 300
Marx, Stephen, 256*n*31
Marxism, 40, 241, 248, 296
masculinity, 6, 175, 179, 181–3, 185, 289
Masson, J. L., 253*n*8
Mathiez, Albert, 300
Matthes, Melissa, 184–6
Mazzotta, Giuseppe, 173*n*27
McCormick, John, 1, 9, 10, 16*n*4, *n*9, 45*n*4, 64, 71*n*35, 164, 171*n*10, 172*n*25, 258*n*52
Medici family, 31, 39–40, 57, 64, 79–80, 87, 121, 162–4, 167–9, 196, 228, 240
Medici Giovanni di Lorenzo de'. *See* Leo X, Pope
Medici, Cosimo de', 79–81, 207–8
Medici, Giovanni de' (Cosimo I's father), 169
Medici, Giuliano de', 96, 242
Medici, Giulio de'. *See* Clement VII, Pope
Medici, Lorenzo de', 79, 163, 282
Medici, Rita, 300
Meinecke, Friedrich, 18*n*22
mercenaries, 31–7, 42, 80, 269–70, 273, 302
Messina, Antonello da, 237
metamorphosis, 195, 197–201, 207–10, 220
Michele, Don. *See* Corella
Migiel, Marilyn, 217*n*57
Miguel, Don. *See* Corella
Milan, 34, 74, 129
militia, 42–4, 50*n*44, 110, 302
militia, citizens', 4, 10, 31–40, 43, 100, 289, 308. See also *armi proprie*
Milton, John, 4, 238, 240, 249
Mineo, Igor, 275*n*15
Mirandola. *See* Pico
Molho, Anthony, 41, 51*n*55
monarchy, 8, 12, 18*n*25, 57, 60–2, 65–6, 125, 129, 137*n*31, 139*n*39, 175–9, 298–9, 302, 306, 309–10, 315*n*81. *See also* hereditary rule, principality
Montag, Warren, 260*n*65
Montagu, Edwin, 284
Montaigne, Michel de, 209, 237–8, 240, 243, 249, 257*n*42, 287
Monte, the, 41
More, Thomas, 168, 225, 239
Morfino, Vittorio, 10, 16*n*9, 29*n*, 51*n*54, 160*n*33
Moses, 2, 21, 64, 73–4, 76, 83, 186*n*1, 241, 256*n*31
Murakami, Haruki, 239–40

myth, 3, 10, 14, 175, 180, 183–6, 186*n*1, 195, 202, 207, 210, 219–26, 229–30, 231*n*1, *n*17, 234*n*39, 249, 299–300, 311

Nabis, 44, 130–1, 139, 186
Nadon, Christopher, 3, 94*n*53
Nagel, Thomas, 200
Najemy, John M., 17*n*14, 50*n*42, *n*44, 155*n*5, 162
Naples, 129, 181
Napoleon, 2, 44
nation/nationalism/nation-state, 10–11, 15, 59, 67, 116, 167, 219, 229, 268, 284, 298, 302, 304, 306–8, 310
Nazism, 219, 223–4
neocon right, 121. *See also* Trump, Donald
Neoplatonism, 6, 14, 78, 199, 204, 207, 247
Nero, 57
Nerva, 65–6, 72*n*40
Neville, Henry, 8
new princes, 10–11, 21, 25, 34–5, 44, 57–9, 62–7, 131, 204–5, 270, 304, 306–7, 310. *See also* founding a state
Newton, Isaac, 283
Nicholas V, Pope, 74
Nicholls, Angus, 232*n*22
Nicolet, Claude, 52*n*63
Nietzsche, Friedrich, 30*n*19, 44
Nifo, Agostino, 129
Noah, 79
nobility. *See* aristocracy
non-violence, 281, 283, 289. *See also* passive resistance, *satyagraha*
Norbrook, David, 17*n*21
Numa Pompilius, 226, 256*n*31

occasion. *See* opportunity
Odysseus (Ulysses), 198, 220
Ogilvie, R. M., 187*n*7
Okin, Susan Moller, 189*n*32
oligarchy, 4, 40, 61, 133
Oppian, 215*n*40
opportunity (*occasione*), 5, 21–4, 26, 28, 44, 98, 105, 127, 311
ordinanza, Machiavelli's, 31–2, 35–40, 270
Ordine, Nuccio, 196, 201–2, 205–6, 216*n*49, 217*n*52
Orr, Robert, 157*n*15
Ortega y Gasset, José, 97, 101, 103, 107, 113, 116
Orti Oricellari circle, 14
Otto di Pratica, 167
Ovid, 6, 96, 199–200, 207, 242–3

Pamuk, Orhan, 236, 240
Parel, Anthony, 17*n*14, 158*n*16, 159*n*24
Parker, Geoffrey, 49*n*33
passive resistance, 290–1
Patapan, Haig, 17*n*15, 261*n*75
Pathosformel, 116, 120*n*44
patria/fatherland, 1, 11, 71*n*39, 93*n*41, 169, 171*n*18, 172*n*24, 188*n*19
patriarchy, 175, 181, 183, 186
patriotism, 1, 11, 65, 167, 177, 282
Patrizi, Francesco, 75–6, 124
Patwardhan, M. V., 253*n*8
Paul, Saint, 110
Paul II, Pope, 74
Pavia, 282
Pavia, Battle of, 165
Pazzi Conspiracy, 168
Pedullà, Gabrielle, 16*n*9, 46*n*4, 51*n*50, 53*n*71, 134*n*4, *n*10, 135*n*16, 136*n*26, 139*n*58, 141*n*78,

Pelagianism, 197
Pelagius, 197
Pellegrini, A. M., 218*n*63
people, the (*il popolo*), 3–4, 9, 38–9, 41, 45, 63, 76, 102, 112, 123–4, 126–8, 131–3, 140*n*68, 141*n*78, 177, 197, 248, 250, 259*n*52, 267, 271, 285, 301, 305–6, 308–11. *See also* plebs, populism
Pericles, 240
Perugia, 129, 146, 151, 156*n*7
Petersen, Anne Marie, 293*n*17
Petrarch (Petrarca), Francesco, 89*n*9, 96, 107, 205, 208, 238, 242–3, 249, 254*n*13
'Petrarch Master', 205
Petrina, Alessandra, 255*n*20
Petrucci, Pandolfo, 129
Pettit, Philip, 9
Petty, William, 300
Philip of Macedon, 59
Philippides, S. N., 187*n*7
Pico della Mirandola, 78–81, 91*n*26, 151, 196, 208
Pierguido, Stefano, 206, 216*n*52
Pieters, Jurgen, 244, 254*n*15
Pino, Giovan Battista, 205
Pisa, 31–2, 163
Pitkin, Hanna, 182–4
Pitt, William, 240
Platina, Bartolomeo Sacchi di, 75
Plato and Platonism, 3, 38, 73, 76–83, 91*n*26, 133, 168, 195–6, 202–5, 207, 223, 228
Platone, Felice, 296
plebeians/plebs, 44, 164, 251
Pliny, 198, 200, 206
Plotinus, 213*n*22
Plutarch, 63, 65, 198–201, 204–7, 209, 214*n*26, *n*30

Pocock, J. G. A., 9, 31, 36, 44, 45*n*3, 103, 145, 168, 213*n*19, 214*n*32, 274*n*10
Pole, Reginald, 54, 68*n*5
Polybius, 23, 60–1
Pompey, 63, 71
Pontano, Giovanni, 21, 75, 88*n*5, 124–5, 127–8
Pope/papacy, 147, 169, 239, 297. *See also* Church, *and names of individual popes*
populism, 4, 7, 9–12, 37–9, 41, 43, 45, 50*n*43, 109, 112, 126, 131–3, 141*n*78. *See also* people
Porphyry, 199
power, 10–11, 28, 45, 56, 58–62, 99, 100, 104, 106, 113–15, 123–4, 126–7, 130–3, 136*n*21, 139*n*52, 153, 172*n*20, 174, 179, 181, 183, 185, 203, 220, 228, 264, 271, 276*n*16
prayer, 25–6, 197
Praz, Mario, 17*n*21, 255*n*20
principalities, 6, 35, 38, 45, 58, 67, 75, 121, 123–34, 134*n*4, 136*n*24, 137*n*31, 139*nn*59–60, 140*n*64, 227–8, 168, 220, 227, 233*n*26, 271, 301, 306–7, 310
Privat, Madame Edmond, 290, 295*n*45
Prometheus, 208
prophecy, prophets, 25–6, 87, 149, 171*n*8, 229, 256*n*31, 290
Proteus, 208, 212*n*14
Proust, Marcel, 236
Provvidera, Tiziana, 218*n*63
prudence, 5, 11–12, 22, 84, 127, 130, 138*n*39, 149–54, 171*n*8, 200, 241
Ptolemy, 149

Quaglioni, Diego, 134*n*9, 141*n*77, 275*n*16
qualità di tempi, 132, 133, 140*n*65, 141*n*78, 145, 148, 154, 156*n*13, 166, 262, 264, 286, 293*n*22

Quintilian, 12, 225
Quran (Koran), 285

Raab, Felix, 17*n*21
Rahe, Paul A., 10, 46*n*5, 47*n*14, 50*n*43, 52*n*63, *n*67
reading, Machiavelli's, 8, 96, 121, 147, 236–7, 241–52, 253*n*9, 255*n*25, 264, 305–6
religion, 6, 26, 68*n*3, 76–9, 81, 87, 112–13, 188*n*20, 197, 212*n*18, 226, 239, 249, 269, 284–6, 288, 291–2, 308, 310. *See also* Christianity
republicanism, 3–4, 8–9, 11, 12, 14–15, 17*n*21, 35, 37–8, 44, 62, 64–6, 71*n*35, 74, 76–7, 101, 111, 124–6, 129, 132, 137*n*27, 145, 168, 177–8, 183–5, 220–1, 225, 229, 273, 275*n*15, 282, 305–6, 310. *See also* republics
republics, 6, 12, 27–8, 33, 35, 38, 43–5, 59, 62–7, 69*n*17, 75, 81, 87, 103, 111–12, 123–7, 129, 136*n*24, 137*n*31, 139*n*49, 168, 173*n*27, 175, 177–8, 184–5, 220, 224, 227, 229, 250–2, 259*n*52, 301, 305–6. *See also* republicanism
revolt/uprising, 4, 11, 32, 36, 112, 169, 175–80, 182–3, 186. *See also* revolution, Tumulto
revolution, 36, 40, 44, 124, 174–5, 178–9, 183, 186, 299
revolution, Roman, 175, 179, 181, 183, 185
revolution, Russian, 248
rhetoric, 7, 9–10, 13–14, 77, 127–8, 193, 195, 199, 203, 205, 220, 224–31, 232*nn*22–23, *n*25, 233*n*26, 255*n*26, 262–3, 266–7, 272, 301, 310
Rhetorica ad Herennium, 225–6, 232*n*25

Ricci, Giuliano de', 257*n*34, 36
Ricoeur, Paul, 230
Ridolfi, Roberto, 150, 158*n*19, 256*n*34
rights, 7, 32, 43, 59, 66, 88, 88*n*1, 101, 104, 131, 201, 221, 226
Rinaldi, Rinaldo, 137*n*31, 141*n*74
Rinuccini, Alamanno, 13
riscontro, 4–5, 145–6, 148–54, 157*n*15, 161*n*35
Rispoli, Tania, 204, 215*n*42, 216*n*47
Rogers, Clifford J., 49*n*31
Romagna, 302
Romanticism, 3, 5, 9, 17*n*15, 221, 223–4
Rome and Romans, 3, 8, 12, 18*n*25, 23–4, 26–8, 29*n*6, 30*n*15, *n*18, 34–5, 37–8, 35, 42–5, 56, 62, 64–6, 71*n*32, 76, 85, 103–4, 109–10, 113, 123, 137*n*31, 147, 76, 162–4, 167, 169, 174–81, 183, 185, 186*n*1, 188*nn*20–21, 226–7, 250, 259*n*52, 268–9, 284, 292, 305–6
Rome, Sack of, 169
Romulus, 21, 30*n*15, 62, 65, 83, 178, 186*n*1, 256*n*31
Rorario, Girolamo, 217*n*61
Rosamund, Queen of the Longobards, 181
Rosen, Stephen Peter, 38, 49*n*41
Rouen, Cardinal of, 270
Rousseau, Jean-Jacques, 9, 71, 283
Rubinstein, Nicolai, 275*n*15
Rucellai, Cosimo, 39, 43–4, 59, 164
Ruggiero, Guido, 17*n*15, 189*n*31
Russo, Luigi, 300–1

Sallust, 38
Salutati, Coluccio, 56–7, 61–3, 73
Sanders, Wilbur, 283
Sandys, George, 199
Sant' Andrea in Percussina, 242

Sasso, Gennaro, 50*n*50, 135*n*13, 136*n*24, 138*n*48, 139*n*53–54, *n*57, *n*60, 140*n*61, *n*64, 150, 152, 158*n*19, 159*n*24
Satan, Machiavelli as, 34, 45, 48*n*23, 54, 67, 239
Saturn, 201
satyagraha, 12, 285, 287–91
Savonarola, Girolamo, 9, 25–6, 78, 82–3, 229, 266, 273*n*2, 276*n*17, 285
Saxonhouse, Arlene W., 189*n*33
Schilling, Michael, 216*n*50
Schmidt, Ronald J., Jr, 246, 256*nn*30–31
Schmitt, Carl, 5, 139*n*49
Schucht, Tatiana (Tania), 259*n*56, 298–9
Scipio Africanus, 84–6, 147, 161*n*35
Scobie, Alexander, 211*n*9
Segni, Lotario de', 206
Sellers, Harry, 218*n*63
Seneca, 104, 113
Senigaglia, 39
Sermon on the Mount. *See* Bible
Sforza family, 80, 129
Sforza, Caterina, 180–1
Sforza, Francesco, 34, 50*n*47, 74, 80–1, 139*n*60, 186*n*1
Sforza, Ludovico, 81
Shaw, Christine, 273*n*
Shelley, Percy Bysshe, 199
Sherberg, Michael, 245–6, 256*n*29
Sherman, William, 240, 255*n*25
Shin, John Juncholl, 189*n*33
Sidney, Algernon, 8
siege warfare, 268, 271
Siena, 129, 165, 171*n*15
Signoria, 39–40
Simonetta, Marcello, 9, 170*n*4, 171*n*13, *nn*15–16, 172*nn*19–21, 173*nn*28–29

Singleton, Charles, 146, 153–4
skepticism, 286–7
Skinner, Quentin, 9, 15*n*1, 17*n*21, 31, 36, 45*n*3, 64, 69*n*17, 71*n*35, 155*n*5, 233*n*27, 241, 274*n*10, 275*n*15, 276*n*19
slander, 111–13, 195
Smith, Thomas, 57
Smuts, Jan, 294
Socrates, 3, 74, 77, 83, 86, 89*n*7
Soderini brothers, 38–9
Soderini, Francesco, 39–40, 50*n*47
Soderini, Giovan Battista, 145–6, 150
Soderini, Pier(o), 32, 37, 39–40, 44, 109, 123, 146–7, 150–1
Soll, Joseph, 241
Solon, 42, 64, 82, 186*n*1
Sophocles, 240
Sorabji, Richard, 213*n*19
Sorel, Georges, 299
soul/souls, 3, 77, 81, 85, 133, 141*n*74, 172*n*20, 195, 198, 204, 207, 237, 288–9, 291
soul-force, 285
South Africa, 281–2, 289–90
sovereignty, 5, 11–12, 16*n*7, 57–9, 101, 113, 115, 129
Soviet state, the, 224
Spackman, Barbara, 187*n*6
Spain, 63, 147, 163, 165, 298
Sparta, 23, 26–7, 34, 43–4, 74, 250, 259*n*52
Spengler, Oswald, 224, 231*n*17
Spenser, Edmund, 200
Spiegel, Jakob, 88*n*5
Spinoza, Baruch, 16*n*9, 30*n*19
Sraffa, Piero, 299–300
Stacey, Peter, 18*n*25, 103–4
statecraft, art of (*l'arte dello stato*), 11, 55, 87, 153–4, 265, 271–3

Stendhal, 236, 240
Stoicism, 76, 103–4, 195, 198–9, 238, 252
Strauss, Leo, 4, 11, 18n22, 54–5, 193, 196, 223–4, 228, 231n17, 232n21, 233n36, 259n59
Strozzi, Lorenzo, 96
Struever, Nancy S., 160n31
Suarez, Francisco, 5
Switzerland/the Swiss, 34–7, 147, 290

Tagore, Rabindranath, 288
Tarcov, Nathan, 46n9, 94n55
Tarquin family, 174–80, 182–3, 214n30, 188n15
Tarquinius Sextus, 176, 179
Tarquinius Superbus, 175, 179
Terray, Emmanuel, 314n77
theriophily, 208–9
Theseus, 21, 83, 186n1
Thoreau, Henry David, 283
Tibullus, 96, 242–3
Tiepolo, 184
Tinkler, John, 225–6
Titian, 184
Togliatti, Palmiro, 296
Tolstoy, Lev, 283
Tommasini, Oreste, 158n19
Tomyris, 75
Torquatus, Manlius, 95n64
Treves, Paolo, 298
tribunes, 3, 9, 164, 177, 251.
Trump, Donald, 219, 223
Tullus Hostilius, 35
Tumulto, Florentine, 168–9
Turin, 247
Turkey, 141n78, 219
Tutino, Stefania, 239
Twitter, 229

tyranny, 8, 11, 38, 54–63, 65–7, 68n5, 124, 129–32, 135n13, 139n56, 141n78, 178, 168, 184, 186, 195, 204–5, 224, 229, 232n21, 251, 266, 305–6

Ulysses. *See* Odysseus
United States, 219
Urbani, Brigitte, 217n54
Urbino, 169
utilitas, 126, 225–6, 232n23, n25
utopia, 168, 230, 298, 302, 304–5, 309–10, 313n35

Valentino, Duke. *See* Borgia, Cesare
Valla, Lorenzo, 74
Van Ginneken, Jaap, 119n36
Varchi, Benedetto, 87
Vatican, 146, 215n42
Vatter, Miguel, 9–10, 159n28, 160n33, 161n35, 201
Vedas, 285
Vegetius, 33
Vegezio, 271
Venice/Venetians, 41, 43, 63, 165, 259n52
Verene, Donald Philip, 234n38
verità effettuale, 1, 82, 163, 263–5, 271, 275n13, 304
Vespucci, Amerigo, 151
Vespucci, Bartolomeo, 151–2
Vettori, Francesco, 46n6, 49n35, 52n59, 96, 160n30, 162–3, 165, 167–9, 170n3, 242–3, 245, 248–9, 273n2, 275n13
Vettori, Paolo, 162
Villacañas, José Luis, 141n73
violence, 4, 12, 18n24, 23, 30n15, 57–8, 62, 65, 67, 99, 109–11, 114, 130–1, 139n53, 174–7, 179–81,

185–6, 187*n*5, 205, 230, 232*n*22, 246, 281–3, 303, 310–11
Virgil, 75, 169–70, 196, 240
Viroli, Maurizio, 6, 71*n*35, 155*n*5, 227, 232*n*25, 233*n*26, 255*n*26
Virtù/virtus/'virtue', 5, 11, 12, 21, 23–4, 28, 34, 44, 56, 58, 60–1, 65, 73, 83, 86, 96–7, 102–3, 105, 116, 127, 153, 197, 222, 225, 227–8, 232*n*23, 241, 247, 270, 288–9, 291, 307, 311
Visconti, Filippo Maria, 74
Vivanti, Corrado, 4
Voegelin, Eric, 15, 223
Volterra, 32

Waley, Daniel, 47*n*19
Walsh, P. G., 187*n*7
war, 5, 22, 33, 35, 37, 42–3, 97–100, 165–7, 229, 262–3, 265–7, 269–70, 272–3, 277*n*30, 289
war, art of, 6, 22, 83–4, 97, 277*n*30

Weiditz, Hans, the younger, 205
Wells, H. G., 243
Whitney, Geoffrey, 199–200, 214*n*26
Wicht, Bernard, 49*n*35
Winter, Yves, 9, 12, 18*n*24, 187*nn*4–5
Wittgenstein, Ludwig, 193
Wolfe, John, 209
Wolin, Sheldon, 187*n*3
women and femininity, 106, 108, 175, 179–84, 289
Wootton, David, 7–8
World War I, 282
World War II, 219

Xenophon, 3, 73–8, 83–8, 88*n*2, 89*n*7, 101–3, 107, 116, 204

Yoran, Hanan, 258*n*49

Zancarini, Jean-Claude, 139*nn*55–56, 273*n*2, 274*n*8, 275*n*15, 276*n*22
Zorzi, Andrea, 180
Zuckert, Catherine H., 46*n*4